Bukharan Jews and the
Dynamics of Global Judaism

D1738660

INDIANA SERIES IN SEPHARDI AND MIZRAHI STUDIES

Harvey E. Goldberg and Matthias Lehmann, editors

Bukharan Jews and the Dynamics of Global Judaism

Alanna E. Cooper

Indiana University Press

Bloomington & Indianapolis

This book is a publication of

INDIANA UNIVERSITY PRESS
601 North Morton Street
Bloomington, Indiana
47404–3797 USA

iupress.indiana.edu

Telephone orders 800-842-6796
Fax orders 812-855-7931

♾ The paper used in this publication
meets the minimum requirements of
the American National Standard for
Information Sciences—Permanence
of Paper for Printed Library
Materials, ANSI Z39.48-1992.

*Manufactured in the
United States of America*

*Library of Congress
Cataloging-in-Publication Data*

Cooper, Alanna E., [date]
 Bukharan Jews and the dynamics of
global Judaism / Alanna E. Cooper.
  p. cm. — (Indiana series in
Sephardi and Mizrahi studies)
 Includes bibliographical references
and index.
 ISBN 978-0-253-00643-1 (cloth : alk.
paper) — ISBN 978-0-253-00650-9
(pbk. : alk. paper) — ISBN 978-0-253-
00655-4 (electronic book) 1. Jews—
Uzbekistan—Bukhoro viloiati—
History. 2. Jews—Uzbekistan—
Bukhoro viloiati—Social conditions.
3. Jews, Bukharan. 4. Bukhoro viloiati
(Uzbekistan)—Ethnic relations. I. Title.
 DS135.U92C66 2012
 305.892′40587—dc23

                                2012024374

1 2 3 4 5 17 16 15 14 13 12

For Moshe

CONTENTS

Reining in Diaspora's Margins

For countless generations, Jewish houses of prayer, schools, neighborhood associations, and markets dotted the landscape of Central Asia's ancient silk-route cities. Although historians are not certain when Jews first appeared in the region, most believe they were among those who were exiled—or whose ancestors were exiled—from the Land of Israel in the sixth century BCE at the hands of the Babylonians. They moved eastward, probably as merchants along trade routes, spreading out as far as the fertile river valleys of present-day Uzbekistan and Tajikistan.

As the centuries passed, their descendants continued to carry the collective memory of exile and loss of the Jewish homeland. Over time, however, their historical experiences became intimately linked to the Central Asian landscape in which they found themselves. So much so, that the Jews whom I met there in the 1990s characterized themselves as "indigenous" to the region. *We arrived here before Islam was introduced to the area, and before the Uzbek dynasts conquered the territory,* they explained.

Even their language testifies to their deep Central Asian ties. Like Jews around the world, they spoke a dialect that set them off as a distinct community, separate from the non-Jews among whom they lived. Unlike the Ashkenazi Jews of Eastern Europe, however, whose language was derived from experiences in a previous diaspora home, the language of Central Asia's Jews evolved within the confines of Central Asia itself. Whereas Yiddish—a Germanic language—marked Ashkenazi Jews as outsiders in Poland, Judeo-Tajik is one of the many variants of Tajik (a Persian language) spoken in the region by Jews and Muslims alike.

In spite of their deep roots, the ties that bound the Jews to Central Asia were, nonetheless, not strong enough to withstand the changes that swept through the region at the end of the twentieth century. As soon as the USSR dissolved, these Jews (who lived in the Central Asian territories that had been incorporated into the Soviet Union in the 1920s) began emigrating en masse.

I met many of them as new arrivals in an immigrant school in New York, where I taught in 1993 (and which I describe further in the book). Curious to learn what it was like to be Jewish in Uzbekistan and Tajikistan, I asked my students to tell me about the homes, schools, synagogues, and neighborhoods they had left behind. They began to answer my questions, but the language and cultural barriers that stood between us proved serious obstacles, and we quickly reached the limits of conversation. *If you want to know the place we call home,* they concluded, *you will have to go visit for yourself.* Several years before, this would not have been possible. Now, however, Soviet restrictions on tourism had been lifted and travel to the region was a real possibility. My curiosity was piqued.

But you had better go quickly, they warned. The rise in nationalism and antisemitism, coupled with economic instability and a fear that the window of opportunity for leaving might be short-lived, had led to rapid chain-migration. Everyone's aunts, uncles, cousins, grandparents, and friends seemed to be packing their bags, leaving, and resettling in Israel and the United States. *Soon it will be too late to see Jewish life in Central Asia,* my students cautioned.

And they were right. In 1989, approximately 50,000 "indigenous" Jews lived in Uzbekistan and Tajikistan.[1] Just a decade later, their population in the region had been reduced to about a tenth of its size. And today, no more than several hundred remain. In a historical instant, Jews have all but disappeared from this corner of the world, and a long chapter in diaspora history has come to a close.

The story of Central Asia's Jews' deep roots and sudden rupture is not an isolated one. Indeed, it is part of a much larger phenomenon: a dramatic demographic shift that has occurred over the past century. Whereas today more than 80 percent of the world's Jewish population is concentrated in the United States and Israel,[2] several decades ago this portion of the world's Jewish population was dispersed across regions in which they simply are no more. Gone are the Jewish communities in

Eastern Europe, which were decimated during World War II. Empty stand the Jewish communal structures of the predominantly Muslim countries of North Africa and the Middle East since the Jews' mass departure in the middle of the last century.

As Jewish life the way it once existed in Yemen, Libya, Iraq, Poland, Ukraine, and other locales waned (and in some instances disappeared), anthropologists of Jews and Judaism set to work capturing and documenting it. Lloyd Cabot Briggs, for example, spent time living among the Jews in the Sahara Desert town of Ghardaia in the early 1960s, during the months leading up to their mass departure to France.[3] Barbara Myerhoff elicited narratives from elderly Jews in Venice, California, about their lives in Eastern Europe prior to World War II.[4] Irene Awret used the paintings of artist Rafael Uzan, along with the tales he told to accompany them, to record the contours of Jewish life in a small town in Tunisia prior to the Jews' great migration in 1956.[5] Jonathan Boyarin and Jack Kugelmass translated *yizker-bikher* (memorial books compiled by refugees) to shed light on everyday life in the Polish Jewish communities that were destroyed during World War II.[6] And Joelle Bahloul returned to her hometown to interview the Muslim neighbors among whom her family lived, in her effort to document the dynamics of Jewish–Muslim relations in Algeria prior to the Jews' leaving.[7] While this body of work (which includes many additional contributions) serves to preserve a record of Jewish life that is now gone, it also highlights what has been coined the "diversities of diaspora":[8] the great range of Jewish experience, the malleability of Jewish cultural forms, and the religion's flexibility and dynamism.

Aspects of this book have been inspired by these same concerns. Like Lloyd Cabot Briggs, who frantically worked to capture Jewish life in Ghardaia just before the entire community fled, I traveled to Uzbekistan in the 1990s to document Jewish life in Central Asia before it disappeared in the wake of the Soviet Union's dissolution. I attended synagogue services and participated in life-cycle rituals, spent time cooking with women in their courtyards, joined families at holiday meals, attended Jewish youth-club events, and sat in on classes in Jewish schools. In this effort, I was driven not only by a desire to document Jewish life in Central Asia before it was too late, but also to gain insight into Judaism's adaptability. Along these lines, this book adds to the body of ethnographic literature that describes Judaism as an embodied religion that is articulated through practice and is organically connected to the cultures across the globe in which it has been embedded. This particular case study focuses on Judaism's interactions with the Islamic, Turko-Persian, and Soviet cultures of which it was a part in Central Asia. For readers familiar with Judaism only in its Western contexts, the Jewish practices described and analyzed here will read as lively, colorful depictions of the "other." They illustrate just how variable Judaism can be, and how different Jews can be from one another.

Another critical aspect of the book, however, is not centered on difference at all. For what intrigued me most over the course of my research were not the distinctions I encountered. Rather, it was the curious sense of familiarity that I felt among Central Asia's Jews. Although I, myself, am an Ashkenazi Jew (that is, of Eastern European origin) and fourth-generation American, I was easily and readily welcomed into the homes of people from another cultural world, whose historical experiences had been utterly different from my own, and who were total strangers, except for the fact that we commonly identified as Jews. And once inside their homes, synagogues, and schools, I was struck by the ways in which their religious practices and categories felt so foreign to me, and yet so familiar.

This diffuse and ill-defined feeling of connectedness, which hovered above our differences, led me to wonder how I might understand the relationship between the Judaism with which I am familiar from home, and that which I encountered in Central Asia. This specific question points to broader theoretical issues surrounding the contours of Judaism, Jewish history, and Jewish Peoplehood.

Is there a single Judaism and Jewish People? And if so, how might these entities be defined in light of the great diversity of Jewish forms that developed across the far reaches of the diaspora? Not unique to Judaism, these questions have been given much attention by scholars of Islam, Hinduism, Buddhism, and Christianity, all commonly referred to as world religions or global religions. What exactly does it mean to be a "global religion"? And what is the nature of the relationship between a religion's global and local forms?

Judaism is a particularly fertile site for exploring these questions because its formative development did not take place in the context of empire or state, but rather on a dis-embedded world stage. Unattached to territorial bonds, with no recourse to military might, and without the trappings to enforce temporal authority or religious hierarchy, the Jewish case raises very interesting questions about the mechanisms through which a global religion can be cultivated and maintained. Yet, there is still a paucity of literature which explores this topic.

Traditionally, the work of Jewish Studies scholars tended to be informed by the assumption (sometimes explicitly stated, but oftentimes implicit) that Judaism is located within the texts of a stable canon and is transmitted by learned initiates. Regardless of where and when they lived, all Jewish communities practiced global Judaism, often referred to as "Rabbinic Judaism," if their behaviors conformed to these texts. Within this framework, there is little room for local forms. The technical, rabbinic category *minhag ha-makom* (literally: local custom) allows for some degree of regional variation, but only within parameters imposed by normative Judaism. Outside of these parameters, local practices are considered illegitimate deviations, which emerge among communities that lose, forget, misread, misunderstand, or ignore parts of the canon.

In recent decades, many scholars have criticized this approach, arguing against the assumptions that Judaism possesses an enduring, static essence and normative tenets, and that deviations from these are corruptions of that which is the true and authentic form. This critique is generally coupled with the assertion that Judaism is located within the practice, discourse, ideas, and identity of the people themselves, rather than in a set of disembodied texts. This formula—which asserts the legitimacy of all local forms—suggests that there may be no single Judaism at all, only many local Judaisms.

A handful of scholars have worked to navigate between these two positions by developing theories that accommodate both a global Judaism and robust local forms.[9] Here, I contribute to this project by uncoupling the terms *normative* and *essential*. This book argues that there is, indeed, a normative Judaism, but that it does not have an essential, static, or given form. Rather than being transcendent—above time or place— normative Judaism is created and maintained in an ongoing, dynamic process. This generative model involves continual negotiation and contestation about what is legitimately Jewish and what is not. Global Judaism, then, is a protracted conversation between those voices that come to be labeled as marginal, or peripheral, and those that come to be labeled as central or normative. These labels, though, are never givens, for at every moment they are each in the process of becoming or changing through their ongoing engagement with the other.

Central Asia's Jews provide a compelling starting point for analyzing this dynamic because of their long history at the geographical margins of the scattered Jewish world. At the far edges of diaspora, their relationship with Jews in other parts of the world oscillated between periods of isolation and moments of contact. The periods of isolation were long enough for them to develop their own particular forms of Jewish practices and ideas, which were organically tied to the social and cultural worlds in which they found themselves—not long enough, however, to undo the collective memory of their bonds to Judaism and world Jewry. This memory was activated during punctuated encounters with Jews in other parts of the world. It is this contact, which I refer to as "moments of reunion," that makes up the substance of this book. For it is here, in these encounters, that dramatic contestation unfolded about what "normative" Judaism is, about where the boundaries of Jewish Peoplehood should be drawn, and about who has the authority to decide these critical issues.

This book, then, is neither an ethnography of Central Asia's Bukharan Jews nor an overview of Judaism as a global religion, but a project that aims—in the words of anthropologist Frank Korom—to "capture both simultaneously." In his work on Islam, Korom points out that navigating between the "zigzagging contours of the local and global" poses a serious challenge, for it calls for an interdisciplinary methodology that "bring[s] together the work of the textual scholar in the field of history of religions and the contextual scholar of ethnography."[10] Indeed, an analysis of the pushes and pulls of Judaism's centrifugal and centripetal forces requires the tight ethnographic gaze of an anthropologist, alongside a wide-angle lens on the long durée of Jewish history; a detailed focus on lived-in experiences, as well as an understanding of disembodied religious texts. All of these methodological approaches are brought to bear in the study of the encounters around which the book is structured.

Part 1 opens with an ethnographic account of an encounter between Bukharan Jewish immigrants and Ashkenazi teachers and administrators in a religious school in New York in the early 1990s. Although the immigrant students told me of the Jewish practices and ideas they had brought with them to America, the teachers and administrators spoke of the students as religiously ignorant and saw themselves as facilitating their reconnection to Judaism and the Jewish People. A full examination of this charged interaction calls not only for a study of Bukharan Jews in present-day New York, but also for a journey through time and space to uncover the baggage they carried to it.

Part 2 moves back to the eighteenth century, focusing on an encounter between an emissary from the Holy Land and the Jews of Central Asia. Although no primary sources of this historic meeting remain, for generations dramatic stories about it would be recounted and recorded. The version that came to be popularly accepted depicts the emissary as having found the Jews to be isolated, religiously ignorant, and on the brink of total assimilation into the surrounding society. Through his work, they were reeducated and reconnected with the Jewish world. Another version of this story, which has remained largely sidelined, depicts the Jews as strongly connected to their religion prior to the emissary's arrival, and highlights the debate that emerged between the emissary and indigenous communal leaders about how Judaism should be practiced and who had the authority to decide how it should be observed. In a historiographic analysis—a study of how history comes to be written—this section presents the Center-Periphery Paradigm, a framework historians have invoked to tell the story of Central Asian Jews' past. This section describes how this paradigm functions as a prism through which to construct memory and shows how it is marshaled to articulate and maintain a normative Judaism in the face of diaspora.

Part 3, set in the late nineteenth and early twentieth centuries, depicts an encounter that unfolded on the heels of the Tsarist Empire's encroachment upon Central Asia. After describing the changes that Russian colonialism brought to Jewish communal life in the region, this section draws on an array of archived letters to explore the interactions between the local Jews and Jewish communities in Russia, Western Europe, and Ottoman Palestine. One area of focus is a controversy that erupted in Samarkand about the proper method for ritually slaughtering meat, an issue that had urgent ramifications in the social sphere, the marketplace, and the belly. Letters preserve the voices of the butchers, slaughterers, and householders who became embroiled in the debate, as well as the voices of three individuals who came to dominate the conversation: an Ashkenazi emissary to the region, the chief rabbi of Bukhara, and the Rishon LeTsion (Sephardi chief rabbi in Ottoman Palestine). The writings of these men preserve a rich, technical rabbinic discussion about the religious laws of ritual slaughtering, intertwined with an intimate, impassioned conversation about religious authority. To analyze the contours of this correspondence, two sets of tools are used. An ethnographic lens places the words of these religious leaders within the particular cultural and historical settings they occupy, while the viewpoint of a religious initiate provides entrée into the ways in which these men engaged each other through a world of texts, where the coordinates separating time and place are collapsed. This reading, which is attuned to both the imminent and the timeless, tells a story in which there is no final triumph of either the local or the global. Drawing on a generative model of the Center-Periphery Paradigm, it suggests that Judaism is held together through a dynamic and ongoing struggle to define the meaning of these terms and to identify where they are located.

Here, the book temporarily turns away from the Center-Periphery Paradigm to introduce the *Edah* Paradigm: a very different construct for conceiving of and maintaining Jewish unity. Rather than offering a framework for solidifying a singular, normative Judaism, this paradigm is popularly invoked as a vehicle for accepting cultural diversity among the Jewish People. Analysis of two museum exhibits (one in Jerusalem in 1967 and the other in New York in 1999) highlights how Bukharan Jews—like many other Jewish diaspora groups—are identified as members of a discrete ethnic unit, which is often referred to as an *edah*. The meaning of this term is explored in chapter 7. A simple translation might be "ethnic group," or "historical community." While the exhibits celebrate the group's unique diaspora history and culture, these depictions come at a cost. By their very nature, they treat the group as a frozen form, placing the people who belong to it outside of the flow of history and isolating them from other Jews as well as from the non-Jews among whom they lived.

This critique of the static museum depictions of Bukharan Jews is followed by a reevaluation of the *Edah* Paradigm. Returning to the late nineteenth century, this section draws on a set of community announcements and letters written in reference to a building project in Jerusalem initiated by Central Asia's Jews. These documents show that the Bukharan Jewish *edah* did not come into existence as a result of isolation. Rather, this group identity emerged in Jerusalem—far from the Bukharan heartland—as a result of interactions with other Jewish groups. Those who would come to identify as "Bukharan Jews" distinguished themselves as an *edah* as part of their efforts to legitimize the founding and building of their own communal institutions. This process suggests that the *Edah* Paradigm, like the Center-Periphery Paradigm, works to hold the Jewish world together. However, rather than having an essential or given form, the *edah* category is generative by nature, created and maintained in a dynamic conversation with others.

Part 4, which returns to the Center-Periphery Paradigm, provides an ethnographic description of encounters that have unfolded in the wake of the dissolution of the Soviet Union. Like most of the Jews of the Soviet Empire, Bukharan Jews in Uzbekistan and Tajikistan were largely disconnected from the rest of the Jewish world during the seventy years of communist rule. Since the fall of the iron curtain, however, these ties have been strengthened through outward movement, in the form of massive emigration, as well as inward movement, in the form of travelers and emissaries.

Unlike the previous encounters, which could only be studied through the textual evidence that is left behind, I had the opportunity to witness this one unfold. This part of the book draws on eighteen months of intensive field research carried out in the 1990s, and more than a decade following the stories of the people and institutions to which I was introduced during that first period of fieldwork. Doing research among Bukharan Jews at a moment of great demographic movement sent me to far-flung locales, including New York, Tel Aviv, Samarkand, and Bukhara, and it required the use of multiple languages: English, Hebrew, Russian, and Judeo-Tajik (a Persian language). In each of my various research sites, I lived among Bukharan Jews, conversed with them, watched them interact with one another, and in some cases developed deep relationships, all of which provided me with intimate views of the processes of encounter discussed in the book's first sections. Whereas Part 2 focuses on public memory and the writing of history and Part 3 on public leaders and institutions, this section dwells on common people, men and women alike, and explores the impact of encounters upon individuals' understandings of self.

In Uzbekistan, analysis revolves around interactions between local Jews and representatives of two international Jewish organizations,

Chabad-Lubavitch and the Jewish Agency for Israel. During the Soviet period, Bukharan Jews had developed and elaborated localized forms of Jewish practices and understandings. This was largely a result of the Soviet assault on religion, which severed their connections to Jews in other parts of the world and forced them to practice and transmit Judaism underground. Upon their arrival, the emissaries set about "reuniting" the local Jews with the wider Jewish world by introducing a variety of abstract and global definitions of Judaism and Jewishness. My personal conversations with Bukharan Jews about the emissaries' work reveal their intimate negotiations to come to terms with the new ideas the emissaries introduced without fully discarding their own historical views about Judaism and Jewishness.

Shifting attention away from Central Asia to explore the experiences of those who have emigrated, the next section revisits the popular representation of Bukharan Jews as an *edah*. Whereas Bukharan Jews constituted a single transnational community at the turn of the last century, during the Soviet period the ties that had bound those who inhabited distant locales frayed, and in some cases even dissolved. So too, their historical experiences differed so greatly that much of the cultural resemblance between those who remained in Central Asia and those whose parents and grandparents had emigrated in previous decades was lost. To illustrate, four types of Bukharan Jewish migration experiences that unfolded over the past century are explored. The macro social forces that gave rise to these migrations, as well as portraits of four individuals affected by them, illuminate the range of contemporary views about what it means to be a Bukharan Jew.

While these four depictions capture the multiplicity of ideas about Bukharan Jewishness, they actually tell only part of the story, because each individual is considered in a discrete frame. In fact, immigrants from the various waves pass through shared spaces. Just as I, as an anthropologist doing research in a fractured, transnational field, became aware of the varieties of Bukharan Jewishness, they too come into contact with one another in multiple settings. These encounters, which have become impossible to avoid in the dynamic, post-Soviet era, raise difficult questions about the authenticity of the *edah*. In spite (or perhaps because) of these challenges, great efforts are made to maintain and strengthen it.

Finally, the book concludes by offering the metaphor of "conversation" to define the relationship between global and local forms of Judaism. While Bukharan Jews occupy center stage in this particular set of conversations, the analytical approach used to study them might serve as a model for understanding the Jewish past and for illuminating some of the challenges facing the contemporary Jewish world.

Writing Conventions

The spelling *Bukharan* is used throughout this book in accordance with the convention followed by the *Encyclopedia Judaica*. In citing publications that use alternate spellings, however, these are used. One such widely used spelling is *Bukharian* (appearing in publications including the *New York Times* and the *Bukharian Jewish Times*). The spelling *Bokharan* was once popular, but has largely fallen out of use since the 1970s.

In collecting information for the ethnographic sections of this text, I often carried pen and paper or a tape recorder, which allowed me to capture individuals' words exactly as they were said. These words (sometimes in English translation) are presented in quotation marks. Many of my conversations, however, were informal and spontaneous. I faithfully tried to capture the spirit of what was said to me, but to indicate that they are not verbatim quotes I present them in italics.

To protect the privacy of the people who appear in this book, I refer to many of them by pseudonyms.

The stories of several religious leaders appear in this text. While many of these men are rabbis, revered by their constituents, they are not referred to here by honorific titles. This is partly because these titles are not used with consistency in the Central Asian context. An individual, for example, might be referred to as "Mullah" (a local term) by some, but as "Rabbi" by others. More importantly, assigning honorific titles in this work runs contrary to the book's depiction of religious authority as contested and negotiated. Although individuals' titles cannot be used in this sort of publication, I ask that readers (particularly the followers and descendants of the leaders treated here) not take this as a sign of dishonor. I have worked to treat each public persona who appears in this text with respect—both as leaders and as human beings—while also remaining true to history. I hope the work is read in this spirit.

ACKNOWLEDGMENTS

This work is about the way in which unity can be constructed and maintained in the midst of tremendous flux and dispersion. Indeed, the book itself brings together in a single volume almost twenty years of research and writing, done in many locales. My deep love and devotion to the subject matters have carried me through the process. But this was no solitary enterprise. It could never have been accomplished without the care, support, encouragement, wisdom, friendship, sharing, and dedication of so many whom I met along the way. Some joined me in my endeavors for a few fleeting moments, and with others I have had deeper and more sustained interactions. Regardless, this work is a product of all these relationships.

First, I must thank the people whom this book is about. Although it is not possible for me to list each of the hundreds of individuals who shaped this work by sharing pieces of their lives with me, I extend deep gratitude to all those who did. I am particularly thankful to a few for opening their hearts and homes to me, and for the great time and energy they spent teaching and sharing with me. These include: Yitzhak Abramov, Rivka (Aronbayev) Aharoni, Leora Gevirtzman, Rahel Karayof, Berta Nektalov, Shlomo Haye Niyazov, Geula Sabet, and Nina Yitzhakov. I would also like to mention Sasha Aronbayev and Mikhael Chulpayev, who passed away while still in the prime of their lives. I am grateful for their generosity of time and spirit, and wish I could have been able to share this book with them. May their memory be for a blessing. There are others whose anonymity I have worked to preserve, and am therefore unable to thank by name. I am deeply indebted to these individuals whose lives are so integral to the story I tell here.

Thank you to the community leaders who facilitated my research. These include Eli Aminov and the staff at Moreshet Yahadut Bukhara; Rahel Karayof; Samuel Kassin and the representatives of Midrash Sephardi; Emanuel Shimunov; and Yitzhak Yehoshua. Thank you to Shlomo Tagger and Geula Sabet for providing me with photos of their forebears, and for the permission to print them.

Along my way I have had the benefit of receiving valuable insight, which helped me develop the ideas expressed here. At Boston University, thank you to Frank Korom, Fredrik Barth, Thomas Barfield, and Robert Weller for reading and commenting on the earliest versions of this work. I thank Charles Lindholm for his unwavering encouragement, and for teaching me, in his quiet but steadfast manner, that my work can be rigorous and disciplined, while simultaneously creative and free. My path has intersected Zvi Gitelman at many crucial moments and places in my writing and research: in Cambridge, Ann Arbor, Budapest, Uzbekistan, and of course over the Internet. I thank him for reading and commenting on a number of key sections here, for sharing his expert knowledge, for his gentle prodding, and for his sustained interest. In New York, I thank Jane Gerber for her encouragement and enthusiasm over the course of the many years. I thank Jay Berkovitz who spent countless hours talking with me about my writing during the long commute that we shared between Boston and Amherst. Our conversations were a tremendous help to me in thinking through some of the sections of this book that were most difficult to write.

I am grateful to many people for assisting me in my efforts to decode the rabbinic letters that form the basis of chapter 6. Early on, Seth Farber, Elly Krimsky, and David Weiss-Halivni provided me with information and tools that helped me to read and understand these letters. Later, as I worked to resolve questions about these documents, I had the benefit of assistance from Aharon Oppenheimer, who spent many long study sessions with me. I also thank Shlomo Yaffe for sharing with me his tremendous knowledge. Finally, I thank Ephraim Kanarfogel and Ari Zivotofsky for their detailed reading of individual chapters of the manuscript and providing very helpful feedback.

I thank Hagar Salamon, Harvey Goldberg, and an anonymous reviewer who read the work in its completion as it neared the final stages. Their detailed questions, comments, and suggestions played a critical role in creating a stronger, clearer final product. I thank Seymour Becker for his careful work helping me to refine the sections on Central Asian history. Of course all inaccuracies are my own.

Warm thanks to Shari Lowin, Elitzur Bar-Asher Seigal, Yishai Newman, and Max Malkiel, who all provided help with transliteration, and to Marina Shapiro who helped with translation. Thank you to Kathleen Rose-Johnson for her wizardry in designing the book's cover. Many thanks to all the people who helped with preparation of the manuscript for publication, including Lisanne Norman and Betsy Dean, and to the wonderful team at Indiana University Press: Angela Burton, Peter Froehlich, Daniel Pyle, Janet Rabinowitch, Joyce Rappaport, and the book's formidable project editor, Marvin Keenan, who shepherded the work through its final, critical stages.

The financial support I received from many organizations allowed me to carry out my research in Israel, Uzbekistan, and various locations in the United States. Thank you to the Lady Davis Fellowship Trust, the Memorial Foundation for Jewish Culture, Morton Meyerson, the Sino-Judaic Foundation, and the United States National Security Education Program. I also extend a heartfelt thanks to the Frankel Institute at the University of Michigan. My fellowship year there provided me with the perfect balance of solitude and intellectual camaraderie to allow me to finish writing the final pieces of this book. The notion that Jewish history might be thought of as a conversation was a direct outgrowth of the stimulating conversations I had with the other fellows there that year. I extend special thanks to Todd Endelman and Deborah Dash Moore for convening and nurturing this lively group of fellows, and for their very helpful comments on critical sections of the book manuscript.

I also have many people to thank outside of the academic sphere who have nurtured my work. I thank Dean Solomon who helped me climb out of many pits of confusion and doubt. I thank my dear friend Shari Lowin for her empathy, encouragement, loyalty, and academic kinship. I thank my parents Leonard and Sharon Cooper, and my siblings Ben and Michele Cooper and Ziva Cooper for their never-ending support along the long journey I have taken to bring this book to print. My lovely daughters, Rebecca Lee, Anna Belle, and Miriam Shlayma, were born when I was already deeply invested in my work on this project. I thank them for their sweet laughter and love, which filled me with more happiness than I can express, even in the midst of the most trying moments of the publication process.

And finally, I come to Moshe Shapiro who has been with me through it all: the locales in which I have dwelled, the historical eras I have traversed, the people I have met, and the stages of life I lived through since I began my work on this project. The book bears the imprint of his active involvement in every aspect of my researching, writing, thinking, editing, struggling, and celebrating as the book has moved from the seeds of an idea to fruition. With great love, affection, and gratitude I dedicate to him that which is in part already his.

Bukharan Jews and the
Dynamics of Global Judaism

MAP 0.1
Contemporary Central Asia
Courtesy of The Littman Library of Jewish Civilization, Oxford, U.K.

PART 1

Introduction

First Encounter:
Bukharan Jewish Immigrants in an Ashkenazi School in New York

During the cold war, when tensions between the Soviet Union and the United States were high, the plight of the Jews of the USSR was on the forefront of the American Jewish public agenda. The *refusenik* movement, in particular, was given great attention and publicity. Among its heroes were Anatoly Sharansky, Ida Nudel, Vladimir Slepak, and others who attempted to leave their homes for a place where they could identify as Jews without stigma, and practice their religion without fear. As a consequence of applying for exit visas, they were declared enemies of the state, lost their jobs, and were imprisoned.

While I was growing up in the United States in the 1970s and 1980s, the stories of these *refuseniks* played a formative role in shaping my Jewish identity. I was among the many Jewish youth who signed petitions on their behalf, wrote letters of encouragement to them, sent money to organizations that fought for their freedom, and wore bracelets signifying our solidarity with their plight. These activities sensitized me to the situation of Soviet Jews, but also strongly informed my own ideas about what it meant to be an American Jew. They instilled within me a strong appreciation for the freedom that I had to practice religion and identify proudly as a Jew, all the while maintaining my sense of belonging to America.

In 1991, the Soviet Union dissolved and the Jewish world as I knew it underwent dramatic changes. The Jews of the USSR began to migrate en masse to the United States and Israel, and I was compelled to meet these people whose own experiences had so strongly shaped my understanding of my own Jewish identity. As it happened, this event occurred when I was beginning graduate school in cultural anthropology, and was starting to formulate a research project. It seemed an auspicious time to find entrée into the lives of the Jews who were emigrating. I began studying Russian and took a job at Torah Academy, one of the many private Jewish high schools that had been established in New York to help this immigrant population.

I knew little about the school, other than that it was founded to provide the Soviet émigré student population with a Jewish education, which they had been denied in their home country. I learned much more on the opening day of the school year, the first time I was in the building since my job interview a few months before. I picked up a memo waiting in my mailbox, which in lieu of an orientation was my introduction to Torah Academy's agenda and to the administration's view of my position. Addressed to all staff members, the memo began by describing each student at Torah Academy as a "Jewish soul" that was "thirsting for the beauty of Judaism." The goal of the school, it continued, was to reach out to these students in an effort to quench their thirst, and its raison d'etre was to bring them "closer to Judaism and guide them in their spiritual growth."

This brief statement went a long way to explain the rather puzzling hiring process that had brought me to Torah Academy. After glancing over my resume, and exchanging what seemed to me to be no more than a few pleasantries, the principal had offered me the position of social studies teacher in the girls' division. I would be responsible for teaching four classes, five days a week. The money was meager, the very hasty hiring process was perplexing, but I was a graduate student, excited for the opportunity to have an entrée into the Soviet émigré community, and I agreed without hesitation. Not wanting to draw attention to the fact that I had no prior classroom teaching experience, I cautiously asked the principal before leaving his office if he might advise me on how to prepare for my classes. *Just stay a few pages ahead of the students* were his only words of advice. *Everything will work out fine,* he assured me with a smile, and sent me on my way.

As soon as the school year began and I had the opportunity to meet the other teachers, I learned that Torah Academy was run by an ultra-Orthodox administration, was funded by ultra-Orthodox donors, and was almost exclusively staffed by teachers who viewed the Judaic studies classes as the most vital aspects of the students' education. Many of the teachers who taught math, American history, science, and English in the afternoons also taught religious studies classes in the mornings, and aside from two or three exceptions, none had college degrees. Most were from a relatively tight social and religious circle, lived in a few neighborhoods in Queens, had studied in the same religious academies, and looked to the same Agudat Israel[1] rabbis for guidance. As teachers at Torah Academy, they were fully committed to imparting their particular understanding of Judaism to their students, most of whom were from the Central Asian republics of the former Soviet Union. I learned how strong this commitment was toward the end of the school year when I found out that most of the teachers had not received their paychecks in a timely, regular fashion. In the spring, as a result of a donor's serious lapse in payments, the school's financial crisis reached a peak. At a staff meeting I was surprised to discover that many of the teachers whom I saw each day in the hallways busily rushing from class to class, holding stacks of graded papers in their hands, had not been paid for four consecutive months. More surprising was the fact that there had been so little discussion about this issue in the photocopy room and teachers' lounge, and that I had been utterly sheltered from any knowledge about this situation.

It is this point that brings me to a few words about my place in the school, and the way in which my perspective informs the analysis to follow. Like the other teachers at Torah Academy, I had grown up knowing about the plight of the Soviet Jews who were not permitted to study or practice their religion. Also like the other teachers, I was excited by the school's project of filling this gaping hole left by the communist regime. However, if this task had fallen to my hands, I would have been at a loss. Although I was deeply invested in my own Jewishness, I did not closely identify with any single variant of Judaism and would have been hard-pressed to come up with an approach to teach the religion. As a young child my family belonged to a synagogue affiliated with the Conservative movement, and I attended an ultra-Orthodox Chabad-Lubavitch summer camp. During my teenage years, my parents joined an Orthodox synagogue and sent me to a nonsectarian Jewish high school, in which many different religious perspectives were taught, each given equal weight. For college, I chose to attend Barnard both because of its large, active Jewish student population and also because of the highly liberal education it offered. After I completed my B.A., I remained committed to practicing the religion as an insider, but also enrolled in a Ph.D. program with the intent of studying Judaism and the Jewish world through a critical, analytic approach. As a doctoral student in cultural anthropology, academic inquiry entailed for me an effort to investigate the ways in which Jewish texts were translated into practice. By engaging in my own ethnographic research and drawing on the writings of others, I worked to gain an understanding of the great range of forms the religion had taken on across the far reaches of the diaspora.

At Torah Academy, then, I was primarily driven by a desire to learn about the ways in which my students' experiences in Soviet Central Asia had shaped their practices and understandings of Judaism. I also took note of the great divide between the religious outlook of the school's student population and its teacher population, and was intrigued by the conversations between them in which they negotiated claims to two very different views of Judaism. In short, unlike most of the faculty members, my goal was not to teach Judaism to the students. Rather, it was to enrich my understanding of it through discussions with my students and with the other teachers, and through my observations of the unfolding encounter between them.

In light of what I learned over the course of the year, I was able to make some sense out of the way the teachers handled the lapse in their paychecks, as well as about why I had been sheltered from the situation. Because my educational background, my social world, and my religious views did not neatly overlap with that of the administration, I had not been hired to teach courses that were integral to the school's agenda. My social studies classes, like the math, science, and English classes, were included in the curriculum for the purpose of securing state accreditation. This goal, however, was utilitarian, and was secondary to Torah Academy's central mission.

The peripheral nature of the relationship between the courses I taught and the school's primary agenda explained why I had been hired so quickly and casually. So, too, it explained why I continued to receive my salary in the midst of the school's grave financial troubles. Each time the principal handed me my paycheck and I accepted it, we jointly acknowledged that my work, unlike that of the Judaic teachers, was not organically linked to Torah Academy's core purpose. By contrast, the fact that the teachers who did not receive their paychecks voiced almost no public protest, and continued to work without any clear sense of when they would be compensated, brought into sharp relief just how strongly and authentically they identified with the school's objectives.

These objectives were articulated by a number of teachers in response to my survey question, "What are your goals as a teacher at Torah Academy?" One woman wrote, "I wanted to imbue my students with a love for Judaism, which unfortunately they don't get from the home." Another wrote that her energies were directed toward giving her students "an awareness and appreciation of who they are—as Jews." This teacher pointed out the urgency of her task by explaining that the "students have much opposition from their parents—many of whom find religious observance to be fanatical and a thing of the past." This trope, that the students did not grow up with an appreciation of Judaism and that they had to be taught it from scratch, was strongly articulated in Judaic studies lessons.

Toward the end of the academic year, a number of teachers gave me permission to sit in on their classes, which gave me the opportunity to watch them in action in their effort to "bring the students closer" to their religion. They read religious texts with their students, prayed with them, and taught the religious strictures pertaining to keeping kosher and to observing the Sabbath and holidays. So, too, they taught them moral precepts such as those related to dressing modestly, respecting elders, and refraining from gossip. But more than just teaching the rules of the religion, the teachers worked hard to convince their students to incorporate these practices into their lives. As part of their efforts to "sell" Judaism, the teachers told stories with moral lessons, highlighted the power of divine retribution, described the ways in which religious laws could add meaning to life, and chided those who did not observe them.

The work of the teachers was described in an article about the school that appeared in *New York Newsday* the year I taught there. Proud that his school was featured in the paper, and pleased with the story journalist Susan Berfield told, the principal hung the article on his office door and distributed it to all the teachers. When I picked up the copy in my mailbox, I was drawn to the headline, printed in large bold type, "Heritage 101." This title offered a preview of Berfield's description of Torah Academy's curriculum as an introductory course on Judaism for students who had arrived in the United States, "knowing nothing about being Jewish except to hide it."[2] As a result of the restrictions posed by the Soviet Union, the piece began, the school's students, almost all of whom were from Soviet Central Asia, had been isolated from the rest of the Jewish world for most of the twentieth century. Over the course of this contemporary period of isolation they had forgotten how to practice their religion and had lost their sense of connection to Jewish history and to the Jewish People. They came to the United States with only the vaguest historical memory of their ties to the rest of the Jewish world. Upon arrival, the story continued, many had been fortunate enough to find their way to Torah Academy. Here, they were given the opportunity to learn about their religion and reconnect with their people.

Was the school successful? Did the teachers manage to imbue students with a "love for Judaism" and an "awareness" of who they are as Jews? Was the principal able to bring the students "closer to Judaism" and help them achieve "spiritual growth"? These were all critical questions for the teachers, who had invested vast stores of energy and time in working toward these goals. So, too, they were critical for the administration, whose primary directive was to carry out the mission they shared with the school's donors. Finally, they were essential to the donors themselves, whose funding was conditional on the school's success in meeting its stated goals. The answers to these questions were addressed in staff meetings and memos, and at the school's graduation ceremony, an ideal forum to assure the teachers, administrators, and donors of Torah Academy's success. The caps and gowns, the awards, the formalized speeches, the podium, stage, and performative nature of the event all served to imbue the graduation ceremony's message with a powerful aura of truth. This message was not just that the students had mastered a certain body of knowledge, or that the school had been successful in educating another cadre of young adults. More than anything, the students' receipt of their diplomas signified their passage from a state of religious ignorance to a state of Jewish knowledge and commitment, and from a state of disconnection from world Jewry to connection.

The marking of this transformation was foreshadowed in the invitation to the event, which urged recipients to come witness a "miracle": the transformation of children "from a world of atheism to a world of Judaism." It was the story of this miracle that was featured as the main theme of the ceremony. In the speech delivered by the assistant principal, the students were characterized as "young men and women . . . [who] came from an oppressive, atheist society determined to suppress religion in general and Judaism in particular." He then turned to the audience, asked "Can you believe it?!" and with inflections of amazement continued, "Coming from the society that they did, that they now have the basic bedrock of belief?" This miracle was reiterated in a screening of a promotional film about the school. Against the backdrop of scenes of children actively engaged in a class, the narrator explained, "These young students come spiritually devoid of everything and anything Jewish." As a result of the education they receive in the school, the narrator continued, they develop "strong feelings for *Yiddishkeit* [Jewishness]," are "increasing their level of [religious] observance, [their] homes are being made kosher, Shabbat is being kept, and families are being drawn closer together."

Most powerfully, it was in the speech of the valedictorian that the message of transformation was conveyed. Esther was chosen by her teachers because she seemed to most closely embody Torah Academy's successes. "Today is one of the greatest days of my life," she began, and then, like the others, she invoked the term "miracle" to describe her graduation. Esther affirmed her choice to attend Torah Academy upon her arrival in the United States, which gave her the opportunity to choose "the right path—the path of Torah and *Hashem* [God]" after having lived so many years in the Soviet Union. Each day she spent in the school, she explained, she "grew stronger" in her "resolve to live a Torah way of life," and graduation marked her full commitment to this choice.

Esther's speech was a clear articulation of the final chapter in a tripartite story about Central Asia's Jews that I would come to hear many times over: isolation, encounter, and then the triumph of the educator in reuniting these Jews with the wider Jewish world and with their own Jewish selves. This tale, however, was told by the voices that dominated in the public sphere. In the private, unofficial sphere—in my classroom and in the personal conversations I had with students and their families outside of the school—I heard very different stories.

While the faculty at Torah Academy characterized the students as "Russian Jews," a catchword for "Jewishly ignorant and assimilated," they referred to themselves as "Bukharan Jews." This label was, among other things, a way to distinguish themselves from the only other Jews with whom they had had contact during the long decades of their isolation under Soviet rule; the Ashkenazi Jews, most of whom arrived in Central Asia during World War II after escaping or being evacuated from their homes in Eastern Europe.[3]

Unlike Bukharan Jews who had very low rates of intermarriage, who tended to structure their rites of passage around Jewish idiom, observe key Jewish holidays, and keep kosher throughout the seventy years of Soviet rule, Ashkenazi Jews in Central Asia were generally highly assimilated, both structurally and culturally, into the Soviet Union's Russian population. The reference to themselves as "Bukharan Jews" and to the others as "Ashkenazi Jews," then, implied a comparison between those who continued to practice Judaism and to strongly identify themselves as Jews throughout the Soviet era, and those who did not.

Significantly, Bukharan Jews' practice and identity were strongly shaped by the particular circumstances in which they found themselves in Soviet Central Asia. As a result of having to transmit and practice their religion underground over the course of many decades of Soviet rule, their Judaism had taken on a localized form. Given that the development of their very particular forms of Jewish expression did not occur in conversation with other Jewish populations, however, those who engaged in them were unaware of just how idiosyncratic their practice had become. Their practices, as well as Bukharan Jews' perceptions of them, are explored at length further in this book. The critical point here is that Bukharan Jews did not think of themselves as having forgotten their Judaism, nor did they think of themselves as adherents to a deviant or exotic form of Judaism. Therefore, the gap between Torah Academy's teachers' view of the students' Jewishness and those of the students themselves was immense. So too was the gap in these two groups' understandings of the purpose of the school.

Torah Academy, which was founded to cater to the Soviet émigré population, happened to have been established in Kew Gardens, a neighborhood in Queens that was teeming with Bukharan Jewish immigrants. These newcomers arrived with almost no English skills, with little understanding of the school system in the United States, and with very meager financial resources. The school was appealing to them because tuition was almost fully subsidized, students were given free hot lunches, and parents who were frightened of New York and New Yorkers were given the security of knowing that their children were in school with others like them. Parents did not send their children to Torah Academy with the hopes that they would increase their level of religious observance. In fact, the teachers' great efforts to instill new Jewish values and understandings seemed to have taken many of the students and their parents by surprise.

The great divide between the motives and interests of the administration and teachers, on the one hand, and the parents and students, on the other, gave rise to two different sorts of stories about the school which bore little resemblance to one another. Torah Academy's official narrative presented its students as Jewishly ignorant prior to their arrival in the United States and portrayed their education as a religious transformation. If this public story was well packaged by the school's donors and administration, much in the way of an advertising campaign, the voices of the students were softer, and their narratives were not well articulated. Indeed, they came in many different versions, and no strong spokesperson assembled them together into a single, clear story that might be publicized. I myself only began to tease out the various aspects of their stories after careful listening and reflection on conversations that I had with my students and their family members over the course of that year. These stories began with discussions about their memories of Jewish life in Central Asia. They moved to descriptions of the surprises encountered at Torah Academy, and ended with difficult questions about whether the form of Judaism they had practiced in Central Asia ought to be preserved, about how the Judaism presented at Torah Academy compared with other forms of American Judaism, and about how to characterize authentic Judaism.

In one sense, this book is structured around these very narratives, not necessarily the ones told by the students at Torah Academy but rather by individuals who occupied the Bukharan Jewish diaspora landscape over the course of the past two centuries. In this effort, I carried with me an important lesson about ethnographic research taught by Bronislaw Malinowski, considered one of cultural anthropology's founding fathers. Writing and researching in the 1920s, Malinowski rejected the methods of "arm-chair anthropologists," who wrote ethnographies of indigenous peoples by drawing solely on the data collected by British colonial officials, missionaries, and travelers. These Westerners may have lived in the colonies for years, with "constant opportunities" to observe "the natives" and to communicate with them, but because they were driven by a particular agenda they "hardly knew one thing about them really well."[4] One of the first anthropologists to engage in intense fieldwork himself, Malinowski set up camp in Papua New Guinea, and learned about the people there through their own voices, rather than through descriptions that were filtered through the prism of the colonizer. Keeping this approach in mind, I recognized that much of what has been published on Bukharan Jewish history and culture has been written by Western scholars, many of whom have brought a priori assumptions to bear on their work. To peel away the filters that have informed their scholarship, I would have to seek an understanding of Bukharan Jewish history, identity, social relationships, and practices as seen through their own eyes, and as framed on their own terms.

Yet, this task of listening to Bukharan Jews and working to see the world as they view it is only half the project. At Torah Academy, I was also intrigued by the encounters between the school's student population and teacher population, in which they negotiated claims to two very different views of Judaism. This formative experience shaped the direction of my research as well as the structure of this book. The gateway story this chapter presents, then, is not only intended to provide ethnographic details about the interactions between Torah Academy's ultra-Orthodox, Ashkenazi establishment and the school's Bukharan Jewish immigrant students, an encounter that unfolded in a very particular time, place, and cultural context. It is also meant to serve as a narrative about the efforts of the religious establishment (however that broad and shifting term is defined) to strip Bukharan Jews of features it characterizes as misguided or not authentically Jewish. In this respect, the interactions that unfolded at Torah Academy are not an isolated phenomenon. The book focuses on similar efforts undertaken over the course of two hundred years of history. During this period, a range of Jewish institutions, leaders, and intellectuals have worked to bring Bukharan Jews—whom they have understood to be situated at the margins of the Jewish world (both in terms of their practice, as well as their geographical location)—into alignment with that which they classify as "Center."

At another level, this narrative need not be read as pertaining to Bukharan Jews alone. While this book focuses on the particulars of this group, it offers a more general framework for understanding the ways in which groups—throughout Jewish history—have been labeled and treated by other Jewish groups as marginal, deviant, or backward. Likewise, it is about the efforts of the latter to reeducate and resocialize the former as part of a larger project; that of reining in diaspora's centrifugal forces.

Keeping in mind this broader narrative, the book deliberately began with a story that takes place in the United States rather than in Israel. This starting point serves as a response to a current trend in Jewish Studies scholarship: most works that focus on the dynamics between the Jewish establishment vis-à-vis Jewish groups that are disempowered and marginalized are set in Israel. They call attention to relations between the country's Ashkenazi and Mizrahi Jews (who are of North African, Middle Eastern, and Central Asian extraction), and discussions are generally couched in terms of West and East; colonizer and native; white-skinned and dark-skinned. More specifically, this discourse tends to center on power relations between the country's hegemonic, white, Ashkenazi, Zionist establishment and the disempowered, dark-skinned Mizrahi populations.

This book does not exclude Israel as a site of investigation. Yet, Israel's interethnic and class tensions are not the focus of analysis. Likewise, the work does not exclude power relations from the discussion. However, the colonial and imperialist urge associated with the West's effort to dominate the East, and ascribed by many to the Ashkenazi establishment's exertion of power over Israel's Mizrahi citizens, is not treated as a driving mechanism. Instead, relations among Jewish groups within Israel are regarded as but one manifestation of a phenomenon that has been present throughout much of Jewish history: the project of maintaining a single religion and people in the face of global dispersion. This project extends well beyond the borders of modern-day Israel and begins long before the history of contemporary Zionism or European colonialism.

Rather than drawing on postcolonial theory or an orientalist critique to understand the relationship between Bukharan Jews and the other Jews they encounter, then, it is diaspora studies that informs this work. Along these lines, the final level at which this gateway story—and more broadly this book—can be read is not about Jews in particular. Rather, it is about world religions more generally. At this level, the focus is on the work involved in navigating between diaspora's centripetal and centrifugal forces: the centralizing claims of a global religion in tension with the pulls of varied local beliefs and practices.

Writing Bukharan Jewish History: Memory, Authority, and Peoplehood

Geographical and Temporal Boundaries

On my first day of teaching at Torah Academy, before I knew that my students were immigrants from Soviet Central Asia, I looked at the many faces in my classroom, and was perplexed. Noticing that most had ol-ive skin, deep-brown eyes, and dark hair, I wondered why they looked so different from the fair-skinned Soviet Jews I had seen in pictures. Glancing over the attendance list, I was puzzled further. As I stumbled through the roster of names, most of which I had never heard—Mullo-kandov, Abdurakhmanov, Illyayev, Shalamayev—my students corrected me and snickered among themselves in a language that did not sound anything like Russian.

To gain some insight into my students' backgrounds, I had them fill out cards telling me how long they had been in the country and where they had come from. I learned that most of them had immigrated within the past two years, and that they were from cities that had names with which I was largely unfamiliar: Tashkent, Dushanbe, Novaii, An-dijan, Namangan, Bukhara, and Samarkand. Studying an atlas, I found that they were all located in the newly independent states of Uzbekistan and Tajikistan, which until 1991 had been republics within the Soviet Union.

When I spoke with my students further about their origins, I learned that they did not call themselves "Uzbeki Jews" or "Tajiki Jews." This, in fact, came as no surprise, as I knew from my exposure to the *refusenik* movement that Soviet Jews were marked as outsiders on their identity documents. Rather than being labeled "Russian" or "Ukrainian," for example, the Soviets identified them as "Jews," regardless of the republic in which they were born. What was surprising to me, though, was that no matter which city they were from, they referred to themselves as "Bukharan Jews." Why they used this label and what exactly it meant to be a Bukharan Jew was not clear to me, and when I asked them about it, I got no simple response.

My students, all recent immigrants to Queens, New York, tended to speak in a certain characteristic way about what it meant to be a Bukharan Jew. However, as I learned more about the Bukharan Jews living in Queens, I found that among this community of some 30,000 people were several thousand who had immigrated in the 1970s (when there had been a slight ease of migration restrictions from the USSR). Furthermore, there was another small group of people who had immigrated (or whose parents had) in the 1920s, just as Central Asia was being incorporated into the vast Soviet Empire. Each of these immigrant groups had a different way of explaining why they were called "Bukharan Jews" and each had different ways of characterizing the essential features of "Bukharan Jewishness." For example, those who had left Central Asia in the 1920s pointed out that many of the recent immigrants had abandoned "traditional" Bukharan Jewish culture as a result of their exposure to three generations of Soviet atheist, communist policy. The newcomers, on the other hand, spoke about the culture of Bukharan Jewish old-timers as having been spoiled by the Western, American values that they had adopted.

The question of what Bukharan Jewishness is all about, and who might be considered most representative of the Bukharan Jewish population became more complicated when I considered the variations among those who had lived in different areas of Soviet Central Asia: those who immigrated from the city Bukhara itself, versus those who came from other cities and towns; those who immigrated from cities that had been strongly influenced by Russian culture, such as Uzbekistan's cosmopolitan capital, Tashkent, versus those who came from small towns on the margins of the Soviet sphere of influence; those who immigrated from Uzbekistan where the national language is Uzbek (a Turkic language, which the Jews generally did not use), versus those who came from Tajikistan, where the national language is Tajik (a Persian language, which the Jews spoke).

The problem became knottier still when I left New York to go to Israel to conduct further research among immigrants, and then to Uzbekistan to seek out those who still remained there. As I accumulated many different, and often contradictory, descriptions of Bukharan Jewish culture, history, values, and identity, the task of presenting a coherent picture of the people I was studying became increasing complicated. But it is precisely this complication that fascinated me and drew me to follow the people who call themselves Bukharan Jews, on an ethnographic venture that cut across continents, and on a historical quest that cut across languages, perspectives, and time periods.

It is a difficult task to present introductory notes that describe who Bukharan Jews are, for it is this very question and the contested nature of its answer that make up much of the substance of the book. The book, therefore, is structured in a way that allows the answer to the question "Who are the Bukharan Jews?" to unfold as it did for me during my travels from one research site to the next. For now, I introduce them through an overview of their past. This section addresses the various ways in which this past might be told depending on the perspective of the historian.

Jewish History in Central Asia

Little information is available about how and when Jews first appeared in Central Asia. While some claim that they were among the lost Israelite tribes, the data available suggests that the first to arrive were probably among those who were exiled (or whose ancestors were exiled) from the Land of Israel in 586 BCE at the hands of the Babylonians. When the Persians conquered the Babylonians seventy years later, the Jews were permitted to return to their homes. Yet, many chose not to. Some turned eastward, spreading out from Babylonia (contemporary Iraq) into the territory that is today Iran, probably moving as merchants along trade routes.[1] Some moved farther east to Afghanistan and northeast to the fertile river valleys and oases of the region known as "Transoxiana,"[2] ruled by the Persian Archaemenids. It was not until the sixteenth century that the name "Bukhara" was assigned to this territory. This occurred when Uzbek dynasts (of Turkic lineage) rose to power and divided the land into two loosely governed territories called "khanates": Bukhara and Khworizm (later Khiva).[3] While Jews could be found across the region encompassed by these two khanates (and later a third, Kokand),[4] they clustered primarily in the cities of Samarkand and Bukhara,[5] both silk-route hubs located within Bukhara Khanate.

In the 1920s, on the heels of Russian expansion into the area, the names delineating the region changed again. Beginning in the latter half of the nineteenth century, the Russians whittled away at the borders of the khanates until they were fully incorporated into the Soviet Union and then dissolved. In their place stood the newly created republics of Uzbekistan and Tajikistan, which became independent states when the Soviet Union collapsed in 1991.

Over the course of their history, first in Transoxiana, then in the khanates of Bukhara and Khiva (and later Kokand), and finally in Uzbekistan and Tajikistan, Jewish life became integrated into the Turko-Persian "composite culture"[6] dominant in the region. Yet, from the eighth century on (when Islam was introduced to the area), Jews also stood out as one of the few "numerically insignificant" minorities among the population's Muslim majority.[7] To understand the Jews' status as both insiders and outsiders, some explanation of the region's political organization is in order.

When the Soviets undertook the task of redrawing the map of Central Asia in the 1920s, this did not prove a difficult challenge. They faced little local resistance as the khanates' boundaries had not coincided with existing linguistic or ethnic borders. Nor was the khanates' territorial organization linked to strong political loyalties or economic ties. Instead, as historian Seymour Becker points out, the khanates' borders "simply reflected the relative strength of the amir [or khan] vis-a-vis his rivals in any given period," and that strength, which "was entirely a matter of the fortunes of war and politics," was unstable and volatile.[8] Within this fluid geographical context, the populations did not develop a sense of belonging to or identification with the khanates in which they lived. This geopolitical pattern is critical for understanding the relationship between the region's Jews and their non-Jewish neighbors.

Given that the peoples of the region did not derive their sense of identity from the khanates they inhabited, and that they had no sense of national identity, the Jews—unlike Jews in other parts of the world where nationalist movements were beginning to burgeon by the nineteenth century—were not viewed as foreign inhabitants. Instead, the Jews' sense of inclusion in, or exclusion from, the population amid whom they lived was derived from two other aspects of the region's social patterns. The first was linked to the dynamic between the sedentary and nomadic peoples, and the second was related to the fact that unlike the majority of people in Central Asia, they were not Muslim.

Regarding the sedentary–nomadic division: the region's Jews were sedentary, like most others who lived in the khanates' urban centers. Among these sedentary peoples, however, a distinction was drawn between the Tajiks and the Uzbeks. The Tajiks, who were of Persian stock, had always lived in the settled areas, whereas the Uzbeks, who were of Turkic stock and were descendants of the region's nomadic conquerors, had become sedentary over time. Nineteenth-century travelers such as Eugene Schuyler noted stereotypical differences between the Uzbek and Tajik settled peoples. Schuyler portrayed the former as straightforward, honest, and simple, and the latter as shrewd and tricky urbanites.[9] The Uzbeks also tended to identify themselves with their tribal lineage, stating, "I am an Uzbek, the clan of Jalayer or Kalagar," for example; whereas the Tajiks tended to identify themselves by their residential heritage, saying, "I am a man of Tashkent," for example.[10]

Despite these caricature-like portrayals of the differences between the Uzbeks and Tajiks, contemporary scholars posit that these identities were not significant boundary markers.[11] Neither was strong enough to unify its group in a call for special rights or distinct sovereign territories. Nineteenth-century travelers note that Uzbeks and Tajiks lived side by side,[12] they did not distinguish themselves with much "precision, consistency or linguistic significance,"[13] nor did they have distinct cultural traditions.[14] Indeed, the Uzbeks and Tajiks shared a strong sense of commonality with each other relative to the Kyrgyz, Turkomen, and Kazakhs, who were still largely nomadic.

Thus, while the terms *Uzbek* and *Tajik* did carry some historical value for the people who asserted these identities, their shared culture, which set them off from neighboring nomadic groups, more strongly informed their conceptions of who they were. In this sense, the Jews very much belonged to this group, sharing most elements of the settled peoples' culture, including dress, cuisine, architecture, language, and customs.[15]

Yet, living in a predominantly Muslim society, Jews were marked as outsiders. As in all areas of the world where the rule of the Islam prevailed, Jewish inhabitants (like Christian inhabitants) were classified as *ahl al-kitab* ("people of the book") and were conferred the status of *ahl al-dhimma* ("people of the pact"). This status allowed them a degree of tolerance and protection in return for their acceptance of certain discriminatory measures.[16]

In Central Asia, as with other areas under Muslim rule, these measures included numerous prohibitions.[17] Jews, for example, were allowed to repair existing synagogues but were not permitted to build new ones. They were allowed to build homes as long as they were no taller than any Muslim home in the area. They were not permitted to ride donkeys or horses but had to transport themselves by foot alone. They were required to pay a special poll tax, which the Muslim receiver acknowledged by delivering a slap in the face. Not permitted to wear elaborate, fashionable belts, Jewish men could only close their robes with a "simple rope." So, too, Jewish men were not permitted to wear turbans, the head covering worn by Muslim men. Instead, they were allowed only a particular style of hat called a *tilpak,* which signified their identity as Jews. Their homes were also marked as Jewish by a dark or dirty cloth that they were forced to nail to their front doors. Finally, the evidence of a Jew was inadmissible in any court case that involved a Muslim. Such restrictions were not evenly enforced during the many centuries that Jews lived in Central Asia under Muslim rule. In periods of economic and social stability, the restrictions were generally relaxed, whereas in times of hardship or crisis, they tended to be more strictly enforced.

In the late nineteenth century, Russia's expansion into Central Asia brought improvements in communication and travel conditions, new avenues for trade, and new forms of technology. Russian colonial efforts also introduced Western secular ideologies to the region. As new worldviews challenged the old religious, traditional ones that were dominant in the area, the stigma attached to the Jews was softened and the label *dhimmi* began to lose its meaning.

The distinction between Muslim and Jew continued to erode as a result of the antireligious policies the Soviets imposed on Central Asia when the area came under their control. Synagogues were shut down, as were mosques. *Khomlos*,[18] where young children studied Jewish traditional teachings, were shut down, as were *kitabs*. The Soviets also saw to it that celebrations of rites of passage, such as weddings and births, came under control of the state. Public aspects of these events were structured around civil idiom, rather than around traditional religious practice. The result was a further blurring of differences between Jews and Muslims.

The fading of these differences, however, should not be overstated. Soviet antireligious campaigns were not as harshly enforced in Central Asia as they were in western parts of the USSR. Furthermore, the region's slow pace of industrialization and urbanization allowed the traditional organization of society to remain largely intact during the course of Soviet rule.[19] People had little incentive to leave their home villages and towns in search of employment, education, or high culture. Geographic mobility, therefore, remained low and social boundaries remained high. In Uzbekistan, intermarriage between Uzbeks and non-Uzbeks was rare[20] and the locals maintained use of their native language (as opposed to Russian) as their first language.[21] Similar patterns were found among Central Asia's Jews. Almost every city and town in Uzbekistan and Tajikistan that was home to a Jewish community had a Jewish *mahalla* (residential quarter). Throughout the Soviet era, Jewish populations remained concentrated in these *mahallas* which functioned as centers of Jewish life. The communities' physical boundaries reinforced their social boundaries. Rates of intermarriage with non-Jews remained low[22] and a strong sense of Jewish identity persisted.

Relationship between Central Asia's Jews and the Wider Jewish World

Although the students I met while teaching in Queens brought their Jewish sense of identity with them, to me they seemed unfamiliar. They did not look like any Jews I had ever met; they spoke a language I had never heard; and the Jewish marriage and mourning customs that they told me about were different from any I had ever seen. I assumed that because we were all Jews, my students and I *were* historically connected, but wondered how, and began to search for information about the ways in which my Ashkenazi Jewish past intersected with theirs. I turned to books that covered the broad sweep of Jewish history, hoping that I might learn about their place in the story. I looked in popular works as well as scholarly ones, but was unable to find the information I sought.

Changing my strategy, I set out to look for information about Bukharan Jews in more specialized journals and books, which focused on narrower topics such as the Jews of the Soviet Union and Mizrahi Jews.[23] Through this search, I discovered that a few academic scholars— including Yitzhak Ben-Zvi, Walter Fischel, and Michael Zand—had, in fact, written histories of Central Asia's Jews. Through their works it became clear (or so I thought at the time) why I had been unable to find information about how their past intersected with that of the world's other Jews. According to these three scholars, the social and religious ties between Central Asia's Jewish communities and the rest of the Jewish world remained relatively strong for many centuries. In the thirteenth century, however, these connections began to weaken and then dissolve, leaving the Jews of Central Asia totally isolated from the rest of the Jewish world. These Jews, it seemed, were excluded from general narratives of the Jewish past because they simply did not occupy the same stage upon which much of Jewish history unfolded.

A rapid historical overview draws attention to this story of progressive isolation. Historians highlight the connections between the Jews of Central Asia and the prosperous, influential Jewish community of Baghdad prior to the thirteenth century.[24] Citing the writings of the early tenth-century chronicler Nathan the Babylonian, Zand explains that when religious issues arose in the Central Asian province of Khorasan, the Jews there would confer with the scholars of Baghdad's prominent Jewish institution, Pumpedita Academy, and defer to their opinions.[25] Zand brings a further citation from Nathan the Babylonian regarding a "bitter controversy" that took place between the Exilarch (Jewish political leader in Baghdad) and the Gaon (Jewish religious leader) of the Pumpedita Academy surrounding the distribution of revenues received from the Jewish communities of Khorasan.[26] These two points suggest that the Jews in tenth-century Central Asia paid taxes toward the upkeep of Jewish institutions in Baghdad, and considered themselves bound to the religious decisions made there.

Additional documentation regarding the relationship between the Jews in Central Asia and Baghdad's Jewish communal institutions can be gleaned from the report of twelfth-century traveler Benjamin of Tudela. A significant section of his travelogue is devoted to a description of Baghdad, one of the largest cities he visited. Among other things, he provides an extensive depiction of the Exilarch, whose influence, Benjamin explains, extended to Jewish communities across the far reaches of the Muslim caliphate. He writes:

> In Bagdad there are about forty thousand Jews. . . . And at the head of them all is Daniel the son of Hisdai. The Jews call him "Our Lord, Head of the Exile." . . . The authority of the Exilarch extends over all the communities of Babylon, Persia, Khurasan and Sheba which is El-Yemen, and Diyar Kalach and all the land of Mesopotamia, and over the dwellers in the mountains of Ararat and the land of the Alans. . . . His authority extends also over the land of the Sawir, and the land of the Turks, unto the mountains of Asveh and the land of Gurgan. . . . Further it extends *to the gates of Samarkand,* the land of Thibet, and the land of India.[27]

According to this testimony, the authority of the Exilarch, which extended to Khorasan and "to the gates of Samarkand," connected the Jews of Central Asia to Baghdad, the heart of religious life for much of the world's contemporary Jewish population.

Ben-Zvi, Fischel, and Zand explain that these ties were severed in the thirteenth century when Genghis Khan and his army swept through the area, leaving death and destruction in their wake. Despite the (supposed) isolation that followed, these authors draw attention to the close connections maintained between various Persian-speaking Jewish communities that lived in the territories that would become Iran, Afghanistan, Uzbekistan, and Tajikistan. These ties remained strong and intact, joining the Jews of this broad region into what Zand calls a "single community," which shared a common liturgy and created a shared library of Judeo-Persian biblical commentary and poetry.[28]

It was not long, though, before these ties were severed as well. With the ascent of the Safavid dynasty and their adoption of Shi'ism, Iran dissolved political and economic relations with its Sunni neighbors, including the khanate of Bukhara. As a result, Zand argues, the Jews of the two areas were unable to maintain contact, and the single community became divided into two distinct entities. In the eighteenth century, the Jews of Bukhara sank into further isolation as a result of "constant hostilities" and the eventual severance of political ties between Bukhara and Afghanistan.[29]

Cut off from the rest of the Jewish world, the Jews in Bukhara are described as having reached a state of "spiritual exhaustion," "religious dissolution," and "ignorance."[30] A new chapter of their history opens as the eighteenth century draws to a close. At this moment, historians introduce Yosef Maman, an emissary to Central Asia from Palestine, and portray his arrival as a pivotal juncture in Bukharan Jewish history. Fischel writes:

> Cut off from the rest of [the] Jewish world, in the heart of Asia, they would have suffered the fate of the Jews in China had Providence not led to their re-discovery through a "Messenger from Zion" . . . Rabbi Joseph Ma'man al-Maghrebi.[31]

Like Fischel, Zand and Ben-Zvi explain that Maman rejuvenated religious life in Central Asia, ushering the Jews there back onto the stage of Jewish history.[32]

Later, I will return to the story of Yosef Maman, which is so central to the way that Bukharan Jews and their history have been understood. Close analysis will call into question this popularized portrayal. For now, let it suffice to say that the story of Maman is a compelling one because it appears to encapsulate the whole of Bukharan Jewish history: the story of a remote people whose ties to the Jewish world weakened over centuries of isolation, but who were rejoined through the work of an emissary who arrived from a center of the Jewish world.

Perhaps, though, the story is so compelling because it is not only shorthand for the long diaspora history of Bukharan Jews, but because it is, in fact, shorthand for a widely accepted view of all of Jewish history—a history of a diaspora people, scattered across the globe, who have maintained a sense of unity through the prominence of important centers. This approach rests on the premise that far-flung communities remain bound to the Jewish People as long as they maintain connections to the center (or a center) of the Jewish world. The loosening of such connections poses the possibility of such communities becoming "lost." If and when they are "found," they rejoin the Jewish world upon their re-socialization and acceptance of the norms from which they had strayed during their history of isolation. This dynamic has allowed for the maintenance of the religion's integrity and the people's unity. This is one very standard approach to Jewish history, but as we shall see, a more nuanced rendition of the Bukharan Jews' complex story allows for a more accurate view of the past.

Jewish History as a Narrative

In his book *Zakhor*, which analyzes the Jews' relationship to their past, Yosef Yerushalmi notes that the act of remembering has always been "a central component of Jewish experience." Yet the study of history though a detached academic lens "played at best an ancillary role among the Jews, and often no role at all."[33] Indeed, it was not until the nineteenth century that Jewish history as a discipline was inaugurated with the formation of *Verein für Kultur und Wissenschaft des Judentums* (the Society for Culture and Science of the Jews) in Berlin.

Inspired by the Enlightenment's spirit of rationalism, Wissenschaft scholars treated the study of the Jewish past as a social science rather than as sacred history. In their "battle" to "emancipate the historian from the authority of the theologian,"[34] they reacted against the traditional understanding of Judaism as having "simply drop[ped] down from heaven" and then "transmitted without change from generation to generation,"[35] and argued that Judaism, like any other social and religious institution, had a history that unfolded within a wider political and social context and that it could be studied within the framework of modern scholarship.[36]

In spite of their new critical approach to the past, Wissenschaft scholars never problematized the given nature of Jewish Peoplehood. Unlike contemporary academics who are aware of and acutely concerned with the contingent and situated nature of national, ethnic, and religious forms and identities, these nineteenth-century scholars never called into question the existence of the objects of their study. Rather, they took it for granted that there was a single entity called *The Jewish People* and a normative religion called Judaism. Given this starting point, they did not debate whether or not it was possible to write a singular narrative of the Jewish experience. If there was, after all, a "Jewish People," then surely it was possible to write their story. Given that most of the Jews' history unfolded in a diaspora context, however, this proved a difficult challenge.

How could a single narrative encompass the story of Jews in such far-flung regions as the Middle East, Europe, and North Africa? Historian Michael Meyer aptly summarizes this problem:

> Once the Jews became scattered among the nations . . . their history no longer possessed the unity of a nation dwelling upon its own soil. . . . Jewish historians have had to search for the common bond which united Jews undergoing very different historical experiences . . . [and] have been pressed to come up with some thread running the entire length of Jewish history.[37]

In the face of this challenge, nineteenth- and early twentieth-century European Jewish scholars worked to identify "integrating patterns" that could be used to construct a "coherent, unified account of the whole of Jewish history" into which they could insert the details of the Jews' great range of experiences.[38] While a diverse number of such "integrating patterns" emerged, historian Robert Seltzer identifies two ideal types: one, which has been labeled "theological and metaphysical," and the other "secular and anthropocentric."[39]

As representative of the former, Seltzer points to the work of Heinrich Graetz. Informed by German idealism and Hegelian philosophy, Graetz's scholarship focused on the development of Jewish ideas, as opposed to emphasis on the history of Jewish People. A leading exponent of the latter was Russian Jewish historian Simon Dubnow, who viewed Jewish history through a sociological lens and focused primarily on Jewish communal life.[40]

Regardless of the difference between their approaches, a critical similarity existed between them. While Graetz's story revolved around the evolution of an idea, and Dubnow's around the tenacious survival of a people, both unabashedly spun a singular narrative of Jewish history by following the respective threads of their stories over the course of the grand procession of time. But what about space? How were Graetz, Dubnow, and their contemporaries able to incorporate their linear, diachronic patterns into a complex synchronic weave that crisscrossed the globe in complicated ways? How, in other words, could they move forward in time, while also taking into account the myriad events occurring at any given moment within Jewish communities dispersed throughout the world?

Both scholars resolved this dilemma by focusing their narratives around a series of Jewish centers. Rather than writing about every Jewish community at each moment in time, they identified hegemonic centers that served as focal points for their stories. Baghdad, for example, was identified as the geographic focus of the Jewish story during the years that it served as the place where the Babylonian Talmud was compiled and from which it was then disseminated. When Baghdad lost its influential position, the story of the Jews living there falls into the background and the Jewish community in Spain becomes the focus, taking up a leading role in Jewish cultural and religious activity. These shifting centers were presented as nodes through which the essence of Judaism and the Jewish People developed and emanated. Through them Jewish "historical life spread out over the wide periphery," thus providing a sense of unity to the story of Jewish history.[41] Graetz explains:

> One should not let oneself be deceived by the seeming lack of cohesion and unity displayed by post-Talmudic Jewish history when it is viewed from the outside, making the Jewish race appear to fall into as many entities as there were communities. . . . It has, on the contrary, established quite definite and prominent centers from which historical life flowed out to the widely extended periphery.[42]

Like Graetz, Dubnow also used the language of centers and peripheries:

> The history of the stateless period [, which began] after the Jews lost their unified center, must be subdivided in accordance with clear-cut geographical considerations and along lines corresponding to shifts in the center of national hegemony within the Jewish people. Each epoch is determined by the fact that the dispersed nation possessed within this period one main center, or sometimes two coexisting centers, which assumed the leadership of all other parts of the Diaspora.[43]

The approach that Graetz and Dubnow used to construct a "coherent, unified account of the whole of Jewish history" had a tremendous influence on the way the discipline developed for decades to come.[44] Following in their footsteps, generations of Jewish historians focused on the rise and fall of centers as a means to frame their unified narratives of the Jewish People and religion.

Since these centers were defined by their influence on the Jewish population across the globe, historians' documentation of Jewish life within them generally focused on their public, political, and intellectual contributions. There was, therefore, an intimate link between the center-based narrative and the presentation of Jewish history in elitist terms. Jewish historians' concerns focused around the ideas and accomplishments of the literate, scholarly classes and the activities of the wealthy and political leaders. Generally excluded from this presentation of history were the strands that did not bolster or enforce the center's hegemony. A list of these strands included religious movements considered deviant, such as mysticism; Jewish individuals who did not hold public community roles, such as women; and groups of Jews who did not contribute to the production of widely accepted rabbinic texts, such as Mizrahi Jews.[45]

The absence of these strands from the grand narrative of Jewish history brings us back to the discussion of Central Asia's Jews. Throughout the ages, they have lived at the far margins of areas traditionally considered centers of the Jewish world. They have, therefore, been treated as irrelevant to the story, and have been largely excluded from Jewish histories published by scholarly as well as popular presses. Zand, Fischel, and Ben-Zvi are among the few historians who have told discrete histories of the Central Asian Jewish communities. Their works, though, are primarily aimed at explaining and detailing a process of disconnection and alienation from world Jewry. These stories of increasing isolation, told from the vantage point of the world's shifting Jewish centers, treat the periods during which Central Asia's Jews had little contact with the center as unimportant—even illegitimate—chapters in Jewish history. And when Central Asia's Jews were finally reconnected to the center through Yosef Maman, the story told about this reunion is not about them at all, but rather about the center's triumph in holding together a unified Jewish world.

A Story of Reunions

In the many decades that have passed since Graetz and Dubnow wrote their monumental works, the study of the Jewish past has undergone a major paradigm shift, which has opened up new avenues for telling the story of communities that do not fit neatly into traditional master narratives of Jewish history.

In the United States this change was linked to the social turmoil of the 1960s and 1970s. The civil rights movement and the antiwar movement, the feminist revolution, and the challenge of youth to the establishment brought people who had until then occupied the margins of the country's political and social institutions into vocal, visible positions. At this same time, Israel was experiencing its own social revolution. Israeli Jewish immigrants from Muslim lands began protesting against widespread discrimination. The Labor party, composed of the country's old Eastern European guard, was voted out of power for the first time since the foundation of the state. Dissent arose against the annexation of territories that had been acquired in the Six Day War of 1967, and the rights and aspirations of Arabs living in those territories were placed on the public agenda.

In very different circumstances, but for similar kinds of reasons, voices that until then had been silenced began to be heard in political and academic institutions in both the United States and Israel. So, too, attention to the works and lives of those who had traditionally occupied the centers of power (intellectuals, men, politicians, the wealthy) gave way to a growing interest in the voices and experiences of immigrants, women, the working class, and the disenfranchised. Scholars of Jewish history have responded to these changes accordingly, turning to areas of study that had been previously overlooked.[46]

Additional avenues for exploring the Jews' past were opened up in the 1980s and 1990s. With the advent of postmodern theory, new epistemological understandings began to challenge universal, detached narratives of history. As voices of contestation are integrated into multiperspectival histories, it is becoming increasingly more acceptable to write about streams of Judaism that had once been considered deviant, and the experiences of people once considered unimportant. While the case should not be overstated, as Jewish Studies still remains a relatively traditional field of study, these changes have allowed contemporary scholars to turn away from the old exercise of identifying and tracing the development of the essence of Judaism and Jewish people.[47]

One recent work which nicely illustrates this contemporary understanding of the Jewish past is David Biale's "new history" of the Jews.

Unlike traditional histories, this thousand-plus-page tome, titled *Cultures of the Jews*, does not narrate a story of the Jewish People: there is no plot, no crisis, and no resolution to draw the reader through the book. There is, in fact, no single author or voice to steer the reader through an epochal Jewish journey across time and space. Instead, the book, which draws on an elastic, multicultural approach to understanding the Jews' past, provides a collection of articles written by scholars from a wide range of disciplines, "archeology, art history, ancient Near Eastern studies, cultural history, literary studies, and folklore." The articles each employ a different set of tools and perspectives to analyze their "imprecise" object of study—the Jews. Not only are these scholars' efforts diverse, but so are the various groups they study. Jewish communities whenever and wherever they may be are equally legitimate subjects in their discussion.[48] Indeed, it is the differences between the various Jewish communities, which highlight the flexible and adaptable nature of Judaism across time and space, that are the focal point of the book.

If Biale's book represents the contemporary celebration of Jewish multiculturalism, it also represents a crisis that has grown out of this approach. The questions posed in the introduction belie a growing sense of doubt in the academy: "[C]an we speak at all of *a* Jewish history, a common narrative. . . . Is there or was there *one* Jewish people with one history? Is there or has there ever been one Jewish religion called Judaism?"[49] Given the Jews' expansive range of diaspora experiences, and given current concerns with the constructed and contingent nature of group identity, it is not surprising that scholars today are calling into question the notion of a single Jewish People and single, normative Judaism.

What is surprising, though, is that until very recently the answers to such questions have been taken for granted: that in spite of their age-old, far-reaching dispersion, which gave rise to such a great range of Jewish religious and cultural expressions, Jews considered themselves to be a common people and religion. Moreover, even today, in spite of an awareness of diversity and change, many sectors of the Jewish world continue to speak of Judaism (as opposed to Judaisms) and Jewish Peoplehood (often invoking the term *klal yisrael*). So, if scholars are to argue that neither Jewish Peoplehood nor Judaism are sui generis, they must also address the question of why they have appeared to be so. What are the mechanisms through which this sense of commonality has been maintained?

It is this very question that frames this book. Drawing on the case of the Bukharan Jews, I will show—not unlike the Wissenschaft scholars—that a single global Judaism was, in fact, preserved through the hegemony of dominant centers. But I will also demonstrate that this dominance was constructed through social and political processes. While Jewish history has largely been written as though the positions labeled "center" (and hence "normative") and "periphery" (and hence "marginal") are sui generis, in fact, they are not ontological categories. Their definitions are not self-evident nor is their hierarchical relationship fixed, enduring, or in the nature of things.[50]

The case of the Bukharan Jews presented in this book demonstrates that the authority of the world's shifting Jewish centers has been constructed through an ongoing engagement with the peripheries. It is only through conversation and negotiation with the peripheries that the authority of centers is legitimized, and that they come to be viewed and labeled centers in the first place. Peripheries are likewise constructed through this dynamic process. The confrontation and struggles between them, then, offer a key point of entry into understanding the dynamics of global Jewish history.

Here, the story of the Bukharan Jews becomes relevant, for throughout much of their history they were relegated to a position of "marginality" in the Jewish world. This position, though, should not be taken for granted, for it was not fixed, nor was it self-reproducing. Rather, it was the outcome of a complex, protracted relationship with Jews in other parts of the world. Oscillating between periods of isolation and moments of contact triggered difficult struggles to define what "normative" Judaism is, to identify the boundaries of Jewish Peoplehood, and to determine who has the authority to decide these critical issues.

The de facto "center" always emerges triumphant, allowing for the maintenance of a single Jewish religion and people. This triumph, however, has come at a cost to the local forms of Jewish practice, belief, and sense of identity that emerged during periods of isolation. This book, which is neither a celebration of the center's triumph, nor a lament for the periphery, is meant to lay bare the dynamic mechanisms at work in maintaining a people and a religion over the long centuries and far reaches of their diaspora experience.

One such mechanism has been the creation and promulgation of historical narratives about moments of reunion between areas that are considered—de facto—to be "centers," and areas—like Bukhara—considered to be "on the margins." We turn our attention to this process of writing history in the chapter that follows.

PART 2

Eighteenth-Century Conversations

THREE

An Emissary from the Holy Land in Central Asia

Much is at stake in writing the past of the Bukharan Jews, for their story —ostensibly about a small, marginal diaspora group—actually encapsulates the dynamics of Jewish history and Jewish People in the broadest sense. Nowhere is this better illustrated than in the tale of an eighteenth-century Sephardi emissary from Ottoman Palestine, and his encounter with Central Asia's Bukharan Jews.

The Story of Yosef Maman

At the end of the eighteenth century, a young man by the name of Yosef Maman is said to have set out from his home in Safed. He headed eastward as an emissary of the Holy Land, driven by a desire to educate Jews living in the far reaches of the diaspora. Over many generations of isolation from important centers of Jewish learning, explains historian Avraham Ya'ari, these communities had lost their sense of connection to the Holy Land and to the Jewish People, and had strayed from the dictates of Judaism. The hardy, charismatic Maman, who was not much older than twenty, was determined to reunite them.

In his travels, Maman passed through Bukhara and stumbled upon Jews there, finding them to be in a particularly dire situation. These Jews, Ya'ari continues, had only the vaguest historical memory of their connection to the rest of the Jewish world, and had forgotten how to practice their religion properly. Maman stayed there, reached out to the ignorant but interested, and began teaching them the laws, traditions, and history that they had forgotten during the long years of their isolation. Maman's students were so taken by him that they pleaded with him to remain in Bukhara. He agreed, settled in the community, married there, and remained until his death at the age of eighty-one. Over the course of his life, Maman taught many among the local Jewish community and trained a generation of religious leaders. It was through him and his work that the Jews of Bukhara reconnected to Judaism and to the wider Jewish world.

Thus concludes this chapter in the history of the Jews of Central Asia. In the opening scene is a Jewish community living in religious darkness, isolated and ignorant of religious law and tradition. In the second scene, the emissary arrives, bringing spiritual nourishment and the light of the Land of Israel with him. And in the final scene, a religiously enlightened community reconnects to their Jewish heritage and to world Jewry.

Ya'ari wove this three-part historical narrative from a variety of sources, and published it for the first time in 1942 in the preface to his *Sifrei Yehudei Bukhara* (The Books of the Jews of Bukhara). This volume consists of annotated lists, organized by year, of every book published by Bukharan Jews between 1842 and 1939. When it first appeared, the work probably generated little interest in the academy, and it has remained of little relevance, rarely cited in the annals of scholarly literature or in popular accounts of the Bukharan Jews' past. Yet, over the years, this tale of Yosef Maman, once tucked away in an obscure book, has become one of the most well-known stories of Bukharan Jewish history, cited in popular and academic accounts alike. This chapter and the next tell how the Maman tale, first published in the margins of scholarly literature, has come to be told and retold as a definitive moment in Bukharan Jewish history.

The Story's Journey

Ya'ari's preface to his 1942 work provides one of the earliest written histories of Bukharan Jews.[1] He introduces readers to the group through a brief discussion of the mystery that surrounds their origins in Central Asia. Because of a dearth of written texts and archeological data, Ya'ari explains, it has been impossible to determine when Jews first settled in the region. It is certain, however, that they were there since the fifteenth century (if not before) and that they hailed from Persia. Until the end of the eighteenth century, these Jews were "totally cut off from all other Jewish communities."[2] Their isolation was so complete, he continues, that Jewish communities in Europe and the Middle East (including the Holy Land) knew nothing of their existence. This very cursory overview brings Ya'ari to a discussion about the moment the Jews of Central Asia were brought back into contact with the wider Jewish world after their centuries of isolation, through their dramatic interactions with the emissary Yosef Maman.

In 1947, Ya'ari edited and published *Masa be-Eretz ha-Kedem: Surya, Kurdistan, Aram-Naharayim, Paras ve-Asya ha-Merkazit* (Journey to the Land of the Orient: Syria, Kurdistan, Mesopotamia, Persia, and Central Asia), the travelogue of the nineteenth-century adventurer Ephraim Neumark. In his introduction, Ya'ari provides ethnographic and historical notes about the various Jewish communities Neumark visited, including Bukhara. Here, he retells the history of the Bukharan Jews and their interactions with Maman.

Four years later, Ya'ari again relates the Maman story, this time in a brief segment of his massive 947-page book, *Shluhei Erets Yisrael* (Emissaries of the Land of Israel), which traces the 2,500-year-long history of emissaries from Israel across the far reaches of the Jewish diaspora. In this publication, like the previous two, the story of Maman is buried among a myriad of details devoted to subjects other than Bukharan Jewish history.

Ya'ari's account of Maman soon found its way into the hands of a few historians who retold it in a number of more accessible publications. In 1952, Yitzhak Ben-Zvi included it in a chapter on the history and culture of the Bukharan Jews, which appeared in his widely circulated *Nidhei Yisrael* (The Remnants of Israel).[3] This popular book was reprinted in 1956 and then again in 1965, and disseminated beyond a Hebrew-speaking audience through its publication in English,[4] as well as in French, Spanish, and Yiddish. In 1964, Walter Fischel included Ya'ari's Maman story in his chapter "The Leaders of the Jews of Bokhara," which appeared in the book *Jewish Leaders,* edited by the prominent Orthodox rabbi and leader Leo Jung. And in 1975 it appeared again in a lengthy article on Bukharan Jews, written by historian Michael Zand and published in the *Encyclopedia Judaica Yearbook.*

In the 1990s, as a result of the great influx of Bukharan Jews from Central Asia into Israel and the United States on the heels of the Soviet Union's dissolution, this group became the object of much popular interest. Folk festivals, museum exhibits, and musical performances have showcased Bukharan Jewish culture. So, too, journalists have written about them in newspaper articles, popular magazines, and Internet sites. As a result of this attention, the Maman story—first published a half-century before in Ya'ari's esoteric works—found its way into the popular media (in publications such as *The World and I, Eretz,* and *The Chicago Sentinel*).[5] It was in this format, where scholarly references and footnotes are not provided, that I first encountered the tale.

In the earliest stages of my research, I took for granted the veracity of this popular version of the story. It was so common and told with such a sense of givenness that I did not think to question it, and even retold it myself in my earliest research proposals. Over the years, however, I began to trace the history of the tale's evolution backward from these popular media accounts, to the work of historians Zand, Fischel, and Ben-Zvi, and further back to Ya'ari's three publications.

Construction of the Story

Having arrived at Ya'ari's publications through this process of back-tracking, I still had further to go to find the historical sources that Ya'ari himself had used to compose the story. Tracing these five nineteenth-century texts, pulling them off the library shelves, and reading through them in the original, I discovered that not one of them was composed by someone who had himself met Yosef Maman. Indeed, the annals of history have not preserved even a single account of a direct, firsthand interaction with him. All secondhand memory reports, Ya'ari's sources are the notes of Western travelers who passed through Central Asia in the nineteenth century after Yosef Maman was gone, as well as one report by a descendant of Maman who was born long after his forebear died. These men all learned about Maman through listening to the recollections of others. Their layered accounts, each of which offers a different perspective and set of details, together provide a fascinating window into the journey of the Maman tale from a collection of second- and thirdhand stories told by a variety of people at different times into a reified chapter of Bukharan Jewish history.

DAVID D'BETH HILLEL

Ya'ari's earliest historical source was the travelogue of David D'Beth Hillel,[6] an Ashkenazi Jew who was born in Lithuania to a family of rabbis and religious scholars. As a child, D'Beth Hillel moved with his family to Ottoman Palestine, where he spent eight years studying with students of the Vilna Gaon. In 1824, when David D'Beth Hillel was likely in his twenties,[7] he set out on an eight-year-long trip. He began by journeying through the Land of Israel, moved on to Lebanon and Syria, and then made his way through the mountainous regions of Turkish and Iraqi Kurdistan, Azerbaijan, Mesopotamia, and Persia. From Persia, he sailed to India, where he arrived in 1828, spent about two years, and published his fascinating travelogue in which he describes the Jewish communities he encountered as well as the peoples among whom they lived.[8] For our purposes, the relevant section of his book is a single footnote in his section about Baghdad.

In this footnote, D'Beth Hillel explains that he was aware of a Jewish community in Bukhara, and "was very anxious to meet" these people during his travels. Though he never did manage to reach this area of the world, his wish to become acquainted with Jews from there was fulfilled during his visit to Baghdad. There he encountered two men, a "father and a son" who were from Bukhara, and who were on their way to "visit Judea." Communicating in Hebrew, D'Beth Hillel became "very well acquainted" with these two "fair and handsome" men, who shared with him information about the Jewish community in their home city. They told him that the three thousand Jews there used to be "very ignorant of the Hebrew language and customs," having "no Hebrew books nor manuscripts, nor anything relating to the Hebrew law," except a few handwritten prayers. They were saved from their dire state by a "traveller, an African Israelite from Judea by the name of Rabbi Joseph Marobi [Rabbi Joseph the Westerner]." This rabbi had "passed" through the area about thirty-five years earlier (around 1797) and found the people to be "so ignorant" of Jewish law that he "would not even eat with them."[9]

D'Beth Hillel does not seem to have gleaned any information about the local Jews' initial interactions with Maman. Were they offended that Maman would not eat with them, embarrassed by their "ignorance," or simply grateful to learn the Jewish ritual dietary laws from him? D'Beth Hillel did learn that at least some members of the community (including this father and son) had been drawn to Maman's teachings and religious messages, and "attended him as their Rabbi and teacher of law." He served them in this capacity and worked to improve the area's Jewish library by sending letters to Jewish communities in Eastern Europe and the Ottoman Empire, requesting shipments of religious books. D'Beth Hillel concludes his footnote by stating that these men now follow the customs Maman taught to them and that they have "a good knowledge of the Hebrew books and customs, and fear God."[10] D'Beth Hillel's report is best representative of Ya'ari's tripartite schema of isolation, reunion, and return.

JOSEPH WOLFF

The next account upon which Ya'ari draws to construct his portrait of Maman is the travelogue of Josef Wolff. Wolff was born into a German Jewish family, and converted to Christianity at the age of seventeen. He wholeheartedly committed himself to his new religion by becoming a missionary who traveled through much of the Middle East and Asia in an effort to convert Jews wherever he found them by "proclaim[ing] the Gospel of the kingdom of Christ" among them.[11] He traveled to Bukhara in 1832, and stayed from March 4 until March 21. There, he met and conversed with local Jews about their community and leaders. In *Researches and Missionary Labours among the Jews, Mohammedans and Other Sects* he provides a record of these conversations, stating (among other things) what he learned about "Joseph Mooghrebee" (Joseph the Westerner). In this section, Wolff not only describes Joseph Mooghrebee's "widespread influence," but also lists the practices in which he engaged that raised "doubt [about] his orthodoxy."[12]

According to Wolff's account, Joseph Mooghrebee, the son of Rabbi Moshe Maimon, married while in his hometown of "Tituan," Morocco, while still in his teens. Not long after, the young man left his bride and set out on a one-way trip to Ottoman Palestine, thence to Baghdad, and from there to Bukhara, where he arrived sometime before 1771 at the age of twenty. Although young and alone, Joseph Mooghrebee must have been highly self-confident, for he was unequivocal about calling attention to the "great ignorance" of the people he encountered there. His assessment, according to Wolff's report, was that these Jews had forgotten "their laws, rites and customs." With no rabbi to teach them "the Law of Moses and the Prophets, or who was able to tell them what was clean and unclean," they were even given to eating the "meat of the Musselmans." Deeply dismayed by all that he saw, Joseph Mooghrebee is said to have exclaimed, "Woe is me, Oh my brethren! to find you in such a condition, that you have forgotten the Law of Moses and the Prophets, and the words of the wise men!" Swiftly, he took action to rectify the situation. He taught them to "kill animals according to the law of the Jews" and "ordered them to perform ablution." He recruited people to travel to some of the important Jewish publishing centers (Constantinople, Vilna, and Leghorn) to purchase volumes of the Talmud. He sent abroad for a scribe to come to Bukhara to write Torah scrolls, and taught religious texts and principles to many students. All of Maman's work resulted in a resurgence of religious activity. Jewish life in Bukhara became so vibrant that it was not long before the local Jews began to refer to their city as a "little Jerusalem."[13]

This charismatic and influential Joseph Mooghrebee also had a dark side, however. His close pupils spoke not only about his piety and religious leadership, but also of his questionable, unorthodox practices. Wolff was told, for example, that he taught his students that "it was no sin to drink milk immediately after meat, provided that none of the unlearned Jews were present." This teaching seems to have been linked to Joseph's understanding about the structure of the Jewish religion, which "may be divided into two parts: the one part to be taught to all, and another part reserved for wise men." Finally, Wolff recorded a conversation that he had with a rabbi who reported that Joseph Mooghrebee was known for pleading with God, "Oh Lord, King of the worlds, when will the time come that the followers of Jesus will take possession of these countries!" Despite these questionable practices, Wolff concluded that Joseph Mooghrebee was respected over the course of his long life. When he died there at the age of eighty-one, he was "lamented by every Jew of Bokhara" who referred to him as "the 'Light of Israel.'"[14]

EPHRAIM NEUMARK

After Joseph Wolff's travelogue was published, fifty years would pass before any other traveler would make his way through Bukhara and record information on the protagonist of our story. This next traveler, Ephraim Neumark, was born in Poland in 1861. At the age of twenty, he fled to Ottoman Palestine, settling in Tiberias. Three years later, he left his new home and set out on his travels east to Syria, Kurdistan, Iraq, Persia, and Central Asia. When he returned, he published a record of his travels in the Hebrew newspaper *Ha'asif*.[15]

Neumark begins his entry on Bukhara in the past tense: "These Jews who were so far from their brothers, were also far from Torah," and then goes on to explain that this situation changed eighty years before his own arrival in the city. At the dawn of the nineteenth century, a wise man "of the West," referred to as "Hakham Yosef Maman," arrived in Bukhara.[16] The Maman in Neumark's version—unlike the protagonist in the versions of D'Beth Hillel and Wolff—does not remark on this community's ignorance or dire religious condition.

Neither reprimanded nor rebuked by him, the people of Bukhara found Maman to be "honorable." They "pleaded with him and prevailed upon him to remain in Bukhara," and he agreed.[17] Neumark then discusses the details of a particular interaction between Maman and the local Jews. Unlike the other texts, in which Maman's voice alone is heard, in this interchange we hear the voices of the people among whom he had come to live.

Maman once saw people coming from the bathhouse on Shabbat. According to Neumark, Maman deemed these people to be *anashim ksherim* (pure people) and "asked them about this" practice. They explained that "the law explicitly permits this." Maman expressed doubt, and the people understood that "he did not believe them." In response, they "brought the book to him and showed him that it is written, 'In a city where there is a bathhouse, [you may] wash on the Sabbath!'" While Maman's answer to them is not recorded, Neumark interjects his own commentary. The people, he tells us, "did not pay attention to the end of the section" of this text, which, Neumark explains, in fact prohibits using the bathhouse on Shabbat. According to Neumark, this incident was the first in which Maman succeeded, "Little by little . . . to teach them Torah."[18]

In addition to his portrayal of the changes Maman brought to Bukhara, Neumark describes another development that occurred around this same time period. In this section of Neumark's text, it is not the arrival of a religious emissary from abroad that serves as a turning point. Rather, it is the arrival of the Russians to Central Asia. Prior to Russian expansion into the region, Neumark tells us, the local Jews "had very few [religious] books" because they were "far from any printing house." As a result of improved communication and travel, this situation changed rapidly in the nineteenth century. The "way to Russia was opened," the Jews of Bukhara began to travel there, and when they returned home, they "brought back from there whatever books their hearts desired." Some even chose to stay, to study in the religious academies in Moscow. As a result of these new connections, Neumark concludes, the "*edah* of Bukhara has become a very important *edah* in Israel. . . ."[19]

ELKAN ADLER

Elkan Adler, son of Britain's Chief Rabbi Nathan Adler, was a book collector who traveled to far-flung areas of the world in pursuit of his hobby. Among his many ventures was a trip to Central Asia in 1897. Immediately upon his return, he wrote an article about this expedition, titled "The Persian Jews: Their Books and Their Ritual," which was published in the *Jewish Quarterly Review.* Hoping to satisfy the curious reader, who may have wondered how he had gone about acquiring his collection, Adler explains that he went through the Jewish neighborhoods, "from house to house," to "beg for a sight of all the books the inhabitants possessed." With an interpreter alongside him, he visited some one hundred homes in Bukhara and Samarkand, examined the owners' books, and then put in "bids" for those he wanted.[20]

Following this introduction, Adler goes on to list the books he acquired in Central Asia, along with many details about them. Through his assiduous work in copying their colophons and inscriptions, we gain insight into the books' travel histories, such as where they were printed or copied, when and by whom, as well as information about who owned them. This list, and Adler's analysis of it, suggest that the Jews of Central Asia were surprisingly well connected with many Jewish communities in the West. Particularly noteworthy is that these ties, which Maman may well have had a hand in strengthening, were in place long before the emissary's arrival.

One book that illustrates the long-standing connections of Central Asia's Jews to other parts of the Jewish world is the *Aruch of Rabbi Natan of Rome,* a lexicon of terms found in the Talmud and Midrash. The work was written in Rome in 1101, and was brought to print there in 1469. A copy of this printed book traveled to Isphahan, Persia, where in 1502 a scribe penned a copy that made its way to Bukhara. It was safeguarded in Bukhara, where Adler was finally to purchase it in 1898.[21] A second example is *Sefer Tola'at Ya'akov,* a mystical exposition on the ritual of prayer written in 1507, which was printed in Constantinople in 1560. In that same year, Joseph ben Moses Kalantar acquired a copy of the book in Constantinople (inscribing it with his name and the date). Sometime between then and 1724 (when a scribe added fifteen pages of Hebrew manuscript to the printed text), this book traveled to Bukhara, where Adler bought it in 1898.[22] Still another example is *Hilkhot Shehita u-Vedika,* which outlines the laws associated with ritual slaughtering. This work was printed in Venice in 1574, and sometime between then and the time Adler traveled it was copied into manuscript form and brought to Bukhara.[23]

These books and others[24] tell the story of a Jewish community that may not have been as isolated or ignorant prior to the eighteenth century as our other travelers indicated. It is no coincidence, then, that Adler does not depict Maman as the founder of the Jewish library for the Jews in Bukhara. Although Maman may have helped to enhance their collection, Adler's data suggests that they had been managing without him.

Still, Maman is hardly absent from Adler's story. Indeed, like D'Beth Hillel, Wolff, and Neumark, Adler writes about Maman's role in initiating a revolutionary moment in the life of the Jews in Bukhara. However, the dramatic change that he highlights is not related to their level of religious observance or to their knowledge of Jewish texts. Instead, Adler writes about a change that Maman brought about in this Jewish community's understanding of its own history, and consequently altered its very sense of identity.

Adler's discovery of Maman's impact in this realm rested on his analysis of the prayer books he collected while in Central Asia. The most unusual among them were two manuscripts "containing the old Persian

[Jewish] Ritual, a complete liturgy."[25] These stood out among the other prayer books Adler found, which were produced in the nineteenth century, were printed (rather than handwritten), and contained Sephardi[26] rather than Persian liturgy. On the basis of these findings, Adler concludes that the Jews in Bukhara were originally "Persian Jews" and that they continued to remain closely connected to and identified with this part of the Jewish world for most of their history.

Only in the nineteenth century did the Jews of Bukhara switch to Sephardi liturgy. And who should be responsible for this switch? None other but Maman, Adler explains: "There seems to have been a curious reason for this. Some 150 years ago [around 1730] . . . a learned man" appeared in Bukhara. This man, whom Adler refers to as R. Abraham Mammon, "journeyed from Morocco" and when he arrived in Bukhara he "persuaded his co-religionists that like himself, they were descended from the Jews exiled from Spain and Portugal." He succeeded, according to Adler, not only in revising their past, but also in convincing them that it was "their duty" to "conform" to the same ritual as he. In short, Maman is viewed by Adler as having severed the Bukharan Jews' historical and ritual connections with the Judeo-Persian world, in exchange for those with the Sephardi world.[27]

PINHAS HAKHAM

The fifth and final account that Avraham Ya'ari uses to piece together his story about Yosef Maman is a text by a young man named Pinhas Hakham, who was born in Bukhara in 1876 and died in Jerusalem eighteen years later. This piece stands in marked contrast to the others in that it is not written by a foreigner who traveled to Central Asia from afar.

A member of the local community, Pinhas Hakham did not view the Jews of Bukhara as either remote or exotic. He probably did not identify with Yosef Maman's sense of "discovery" of his long-lost brethren, and provides no ethnographic description of Bukharan Jews as they may have been seen through Maman's eyes. What captured Pinhas's imagination, instead, were the teachings and messages Maman brought with him from the faraway Holy Land.

Pinhas's writings are also different from the others in that they are closer to a primary source. The texts provided by D'Beth Hillel, Wolff,

Neumark, and Adler are their records of stories that others told them about our protagonist. They are, in other words, stories of others' stories. Pinhas Hakham, by contrast, was a descendant of Maman and had access to works written in Maman's own hand. Strictly speaking, Pinhas's text is not an original, but rather his translation (into Hebrew) of Maman's writings. Nevertheless, it appears to have been filtered through one less interpretive lens.

This text is contained in a book titled *Sefer Zekher Tsadik* (Book in Memory of a Righteous One), originally published in 1894 by Pinhas Hakham's grieving father shortly after his son's untimely death. It contains eulogies that were delivered to honor the memory of the deceased, as well as pieces that Pinhas himself wrote during his short life. Among these is a text that begins, "When I was in the land of my birth, Bukhara, I . . . Pinhas Hakham, found books written in Spanish writing,[28] and I could not read them, nor could others. But from the chapter headings, it seemed that they were words of Torah. So I took them with me."[29]

With these books in hand, fourteen-year-old Pinhas arrived in Jerusalem, and set before himself the task of learning to read them. When he was able to decipher them, he discovered that they were "pleasant lessons written by the holy hand" of his ancestor, "Light of the West, the emissary, Hakham Rabbi Yosef Maman Ma'aravi." Although Pinhas never met his great-great-grandfather, he refers to him as both his "teacher" and his "rabbi," indicating the power and longevity of Maman's influence. Maman, Pinhas explains, came to Bukhara in 1793 "as an emissary from the holy city of Safed to the cities of Persia and Bukhara." On the first Sabbath after his arrival, he "delivered a sermon in the synagogue" and left behind a written record of it. This sermon, as it appears in *Book in Memory of a Righteous One,* addresses the importance of donating money toward the upkeep of the graves of the rabbis who are buried in the holy city of Safed, and is built upon citations from biblical and rabbinic literature. Pinhas translated it into Hebrew so that the "memory" of his forebear "may endure."[30]

David D'Beth Hillel, Joseph Wolff, Ephraim Neumark, Elkan Adler, and Pinhas Hakham each provide a description of a charismatic figure who arrived in Bukhara from the West sometime in the eighteenth century, and who had a significant impact on the Jewish community there. Given the variation in the five men's religious and cultural backgrounds,

the differences in their reasons for writing and for travel, and the sev-
enty-year disparity between them (D'Beth Hillel having traveled first in
1828, and Elkan Adler having traveled last, in 1897), it should come as no
surprise that their reports differ in significant ways. These differences
open up intriguing questions about Maman: what kind of man was he,
and what sorts of change did he effect in Bukhara?

At the simplest level, the contradictions between the reports call
into question the basic data surrounding the sequence of events that unfolded. What, for example, was the man's name? Four of the reports con-
cur that his first name was Joseph (or Yosef), yet Adler refers to him as
"Abraham." When did the emissary arrive in Bukhara? Pinhas Hakham
and D'Beth Hillel agree that it was in 1797, and Neumark dates his arrival
to just a few years after that. Wolff's report, however, indicates that it was
sometime prior to 1772 and Adler states that it was around 1747. Maman's
biography becomes murkier with regard to details of his travel route.
Wolff reports that he traveled as an emissary from Jerusalem, and went
from there to Baghdad and on to Bukhara. Pinhas Hakham, on the other
hand, reports that Maman traveled as an emissary from Safed, going
from there to Persia and on to Bukhara. Finally, the reports contradict
one another regarding the length of time Maman remained in Bukhara.
While Joseph Wolff writes that he lived there for sixty-one years, D'Beth
Hillel writes only that he "passed" through the area.

Beyond these factual discrepancies are more difficult questions
about the protagonist's character. What sort of man was he? Was he respected, honorable, and wise, as the reports of D'Beth Hillel, Neumark,
and Pinhas Hakham indicate? Or was he deceptive and hypocritical, as
Wolff and Adler suggest—a man who abandoned his bride in Morocco,
flirted with Christianity, disobeyed religious dietary proscriptions, and
duped the local Jews into believing a false story about their own past?

The stories not only present contradictory portraits of Maman, but
are also unclear about their characterization of the state of the Bukharan
Jewish community prior to his arrival. Neumark remarks that they were
"far from Torah," whereas D'Beth Hillel uses sharper language, characterizing the Jews there as "very ignorant of the Hebrew language and
customs." Harsher still is Wolff's assessment of them as having forgotten
"their laws, rites and customs." From the writings of Pinhas Hakham,
on the other hand, a very different picture emerges. Although Pinhas

is silent about the extent to which the Jews there were learned or ignorant, several assumptions may be made from his account. The context of Maman's first speech, which was delivered on Shabbat in a synagogue, suggests that they had not forgotten Jewish rites and customs. Likewise, the content of the speech—an esoteric lesson on the holiness of the Land of Israel and the mystical powers of deceased spiritual leaders—suggests that Maman was addressing an audience that shared many of his religious assumptions, rather than one in need of a remedial lesson on the basic elements of religious observance. Finally, the structure of Maman's talk, which was built upon a complex set of rabbinic arguments, indicates that the people were well versed in Jewish textual tradition. The books Adler collected while he was there support Pinhas's alternative portrayal.

Finally, the discrepancies in the reports raise questions about Maman's impact in Bukhara. Did he instigate a revolutionary change in Jewish life there, and if so, what was the nature of this revolution? D'Beth Hillel stresses that through Maman the Jews attained "a good knowledge of the Hebrew language and customs."[31] Wolff reports that Maman taught them how to observe some of the basic religious laws, including the slaughtering of animals "according to the law of the Jews" and performing "ablutions."[32] Wolff, too, emphasizes Maman's contribution to the level of Jewish literacy by training teachers and sending for books. Neumark, by contrast, attributes this to the larger historical circumstances related to Russia's encroachment upon Central Asia, rather than to Maman.

The story of revolution that Adler tells is very different from those of the others. He focuses on the switch in liturgy from their historically rooted practice to the Sephardi practice that Maman himself followed.[33] Finally, Pinhas Hakham, who tells of the eagerness of the Jews in Bukhara to learn about the Holy Land from someone who had firsthand knowledge, offers no indication that Maman brought about a revolutionary change at all.

Writing Maman's Biography

Although differences between these various accounts complicate the effort to write a biography of Yosef Maman, they did not deter Avraham Ya'ari. He contends with the contradictions by winnowing through the data, classifying some of the reports (or some aspects of them) as trust-worthy and others as unreliable, and by retaining some pieces of data contained within them and discarding others. Ultimately, he emerges with the following single, coherent life history:

> Rabbi Yosef, the son of Rabbi Moshe Maman, was born in Tetuan, which is in Morocco. He moved to the Holy Land and settled in Safed. As an em-issary of Safed he went to Persia and to Bukhara. He arrived in Bukhara when he was 20 years old, which was in the year 1793.[34]

Aware of the discrepancies surrounding the emissary's date of ar-rival, his route of travel, the amount of time he spent in Bukhara, and even his name, Ya'ari simply identifies the inconsistencies as errors, and buries reference to them in a single footnote. For example, he dismisses the possibility that the protagonist's name may have been "Maimon" with the claim that Wolff recorded the name "incorrectly" and con-cludes that his reports should "not be trusted." Similarly, he ignores the possibility that Maman may have arrived in Bukhara as an independent traveler, by stating that Neumark "did not know" that Maman was an emissary from the Land of Israel. And rather than acknowledging and interrogating the discrepancies between the dates of Maman's arrival in Bukhara, he states that Adler "mistakenly said that the time of his arrival in Bukhara was about 50 years earlier than it actually was."[35]

What methodological approach does Ya'ari take in deciding which data to dismiss and which to retain? Did he, for example, dismiss reports written later in time in favor of those written earlier (and therefore closer to the event)? Did he privilege the reports of a Jewish traveler over those of a Christian missionary? Or did he dismiss the reports of a traveler who spent little or no time in Bukhara, in favor of a descendant of Ma-man who himself grew up in Bukhara? Ya'ari provides the reader with no such justification for his decisions, and my own attempts to uncover a logarithm fail to identify a systematic methodology. More problematic is the inconsistent manner in which Ya'ari relies on some of the very same reports that he discredits. For example, although he dismisses Wolff as generally "untrustworthy,"[36] he goes on to use Wolff's data to determine Maman's age upon his arrival.

Why does Ya'ari choose to spin a coherent, single narrative of the life of Yosef Maman, rather than call attention to the contradictions in his data, addressing their implications? And why is he unequivocal in his story of Bukharan Jewish isolation and reunion, despite the weak data upon which his claim rests? In addressing these questions, this section moves away from Yosef Maman, and turns to his biographer to explore his motivations.

Ya'ari's concern with the Jews of Bukhara was but one tiny segment of his scholarship, which includes tens of books and well over one hundred scholarly articles. Nevertheless, his work on this community typifies his broader interest in Jewish communities across the vast stretches of the Jewish diaspora. Among other aspects of their history and culture, he was interested in the diverse texts produced by Jewish communities around the globe. His work *The Books of the Jews of Bukhara* (in which he first published the story of Yosef Maman) is one of among several of his annotated bibliographies, including *Ha-Dfus ha-Ivri be-Kushta* (Hebrew Printing in Constantinople) and *Ha-Dfus ha-Ivri be-Artsot ha-Mizrah* (Hebrew Printing in Eastern Countries). Ya'ari's interest in the great range of Jewish cultural expression also manifested itself in his attention to Jewish ritual practice. For example, he collected information about various traditions surrounding the holiday of Simhat Torah, publishing them in his book *Toldot Hag Simhat Torah: Hishtalshelut Minhagav bi-Tfutsot Yisrael le-Doroteihen* (The History of the Holiday of Simhat Torah: The Development of Customs among the Jewish Diaspora over the Generations). He also provided information about the great range of *haggadot* used at the Passover *seder,* which he published in his book *Bibliyografya shel Haggadot Pesah me-Reshit ha-Dfus ve-ad Hayom* (Bibliography of Passover Haggadot: From the Beginning of Print until Today).

Ya'ari was attentive to ethnographic descriptions of various Jewish groups, as seen in his considerable work compiling and editing travelogues of Jews who journeyed to the far reaches of the diaspora. Included among these is his edition of Ephraim Neumark's travelogue of his journey to Syria, Kurdistan, Iraq, Persia, and Central Asia,[37] as well as his edition of Ya'akov Sapir's travelogue of his journey to Yemen.[38]

Although Ya'ari had a keen interest in exploring and publicizing expressions of Jewish cultural diversity, he was not disturbed by the questions vexing contemporary academics about whether there is a single Jewish People with a single history and religion.[39] As an Israeli scholar, writing at the time of the foundation of the State, Ya'ari was aligned with the establishment generally, and with the Jerusalem School of Jewish history, in particular. Like the school's leading proponent, Ben Zion Dinur, he was convinced of the unified nature of the Jewish People and their past.

Dinur understood Jewish history to be the story of a nation that maintained its unity "complete and unbroken," throughout their age-old diaspora experiences. He argued that the "organic unity" binding the scattered Jewish populations had been maintained by "memories of a common past," and by their common homeland.[40] This homeland connected Jews across the world because it served as a common focal point for their yearnings and hopes for the future. But more than a center of sentiment, the homeland was also a focal point for the active articulation of Jews' common fate and destiny. The Jewish presence there was supported throughout the ages by funds collected throughout the diaspora. Regardless of how small, the population that lived in the Holy Land was a "common project" of the dispersed Jewish population. In this capacity it served as a vehicle for articulating the "combined" nature of the Jewish nation.[41]

A contemporary of Dinur's, Avraham Ya'ari was a scholar and a bibliophile who worked at Israel's national library during the time of Israel's emergence as an independent state. Like other academics in the Jerusalem School, his scholarship was intimately connected to his work promoting Zionism. Although he celebrated the great variety of cultural expression that emerged over the long course of the Jews' diaspora history, he believed that Jews remained a unified nation throughout. It was the Land of Israel as a common national center, he argued, that served to maintain this unity.[42]

In writing about the mechanisms through which the Holy Land served as a centralizing force, Ya'ari elaborated upon Dinur's approach. Whereas Dinur drew attention to the efforts of the world's scattered Jewish communities to support the Jewish population in the Holy Land, Ya'ari emphasized the efforts of those who lived there themselves. In his monumental book *Emissaries of the Land of Israel,* he wrote of local efforts to train and send emissaries from the Holy Land to the far reaches of the Jewish diaspora, to spread the teachings and the spirit of the Center. Through their work, Ya'ari argued, the Holy Land bound the Jewish world together not only through receiving, but also by giving.

Here, Ya'ari's story of Yosef Maman becomes relevant, as it encapsulates his broad understanding of the way in which the work of the emissaries facilitated the enduring relationship between homeland and diaspora. In *Emissaries of the Land of Israel,* he describes "emissary work from the land of Israel to the diaspora" as "a continuous institution" that functioned over the course of almost two millennia, "from the time of the destruction of the Second Temple [71 CE] until today."[43] While he acknowledges that the logistics of emissary work have changed over time, he claims that its aims have always remained the same: "to strengthen the connection between the Land of Israel and the lands of the diaspora."[44] Emissary work was not random, spontaneous, or subject to particularities of history or to the whims of individuals, Ya'ari explains. Rather, it was an enduring institution with canonized expectations, regulations, and goals.

Given this context, Ya'ari's story of Maman is not about one particular man or one particular Jewish diaspora community. Rather, it is the story of Jewish diaspora history writ large. The particulars read as follows:

> The centuries-long severance of the Jews of Bukhara from the rest of the Israel brought them to a state of spiritual decay which would have surely ended in total assimilation had it not been for an emissary from the Land of Israel who arrived at the end of the 18th century. He brought news to them from the Land of Israel, he aroused their self-awareness, he formed connections between them and the rest of Israel, he fought against their illiteracy, he taught them Torah and the Jewish commandments, he circulated [religious] books among them, he established teachers for them, and he transformed them from an atrophied limb into a living limb of the body of the nation of Israel. With the appearance of this emissary in the land of Bukhara, the Jews of Bukhara entered the stage of Jewish history. The name of this emissary is Rabbi Yosef Maman.[45]

Maman, like every emissary, served as a human bridge, binding the diaspora and the homeland together through his work, which was a two-sided enterprise. One side was the "taking," which involved the collection of donations from Jews of diaspora communities, to be used as sustenance for the Jewish inhabitants of the Holy Land. The other side of the emissary's work was "giving." He would bring peoples of the diaspora news from the Land of Israel, spiritual invigoration, and religious guidance. Put another way, the diaspora communities provided the practical material means for the homeland's sustenance, while the homeland provided the Jewish communities of the diaspora with spiritual nourishment. Although this relationship was reciprocal, it was unbalanced. Ya'ari explains this in poetic and symbolic terms:

> This emissary had a spiritual task; he had to bring news from the Land of Israel into the darkness of the diaspora, to bring holy vision into secular reality, and to bring the stirrings of redemption into the mundane of foreign lands. He had the responsibility to wake the nation from their spiritual slumber.[46]

Diaspora in this description is dark, secular, and mundane, whereas the Land of Israel is holy, spiritual, and the locus of redemption. Without ties to the homeland, the Jews in Bukhara (and all other diaspora lands) could not preserve their connection to God, Jewish history, or the Jewish religion. Disconnected for centuries, their community withered and stood on the brink of spiritual death. Looking at the relationship from the other perspective—had the connection between the Jews in Bukhara and the Jews of homeland been totally severed, the homeland would have suffered loss of a limb, but the heart and soul of the Jewish People would have remained unaffected.

In sum, Ya'ari's portrayal of Maman's moment of contact with the Jews in Bukhara is shorthand for his broad understanding of diaspora history. When they were at home, the Jews were a people, living in a state of unity and wholeness. Sharing the land that was their own, they were tied to one another, to their history, to the traditions of their ancestors, and to God. For a few generations after their exile, their memory of home served as a thread tying them to their normal state of unity. With the passage of time, however, this thread weakened and frayed. The emissary came to mend the link. By bringing spiritual messages from the homeland, teaching the language of homeland, and reteaching the religious laws that the dispersed peoples had forgotten, he repaired the fissures that had disrupted the unified relationship.

In this model, the respective positions of the homeland and the diaspora are fixed and enduring. The former is the spiritual, national center and is the source of life, whereas the latter is mundane, peripheral, and dependent upon the center. The center's emissaries, therefore, need not work to legitimize their efforts to bring "holy vision into secular reality"[47] or their efforts to mend the fraying ties between diaspora communities and the homeland. Nor must they explain why the practices of the diaspora communities (that are not in line with those of the center) are illegitimate. The fact of their having strayed from that which is understood—a priori—to be normative makes them, by their very nature, deviant and needing repair.

This framework helps to explain why in Avraham Ya'ari's story we hear the words of the emissary ("Woe unto me, Oh my brethren! to find you in such a condition . . .") but do not hear the response of the Bukharan Jews themselves. In Ya'ari's paradigm of homeland–diaspora relations, there exists no possibility for conversation or debate. There can be no negotiation between homeland and diaspora because the terms *center* and *periphery* (and their attendant locales) are not constructed, and they do not evolve. They are what they are, and what they have been; sui generis and fixed.

Outside of this paradigm, however, one cannot help but wonder the following: Did the Jews of Bukhara not question the authority of this young man, a stranger who was born in faraway North Africa, and who had no one to vouch for him and no claim to authority other than his own personal testimony of having lived briefly in Ottoman Palestine?[48] Indeed, Neumark suggests that they did, in his description of the argument between Maman and the local Jews over the use of the bathhouse on Shabbat.

In this significant exchange—the only record of a conversation between Maman and the locals—it is they who speak and the emissary who is silent. Ya'ari, however, omits this interchange. In doing so, he does not merely leave out a detail of the story. Much more significantly, he precludes the possibility of a counter-narrative—a version of the story that calls into question whether or not Maman was a hero, and thus begins to blur the distinction between that which is "center" and that which is "periphery."

The Journey of a Story: A Road Not Taken

Somewhere along the line their adherence to Judaism lapsed. When Joseph Maman, a young Moroccan emissary from Safed, visited the community in 1793, he found it on the verge of spiritual extinction.

There were no religious books, not even a Bible and no Jewish practices. Indeed, the people had virtually forgotten they were Jews.

Maman, or Joseph Hamaaravi as he called himself, gave up his travels and settled in Bukhara in order to teach the Jews the basics of their religion. . . . During the 61 years Maman served the community, there was such a strong religious revival that the community came to be known as "Little Jerusalem."[49]

This retelling of the Maman story, which appeared in the *Jerusalem Post Magazine* in 1979, is written with such a sense of givenness that it veils the tale's back-story: the journey through which it traveled from its obscure beginnings to become the most commonly accepted narrative of the Bukharan Jews' past. Likewise, this version of the tale provides no indication of the junctures along the way where it may have taken a turn to become something other than it did. I conclude this chapter by reflecting on one such pivotal point.

In 1820, Baron Egor Kazimirovich Meiendorff traveled as part of a Russian envoy to Bukhara. Upon his return, he published a book about his trip in which he recorded a conversation he had had with a rabbi, whose name he does not mention, who hailed from North Africa. This rabbi, Meiendorff tells his readers, reported that when he arrived in Bukhara, he found the Jews there to be "in a state of the greatest ignorance." He remained, "established a school," and "ordered books." He was so successful in his work that by the time Meiendorff visited, "all the Jews of Bokhara" had learned "to read and write" and to "study the Talmud."[50]

These details sound strikingly similar to the descriptions that other travelers provided about Yosef Maman, with one noteworthy exception: the rabbi's place of origin. Neumark writes that Maman was from Tetuan (a city in Morocco). Adler, likewise, records that Maman was from Morocco. Meiendorff, on the other hand, places this unnamed rabbi's home in Algeria.[51]

Ya'ari omits this reference. Years later, however, Walter Fischel includes it in his discussion of Yosef Maman.[52] With Meiendorff's information on hand, Fischel's own rendition of the Maman story could have taken one of two different directions. He could have chosen to use the data included in Meiendorff's report to interrogate Ya'ari's version, or he could have smoothed over the discrepancy Meiendorff provided, and remained loyal to Ya'ari's version. We know, of course, how the story turns out. Ya'ari's version triumphs in part because Fischel continued to disseminate it. Choosing to ignore the discrepancy, Fischel states—with no justification—that the rabbi whom Meiendorff met was Yosef Maman from Morocco. Offering no explanation, he follows this assertion with a quotation that states that the rabbi was from Algeria. In overlooking this contradiction, Fischel reiterates Ya'ari's presentation of history as well as the Center-Periphery Paradigm Ya'ari promulgates.

In the next chapter, we will see that other writers challenged this version of the Center-Periphery Paradigm by asserting a different account of the Maman story. I present these alternate versions of history, which have been obscured until now, in order to recover a perspective that has been forgotten. More than that, I address why and how it is that one version of the Maman story comes to be taken for granted as scholarly and normative, whereas the other comes to be dismissed as marginal folk history.

FOUR

Revisiting the Story of the
Emissary from the Holy Land

In addition to recounting Avraham Ya'ari's story of Yosef Maman, the previous chapter narrated the journey of Ya'ari's tale from obscurity into mainstream literature. This meta-narrative suggests that Ya'ari's depiction of Maman became accepted as a definitive moment in Bukharan Jewish history due to factors other than its accuracy. Indeed, the sources invite alternative possibilities for portraying this past. While Walter Fischel and others did not accept these invitations, two historians did. Their stories, however, have largely fallen into oblivion. This chapter resuscitates them, providing another framework for understanding the Bukharan Jews' past. These two histories—as well as the meta-story of how it was that they came to be eclipsed—also allow for a reexamination of the dynamics of Jewish diaspora history, writ large.

A. Z. Idelsohn's Fractured Presentation
of Yosef's Emissary Work

A. Z. Idelsohn's brief article on Bukharan Jews appeared in a Hebrew-language journal almost thirty years before Ya'ari's works were published.[1] In this piece, Idelsohn recounts the whole of Bukharan Jewish history—from the Jews' origins in Central Asia until the present—in just three pages. Toward the end of his summary, Idelsohn writes of two emissaries who had an impact on Jewish life there: Rabbi Yosef, who came from Iraq, settled in Bukhara, and taught the people Torah, and Yosef ben Moshe Maman from Tetuan,[2] who arrived via Persia and convinced the Jews in Bukhara that they were descendants of Jews exiled from Spain in the fifteenth century.[3]

Ya'ari later drew on the same travelogues that Idelsohn cites. However, he dismissed some of their data in order to create a single, seamless narrative. By contrast, these discrepancies posed no difficulty for Idelsohn; the reports differ from each other simply because they refer to different people. Moreover, while Idelsohn's presentation of the past focuses on two emissaries in particular, his narrative does not limit the possibility that others may have arrived. In this depiction, in which emissary work is not carried out by a single individual who arrives at one moment in time, there is no revolutionary instant sandwiched between a distinct "before" and a moment "after." Without such a turning point, the binary nature of Ya'ari's categories falls away. There is no clear-cut distinction between a period of atrophy and assimilation on the one hand, and a period of vibrant education and literacy on the other. Likewise, the distinction between the "isolated, marginal community" and "the center" is blurred. Idelsohn's narrative, in short, suggests that the emissaries' arrivals occurred within the context of a long-standing and complex relationship between the Jews of Bukhara, the Holy Land, and nearby Jewish communities. In this model, the definition and naming of the categories *center* and *periphery* are opened to contestation.

What happened to Idelsohn's account? Unlike Ya'ari's story, which journeyed from obscurity to popularity, this one has languished. It was published in the first volume of the journal *Mizrah u-Ma'arav* (East and West), which was founded in Palestine in 1920 (shortly after Britain assumed control of the mandatory authority). At that time, the rate of Jewish migration from Eastern Europe had reached an all-time high and the political and cultural prominence of Palestine's Sephardi and Mizrahi[4] Jewish population, which had been the majority until 1880, was rapidly becoming eclipsed. The journal represented a scholarly effort to incorporate these Jewish groups into the story of the Jews' nineteenth- and early twentieth-century migration to and settlement in Palestine. It was one of the earliest works that aimed to give greater attention to communities that until then had been marginalized in this body of literature. In their introductory volume, the editors explain: "There are certain [Jewish] communities with very small populations . . . but the whole world nevertheless knows of their happenings. . . . On the other hand, there are some large, important communities but no one knows a thing about them because no scholar has arisen to save them [from oblivion]. . . . This is exactly what has happened to the Sephardim of North Africa and the [Jews] of the East. . . ."[5] *Mizrah u-Ma'arav* aimed to work toward undoing this imbalance in scholarship.

The journal, however, was not a success. Only five volumes were published. Today, though they sit on the shelves of the National Library of Israel (in Jerusalem), they are in few other collections. Likewise, Idelsohn's article is hardly accessible to the general public. Ya'ari did discover it when he conducted his own research in Jerusalem, and used its information, drawing on the sources Idelsohn cited. However, Ya'ari used these same sources to reach different conclusions, and cited Idelsohn only to criticize him, writing: "And Idelsohn did not have the sense [to realize] that these two Yosefs were one and the same: Rabbi Yosef Maman, emissary from the Holy Land."[6] In the shadow of this disparaging comment, Idelsohn's article has remained obscure—along with the other pages in the journal in which it was published—not to be cited again until now.

Nissim Tagger's Fractured Story of Yosef Maman

The journey of Nissim Tagger's presentation of Yosef Maman follows a similar pattern. His version appears in his *Toldot Yehudei Bukhara* (The History of the Jews of Bukhara), published in 1970.[7] In this critical decade of Israel's history, Sephardi and Mizrahi Jews were beginning to protest the widespread discrimination they had suffered at the hands of the country's bureaucratic institutions, which were run primarily by Ashkenazi Jews. Raising their voices in an effort to have their history and culture included in the nation's public view of itself, Sephardi and Mizrahi authors began to publish books that told the stories of their communities. Without betraying the nationalist cause, Tagger (and others like him) looked for ways to highlight the contributions Mizrahi Jews had made to the state. It is in this context that Tagger wrote his history of the Jews of Bukhara, presenting a story of Maman that is radically different from that of Ya'ari, who was closely aligned with the Ashkenazi establishment.

Tagger wrote his book with two audiences in mind: Bukharan Jews (those who had immigrated to Israel as well as those who remained in Central Asia), and the wider Jewish public. In addressing both audiences, he wrote in two languages, which appear side by side: Hebrew and "Bukharit."[8]

The introduction to his book speaks to both these groups:

> The Bukharan Jews had a rich history . . . [and they had] superior quali-
> ties: Their refined Zionism, their welcoming of guests, their generosity,
> and above all, their faithfulness to the eternal values of the nation [of
> Israel]. . . .
>
>   For this reason, I have decided to publicize everything about their his-
> tory that I have gleaned from various sources, in order that all of our di-
> aspora brothers and our brothers in the Land of Israel will know the past
> of this great tribe [shevet] which is called the Bukharan Jewish tribe. . . .
> Books like these have the power to bring hearts close together; they allow
> that which separates us to become distant; and they facilitate the ingather-
> ing of the exiles. . . .[9]

With this opening statement, and with his decision to write in two languages, Tagger embraces two separate goals: to highlight the particular
talents and strengths of Bukharan Jews, while simultaneously working
to facilitate Jewish unity. In doing so, he emphasizes the notion that the
Jewish People is divided into subgroups (which he calls "tribes"), each
with qualities that should be highlighted and celebrated, while also em-
phasizing the notion that Jews belong to one unified group that shares a
common history, tradition, and destiny.

Tagger himself straddles both the particular and the universal. He
draws attention to his own genealogical descent from Yosef Maman, as
well as his descent from Yosef Hasid, who—according to Tagger's own
report—was an important leader of the Jewish community in Bukhara
before Yosef Maman's arrival. An embodiment of both Bukharan Jewish diaspora tradition (as a descendant of Yosef Hasid) and of a unified
Jewish People (as a descendant of Yosef Maman), Tagger contains the
seeds of contestation within his own biography.

Tagger's tension-ridden approach structures his presentation of Yosef Maman's story. On the one hand, he attributes Bukharan Jews' love of
the land of Israel to Maman, and he praises Maman for increasing Jewish
knowledge in Bukhara by building up schools that made Torah study
accessible to all.[10] Yet Tagger is also highly critical of Ya'ari's "twisted
and distorted" portrait of Maman as the savior of Bukharan Jews, and
he structures his own story of Maman as a rebuttal to Ya'ari's. He writes:

> Bukharan Jews were not cut off from the other [Jewish] diaspora groups, as some have claimed.... [Religious] wise men flowed to Bukhara from all the diaspora lands of the east. Many settled in the lands of Bukhara and had many students there.... Though others have claimed differently, the Jews of Bukhara had great Torah scholars in every generation.... [They were not] left without spiritual leaders.
>
> Further on we will discuss the claim that the great rabbi Yosef Maman found the Jews of Bukhara to be very far from traditional Judaism. This is unequivocally false. There was never a break in their traditional and religious way of life.[11]

With these bold statements, Tagger refutes Ya'ari's basic assumption that the Jews of Bukhara were isolated from contact with other Jewish groups. Accordingly, his description of Maman's first moment of contact with Bukharan Jews differs dramatically from that of Ya'ari.

Whereas Ya'ari depicts an encounter between the learned and the ignorant, in Tagger's depiction the encounter takes place between the emissary who had come from abroad and the already existing local religious establishment that had an integrity of its own. When Maman arrived in Bukhara, Tagger writes, the community leaders Yosef Hasid and Yitzhak Kohen "received [him] with great honor."[12] This reception, however, does not suggest harmonious relations. Rather, it portends dialogue—even confrontation—between the local leaders and the foreign emissary.

Indeed, it was not long before conflict erupted:

> [Maman] did not live peacefully during the first years because there was a second *hakham*[13] in Bukhara at the time by the name of Hakham Zechariah Matzliah, from Yemen. Strong arguments between the *hakhamim*[14] erupted, which caused a division of the community into two factions. The *hakhamim* did not identify with one another; not in their ideas, and not in their traditions. Hakham Zechariah did not honor the Zohar ... while Hakham Yosef [Maman] Ma'aravi revered the Zohar very much....
>
> Their arguments over the Zohar seeped into other domains, such as [laws concerning] ritual slaughter, ritual bath, and primary style of prayer, and caused the community to split into two factions.
>
> Hakham Zechariah forwarded the traditions of the Persian Jews, which were similar to those of the Jews of Yemen, while Hakham Yosef wanted the Jews of Bukhara to follow the traditions of the Jews of Morocco and other Jews who had come out of Spain. The argument between the teachers extended to their camps of students, and each side began to slander the opposing side. It got to the point that [each faction] imposed a *herem* [religious ban] on the ritual slaughtering of the opponent.[15]

This section of Tagger's story offers a new way to look at the reports
that appear in the travelogues. Taking the words of D'Beth Hillel and
Wolff at face value, Ya'ari suggests that Maman would not eat the local
Jews' food due to their ignorance of Jewish teachings and their conse-
quent deviance from normative religious practice. Tagger's account, on
the other hand, shows how the definitions of "acceptable" and "normative" religious practice are defined in the context of social and political
relations. This section of Tagger's story also offers a new way to look at
the switch to Sephardi liturgy explained by the historian and book collector Elkan Adler. Adler wrote that Maman "persuaded" the Jews of
Bukhara that "like himself, they were descended from the Jews exiled
from Spain and Portugal, to whose ritual it was therefore their duty to
conform,"[16] portraying the Jews of Bukhara as passive acceptors of Maman's authority. Tagger, instead, depicts a struggle between those who
supported Maman and those who did not. The struggle, according to
Tagger, was resolved in the following manner:

> [In the end] the Jews of Bukhara accepted the opinions of Hakham Yosef
> and to this day they continue to pray according to Sephardi traditions.
>   The students of Hakham Yosef claimed that if it were not for their
> rabbi, the Jews of Bukhara would have assimilated and become distant
> from Judaism. . . . Contrary to their opinion, the students of Hakham
> Zechariah claim that before Hakham Yosef arrived in Bukhara . . . there
> were rabbis in Bukhara. . . . The Jews of Bukhara knew what Judaism was
> and were not ignorant.[17]

In effect, the switch to Sephardi liturgy occurred because the students of Maman won the struggle for religious authority in Bukhara. It
was these students, the victors, who propagated the story that their community was in a state of spiritual dissolution prior to Maman's arrival, as
well as the story that his arrival signaled revolutionary changes in their
religious life. The students who lost the struggle, on the other hand, were
silenced. So, too, their story, which tells of the religious leaders who preceded Maman, is silenced. According to Tagger, the pre-Maman myth
that Ya'ari presents is simply propaganda of the winning side.

A final point of contention between Tagger's and Ya'ari's versions of
the Maman story surrounds their conflicting views of the mechanisms
by which Maman was able to win the religious struggle in Bukhara.
Tagger writes:

The faction of Hakham Yosef prevailed and won because in the meantime two daughters were born to Yosef Maman. The first, Sara, married the brilliant, renowned scholar from Meshed, Mullah Avraham Kohen, and the second, Miriam, married Mullah Niyaz, the grandson of the Nasi Mullah Yosef Hasid, the richest man in Bukhara who was among the close associates of the emir. Mullah Niyaz was very influential and after he became Hakham Yosef's son-in-law, he built up his father-in-law's camp so that it became very powerful.[18]

According to Tagger, Maman did not prevail because he was infused with the holiness of the Land of Israel. Rather, it was his marriage ties, which allied him with the community's preexisting financial and religious authority structure, that allowed him to prevail.

In Ya'ari's version, religious authority and legitimacy are contained within the Holy Land and Maman derives his power from there. In Tagger's version, religious authority and legitimacy are contained within the diaspora community itself and Maman rises to power through his association with the host community's inner resources.

The Fate of Nissim Tagger's Story

Nissim Tagger's complex presentation of the Maman story has much to teach us not only about the nineteenth-century social history of the Jewish community in Bukhara. His narrative also suggests how Avraham Ya'ari's rendition of this chapter in history would come to eclipse his own.

Just as Maman aligned himself with the establishment in Bukhara, Avraham Ya'ari himself was aligned with Israel's national establishment at the time of his writing. Whereas Nissim Tagger's voice came from the margins, Ya'ari was trained within the university system, conferred legitimacy by it, and worked within it. Neither of these men published their stories in widely accessible volumes. However, when later historians wrote more popular versions of Bukharan Jewish history, they turned to Ya'ari's work, which had the trappings of mainstream scholarship.

The fact of his researching and writing from within the state's institutional infrastructure did not stand alone. He also drew upon conventions that were accepted in the establishment. More specifically, Ya'ari relied upon written data to weave his story of Yosef Maman, whereas Nissim Tagger drew primarily on information about his family that he received through oral transmission. He wrote, "Everything which I have written about the period of Hakham Yosef, I heard from my mother's mouth."[19]

While scholars today embrace oral history as a legitimate means to access the past, Ya'ari was operating within a scholarly framework in which this approach was largely dismissed. Indeed, the illegitimate nature of oral history was so taken for granted that it formed the basis of Ya'ari's critique of Idelsohn's rendition of Bukharan Jewish history. In the introduction to his article, Idelsohn explains that he collected much of his information from testimonies of Bukharan Jews themselves. Singling out Idelsohn, Ya'ari responds, "Those who have written about the Jews of Bukhara on the basis of that which they heard from the mouths of the Jews of Bukhara themselves were imprecise in their reports, distorting the information, and twisting the rumors so that they are no longer recognizable."[20] Of course, the texts upon which Ya'ari himself relied were simply written records of spoken testimonies. Yet, he overlooks the blurry nature of the boundary that separates "written history" from "oral history." Categorizing the two as mutually exclusive, he treats textual evidence as authoritative, and oral testimony as illegitimate.

In addition to the trappings and the methodological conventions, the content of Ya'ari's history also reiterated and supported a state-sponsored narrative: the story of the Land of Israel as the Jews' enduring center, holding together the dispersed people and their religion. Ya'ari's voice was another layer added to that which was already accepted as a "normative" rendition of history. This particular construct is so powerful because it is not limited to a description of the role that the Land of Israel played within the Jewish past. Rather, it is part of a broader, deeply rooted, and widely accepted paradigm of the Jewish diaspora held together through shifting centers of authority, which have included Bavel (Iraq), Spain, Ashkenaz, and Eastern Europe. Perhaps Nissim Tagger's rendition of the past remained on the margins because it interrogates this paradigm by posing unsettling questions about the relationship between Jewish unity, on the one hand, and the authority and autonomy of various diaspora groups, on the other.

Finally, Ya'ari's history contains the most basic elements of a story, presented in a clear and predictable sequence. It has a beginning point (religious ignorance), a middle, which might be classified as a "breach" or "disruptive event" (Maman's arrival),[21] and a conclusion that offers a resolution (Bukharan Jews' return to the stage of Jewish history). In this story, the protagonist is clearly identified, as are his heroic qualities. He is the agent of change who moves the story along a triumphant trajectory. Ya'ari's narrative may have been repeated and popularized because it follows an easily defined sequence, one that is predictable and familiar.

Tagger's narrative, by contrast, conforms to no such sequence. Its complexity is largely due to its multivocal nature, in which the reader is provided with the opportunity to identify with both the students of Maman as well as with those who opposed him. Above the din of their contention, Tagger's own narrative voice wavers, leaving the reader wondering whether the protagonist should be viewed as a hero or a rogue.

Just as Tagger's portrait of Maman's character is surrounded by uncertainty, so, too, it is unclear what lesson his story is meant to relate. Whereas Ya'ari's narrative offers a singular teleological argument about how diaspora history unfolds, Tagger offers three separate messages: first, he characterizes the Bukharan Jews as an *edah* and a *shevet* with particular qualities and traditions that should be celebrated. Second, his assertion that "without interruption wise men flowed to Bukhara from all the diaspora lands of the east" contextualizes Torah study in Bukhara as intimately connected to a broader religious community. He distinguishes between this eastern community and the Sephardi world, and takes issue with Maman for imposing his Sephardi traditions on the local Jews, and for not recognizing the legitimacy of the traditions of the Jews of Persia, Yemen, Afghanistan, and Iran. Finally, Tagger celebrates Jewish unity, praising the Jews of Bukhara for their commitment to the Land of Israel, and for their faithfulness to "the eternal values" of the Jewish People. These three different messages leave the reader unsure about whether Maman's arrival should be viewed as good or bad.

Rather than promulgating a moral message, Tagger illuminates the mechanisms through which Maman came to be remembered as a hero. Unlike the popular version of the Center-Periphery Paradigm that assumes these categories to have essential and enduring qualities, he describes the process whereby the center becomes defined as such, and comes to dominate over that which becomes the periphery.

But this chapter and the previous one are not only about Yosef Maman and the people with whom he interacted. Using Tagger's generative paradigm as the framework, these chapters also illuminate how his own depiction of history (and Idelsohn's earlier version of it) came to be relegated to the margins and dismissed, at best as a grandmother's folktale, and at worst as a "twisted" and "distorted" presentation of the past. So, too, Tagger's generative version of the Center-Periphery Paradigm sheds light on how it is that Ya'ari's rendition came to be taken for granted as both normative and true. These two processes did not occur parallel to each other, but in relationship to one another, through intertextual conversation and contestation.

In the chapters to come, two additional encounters between the Jews of Central Asia and those in other parts of the Jewish world are analyzed. The Center-Periphery Paradigm will be invoked; however, through using Tagger's framework as a model, these terms will be treated as unstable, defined and redefined through dynamic and ongoing exchange.

PART 3

Nineteenth-Century Conversations

FIVE

Russian Colonialism and Central Asian Jewish Routes

The story of Yosef Maman's arrival in Central Asia at the turn of the eighteenth century signifies the onset of new forms of engagements between the Jews of Bukhara and the Jewish world that lay to the west. These relationships intensified in the nineteenth century as Imperial Russia encroached on Central Asia, bringing the region under its control. Taking advantage of improved conditions for travel and communication and of new mercantile opportunities the Russians brought with them, Bukhara's Jews formed new far-reaching trade relationships. A well-traveled, nouveau riche class emerged, focused on material acquisition as well as on using their recently obtained financial resources to enhance their spiritual lives. Pilgrimage to the Holy Land became fashionable, and importing religious teachers from there also gained popularity. Through these connections, the Jews of Bukhara were drawn into extensive conversations about religion with rabbinic authorities in Ottoman Palestine.

The next chapter (chapter 6) will trace the contours of these charged debates; we will analyze these in a manner akin to the way in which the debates between Maman and Central Asia's local religious authorities were studied. The current chapter sets the stage by providing a political and historical context for these colorful and complex international religious conversations.

Russian Territorial Expansion

We begin by widening the angle of our lens beyond Bukhara and even beyond Central Asia. We zoom out so far that our picture encompasses

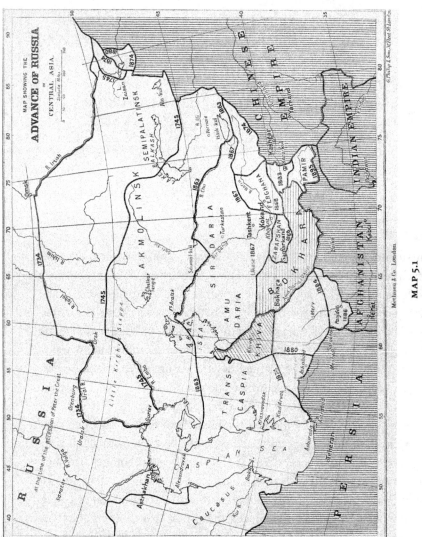

MAP 5.1

Map of Russia's moving frontier, as it appeared in a nineteenth-century travelogue
From Francis Henry Skrine, Heart of Asia (London: Methuen & Co., 1899)

Europe and the large-scale negotiations between Russia and Britain for control of massive areas of land. One object of this Great Game was domination of Central Asia.

As early as the eighteenth century, Russian eastward expansion moved across the Kazak steppes, bringing the nomadic people of the territory today known as Kazakhstan under their governance. Turning southward, the Russians headed toward the Syr River in the direction of Central Asia's three khanates (or kingdoms) of Bukhara, Kokand, and Khiva. In 1865, General Mikhail Chernyayev and his troops reached Tashkent, one of the first important urban centers in his path. At the time, the city belonged within the realm of the Kokand Khanate, but control over it was being contested by Bukhara. In an effort to weaken both kingdoms and to exert Russian power in the region, the general conquered it, bringing it under tsarist control. Tashkent became a base for further expansion and within two years was designated as administrative headquarters of Russia's newly created Central Asian administrative unit, the Turkestan Government-General.[1]

In 1868, following war, the emir of Bukhara was forced to sign a treaty in which he ceded Samarkand, once an important silk-route city, to the Turkestan Government-General. By signing, he also agreed to a set of provisions that facilitated the activities of Russian merchants within the boundaries of the Bukharan emirate. As the treaty was being composed and negotiated, the question of whether Russia should actually occupy and take full control of the Bukharan emirate was raised. While the Turkestan administrators were in favor of occupation, the tsar was not. Orders were issued from St. Petersburg not to add to "the burden of territorial conquests." In response, assistance was provided to the emir to help him regain control of his shrunken emirate. The emir thereby retained sovereignty, but became dependent on Russia to stabilize his fragile crown. After 1868, he was described as "a sort of guilded marionette" controlled by Russian hands.[2]

In 1873 Russian troops attacked the khanate of Khiva. Unlike the Bukharan emirate that retained nominal sovereignty despite its loss in territories, Khiva was fully defeated and "reduced to the legal status of Russia's protectorate." Its capital was occupied and its khan was forced to declare himself an "obedient servant" of the tsar.[3] Pushing east, the khanate of Kokand was incorporated into Russian Turkestan by 1876.[4]

With that conquest, the city of Kokand and the cities of the Fergana Valley (Fergana, Kokand, Andijan, and Namangan) were brought directly under Russian rule.

Russia's Textile Market and Central Asia's Jews

One aspect of Russia's motivation for conquest was territorial expansion in response to competition with British India for supremacy in the region. Another vital aspect of Russian expansion was its search for resources, in particular to meet the demands of a growing textile market.

While the advent of new technology had recently made possible the mass production of cotton textiles, a shortage of raw materials impeded production expansion. Control of Central Asia presented an excellent opportunity for meeting the growing demand. Cotton was a natural crop in the area, grown long before the arrival of the Russians, but only on a small scale alongside other crops cultivated for local consumption. Russian merchants became involved in the business of intensifying cotton production in Central Asia by importing high-quality cottonseed, and organizing and encouraging local peasants to engage in mono-cropping.[5] The result was a dramatic increase in production. Between 1886 and 1890, the land area used for cotton cultivation increased sixfold. In 1886, no more than 4 percent of Russia's cotton was coming from Central Asia. By 1914, that number had risen to 51.3 percent.[6]

The new market, coupled with Russian military governance, paved the way for improved transportation and communication between Central Asia and Russia. In the 1870s, a telegraph network spread through Russian Turkestan, and in the following decade work on a railroad began. By 1888, the railroad that originated at the Caspian Sea stretched as far as Samarkand.[7] Refinement of industrial technology was accompanied by a need for merchants to finance peasant farmers to expand production and for entrepreneurs to buy cotton and sell it to Russian textile manufacturers.[8] It is at this point in the history that the story of the Central Asian Jews becomes relevant.

Before the arrival of the Russians, Central Asia's Jews were primarily engaged in small-scale business, and were known as "able traders" with "an enviable reputation [as people] with whom it was profitable to do business."[9] They also worked in a wide array of crafts,[10] but were known in particular for their specialty in the area of textile dyeing.[11] Their commercial interests and their expertise in dyeing intersected with their involvement in dye-trade, a market which they dominated in nineteenth-century Central Asia. Jewish merchants from Baghdad would purchase dye in India, sell it to Herati Jewish traders; the latter, in turn, sold it to Central Asian merchants who brought it back to sell in their hometowns.[12] Given the Jews' well-developed business connections, trade skills, and dealings in areas related to textile production, their transition into the business of trade, processing, and manufacturing of cotton and cotton textiles in the latter half of the nineteenth century was natural.

Recognizing that the Jews were uniquely situated to assist the Tsarist Empire in its efforts to corner the market in the production and trade of textiles in the region, Russian authorities implemented policies to assist them toward this end. While Jews who lived in Russia then were allowed to reside only within the confines of the legally defined territory called the Pale of Settlement, Central Asia's Jews were granted special trading rights and residence privileges in Russia and in Russian Turkestan.[13] And unlike many Jewish merchants in the western parts of the empire, whose trading rights were restricted due to high membership fees in merchant guilds, Central Asia's Jews were not required to join guilds. With few obstacles, they were permitted to engage in commerce, to participate in trade exhibitions, to live and to own nonmovable property in Russia proper. They were even granted the right to become Russian subjects.[14] Annette Meakin, an Englishwoman who traveled to Central Asia in 1896, wrote about how the Jews there were regarded differently than Jews living in Eastern Europe: "'We trust the word of a Bokharan Jew,' said a Russian banker, when I was asking him about them. 'A Bokharan Jew could go to Russia and bring all Moscow back on bare credit. Everyone would trust him. Polish and Lithuanian Jews may not live in Moscow, but the Bokharans have a right to settle there.'"[15] The result was an emergence of a cosmopolitan, nouveau riche class that came under the influence of contemporary European culture.

Commerce and Cosmopolitan Connections

As European travel to Central Asia increased in the nineteenth century, a wealth of ethnographic information about the local peoples was published in the reports and travelogues of diplomats and adventurers. The Jewish minority, which belonged to the region but stood out because of their differences, drew particular interest. One common theme emphasized in the writings of Western travelers was the Jews' tremendous mobility. Though Central Asia was their home, many had taken advantage of new business opportunities, venturing as far east as India and China, and west to Moscow and Europe.

In the 1870s, Eugene Schuyler, an American diplomat in Russia, published a report on the region. Among the fascinating ethnographic details he provides about the people there, he tells of a Jewish man who approached him, hoping to make a sale of "Greek coins and engraved gems." Schuyler engaged him in conversation and learned the following:

> He and his father went to India on a trading expedition, and then resolved to go to Europe; but in order to do so they were obliged at Bombay to make themselves British subjects and to take out British passports. After staying for more than a year in London, the father returned to Bukhara, where he now is, while the son went to Paris, where he remained three or four years, and then found his way to Samarkand. He speaks English fairly, and French very well.[16]

Elkan Adler, the British book collector who journeyed to Central Asia in the late 1890s, also took note of the local Jews' extensive travel:

> Perhaps I was prejudiced in their favor, but they certainly struck me as most intelligent and hospitable. Many of them were great travellers. One man had been to China; several had visited India by way of Afghanistan and the Khyber Pass. . . . Most of the travelled Jews of Bokhara have been to Moscow, many to Paris, and some to London. One good man had been five times to Moscow.[17]

Likewise, Ole Olufsen, a Danish lieutenant and adventurer who traveled to Bukhara in the late 1890s, noted that "many of the apparently primitive Jews who looked highly archaic in the bazars in their caftans had visited both London and Paris."[18]

Those who traveled to France and England were influenced by styles popular in Europe at the time and became conduits of cultural exchange. For example, Ephraim Neumark, who traveled to Central Asia from Palestine in the mid-1880s, remarked:

> Their standard of living used to be low, but in the past few years they have started to imitate the ways of Moscow, which is one of the places where

they do business. Now you can see a strong European influence in their homes. In particular, they like to bring back silverware from Moscow.[19]

And Schuyler, writing about the same coin dealer referred to earlier, wrote:

> It was amusing to see him in his little Paris coat a thorough European among his countrymen in their caps and long gowns.[20]

In addition to bringing European material culture back with them to Central Asia, Jews also acquired language skills, invaluable for trading purposes as well as for an exchange of culture and ideas. Olufsen notes:

> They [the Jews] now employ Usbegic or Tadjik [the local] language[s], but many of them are also able to speak French, Russian or German.[21]

Finally, Ephraim Neumark comments on the Jews' efforts to import books published in locales far beyond Central Asia's boundaries:

> The road to Russia has been opened up to the Bukharan [Jew]s and they have begun to come to Moscow to trade . . . and from there they have brought every kind of book that their hearts have desired.[22]

These interesting pieces of information contained in the publications of Western travelers provide a glimpse into how rapid changes in Central Asia affected the lives of Jews living there. However, the descriptions provide little information about ways in which Jewish community life was affected. Drawing on biographical sketches written by contemporary Bukharan Jews about their forebears, the following section explores ways in which Jewish communities experienced change in the three cities where they were most highly concentrated: Tashkent, Bukhara, and Samarkand.

TASHKENT

In 1988, Binyamin Ben-David published a brief family history that provides a window into Tashkent's nineteenth-century Jewish community. His story begins in 1865, the year that marked a turning point for his great-great-grandfather, Yehuda. Forty years old at the time, married, and the father of five children, Yehuda was living in his hometown of Shahrisabz. Sensing that fortuitous changes were about to occur, he took his family to Tashkent, two hundred miles away, and joined the city's tiny Jewish community. Within a year of his move, Tashkent was incor-

porated into Russian Turkestan and Yehuda and his family found themselves among a flock of Jewish entrepreneurs who arrived in the city to
take advantage of the favorable market conditions the Russians provided.

Among Yehuda's five sons was Yissakhar, who was nineteen when
the family moved to Tashkent. Soon after their arrival, Yissakhar became a *bozarchi,* a small-scale merchant, who sold textiles at the weekly
bazaars held in villages that encircled the outskirts of the city. Yosef,
another son, was only nine years old when the family moved to Tashkent, but even at this young age he found an outlet for his entrepreneurial spirit—peddling tea and matches. As Yosef grew up, he continued
to engage in business, expanding his repertoire. By the time he turned
eighteen, he joined the textile business established by Yissakhar. Years
passed, the brothers' volume of trade grew, and they became well connected with merchants in the same industry who worked in Moscow.

When Yosef and Yissakhar had children themselves, they were
brought into the business. Yosef sent one son to live in Moscow to oversee
business there. Through him, the family gained a trustworthy reputation
and was able to obtain significant bank loans. Among their early and
wisest major investments was a cotton gin, one of the first in Tashkent.
Business expanded and the family continued to buy and manage other
cotton gins in the Central Asian regions that had come under Russian
control: one in Kokand, another in Namangan, and still another in An-
dijan. In addition to their involvement in production, the family continued to work in sales, building up a wholesale warehouse for textiles that,
at the turn of the century, was designated as the fifth largest in Tashkent.

Yissakhar had a son named Natan, who joined the company at a
young age. He was entrusted with aspects of the business that involved
long-distance travel and trade. By the time he was twenty, Natan was
traveling west to Moscow and as far east as China to fill in wherever help
was needed. Much later in his life, Natan reflected on the hardships the
business had demanded during these years:

> I was on the road for eleven months [a year]. For six months I would
> manage the cotton gin in Kanivadam. For three months I would sit in for
> Uncle Benyamin who was in Moscow. And for two and a half months I
> would live near the border of China, also working for the company. I was
> [in Tashkent] with the family for only two and a half weeks during the
> whole year. This is how I worked for four years.[23]

In the face of these difficult working conditions, Natan felt he was not fairly compensated by the company. Family tensions surrounding individual responsibilities and company holdings deepened, eventually leading Natan to cash out and begin his own business. He wrote:

> So I left the company with 125,000 rubles in capital . . . [and] traveled to Moscow. I already knew the city well. I bought merchandise [there] for a sum of 800,000 rubles in installments. I sent all the merchandise to Turkestan and I sent a telegram to my brother-in-law, Eliyahu, telling him that I would be traveling to Berlin and that I would return to Tashkent in exactly one month. . . . Over the next year and a half, I traveled to Moscow eight times. I made 1,200,000 rubles and I became a great competitor of "the company."[24]

The Ben-David family story illustrates how Jews in Russian Turkestan were able to further their financial growth by taking advantage of the tight social connections and ease of mobility between Moscow and Central Asia in the late nineteenth and early twentieth centuries. It also gives some indication of how the economic attractions of Russian rule resulted in the growth of Tashkent's Jewish community. Whereas Ben-David reports that the city was home to only twelve Jewish families when Yehuda moved there with his family in 1865, by 1872 the Jewish population had grown to a total of 419 people, and by 1898, the number had further increased to 2,053.[25]

Despite the growth of the Jewish population, however, the community's infrastructure remained relatively weak. In 1885, traveler Henry Lansdell, for example, described the only synagogue in Tashkent that serviced Bukharan Jews as "a miserable shed with a lean-to roof of poles, wretchedly covered." He explains the "ill-furnished condition" of this rented space "by the fact that almost all the Jews in Tashkend are traders and sojourners only."[26]

Because many of the Jews in Tashkent were traveling merchants who, unlike Yehuda, did not settle in the city with their children, few Jewish schools were organized. In the 1850s, when the Jewish population in Tashkent consisted of no more than a handful of families, twenty students were enrolled in *khomlos*. These traditional schools (the equivalent of Eastern European *heders*)[27] were to educate boys alone, with the course of study focusing on religious texts. Students would begin to attend a *khomlo* at the age of four and might continue until they reached bar mitzvah age, when they were expected to begin to contribute to the family income.[28]

By the end of the century, although the Jewish population had grown tremendously, there were only three Jewish schools in Tashkent serving one hundred Bukharan students. The administrators of these more modern schools emphasized secular studies alongside religious ones, and allowed girls to attend. The inclusion of girls in the student rosters demonstrates starkly just how tiny the segment of the Jewish population was that was being served by these institutions.[29]

Religious authority in the city also appears to have been weak. There is, in fact, no evidence of any rabbis in Tashkent until 1903. In that year, Shlomo Tagger,[30] who was working in Samarkand at the time, was recruited by some of Tashkent's wealthy community leaders, who persuaded him to move there to serve as their rabbi.[31] Even so, he was not authorized to serve as a *dayan* (religious judge). Therefore, when issues such as divorce cases arose in Tashkent, requiring the arbitration of a *beit din* (Jewish court), they had to be settled outside of the city.[32]

In the chapter that follows, where we examine negotiations between Central Asia's local religious authorities and the religious authorities in Ottoman Palestine, we will see that Tashkent was hardly involved in these conversations. The Jews who lived there were almost all newcomers. Having moved away from Central Asia's traditional Jewish population center to the heart of Russia's colonial enterprise, their communal religious infrastructure was weak and they had no indigenous leadership. No longer marked as *dhimmi,* they also had greater freedom to choose how they wished to express their Jewish identity.

In ancient Bukhara, on the other hand, where Jews trace back their history for many, many centuries, they strongly identified with an indigenous tradition, grounded in the local landscape. There, much more was at stake in nineteenth-century conversations between local and global religious authorities.

BUKHARA

In an oft-told legend depicting the arrival of Jews in Bukhara, their origins are traced back to the days of a powerful new king who was engaged in establishing his reign over the land. Intent on glorifying his court and capital city, this unnamed ruler searched far and wide for the best architects, craftsmen, and designers. In his quest to find a master weaver, he learned of a Jewish craftsman residing in Iran who was renowned for his work in designing and spinning magnificent golden carpets. The king sent an envoy to convince this weaver to relocate to Bukhara to join the craftsmen of his court. The weaver agreed, but only on condition that he could bring nine others with him so that he would have a quorum of Jewish men with whom to pray. With this small group, the community, which came to be known as "Bukharan Jews," was established.

In another version of this story, the main character is not a carpet weaver, but rather a doctor of great prominence. And in still another version, the king's recruiting efforts were not directed toward a single Jewish craftsman (such as the weaver) but rather toward a group of Jewish craftsmen, each with a different specialty.[33]

This narrative, in which the Jews' arrival to Bukhara coincides with the development and growth of the city, establishes a link between the Jews' understanding of their own past and the history of the broader urban landscape they occupied. While the legend does not situate the story in any particular historical period, it may refer to the tenth century, the time that the Abbasid caliphate, which ruled over the entire Muslim world from its capital in Baghdad, weakened and finally collapsed. In the wake of Abbasid reign, a number of Muslim dynastic rulers emerged with their centers in a variety of locales: Karaiwan in North Africa under Fatimid rule, Spain in the West under the Umayyad rule, and Bukhara in Central Asia under Samanid rule.

In Spain, the Umayyads worked to build up their capital in Córdoba through patronizing the arts, sciences, literature, philosophy, and religious studies. The Jews were able to take part in this cultural efflorescence, the community flourished, and this period became renowned in Jewish history as a "golden era." Like the cultural efflorescence in Muslim Spain, Bukhara in this same period "rose to a position of cultural preeminence" as a center of the arts, scientific innovation, and spirituality in the Muslim world.[34] The work of poets Firdausi and Rudaki, of the physician and philosopher Avicenna, and of the religious scholar Muhammad Bukhari, famous for his collection of *hadith* (Sahih Bukhri), are all testimony to the creative growth of that era. However, unlike in Spain, little historical documentation is available about Jewish cultural life in Central Asia from this period. The legend of the Jews' arrival may nevertheless be exemplary of the sense among the local Jews that their past—like that of the Jews of Spain—was intimately linked to this glorious era of cultural productivity.

Other legends, too, demonstrate the way in which Jewish community life was intertwined with the history of the city's local landscape. The story of the establishment of the synagogue in Bukhara's old Jewish quarter, which still stands today, is perhaps most indicative of this intimate relationship. According to legend, the home of an elderly Jewish widow who lived in the early seventeenth century was located a short walk away from where the synagogue stands today.[35] When the vizier of Bukhara initiated a project of urban renewal, he commissioned the construction of an ensemble of buildings: an inn, teahouse, and madrassah, which would surround a water reservoir. The home of the Jewish elderly widow was situated precisely on the spot where the pool was to be built, and she refused to sell it. After much prodding, she and the vizier reached an agreement in which she would give up her house and the property on which it stood in exchange for an adjacent piece of land where the Jewish community would be permitted to build a new synagogue. Today the Labi-Hawz pool and surrounding architectural ensemble—an urban oasis, and a popular tourist destination—still stand, and are emblematic of Bukhara's long, rich history. The house of worship, which the old widow secured almost four hundred years ago, also still stands. Referred to by the local Jews as the Labi-Hawz synagogue, it embodies their sense of deep roots and connection to this historical urban space.

In the 1860s, the emirate of Bukhara was reduced to a Russian dependency, yet for some time Jewish life in the capital city remained relatively unchanged. Indeed, throughout the emirate, Western influences remained "still few and weak" into the 1880s, and the restrictions placed on Jews "continued to be enforced."[36] When a telegraph line was constructed in the 1880s, it became Bukhara's "first modern link to the outside world," followed shortly thereafter by the railroad.[37] Even so, the Bukhara railroad station was situated eight miles from the city itself in concession to the emir who wanted to avoid provoking the Muslim clergy's hostility to the introduction of infidel ways, as well as in response to his subjects' fears of the steam locomotive, which they referred to as "Satan's Wagon."[38]

During this era, the Jewish community did not move to the new area of the city, which the Russians built, but rather remained in the residential quarters of the old city, where they had lived long before the Russians' arrival. While some of the city's Jews did leave to seek their fortunes in Tashkent and elsewhere, the stories that are told about the Jews of Bukhara are of those who stayed. Unlike the life histories of the Jews in Tashkent, in these tales the emphasis is not on their cosmopolitanism or their wealth, but rather on their traditional piety.

Just as we have information about the late nineteenth-century Jewish community in Tashkent through the family history written by a descendant of the visionary entrepreneur Yehuda Ben-David, in Bukhara information about the community is available through the writings of a descendant of a leading rabbinic figure of the period. In his book, *Zarah Kochav mi-Ya'akov* (A Star Shone Forth from Ya'akov), Yehuda ha-Kohen Rabin writes about his ancestors who served as chief rabbis of the community. The book starts with a description of the late 1700s, when the author's great-great-grandfather arrived from Baghdad and established himself as a leading authority in Bukhara. It continues through the early 1900s, when his own father served the community as a rabbi.

Most relevant for the discussion here is the author's depiction of his grandfather, Yitzhak Hayim ha-Kohen Rabin, who served as rabbi from 1866 to 1896, roughly the same period discussed in Ben-David's article. Below are key excerpts from the biographical sketch, rendered in my own words, but written in a style similar to that of the author.[39]

Yitzhak Hayim ha-Kohen Rabin

In 1866, when Yitzhak Hayim ha-Kohen—son of Bukhara's chief rabbi, Pinhas ha-Gadol—reached the age of eighteen, he married and was appointed chief rabbi and head of the religious courts in Bukhara and all surrounding cities, including those in Russian Turkestan. In this position, Yitzhak Hayim ha-Kohen educated many students to become rabbis, ritual slaughterers, cantors, ritual circumcisers, and teachers. After they received certification in Bukhara City, Yitzhak Hayim ha-Kohen sent them out to serve in cities all across the region "in order to glorify and spread the Torah and to show the nation the path to follow."[40]

Also in his position as chief rabbi, Yitzhak Hayim ha-Kohen cultivated relationships with rabbinic leaders far beyond the boundaries of Central Asia. The holiday of Sukkot provided one opportunity for strengthening his ties with the religious community in Jerusalem. People living in the Land of Israel understood how difficult it was in Bukhara to obtain the four plants necessary for the observance of the holiday (as called for in Leviticus 23:40; citron fruits, palm fronds, myrtle branches, and willow branches). Offering assistance, they would send these items from the Holy Land. Acknowledging their appreciation for these great gifts, the Jews of Bukhara would, in turn, send generous donations to the Land of Israel. Under the guidance of Yitzhak Hayim ha-Kohen, an agreement was made with the religious leaders in Jerusalem about how this money should be used. Some was channeled to Bukharan Jewish leaders residing in Jerusalem to support community organizations there, and some was sent to Sephardi leaders in Jerusalem to support their community organizations. By facilitating these ties, Yitzhak Hayim ha-Kohen strengthened relationships with Jerusalem's important religious leaders.

When Yitzhak Hayim ha-Kohen was forty-five years old, he traveled to the Holy Land to visit the graves of his forefathers, and to pray before them. When he arrived in Jerusalem, he was greeted with great honor by the Rishon LeTsion (the Sephardi chief rabbi of Ottoman Palestine),[41] and by many other important rabbinic leaders. He also visited other holy cities in Palestine—Hebron, Safed, and Tiberius—and was greeted warmly by the rabbis in each place. They all knew of Yitzhak Hayim ha-Kohen because of the generous donations he and his community in Bukhara had sent over the years.

In addition to the strong relationships Yitzhak Hayim ha-Kohen forged with the rabbis of Palestine, he was also very close to the pious, spiritual men of Bukhara. He belonged to a tight circle of friends who took a common vow that the first to pass away among them would visit one of the surviving friends in a dream to inform the others about the afterworld.

When one of them did die, the surviving circle of friends cried for three days. For seven days they eulogized him, and for thirty days they did not cut their hair. Each waited for their friend to visit in a dream, but he did not. Then, one evening the deceased appeared to the wife of Yitzhak Hayim ha-Kohen, and conveyed his apologies through her,

"Please forgive me, my dear friends," he asked her to speak on his behalf, "for not being able to uphold my word."[42] She relayed the message and from that day on, her family knew of her great righteousness.

Yitzhak Hayim ha-Kohen had another friend, Mordechai Zanbor, who did reveal himself regularly after his passing. On the first day of each new month, Yitzhak Hayim ha-Kohen would immerse in a ritual bath, don white clothes, and sleep in a special room hoping his deceased friend would visit in a dream. The last time his deceased friend appeared to him was just before Yitzhak Hayim ha-Kohen's own death. "Within the month," Mordechai Zanbor told his living friend, "you will be here with me." And that is exactly what happened.[43]

Yitzhak Hayim ha-Kohen passed away at the age of forty-eight. While the burial society was preparing his body, one of his hands became so stiff and impossible to move that he could not be dressed in his burial garments. A student of Yitzhak Hayim ha-Kohen's, named Hayim Fahla, approached his deceased teacher and spoke to him. "This is Hayim Fahla speaking," he whispered, and then asked his teacher to extend his arm. The deceased Yitzhak Hayim ha-Kohen responded, extending his arm as instructed.

"And on the Shabbat of my wedding," Yitzhak Hayim ha-Kohen's grandson (the author) writes, "my father told this story. [Speaking] to all of those who were gathered [to celebrate], my father said: 'When my [own] father [i.e., the groom's grandfather, Yitzhak Hayim ha-Kohen] extended his arm to Hayim Fahla this is what it meant: That a day would come when one of his own grandchildren would marry one of the grandchildren of Hayim Fahla. And [here we are] today [gathered for this very event] as my son . . . weds one of Hayim Fahla's grandchildren. May it come to be that the merits of the righteous will protect us.'"[44]

This biography tells of a man who was strongly connected to the Jewish community in Bukhara though his lineage, through his leadership position, and through his bonds of friendship with other spiritual leaders in the city and outlying areas. He traveled as well, but unlike members of the entrepreneurial Ben-David family, he went to the Holy Land on a voyage that was integral to his religious life, which was grounded in Central Asia. Also unlike the Ben-David family, whose kinship and business network stretched far across the globe, Hayim ha-Kohen's network was highly localized. Indeed, his relationships are so intimate that the stories about his friendship circles—particularly those concerning the visitations after death—are difficult for outsiders to penetrate.

At the end of the nineteenth century, when the Russian presence becomes prominent in Central Asia, the conversations and debates that would unfold between local Jewish leaders and those from abroad would touch only peripherally on religious practice in the city of Bukhara. It was in Samarkand, which was a dynamic meeting ground between a local Jewish population with a long history in the city and a new colonial culture, where most of the debates presented in the next chapter unfold.

SAMARKAND

Like the city of Bukhara, Samarkand was home to a large Jewish community long before the Russians' arrival. While historians do not offer a precise date for their origins, the travelogue of Benjamin of Tudela indicates that by the twelfth century there was already a substantial, well-organized Jewish community there.[45] Subject to the vicissitudes of rulers and conquests, however, the population hardly remained constant. The early nineteenth century was a particular moment of demographic change when Jews from Meshed (in contemporary Iran) and Herat (in contemporary Afghanistan) flocked to the city, fleeing persecution in their hometowns.[46] Around this same time, the Jews in Samarkand were able to acquire land for the building of a residential quarter, giving them a stake in the city as well as a strong sense of rootedness and belonging.

The Jewish quarter, which still stands today, is located in Samarkand's ancient city, as opposed to the "new city" that was built by the Russians. It is organized around a series of spidery lines radiating outward in organic growth, rather than in a grid. As in Bukhara, Samarkand's Jews lived near the city's defining ancient architectural structures, including the massive blue-tiled madrassahs that make up the ensemble of the Registan (the city center), as well as the great dome of the Bibi Khanum Mosque built by Tamerlane at the end of the fourteenth century, and the blue cupolas and ornamented stone arches of the Shahi-Zinda mausoleums.

In spite of the long-standing intimate connection between the Jews and their home in Samarkand, the urban landscape also provides evidence that Jews were drawn into broad networks of social and business connections from the latter half of the nineteenth century onward. In 1868, the region was incorporated into Russian Turkestan, and the same trading rights that Jews gained in Tashkent were extended to the Jews in Samarkand. Jewish merchants flocked to the area, which became a connection point for people traveling back and forth to Russia and Western Europe on business.[47] Many settled outside of the Jewish quarter and established residence in the newly built colonial town. Among them were wealthy entrepreneurs who lived in large homes inspired by European styles.

Built in 1911, the ornate house of merchant Kalantarov, with its high painted ceilings and colorfully ornamented walls, stood as testimony to the emergence of a powerful nouveau riche class. When the region was incorporated into the USSR, the Soviets confiscated the home as part of their effort to rid the region of its bourgeois capitalism. The house, however, was left intact and today is home to a museum of Jewish artifacts, standing as testimony to this period of great Jewish wealth.

This wealth was also associated with travel. Whereas travel stories from Bukhara at this time are about religious pilgrimage to the Holy Land, and travel stories from Tashkent are about business, the stories from Samarkand are an interesting intersection of both. Merchants would travel to Europe and on their way (or on their return home), they would journey to Palestine to visit the holy sites. Unlike the situation in Tashkent, the Jews in Samarkand had a long-standing historical connection to their city and were not fully influenced by the secularizing forces of modernity. They retained a local religious sensibility, but at the same time became cosmopolitan, multilingual businessmen. The story of Hizkiya Yissakharov embodies this phenomenon well. His biography, presented below, was stitched together by drawing on information about him presented in two folk histories on Bukharan Jews[48] as well as his biographical sketch provided in *Issacharoff: Tale of a Family,* published by the family on the occasion of their 1998 reunion.[49]

Hizkiya Yissakharov

In 1873, just before reaching bar mitzvah age, Hizkiya Yissakharov left his home in Bukhara to travel with his father to Ottoman Palestine. He settled there, attending school to receive both a religious and a secular education. In particular, he studied languages and was said to have mastered French, Spanish, Turkish, and Arabic alongside Hebrew and his native Tajik. Putting these language skills to use, he worked as a tour guide, meeting Jewish pilgrims in the port city of Jaffa and traveling with them to holy sites and graves in Jerusalem, Hebron, Safed, and Tiberius.

Hizkiya also bought and sold precious stones. Although little is written about this aspect of his career, his international language skills and the personal connections he made as a tour guide surely facilitated this work. In the meantime, his brothers who had remained in Central Asia opened up a wholesale business importing and selling textiles. In 1898, when he was thirty-seven years old, Hizkiya returned to Central Asia with his wife and five children so that he could join his brothers' business. They settled in Samarkand, which had been part of the Bukharan emirate when he was born, but by this time had been incorporated into Russian Turkestan, where Jewish mercantile activity was encouraged and accorded great freedom. As the family company grew, Hizkiya and his brothers joined their cousins, the Babayoffs, to open a branch in Kokand, and later joined the wealthy Borokhov brothers in Tashkent to open another branch.

In Samarkand, Hizkiya's wife Rahel bore five more children. In deciding how to educate them, Hizkiya faced a dilemma, as no teachers there were qualified to provide his children with the sort of religious education he himself had received as a youth in Ottoman Palestine. He therefore turned to Shlomo Tagger, a friend of his from Jerusalem, and reached an agreement to bring him to Samarkand to serve as a teacher for his sons and for the sons of other wealthy Jewish families in the city. In addition to contributing to the religious life among Samarkand's prestigious Jews, Hizkiya is also remembered for his impact on transforming the city's cultural life. His connections to Europe, through his mercantile activities, were said to have "stimulated the development of the community." His home became a gathering place and a center of activity for the Jewish upper class, and he is remembered for influencing the Jews of Samarkand "to behave like European Jews."[50]

Hizkiya passed away at the age of fifty-one in a hospital in Berlin, where he had gone for treatment of a heart condition. In his will, he stipulated that he should be buried in the Holy Land. His son Eliyahu accompanied his father's body to Jerusalem to see his father's wish fulfilled.

The story of Hizkiya Yissakharov exemplifies the traditional and pious quality of the Jewish population in Samarkand, as well as the cosmopolitan attributes of the local Jewish community. A well-traveled, wealthy merchant class emerged there at the turn of the last century, and they formed strong connections with the religious authorities and teachers in Ottoman Palestine. At the same time, they had a long historical memory of their past in Samarkand and were deeply rooted in the local space. Given the intersection of both these qualities, Samarkand became a most interesting, volatile site for contesting religious authority, where heated conversations about Jewish practice unfolded in the late nineteenth and early twentieth centuries. In the chapter that follows these debates are explored.

SIX

A Matter of Meat:
Local and Global Religious
Leaders in Conversation

By the spring of 1904, the slaughtering controversy—which had already been brewing in Samarkand's Jewish community for several years—exploded. Perhaps it happened at Passover time, when the city's Jews sat down to partake of the holiday feast at tables that seemed empty. Surely, they were replete with colorful varieties of salads and fish, but meat was nowhere to be seen.

The city's ritual slaughterers had declared almost every animal they killed to be *treif* (ritually unfit for consumption). The butchers, who were trying to turn a profit, berated the slaughterers for their religious fanaticism. The slaughterers retorted that they were simply following *halakhah* (Jewish law). The anger of the people grew, until the conflict could no longer be contained within the boundaries of the city.

In an attempt to reach a resolution, community leaders called upon rabbis from near and far to intercede. Shlomo Tagger came from Tashkent, Shlomo Kiki came from Shahrisabz, and Ya'akov Shaul Elyashar, who was the Rishon LeTsion (chief rabbi of the Sephardi Jews in Ottoman Palestine), wrote letters from Jerusalem, all to no avail. Perhaps the most poignant failure, though, was that of Hizkiya ha-Kohen Rabin, chief rabbi of Bukhara, who was the son, grandson, and great-grandson of prominent rabbis. While each of his forebears had been revered by Jewish communities across the Central Asian landscape, Hizkiya ha-Kohen Rabin was unable to muster such respect.

With pomp and circumstance he must have alighted from the train that brought him to Samarkand, outfitted in a distinguished karakul hat and *joma* (cloak) of fine silk, much like the garb he wears in his surviving portrait. He gathered the city's ritual slaughterers together, and had them take a public oath before all to see. Under his instructions, the slaughterers vowed that they would cease to follow the rulings of the errant rabbi under whom they had studied. This rabbi, Shlomo Lev Eliezerov, who was of Eastern European extraction, and who had lived in Central Asia for only a short period, had left Samarkand some years before. His students, though, had been so charmed by Shlomo Lev Eliezerov's soft demeanor, his extensive rabbinic knowledge, and his religious fervor, that he continued to hold them under his sway, even from a great distance.

Although they all took the oath as Hizkiya ha-Kohen Rabin instructed, it held no significance, as the slaughterers had formed a secret pact beforehand that they would not abide by it. And so, when Hizkiya ha-Kohen Rabin left Samarkand to go back to Bukhara, these slaughterers simply returned to their old ways. From two hundred miles away, he remained powerless to intercede.

Until now, this strange set of events has been given little attention in the scholarly literature. Perhaps the historians who have written about this period fail to mention the 1904 slaughtering controversy because the archival record ends here, trailing off without resolution, or perhaps the events do not seem to signify a moment that defined or changed the course of Central Asian Jewish history. Regardless of the reasons, I noticed the gap in the literature when I happened upon letters written between the various religious leaders who were involved in the debate. At first I could pick out only small bits and pieces of their content, as most of them were written in archaic handwriting and in a Hebrew replete with acronyms and internal references with which I was unfamiliar. But as I held these documents and examined them, hunched over a desk in the basement of Israel's National Library, I was drawn into their conversation: Who were the men who wrote these letters? What motivated them? What was at stake in their disagreement?

Finding answers to these questions was a slow, painstaking process. Yet the letter writers' intimate and impassioned tones beckoned, furnishing details of a story that gradually began fitting together like pieces of a puzzle. Among them were pieces that had been missing in other encounters I had studied. During the time I had spent at Torah Academy, I had recorded how the administration viewed the school's Bukharan

Jewish students, and had collected notes on the ways in which the teachers spoke about their interactions with these recent immigrants. Yet, their dominant voices had left me with a gaping hole in my understanding of how the students understood this same encounter. Likewise, in my study of Yosef Maman's engagement with Bukharan Jews, the flat historical record—dominated by the voice of the emissary—had left me wondering how the locals viewed their interactions with this emissary from afar. But here, in these late nineteenth- and early twentieth-century letters, in which many different writers engage each other, the encounter between emissaries, local religious leaders, and distant authorities has been preserved in multiple dimensions.

Their conversations tell a human story of the relationships and interactions between individual leaders coming from various geographical regions and different points of view. On a more abstract level, their correspondence offers a rich chronicle of an engagement between Judaism in its local and global forms. Here, I use the term *global* to refer to the relatively stable elements of the shared Jewish canon. These include the black-and-white texts of the Torah, the Talmud, and the *Shulhan Aruch,* which have been transmitted with little variation across time and space. *Local,* on the other hand, refers to the prisms through which these texts are refracted as they are studied, interpreted, and applied in particular places and at particular moments in time. In the case of this slaughtering controversy, the religious leaders who were in conversation with one another shared a common written discourse about the laws concerning ritual slaughtering. Shlomo Lev Eliezerov, Hizkiya ha-Kohen Rabin, Shlomo Tagger, and Rishon LeTsion Shaul Elyashar had all studied the laws as they appeared in the Talmud and the *Shulhan Aruch* (among other texts) and were all working to put them into practice. At the same time, their respective understandings of how these texts should be read and applied differed.

The Jewish legal system allows for a certain degree of interpretative variation, and even has a built-in legal category called *minhag ha-makom* (literally: local custom). Yet there is much ambiguity surrounding the guidelines by which one might ascertain whether a practice is a legitimate local form, or whether it is a distortion of that which is considered (depending on one's perspective) to be the "normative" reading and application of the text. The slaughtering controversy sheds light on the sorts of negotiations that emerge when this ambiguity is high. This case is also compelling because of its urgent ramifications. As we will see, the application of laws related to ritual slaughtering may be felt in the most tangible of ways: not only in questions about religious authority and communal politics, but also in the marketplace and in the belly.

A final word of introduction: analyzing and writing about these documents is fraught with tension, for this exercise must be done using two sorts of lenses simultaneously. On the one hand, the controversy can only be understood within the particular historical and cultural context in which it unfolded. The discussion that follows, then, situates the letter writers within the geopolitical reality they occupied: the rapidly shrinking borders of the Bukharan emirate as Russia encroached upon Central Asia. This process was accompanied by the evisceration of the emir's power, along with the attenuation of authority of local rabbinic leadership. At the same time, the region's Jewish population was being drawn into a trans-local sphere of religious influence. At this very historical moment, the Jewish population in Palestine, which had long been a backwater of the Ottoman Empire, was swelling in numbers and influence. Construction projects were initiated, Jewish institutional infrastructure was strengthened, and travel to the region increased. At the same time, the influence of the region's Sephardi chief rabbi (the Rishon LeTsion) grew. Extending far beyond the borders that had been marked by the Ottomans, his sphere of authority came to encompass segments of Central Asia's Jewish community.

If we read the letters on the slaughtering controversy through the eyes of a cultural historian, these particularities of time and place are essential for understanding their authors' intentions and motivations. Yet, there is another dimension to the conversation that must also be given special attention: a holy one, in which factors related to time and place are suspended. When the letter writers engage on this plane, they share an internal set of rules that transcends local knowledge. To enter this aspect of the conversation, then, we must join them in their virtual *beit midrash* (house of study). Here, Hizkiya ha-Kohen Rabin and his contemporaries sit together with the sages who composed the Mishnah, the Talmud, and the *Shulhan Aruch* in generations past, discussing and debating a common tradition. The details of this conversation may seem trivial or even meaningless to those who have not entered it. But for those inside, no nuance in the texts is too small to parse, analyze, and interpret, for contained within the minutiae are the keys into that which the religion demands for leading a proper life according to command.

What follows, then, is a discussion that uses two sets of tools to analyze the letters surrounding Samarkand's 1904 slaughtering controversy: first, the tools of an ethnographer, who gains entrée into the world of the people whom she studies by seeking to understand their words and actions within the particular cultural and historical settings that they occupy; and second, the tools that a religious initiate uses in his study and discussion of religious texts. Here, in the "ever-fluid dialogue" held between students and teachers, the "ordinary barriers of time can be ignored,"[1] just as the coordinates that separate geographic place are collapsed.

Reading while attuned to both the imminent and the timeless, the local and the virtual, we will see a Center-Periphery Paradigm at work in the slaughtering controversy. The model, however, is not akin to the one Ya'ari invokes in his story of Yosef Maman. Nor is it akin to the message presented at Torah Academy. Rather, it is processual, involving an intense negotiation to determine what exactly "normative" Judaism is, and where its center is located.

Pinhas ha-Gadol and His Son Yitzhak Hayim ha-Kohen

This story, of course, does not begin with the meat-slaughtering controversy in 1904. It starts many years before, prior to Russian domination of the region, when the power of the independent emir extended across the territory of the Bukharan kingdom. In those days, Pinhas ha-Gadol (Pinhas the Great)—who would not live to see the birth of his grandson Hizkiya ha-Kohen Rabin—served as chief rabbi of Bukhara. His authority, closely linked to that of the emir, also extended across the territory of the kingdom.

There are no historical documents available that refer to Pinhas ha-Gadol, only stories and legends about him transmitted orally over the generations, which were recorded in recent years by family members and folk historians.[2] These tales tell of a childhood immersed in religious study. Born into a learned family, the son of a rabbi, Pinhas was encouraged from a young age to devote himself to the study of Jewish texts. He quickly stood out among his fellow students for his sharp intelligence and inspirational demeanor. As he grew older, he took over the leadership of the main yeshiva (religious academy) in the city of Bukhara. So, too, he maintained and expanded the city's religious library, a critical resource for Jews across the region. Students from all over Central Asia came to study under his tutelage and upon completion of their tenure in his yeshiva, they would return to their scattered homes to serve as teachers and leaders.

According to his biographer, the prestige of Pinhas ha-Gadol, and that of his institutions, was also enhanced by his close relations with the emir, with whom he visited and conferred regularly. The emir benefited from the loyalty of his Jewish subjects, and Pinhas ha-Gadol benefited by the bolster to his authority. Eventually, Pinhas ha-Gadol was recognized as chief rabbi of the entire emirate and presided over all the cities within its borders, as well as many beyond.

When Pinhas ha-Gadol passed away in 1858, just before having reached the age of sixty, he left behind four daughters and seven sons. One of these sons, Yitzhak Hayim ha-Kohen Rabin, was ten years old at the time, and continued as a student in the yeshiva over which his father had presided. Considered an adult at the age of eighteen, he married and then took over his father's position.

The year was 1866 and the geopolitical situation in which he found himself was undergoing rapid, dramatic change. The fast-advancing Russian frontier had reached the edge of the Syr River, which formed the northeastern border of the Bukharan kingdom. Tashkent had just fallen under Russian control and was soon to become the administrative headquarters of the Government-General of Turkestan. Two years later, Samarkand fell into Russian hands and became incorporated into Russian Turkestan.

The whittling away of the boundaries of the kingdom and the weakening of the emir's power led to Jewish migration out of the Bukharan emirate into Russian Turkestan. There, the migrants were able to take advantage of the rights the Russians extended to them. Moreover, under the rule of secular rather than religious authorities, it now became possible for people to act outside of the restrictions of the Jewish community, and to challenge rabbinic authority.

Yitzhak Hayim ha-Kohen's biographer (and grandson)[3] pays little attention to this changing political landscape, asserting simply that his grandfather was appointed by the local Jewish dignitaries to the position of "chief rabbi and head of the Jewish courts for all the cities of Bukhara and her branches: Kokand, Tashkent, and all the region of Turkestan."[4] The sparse historical evidence that is available, however, suggests the shrinking of his sphere of authority.

One document that belies a threat to his authority is a letter written by Yitzhak Hayim ha-Kohen himself[5] when he got word of a religious case that had arisen in Samarkand. The issue involved a man by the name of Zhora Kandin who had divorced his wife upon learning that she was involved in an adulterous affair. After their divorce, the woman asked Zhora's forgiveness and pleaded with him to marry her again. He agreed and a rabbi in Samarkand—whose identity remains unknown in the letter—prepared the Jewish wedding contract, and officiated at the ceremony. It was this act that prompted Yitzhak Hayim ha-Kohen to write his letter[6] to the rabbis of Samarkand. He begins:

> I see that you, my friends, have no devotion [to religious precepts, which dictate that a man may not stay married to (or remarry) a woman who has committed adultery]. I have done many searches here. I did search after search. And still I have not even found a hint [that such a thing] is permissible [according to Jewish law].

Yitzhak Hayim ha-Kohen then warns the rabbis of Samarkand about the consequences of their actions. "If you do not act zealously in the ways of God, then [the situation will degenerate to such an extent that] tomorrow a man will come to marry the wife of another man!" Leniency on this one issue—he suggests—is the first step toward the loss of all rabbinic control in Samarkand. First the case of Zhora Kandin, next a man may "come to marry the wife of another man," and finally the situation will deteriorate so far that the rabbis of Samarkand may come to shrug their shoulders and give up, stating, in the words of Yitzhak Hayim ha-Kohen, "Our religious courts are not strong. There is no way that we can issue a punishment."

While Yitzhak Hayim ha-Kohen expresses concern here about a general loss of rabbinic authority, other sections of this same letter indicate that he was also anxious about his own particular shrinking sphere of influence. Along these lines, his comments directed to Yosef Khojenov are particularly telling.

Yosef Khojenov was born in Bukhara within a year of Yitzhak Hayim ha-Kohen, grew up with him, and studied with him in yeshiva there.[7] When both men were thirty years old, Yosef Khojenov moved to Samarkand where he served as a rabbi. Why exactly he moved to Samarkand is unclear, as were the terms of his relationship with Yitzhak Hayim ha-Kohen. Was he to work there as his emissary, as an extension of his arm of authority? Or did he move as an independent agent hoping to garner his own support and constituency, independent of Yitzhak Hayim ha-Kohen? The letter does not answer these questions. It does, however, make clear that the terms of their relationship were still being negotiated several years after Yosef Khojenov had already established himself in Samarkand.

Yitzhak Hayim ha-Kohen writes, "Honorable Mullah Yosef Khojenov, you are called upon. . . . [Refer to] the Talmud, which is in your hands." He then goes on to provide a Talmudic argument to demonstrate why the remarriage between Zhora and his ex-wife is not permissible. Upon conclusion of this argument, Yitzhak Hayim ha-Kohen asks, "For what reason . . . do you not stand firm? If it really is permissible according to the law to return her [to him and remarry them], write to me so that I too will know [why it is permissible]." The comment that follows suggests he was not actually asking Yosef Khojenov for religious insight and guidance: "Find out who it was that gave them a *ketubah* [marriage document], and fine him," he commands; "burn out the evil from your midst. Be done with this. . . ." Yitzhak Hayim ha-Kohen stands firm that a remarriage between Zhora and his ex-wife is not permissible, and that the rabbi in Samarkand who officiated over it was errant.

While Yosef Khojenov may (or may not) have been the one to have conducted the wedding, Yitzhak Hayim ha-Kohen holds him responsible for this breach in religious law. Given this clear position, his question to Yosef Khojenov, "For what reason do you not stand firm?" reads rhetorically, rather than as a sincere query. The tone—with its hint of sarcasm—belies a sense of threat to his authority. The leadership in Samarkand seems to have begun to operate on its own, without deferring to, or even consulting with, the would-be chief rabbi.

Some further light is shed on this intrigue by Ephraim Neumark, a Jewish traveler who journeyed through Central Asia in the 1880s.[8] In his description of the Jewish community in Bukhara, he writes the following about Yitzhak Hayim ha-Kohen: "Many times arguments broke out against" him, and there was "even talk of "dismiss[ing] him from his position." The supporters of Yitzhak Hayim ha-Kohen, Neumark continues, are those who "stand by him" because they "remember the deeds of his faithful ancestors."[9] They remember the days when his father and grandfather occupied the position of Bukhara's chief rabbi, and their loyalty stems from their connection and devotion to the traditions and hierarchy of a world past. Those who are swept up in the new economic and social reality introduced by the Russians do not "remember," or do not care to hold fast to the old ways.

These two documents—Yitzhak Hayim ha-Kohen's letter to the rabbis in Samarkand, and Neumark's brief remarks—suggest that Yitzhak Hayim ha-Kohen's authority no longer extended as far as that of his father. The larger record concerning the leadership of Yitzhak Hayim ha-Kohen's son, Hizkiya ha-Kohen Rabin, provides a clear picture of his continued shrinking of authority. More broadly, this record demonstrates the ways in which Russian colonialism in Central Asia, and its attendant social and economic forces were intimately linked to the evisceration of local religious authority.

Hizkiya ha-Kohen Rabin—Legitimate Successor?

Hizkiya ha-Kohen Rabin was presented with his first challenge from the very moment he stepped into his father's position. The year was 1896. Yitzhak Hayim ha-Kohen had died at the young age of forty-eight, leaving behind a will that stipulated that his son Hizkiya, then age twenty-five, should succeed him. By this time, however, the Russian presence in Central Asia had so radically altered the contours of the Jewish social landscape that succession of a man to the position of his father and grandfather could hardly occur without question or debate.

By the close of the nineteenth century, not only had Central Asia's Jews moved in great numbers to cities located outside the Bukharan emirate's shrunken borders, but they also formed a substantial, wealthy

FIGURE 6.1
Hizkiya ha-Kohen Rabin
Courtesy of Geula Sabet

Rabbinic Succession

Pinhas ha-Gadol
(d. 1858)

Yitzhak Hayim ha-Kohen
(1848–1896)

Hizkiya ha-Kohen Rabin
(1871–1944)

community in Ottoman Palestine. This community (discussed at greater length in the next chapter) purchased land in Jerusalem for a residential neighborhood, which was developed at a rapid pace. By 1897, six years after the project was initiated, 179 houses had been built, as well as three synagogues, a yeshiva, and a religious children's school.[10]

Although residing in Jerusalem, the Jews from Bukhara who lived in this neighborhood continued to see themselves as intimately connected to their family and friends back home, many of whom had provided funds for the building project, and who visited frequently. Nevertheless, the relationship between those who resided in Central Asia and those who lived in Jerusalem was hardly tension-free. One contested issue surrounded the seat of community leadership: Where was the political and religious center of this far-flung community? This question became particularly pressing when decisions had to be made about choosing who should be regarded as the community's primary religious authority.

With the death of Yitzhak Hayim ha-Kohen, tensions surrounding this issue surfaced.[11] Testimony to the difficult negotiations that ensued lie in a letter—currently housed in the National Library of Israel—written in Bukhara in 1897, a few months after Yitzhak Hayim ha-Kohen's death.[12] This letter was prompted by a missive the Jewish community leaders in Bukhara received from Jerusalem, which informed them that the "people of Bukhara who dwell in Jerusalem . . . conferred with one another" about the state of religious affairs back in Bukhara.

Before even getting into the particular issue at hand, the letter writers in Bukhara begin by expressing dismay that such a conference had even taken place, "as though they [in Jerusalem] have the right [to represent] the whole of our community." They continue:

> As though they could appoint an honorable man from among the dear dwellers of Zion . . . to teach the laws and rulings that have been forgotten [here] in this land. This has caused our hearts to tremble . . . that such slander is being recounted.

They—who were born in Bukhara, but who now pray at the remains of the ancient Holy Temple, and who study in the religious academies of Jerusalem—have appointed themselves spokesmen for their Bukharan brethren. In doing so, they call local religious practice into question, claiming that Jewish "laws and rulings" have been "forgotten" in Bukhara. Likewise, they call into question the legitimacy of local leadership.

Those who remain in Central Asia chastise:

> [It is being said that] our rabbi [Yitzhak Hayim ha-Kohen] has left us and that we sit here like sheep with no shepherd. How bleary their vision has become so as not to see the living fruit of the citron tree! . . . a lion who is the son of a lion: Rabbi Hizkiya the son of the Crown; the Great Rabbi Yitzhak Hayim ha-Kohen of blessed memory.

Whereas Zion was the homeland for which the Jews had yearned over the course of their long centuries in Bukhara, now that a group of Bukharan Jews had established a community there, the concepts of *home* and *diaspora* have undergone reconsideration. It is not we who live in darkness, write the community leaders in Bukhara. On the contrary, it is they, those "dear dwellers of Zion," who have been blinded. So dazzled are they by the light of the Holy Land that they have lost sight of what is right, and have become "full of disgrace," "casting blemish" upon that which is holy.

In reevaluating the meaning of "diaspora," those who remain in Bukhara do not regard their brethren who have moved to Zion as having returned "home," but rather as people who have "scattered themselves" from their midst. They—in Jerusalem—are the dispersed ones, in diaspora from the Bukharan homeland. In this case, local geography, traditions, and leadership are valorized over the universal Jewish Homeland.

Given this message, which presents Bukhara as a locale of power, piety, and holiness, what is most curious about this letter is that it is not addressed to the Bukharan Jews living in Jerusalem themselves. Inconsistent with their own claims of authority, and despite their best efforts to maintain their integrity, they address their letter to Ya'akov Shaul Elyashar in Jerusalem, asking him to intercede on their behalf.

Ya'akov Shaul Elyashar held the office of Rishon LeTsion. Created as early as the seventeenth century, this title was conferred by the Sephardi Jews of Ottoman Palestine upon their chief rabbi.[13] The position entailed presiding over a regional council of rabbis, and over a central religious court of law.[14] In 1841 the Ottoman authorities formally recognized this religious-communal position, and conferred upon it the title *Hakham Bashi*.[15]

Although the authority of this office was formally limited to Ottoman Palestine, through informal channels it often extended beyond these borders. One such channel was the leadership-succession debate in the Bukharan Jewish community. In deciding who should be appointed successor to Yitzhak Hayim ha-Kohen, and who should have the authority to make this decision, the now transnational community was drawn into conversation with rabbinic authorities in Jerusalem, looking to the chief rabbi there for permission and guidance. No longer isolated, the Jews in Bukhara simply could not maintain their local voice, acknowledging distant authority even in the very struggle to hold on to their own legitimacy.

In this case, they won the fight. Hizkiya ha-Kohen Rabin did remain Bukhara's chief rabbi. He did so, however, not without strain and compromise. Evidence of their victory appears in a document issued by the Rishon LeTsion in 1901, in which he names Hizkiya ha-Kohen Rabin the *Moreh Tsedek* (literally, Righteous Teacher) of Bukhara, stating that he has taken over his father's position as the "shepherd of the holy flock."[16] Hizkiya ha-Kohen Rabin's position is thus officially sanctioned.

However, it took him four years to obtain this seal of approval, and in the meantime someone else in Central Asia had begun to use the term *Moreh Tsedek* to refer to himself. This person—Shlomo Lev Eliezerov— an emissary from the land of Israel—was named *Moreh Tsedek* of Samarkand, also with the endorsement of the Rishon LeTsion. Thus, while the Rishon LeTsion was certifying Hizkiya ha-Kohen Rabin's authority, he also was constraining it. Whereas in precolonial days the authority of Hizkiya ha-Kohen Rabin's forebears extended across the territory of the expansive Bukharan emirate, with the pronouncements of the Rishon LeTsion it became limited to the area contained within the emirate's shrunken borders (in which Samarkand was not included).

Titles and official pronouncements, of course, do not tell the whole story. Let us turn, then, to examine how the sphere of Hizkiya ha-Kohen Rabin's authority was negotiated on the ground, by analyzing his unfolding relationship with the emissary, Shlomo Lev Eliezerov. This analysis lays the groundwork for understanding the controversy over ritual slaughtering, in which the authority of these two men came into direct confrontation.

The Work of an Emissary: Shlomo Lev Eliezerov

In the 1870s, when the Jewish population of Ottoman Palestine numbered not much more than 13,000,[17] the young boy Shlomo Lev Eliezerov and his parents left their home in Yakovshtat, Russia, for the Holy Land.[18] Their destination was Hebron, where they would join the tiny Chabad community that had been established there approximately fifty years earlier.[19] Like most of the Jewish population in Ottoman Palestine prior to the 1880s, this group was supported primarily from donations sent by Jews from abroad. The heroes of this economic system were hardy men who had the courage, charm, and language capabilities to travel to distant lands to raise funds for their communities back home in Ottoman Palestine. They would generally stay in the diaspora communities for several months, teaching and serving as religious functionaries. The communities would pay these emissaries for their services by sending money—through them—to Ottoman Palestine, and the emissary himself would receive a percentage of this sum as his salary.[20]

Shlomo Lev Eliezerov eventually became such a person. He spent his childhood and early adult years studying in religious seminaries in Hebron. At the age of twenty-five he married, and by the time he reached his mid-thirties, he began his work establishing and running the city's religious communal institutions.[21] Part of this work involved extensive travel abroad for the purposes of fundraising. He embarked on his first mission in 1892, setting forth on a voyage to the Caucasus and from there to Central Asia.[22] Although little is known about his work during this period, a letter that he wrote in 1894 indicates that life in Central Asia was very difficult for him. He and his cosignatories explain that fundraising emissaries from the Holy Land—like themselves—had been arriving with such frequency and had become so numerous that the chief rabbi in Bukhara (Yitzhak Hayim ha-Kohen at the time) had ordered that they be given no donations. Making matters worse, the locals had been instructed not to provide lodging for any of the emissaries. The letter writers lament, "Bitter. It is bitter for us here. The land of Bukhara, which has been called the paragon of beauty in her good and charitable deeds, has become a city without mercy."[23]

FIGURE 6.2
Shlomo Lev Eliezerov

Within a year of sending this letter, Shlomo Lev Eliezerov returned to his home in Hebron. Memories of his difficulties in Central Asia, however, did not deter him from going back to Bukhara: just two years later, he set out again to continue his work there.[24] Perhaps it is no coincidence that his return coincided with the transition of rabbinic authority into the hands of Hizkiya ha-Kohen Rabin after Yitzhak Hayim ha-Kohen's recent death. Shlomo Lev Eliezerov lived as a guest in the home of Hizkiya ha-Kohen Rabin, but remained for only a short while, relocating to Samarkand, where Hizkiya ha-Kohen Rabin's sphere of influence was considerably weaker.

Nevertheless, Shlomo Lev Eliezerov was hardly a free agent in Central Asia. He had been sent by community leaders in Hebron and by the Rishon LeTsion. Although far away, communication, travel, and social connections between Central Asia and Ottoman Palestine were tight enough to facilitate the administration and monitoring of his work there. Those in Ottoman Palestine were concerned about the fundraising ventures of their emissaries, Shlomo Lev Eliezerov included. In Central Asia, he was responsible for collecting funds on behalf of Hebron's Jewish population. In this role, he answered to the Rishon LeTsion, who served as the central administrator of all fundraising activities emanating from the Sephardi Jewish communities in Ottoman Palestine.[25]

Another area of concern was the issue of ritual slaughtering. Emissaries were stationed in various diaspora communities not only to collect money, but also to provide religious functionary services; ritual slaughtering was one such task. It was dirty work that involved handling the blood, flesh, and innards of large animals. It was, however, a vital service for every Jewish community. From a religious perspective, people simply could not eat meat unless it had been ritually slaughtered. From a social, symbolic perspective, the meat that people ingested was a powerful marker of their identity. In Samarkand, where Jews were no longer necessarily marked as such by the clothes that they wore, or by the neighborhoods in which they lived, social boundaries were still delineated by the dietary laws related to keeping kosher. When a Jew refused to dine with an outsider because the latter's meat was not kosher, he asserted his place within the social universe he inhabited.

While Shlomo Lev Eliezerov engaged in many religious activities in Central Asia, the two conditions of his work were to raise money on behalf of those who sent him and to properly carry out his tasks as a ritual slaughterer. Seemingly straightforward, these two responsibilities actually became highly complicated by a number of factors that were open to the interpretation and discretion of those involved in implementing and overseeing them. We shall see that Eliezerov became embroiled in controversy surrounding these open-ended areas, and that he was a master in working the system to obtain his desired results.

Negotiating the Terms of Emissary Work

When Shlomo Lev Eliezerov set out for his second[26] trip to Central Asia, he probably carried with him a small bag of personal belongings, a number of religious books, phylacteries, and a few clothes. One item missing, however, was a signed contract stipulating his responsibilities as an emissary. Why he had not resolved these details before leaving his home in Hebron is unclear. What is unmistakable, however, is that the fact that he waited for almost a year after his arrival to negotiate the terms of his service was highly distressing to the Rishon LeTsion.

In the spring of 1898, a few months after having reached Central Asia, Eliezerov received a letter from the Rishon LeTsion, outlining the terms of his service.[27] Whether he was procrastinating, calculating, or simply very busy, he put off responding to the document for months. Preoccupied with his travels to Jewish communities across the countryside and with his efforts to secure a residence permit for himself, "I said [to myself]," he explained, "that I would wait [to write] my answer . . . until I had a chance to collect my thoughts."[28] In the meantime, however, he received word that the Rishon LeTsion was quite annoyed about the delay in response.

"The time has come to do the will of the righteous," Shlomo Lev Eliezerov admitted to himself and to the Rishon LeTsion. The letter that he finally composed begins with laudatory salutations and with apologies for not writing sooner: "Let me begin by asking forgiveness on account of the fact that I . . . greatly delayed in responding. . . . It was not an act of rebellion. . . . But rather on account of my troubles, which have given me no rest."

After listing his activities, as well as the difficulties he had faced since arriving in Central Asia, Eliezerov turns to the matters at hand. His detailed six-page answer, written in fine calligraphy, responds to both stipulations set forth by the Rishon LeTsion. The fundraising issue was somewhat complicated by Shlomo Lev's background, but not difficult to resolve.

Shlomo Lev Eliezerov belonged to the Ashkenazi-Chabad community of Hebron, a minority population among the Sephardi Jews who lived there. In 1825, not long after Chabad had established a small community in Hebron, they reached a financial agreement with the Sephardi *kollel* (communal organization). Emissaries from the two community groups would raise funds separately but would pool their proceeds. Together, they would pay taxes to the Ottoman authorities, and would then divide up their profits. A total of 40 percent would go to the Chabad *kollel* and 60 percent to the Sephardi *kollel,* with the leaders of each overseeing the distribution of funds to their respective communities.[29] While Shlomo Lev Eliezerov's primary interest was to raise funds as a means to improve the lot of Hebron's Chabad community, he agreed to the Rishon LeTsion's stipulation to work under the auspices of the Sephardi *kollel,* and defer to the central fundraising headquarters in Jerusalem.

The issue of ritual slaughtering proved much more difficult to resolve. The Rishon LeTsion had instructed Eliezerov to follow Sephardi traditions in this area of his work. This stipulation posed a complex dilemma due to the strange cultural situation in which Shlomo Lev Eliezerov found himself. He was of Ashkenazi descent, belonged to the Chabad community, and was trained and certified in ritual slaughtering by the Ashkenazi-Chabad authorities in Hebron. Yet he was sent to Central Asia by the Rishon LeTsion who represented the Sephardi Jewish population of Ottoman Palestine. To make matters more complicated, he was working with people who were of neither Ashkenazi nor Sephardi extraction.[30] What traditions should he follow in his work?

Across the Jewish world, there is universal agreement that for meat to be considered kosher, the animal must be killed by a single precise cut to the throat, and the knife must be checked to ensure that it is sharp and has no nicks. In addition, the animal must be healthy (having no trace of an existing condition from which it would have died had it not been killed for consumption). Each of these areas, however, is open to some interpretation. For example, what is the proper way to check that a knife is sharp and without nicks? Of what material should it be made to ensure that it is of the highest quality?[31] In Shlomo Lev Eliezerov's case, the pressing issue was how to define and evaluate the health of the animal.

For guidance on this issue, Eliezerov referred primarily to the *Shulhan Aruch,* a compendium of religious laws published in the sixteenth century. This text, still used today, is remarkable in that it provides a handbook as well as a discussion. As a handbook, it offers clear, concise, and practical guidelines on observing and properly carrying out religious command for all aspects of life. As a discussion, it preserves the perspectives of its two authors, even in the areas in which they disagree.

Yosef Karo was born in Toledo, and was exiled from there in 1492 along with the rest of Spain's Jewish population. In the wake of this communal upheaval, he wrote his code of Jewish law—a "handy reference work"[32]—by drawing on the writings of three medieval commentators as his guide. Partly as an independent endeavor, and partly as a response to Yosef Karo's legal code, Moshe Isserles, the chief rabbi of Kraków, Poland, wrote a work that was similar in structure and style. Unlike Karo's code, however, Isserles drew on the writings of more recent Ashkenazi authorities who lived in Eastern Europe.[33]

Not long after each had completed his code, the two works were brought to print in a single, interlaced volume. Karo's work served as the base upon which Isserles's was overlaid. The result was one compendium of laws offering separate guidelines for the Jewish communities of Eastern Europe and for those that had been exiled from Spain (*Sepharad*).[34] Published soon after print technology had become widespread in Europe, these religious rulings became standardized, mass-produced, and widely disseminated.

Reflecting on the lasting impact of the *Shulhan Aruch,* H. J. Zimmels remarks that it "rendered permanent the division between Ashkenazim and Sephardim by giving it a firm and legal basis."[35] At the same time, however, it united the Sephardi world and it united the Ashkenazi world by collapsing the differences internal to each. Without the *Shulhan Aruch*, notes Zimmels, "there would not have been merely two legal systems but Judaism would have been broken up into many divisions and subdivisions. . . ." Ashkenazi traditions would have become divided into those of the "German Ashkenazim, Polish Ashkenazim, Lithuanian Ashkenazim, Hungarian Ashkenazim [and] Bohemian-Moravian Ashkenazim." Similarly, Sephardi traditions would have fractured into those of the "North African Sephardim, Egyptian Sephardim, Palestinian Sephardim, and European Turkish Sephardim."[36] The printed and bound word came to unite the Jewish world, while simultaneously concretizing two discrete sets of Jewish practices.

The influence of the work was felt in Central Asia as well, where the Jews had accepted Yosef Karo's guidelines. Acknowledging their adoption of Sephardi practice, the Rishon LeTsion insisted that Shlomo Lev

Eliezerov—despite his Ashkenazi background—follow Sephardi religious guidelines in his work as an emissary among them. One issue related to his work as a ritual slaughterer concerned the technique he would use to determine whether an animal was healthy (just prior to its slaughter).

Karo and Isserles both offer detailed descriptions of how an animal's lungs should be examined to determine if they are free of perforations (indicators of illness). Their guidelines, which draw on intimate knowledge of anatomical structures, were developed in two separate parts of the world, where environmental conditions differed, as did the pathology of animal disease. As a result, the guidelines they offer differ from one another in a number of small but significant details.

In principle, Shlomo Lev Eliezerov did not object to the Rishon LeTsion's instruction that he follow Yosef Karo's guidelines. Indeed, in addressing this stipulation, Eliezerov even provided his own set of textual citations in support of the Rishon LeTsion's position. He writes, "Religious law [halakhah] is not dependent on the custom of the teacher or the examiner, but rather on the custom of the place where he [the teacher and examiner] finds himself." Here, Eliezerov acknowledges that—regardless of his own background—he must follow Sephardi ruling because in previous generations the people of Bukhara had "accepted upon themselves the ruling of the holy Yosef Karo."

Six months after writing these words, Shlomo Lev Eliezerov composed and signed a brief official document that served as his work contract. Consistent with that which he had written previously, he stipulated the following terms and conditions for his work:

> I, the undersigned, was chosen as rabbi and *Moreh Tsedek* in this city of Samarkand . . . to govern the community of God according to the Holy Torah under the obligation of the great famous rabbi . . . in Jerusalem, the Rishon LeTsion Rabbi Ya'akov Shaul Elyashar. . . . He gave me authority and appointed me *Moreh Tsedek* . . . but only on condition . . . that I lead my people [here in Samarkand] according to the traditions of our Sephardi brothers' rabbis and wise men.[37]

If Shlomo Lev Eliezerov had concluded and signed the contract here, the slaughtering controversy would never have erupted. But there was more.

In certain aspects of lung examination, Yosef Karo calls for an approach that is more stringent than that of Moshe Isserles. In these cases,

Eliezerov willingly acceded to the Rishon LeTsion's instructions that he follow Karo. There are other aspects of the examination, however, in which Karo calls for an approach more lenient than that of Isserles. Refusing to accept such leniencies, Eliezerov entered into a negotiation with the Rishon LeTsion about the most appropriate course of action.

He opens his lengthy discourse on this issue by acknowledging that "it is forbidden to forbid something that is permissible." In other words, if the locals treat certain conditions as ritually acceptable (in adherence with Karo's rulings), one is forbidden to take a strict approach (in adherence with Isserles's rulings) deeming those conditions unacceptable. Yet, he goes on to note exceptions in which this ruling does not apply, including the situation in which he currently finds himself. "In this land," he writes, "the people are not *b'nei Torah* [followers of Torah]." Eliezerov reiterates this description of the local Jewish community further in the letter by referring to the local Jews' "evil customs" and their "foolish practices."

His view of the locals as lax in their religious knowledge and practice seems to have fueled his own zealous adherence to and promulgation of stringencies. Although he had been sent to Central Asia to raise funds and to serve as a ritual slaughterer, he viewed his task in much broader terms, working to have the Jews in Central Asia "accept my words; that which I tell them in Torah and in religious law [*halakhah*]" even in areas where his own understanding did not accord with Yosef Karo or the Rishon LeTsion.

Delicately, he rejects their authority, without appearing to do so. Invoking a tone of humility he writes, "in reference to the issue that is before us regarding the strictness of Rabbi Moshe Isserles . . . as opposed to the ruling of Yosef Karo; . . . it is not fitting for a lowly student such as myself to decide between the rulings of [the two]. . . ." Who, then, should decide between these two authorities in situations where they disagree?

Rather than turning to the Rishon LeTsion or any other Sephardi leader for guidance, he looks to the *Magen Avraham,* a commentary on the *Shulhan Aruch* written by the seventeenth-century Polish rabbi Avraham Gombiner. Drawing on the general approach to *halakhah* outlined in this Ashkenazi source, Eliezerov concludes, "it seems that . . . whoever is lenient can also be strict." This potent statement came to shape the wording of the brief official document that served as Eliezerov's contract. In writing this document, he included a single ingenious clause that would give him permission to impose his stringent Ashkenazi interpretation of the law. After agreeing that he would follow the customs of Yosef Karo, he adds, "Only in matters which Yosef Karo permits [*matir*] but Moshe Isserles forbids [*oser*] do I have the permission to be strict [*le-hahmir*], by following Moshe Isserles." This clause portended the trouble that was to come.[38]

Religious Authority in Samarkand

Although the 1904 slaughtering controversy primarily revolved around a debate between Shlomo Lev Eliezerov, Hizkiya ha-Kohen Rabin, and Rishon LeTsion Shaul Elyashar, two other characters were peripherally involved: Yosef Khojenov and Shlomo Tagger, both of whom were religious leaders in Samarkand, living there at the same time as Eliezerov. The relationships within this cast of five characters help to explain the contours of the debate.

Yosef Khojenov, whom we met earlier in this chapter,[39] was raised and trained in Bukhara's religious academies. He moved to Samarkand in 1879 at the age of thirty, and seems to have come to be regarded as the chief rabbi in the city. He served in this position for several years, and then left for Ottoman Palestine. He lived in Jerusalem for about a decade and was involved in building the Bukharan Jewish residential quarter. In 1890, Khojenov left Jerusalem and returned to Samarkand. Little information is available about the role he played upon his return to this city. Archived letters, however, do provide a window into his activities there during this time, as well as some information about his relationship with one other religious leader in the area: Shlomo Tagger.

Unlike Khojenov, a native of Central Asia, Shlomo Tagger (pictured on p. 110) was born and raised in Jerusalem. Through marriage, however, he developed strong ties to the Bukharan Jewish community. When he was twenty-three years old (and still living in Jerusalem), he married fifteen-year-old Miriam, the daughter of a wealthy Jew from Bukhara living in Palestine.[40] Around this time, Tagger grew closely connected to the wealthy merchant Hizkiya Yissakharov,[41] whom he met in Jerusalem. When Yissakharov left Jerusalem to return to Central Asia and join his brothers' business, he invited Tagger to come with him to serve

FIGURE 6.3
Shlomo Tagger
Courtesy of Shlomo Tagger (grandson)

as a religious teacher for his children.[42] Shlomo Tagger agreed and went
to work in the small private school that Yissakharov opened for the children of Samarkand's wealthy Jewish families, teaching them Hebrew,
Torah, and Talmud. In addition to his work in the school, Tagger also
took an active role in arbitrating religious issues that arose in the city,
particularly cases involving the status of women (surrounding divorce
and ritual purity).

When questions arose that Tagger was unable to answer on his own,
he would turn to Khojenov for discussion. When the two men were not

able to reach agreement between themselves, they would consult with authorities outside of Samarkand. A record of this decision-making process is preserved in a letter Tagger wrote to the Rishon LeTsion,[43] which reads as follows:

> Forgive me for continually burdening you with questions. For who am I to approach kings? But what am I to do? The people are always knocking on my door with various questions. And to whom should I turn for help, if not to [you] our father, our shepherd, the master of Torah. In particular regarding the strict laws of *niddah*.[44]
>
> When the following question was put to me, I was astonished. This issue is not mentioned at all in any of the books of the *ahronim* [later commentators].
>
> Yesterday I was in the rabbinic court . . . and Rabbi Khojen[ov] was there. I argued with him over this issue. . . . So we decided to draw up the question to send it to you. And here it is:
>
> We are asking about a woman whose teeth were in constant pain because of cavities. She went to a doctor and he filled the cavities with lead. . . . The question is whether this [lead] is considered a *hotzetz le-tevilah* (barrier when she immerses in the ritual bath),[45] or not?

After outlining these details, Tagger goes on to discuss the logic of why a cavity filling might be considered a *hotzetz le-tevilah* and the logic of why it might not. He ends by posing the question again and asking for a response from the Rishon LeTsion. In this case, Tagger was approached with a question, searched for the answer himself, but was unable to locate it. He then consulted with Khojenov. Together, they were still unable to reach a satisfactory answer, and therefore turned their question over to the Rishon LeTsion in Jerusalem.

Records also indicate that Tagger consulted with Hizkiya ha-Kohen Rabin in Bukhara on issues requiring specific local knowledge. For example, in a case involving a woman's marital status, Tagger wrote to Hizkiya ha-Kohen Rabin in Bukhara.[46] "A poor woman," he explained, whose husband had passed away several years before, had been left an *agunah* (abandoned wife) on account of this man's younger brother. Technically, Jewish law required the widow to marry this younger brother. Yet, he was only fourteen years old. In a bind, the woman's only choice to be freed "from the shackles of her status as *agunah*" (so that she might remarry) was for the younger brother to perform the *halitzah* ritual (which releases the widow and the brother of the deceased from the religious obligation to marry one another). The boy, however, was far away in Bukhara, and Tagger was unfamiliar with the Jewish community there. With a request for help, he turned to Hizkiya ha-Kohen Rabin: "The woman's name is Ima the daughter of David Kohen Kavas. I do not know the name of the *yavam* [the deceased's younger brother]. May I please request that you arrange [the] *halitzah* [ritual] for them. . . ."

For this question, which required knowledge of the local social situation, Shlomo Tagger was able to turn to Hizkiya ha-Kohen Rabin. However, when questions arose that required the extrapolation and application of more general legal principles, Tagger would turn to the Rishon LeTsion. For example, he wrote a lengthy letter to the latter regarding the case of a thirty-year-old *agunah*, Pnina, who was the mother of young children and had "no means of support."[47] Her husband, a peddler, had disappeared several years earlier while traveling around the countryside selling his wares. "Word spread all around our area that he was killed by bandits who stole his goods and his money," Tagger explains, yet no trace of his body had been found, and the only information available about his fate had come from discussions with non-Jews in the region who claimed that "he was killed by infamous murderers." This information was not enough to confirm Pnina's status as "widow" according to religious law. To relieve her of her status of *agunah* so that she might remarry, Shlomo Tagger set about searching for people who would testify in a Jewish court to knowledge of her husband's murder. He sent a letter to the hometown of the deceased "requesting that they post a notice in the synagogue and in the house of study, asking if any woman or man knows anything" about his disappearance. Only two people were found to testify, but even they had not been witnesses to the murder. Tagger nevertheless recorded their testimonies, submitted them with his letter, and asked the Rishon LeTsion to review the details of the case to decide if there was sufficient proof to verify Pnina's status as a widow.

These letters written from (and about) the various religious authorities in Samarkand provide insight into the dynamics of how religious issues were arbitrated in the city. First, we learn that Shlomo Lev Eliezerov was not the only religious authority in Samarkand between 1897 and 1901, the years in which he lived there. At least two others were present: Shlomo Tagger, a native of Jerusalem who was nonetheless closely connected to the Bukharan Jewish community through marriage ties, and

Yosef Khojenov, who was also not native to Samarkand, but was native to Central Asia.

Despite their presence, however, there are no records of their involvement in religious matters between 1897 and 1901. Their silence during this period suggests that Eliezerov left little room for other religious authorities, and that they began to take positions of arbitration only after he had left the region. Once he had returned to his home in Hebron, Tagger and Khojenov appear to have conferred in some instances to resolve religious issues. When they were unable to come to a decision, questions would be directed to Hizkiya ha-Kohen Rabin in Bukhara if they were of a local nature, and to the Rishon LeTsion if they were more general.

The Slaughtering Controversy

With this historical background, we return to the issue with which this chapter began: the controversy over ritual slaughtering that erupted in Samarkand. Just a few years before, Shlomo Tagger, Yosef Khojenov, and Shlomo Lev Eliezerov had all lived in Samarkand. By 1904, however, the social landscape had changed dramatically. Eliezerov had returned to Ottoman Palestine, and Tagger had moved to Tashkent, wooed away by a larger salary and a more defined position of authority.[48] What became of Khojenov is unclear, but he is not referred to or heard from subsequent to 1902, suggesting that he might have returned to Jerusalem.[49] When questions about religious practice arose, the city's Jewish residents found they had no local religious authority to whom they could turn. With this vacuum in authority, Samarkand became fascinating territory: a city that several religious leaders attempted to bring into their sphere of influence by exerting their authority from afar. This dynamic was at work in 1904.

We learn about the controversy through a letter written by Samarkand's community leaders to the Rishon LeTsion in Ottoman Palestine.[50] They begin by explaining that a conflict had arisen between the ritual slaughterers and the butchers of their city. Although Shlomo Lev Eliezerov no longer lived in Central Asia, it was he—the letter writers explain—who was the source of the conflict.

The city's ritual slaughterers had all trained under Eliezerov and continued to follow his strict reading and application of the *Shulhan*

Aruch. The result of his stringent approach to examining the animals' lungs after their slaughter was that a great proportion of them were declared *treif.* Deemed unfit for consumption, these animals could not be sold in the kosher market, and the butchers were suffering a loss in profit.

The letter writers go on to explain that they—Samarkand's community leaders—had invited Hizkiya ha-Kohen Rabin to travel to Samarkand (from Bukhara) in order to arbitrate the dispute. They write:

> Almost a year ago, our friend, Rabbi Hizkiya [ha-Kohen Rabin] from Bukhara, came here in response to the request of the [Jewish] leaders of the city. [We asked him] to investigate the ritual slaughterers and their customs.
>
> [After looking into the matter], he finally had the city's three ritual slaughterers swear that from that day on, in every situation where there is a disagreement between Yosef Karo and Moshe Isserles regarding how the lungs should be examined [to determine if the animal is kosher] . . . they would follow the method put forth by Yosef Karo.
>
> The ritual slaughterers accepted this strict oath upon themselves, swearing on the Torah in front of all the city's [Jewish] leaders.

Despite Hizkiya ha-Kohen Rabin's visit to Samarkand, and his stipulation that Samarkand's ritual slaughterers take a public oath that they would use the Sephardi method of ritual slaughtering and examining as outlined by Yosef Karo, his efforts failed. The slaughterers, it seemed, had "conspired between themselves that they would not abide by this oath and would pay it no mind." Hizkiya ha-Kohen Rabin was unable to overcome the impact Shlomo Lev Eliezerov had upon his students.

The letter writers then describe the continuation of the controversy. In this next chapter of the story, a single culprit is identified: Yehuda Derabandi, a local who had apparently been Shlomo Lev Eliezerov's most loyal follower, and who put little stake in Hizkiya ha-Kohen Rabin's religious leadership:

> [After Hizkiya ha-Kohen Rabin returned to Bukhara] the arguments between them [the slaughterers] and the butchers did not cease. They [the butchers] screamed loudly about their loss of income. Finally, the ritual slaughterers made it known that it was Yehuda Derabandi [apparently a student of Shlomo Lev Eliezerov] who taught them [to follow] the method of examining [transmitted to them by Shlomo Lev Eliezerov].

[Yehuda Derabandi] had told them not to abide by the [public] oath that they had taken, since they had previously sworn themselves faithful to Rav Shlomo Lev [Eliezerov]. When the community was made aware of all of this, they became very angry with . . . [Derabandi] and they expelled him.

The next section of the letter discusses what happened after Yehuda Derabandi was expelled:

After he left, we were forced to turn to Rabbi Yehuda Kastil (who is an emissary from the land of Israel) with a request. [We asked him] to go with the ritual slaughterers to the butchers to oversee [their work].

. . . [Yehuda Kastil], however, is a teacher and the parents of his students refused to permit him to engage in this kind of work because [if he did, their children] would miss out on Torah study.

Their hope that Yehuda Kastil would resolve the controversy was dashed. With nowhere else to turn, the letter writers explain that they consulted again with Hizkiya ha-Kohen Rabin in Bukhara. Although he failed the first time, they held out hope that he might be able to provide them with a solution to their problem. Hizkiya ha-Kohen responded to their request with a helpful suggestion recounted in the next section of their letter (in which the voice switches from that of Samarkand's Jewish leaders to that of Hizkiya ha-Kohen Rabin himself).

[Hizkiya ha-Kohen Rabin responded to our plea with the following suggestion:]

The ritual slaughterer, Rabbi Shlomo Kiki (who is an emissary from Land of Israel), left [this city, Bukhara] a few days ago . . . [destined for] Shahrisabz to serve as a ritual slaughterer there.

If you can get him to come to your city to serve as a ritual slaughterer for a few months, that would be good. [He is not urgently needed] in Shahrisabz [anyway, because] they still have a ritual slaughterer there.

If you ask me about this man, [I will tell you] that he had done this kind of work here in Bukhara and I found him to be well versed and talented in every detail.

Following the advice of Hizkiya ha-Kohen Rabin, the leaders in Samarkand brought Shlomo Kiki to their city, hoping his presence would provide the local butchers an alternative ritual slaughterer to whom they could turn, who was not part of the Derabandi-led, Eliezerov-inspired cabal. Alas, this solution, too, proved to be of no avail. In this case, it was actually the Rishon LeTsion who undermined the efforts to resolve the conflict, as explained in the next section of the letter:

> So, we followed the advice of this rabbi [Hizkiya ha-Kohen Rabin, and brought Shlomo Kiki to Samarkand]. But even this brought no respite [to the problem] because we were told that when this man [Shlomo Kiki] had come before you to get a certificate verifying his ordination as a ritual slaughterer you did not want to receive him.

Again, Hizkiya ha-Kohen Rabin's authority is challenged; first by the students of Shlomo Lev Eliezerov in Samarkand, and now by the Rishon LeTsion himself. Left with nowhere else to turn, the people of Samarkand plead with the Rishon LeTsion to reconsider his decision. It is here, toward the end of the letter—after having recounted all the details of their tribulations—that they finally reach the heart of the matter:

> What are we to do? Time is pressuring us, and there are no ritual slaughterers like him [Shlomo Kiki] in the whole of the region. . . . From the day that he came to our city, the continual quarreling that we are so sick of, that has been going on between the ritual slaughterers and the butchers, ceased a bit.
> We pray that your anger against this man will subside. Although he sinned against you, do not disappoint us by [issuing] holy edicts against this ritual slaughterer, because we are in a time of trouble.

Adding to their plea, Samarkand's Jewish community leaders outline one final dimension to the crisis. Until recently, Muslim clerics in nearby cities viewed meat that had been ritually slaughtered by Jews to be ritually fit according to Islamic law. This ruling meant that if a Jewish ritual slaughterer declared an animal to be *treif* upon examining the lungs, the meat could be sold rather than discarded. For reasons not made clear in the letter, there had been a recent change in the status quo. The writers explain, "An edict which the Muslims have established and enacted . . . has already spread across the cities of Tashkent and Kokand, etc., not to eat meat slaughtered by Jews." In Samarkand, the growing abundance of meat classified as Jewish ritual-refuse seems to have posed a threat to the status quo there as well. The writers continue, "Here, too, in this city they have requested to do the same." With the grave possibility of financial loss looming, the letter writers conclude their appeal to the Rishon LeTsion.

This long letter appears to have been intercepted by Shlomo Tagger, who was then serving as a religious leader in Tashkent. Having gotten word of the trouble in Samarkand, he visited to see if he could arbitrate the dispute himself. After collecting information from the people there, he wrote to the Rishon LeTsion to offer his perspective on the matter:[51]

> Two days ago I came to Samarkand. I agreed to come because of the pressures and requests of my people. I see that there is no way to mediate peace in the community other than to get rid of the previous ritual slaughterers . . . [who have] caused great distress to the community. . . . I have already written about this . . . but hearing it is not the same as seeing it, and I can see what will come of all this.
>
> . . . so much [meat] was declared unfit and impure. Not even [as much as] ten percent [of that which was slaughtered was declared fit]. It is therefore my hope that you will take my words with love, as I am a faithful servant.

Shlomo Tagger then goes on to highlight the social ramifications of the controversy: "The community is in great distress" because "the poor are lacking meat and there is none for the sick," and the Muslims have issued a threat. Boldly, Tagger then gets to the heart of the letter: "It is for this reason that I have come before you: to request that you not issue any edict on the matter. . . ." And again, "I [therefore] ask you not to get involved in this matter." Tagger's genteel tone and words of respect do not disguise his bald request that the Rishon LeTsion mind his own business. He should leave the determination of whether Shlomo Kiki might serve as a ritual slaughterer in the hands of the authorities who are there, on the ground, because they have an understanding—which the Rishon LeTsion cannot—of the way in which religious edicts on this matter affect the local community—their economy, their poor, their gustatory experiences, their internal community relations, and their relations with their Muslim neighbors.

Revisiting the Center-Periphery Paradigm

Did the Rishon LeTsion compose a letter in response, and if so, what did it say? Was the slaughtering controversy resolved after this particular crisis, and if so, who prevailed? The archival record trails off here, providing no answers to these questions. Yet, the very fact of nonclosure is an end in itself. It suggests that this turn-of-the-century encounter between Bukhara's Jews and those in Ottoman Palestine is embedded in an ongoing relationship, with no absolute beginning or end, and likewise no clearly defined center or periphery.

By way of explanation, a comparison to the Yosef Maman story is helpful. When Maman arrived in Bukhara, he was said to have described the local Jews as "far from Torah," and he set about reconnecting them to Judaism and the Jewish world. Similarly, when Shlomo Lev Eliezerov arrived in Bukhara a century later, he declared that they were not "followers of Torah," and like Maman, he undertook the task of teaching them that which he believed they had forgotten, and correcting them in areas where he believed they had strayed.

Yet, by contrast to the popularized account of Yosef Maman's encounter with the Jews in Bukhara, the Jews of late nineteenth-century Samarkand can hardly be said to have been religiously enlightened and returned onto "the stage of Jewish history"[52] through their encounter with the Jewish center. First, there is no clearly defined center in this case. The various religious leaders who claimed to represent proper or normative Judaism (the Rishon LeTsion and Shlomo Lev Eliezerov, in particular) disagreed among themselves about how rabbinic texts ought to be read and put into practice. Second, unlike the popularized rendition of the Maman story, Shlomo Lev Eliezerov arrived in a community that had a preexisting local structure of religious authority. Furthermore, the community's religious leaders were hardly isolated or out of touch with Jews in other parts of the world. Indeed, Eliezerov's arrival coincided with a debate between Bukharan Jews living in Jerusalem and those living in Bukhara about where community authority was located; a conversation that called into question the relationship between the terms *home* and *diaspora*.

Just as the terms *center–periphery* and *homeland–diaspora* are blurred, so too are the characterizations of the protagonists of this nineteenth-century encounter. Whereas Yosef Maman is the hero in the popular account of his story, the archival record of the slaughtering controversy does not tell us whether Shlomo Lev Eliezerov should be seen as a hero or a rogue for his labors in Samarkand, or whether Hizkiya ha-Kohen ought to be considered a noble leader or a failure for his efforts to maintain authority in the face of impossible adversity. Finally, the existence of several other protagonists suggests that the slaughtering controversy was not about local Judaism (embodied by Hizkiya ha-Kohen Rabin) championing over the global Judaism (embodied by Shlomo Lev Eliezerov) or vice versa. Shlomo Tagger most strongly represented the blurring of the categories "local" and "global," for he was identified with both. He himself grew up in Ottoman Palestine, and when he arrived in Bukhara he continued to defer to the distant authority of the Rishon LeTsion. Yet he was married to a Bukharan woman. Through her and through the time he spent in Samarkand and Tashkent, he became so connected to the community that he came to see and understand the slaughtering controversy from the perspective of the locals. His letter to the Rishon LeTsion, which reflects this empathy, is not a disembodied discourse on Jewish law, but a plea that Jewish legal arbitration take into consideration local market conditions and social implications.

Like the popularized account of the Yosef Maman tale, the slaughtering controversy might be characterized as an encounter between center and periphery, and between local and global Judaism. Yet, unlike that account, these stations are neither given nor stable. Instead, the generative version of the Center-Periphery Paradigm invoked by Nissim Tagger (in his rendition of the Maman story) teaches that they are defined and redefined through contestation. It is precisely through this contentiousness that Central Asia is drawn into deeper and tighter relationships with other parts of the Jewish world.

SEVEN

Building a Neighborhood and Constructing Bukharan Jewish Identity

The previous chapters outlined two versions of the Center-Periphery Paradigm, shedding light on the mechanisms involved in maintaining a normative Judaism in the face of diaspora. The current chapter switches to an examination of a very different construct used to conceive of and maintain Jewish unity: the *Edah* Paradigm. Rather than attempting to solidify a singular, normative Judaism, this paradigm accepts and even celebrates cultural diversity among the Jewish People. It does so by defining diaspora groups as discrete units, *edot* (plural of *edah*),[1] and by legitimizing and celebrating their unique histories and traditions.

The *Edah* Paradigm and Its Foundations

Over the course of their diaspora experience, Jews' diverse histories and environments have given rise to a great range of Jewish religious and cultural forms. The Bukharan Jews' encounters with Yosef Maman, with Shlomo Lev Eliezerov, and with the administration and teachers at Torah Academy highlight how differences in religious practice open up questions about how Judaism as a religious system ought to be practiced, about how far the definition of "normative" Judaism can be stretched, and about who has the authority to answer these questions. Cultural differences lead to a different set of questions—those which address the character of the Jewish People. Can Jews be considered a single people, given the pronounced differences between their cultural expressions, language, costume, cuisine, and music? If so, how might unity within such diversity be understood?

While versions of the Center-Periphery Paradigm are used as vehicles to contend with the challenge of religious difference, the *Edah*
Paradigm is popularly used to contend with cultural difference. Within
this framework, the cultural heritages of various diaspora groups are
not viewed as having deviated from "authentic" Jewish culture. Rather,
each group is understood as an *edah;* a discrete unit with its own unique
history, a well-defined territory that came to be thought of as its "diaspora homeland," with a set of traditions and character traits that are
generally treated as ontological, rather than as having developed over
time through interaction with non-Jewish neighbors.[2] By legitimizing
and celebrating the unique history and traditions of each, this paradigm
allows for a great range of diversity among Jews while maintaining the
notion that they belong to a single people.

The *Edah* Paradigm is deeply rooted in the Jewish imagination, and
has strong links to the biblical portrayal of tribal relationships among
Ancient Israel: wandering through the desert after having left Egypt, the
Israelites were organized into tribal units. The members of each were
bound to one another through their respective ancestral ties, each to a
son of the patriarch Jacob. In the Land of Israel these tribal units were
joined within a single kingdom. Each was assigned its own distinct territory, delineated by the word of God.[3] So, too, each had particular attributes and destinies.[4] Each tribe was also represented before God through
the High Priest, who wore a breast plate inlaid with twelve stones; each
stone was a different color, representing the uniqueness of each particular group.[5] This biblical portrayal of the Children of Israel as divided into
tribes provides a powerful conceptual framework for viewing the Jewish
People as a common, united group composed of different subunits.

With its foundations in the Bible, this paradigmatic representation
has persisted and has reemerged in various guises at different points in
Jewish history. For example, in his introduction to the twelfth-century
legal code, the *Mishneh Torah,* Moses Maimonides explains, "The whole
of the Law was written by Moses our Teacher before his death, in his own
hand."[6] While there was a single authentic scroll—Maimonides tells his
readers—Moses also "presented a scroll to each tribe" so that each of
the various subgroups might have a copy of their own. Likewise in the
sixteenth-century century legal code, the *Shulhan Aruch,* the section
on prayer recommends that synagogue sanctuaries be built with twelve

windows.[7] Later interpretations of this text suggest that the twelve windows represent the twelve tribes, and are meant to remind those using the space that their prayers unite them with all of the Jewish People.[8]

In the early years of Israel's statehood, the twelve-unit tribal structure was invoked in romantic portrayals of the various diaspora groups' migration to Israel as a return home. For example, in his book *The Exiled and the Redeemed,* Israel's second president, Yitzhak Ben-Zvi, framed the massive waves of immigration into the newly formed state of Israel as a fulfillment of Ezekiel's prophecy that all of the "tribes" of Israel would one day be gathered "from among the nations, whither they are gone" and brought back "into their own land."[9] In the body of the book, which is devoted to ethnographic descriptions of Jewish groups (from Yemen, Kurdistan, Afghanistan, India, Bukhara, and the Caucasus), Ben-Zvi shifts between sometimes referring to them as tribes (*shevatim*) and other times as *edot.* This conceptual framework is echoed more recently in a cookbook published in Israel. The work, *Ha-Mitbah shel Kur ha-Hitukh* (The Melting Pot Kitchen), provides recipes and accompanying photographs for twelve ethnic meals, each representing one of Israel's *edot.* (See page 238 of this book for the Bukharan Jewish example.)[10]

In contemporary Hebrew, the term *tribe* (*shevet*) is generally no longer used to refer to Jewish diaspora groups. In a few interesting exceptions, however, a one-to-one correlation is drawn between a particular tribe of Israel (as listed and described in the Bible) and a particular *edah.* The Jews from Ethiopia, for example, are popularly referred to as descendants of the tribe of Dan.[11] Likewise, a group in Manipur, India (on the border of Myanmar), that claim to be Jewish identify themselves as belonging to the tribe of Menashe.[12] Several hundred members of this group moved to Israel in the early twenty-first century, and are popularly referred to as "Bnei Menashe" (the children of the tribe of Menashe).

In most other cases, a one-to-one correlation is generally not drawn between the various *edot* and particular tribes of Israel.[13] The Jews of Yemen, for example, are often described as the "Yemenite *edah*," but are generally not identified as members of a particular tribe. Likewise, the Jews of Bukhara are often described as the "Bukharan *edah*" and in popular media are even identified at times as lost tribesmen, but rarely are recognized as descendants of a particular tribe. Nevertheless, salient symbolic features of the twelve-tribe construct are carried over to the conception of *edot* as distinct groups, but each an integral part of the Jewish People.

In this model, variations between *edot* are presented and understood to be ordered, predictable, and even sacred, rather than random or idiosyncratic. Regional differences within any particular *edah* are generally dismissed, as is historical change. Finally, the notion that the customs of each *edah* may be attributed to cultural borrowing from non-Jewish neighbors is also downplayed, for if the practices of the various diaspora Jews are viewed as having been adopted from the surrounding peoples in a patchwork fashion, they come to appear disorderly and inauthentic. By contrast, if they are *edot,* each with distinct qualities and history, separate both from other Jews and from the surrounding people among whom they live, the particularities can be regarded as legitimate and even celebrated.

Representations of Bukharan Jews as an *Edah*

Like other *edot,* Bukharan Jews are popularly portrayed as a Jewish diaspora group with colorful cultural attributes that are static and enduring. These traits are not regarded as having developed through dynamic conversation with their non-Jewish neighbors or even with other Jewish groups. This portrayal is elaborated and explored below, in an analysis of two museum exhibits devoted to the group.

In 1967, the Israel Museum in Jerusalem inaugurated its Ethnological Department, established for the purpose of "systematic study of material culture in Israel."[14] The department's first exhibit was a display of the material cultural of Bukharan Jews, consisting primarily of personal luxury items such as jewelry, fine dishware, and richly embroidered robes and caps. The introduction to the catalogue explains that these items were collected from individuals whose parents or grandparents had emigrated from Central Asia in the late nineteenth and early twentieth centuries.

For the reader with historical knowledge, the objects provide a window into consumption patterns of the Bukharan Jewish nouveau riche class, which emerged during the late tsarist period on the heels of Russian colonialism. The curators, however, did not use these items to tell the historically situated story of the Bukharan Jews' rise to wealth and cosmopolitanism. Rather, the items on display float against blank

FIGURE 7.1
"Bokharan Jewess and Child," drawing by Abel Pann

FIGURE 7.2
Muslim women in Samarkand, 1870s
Eugene Schulyer, Turkistan (New York: Scribner, Armstrong & Co., 1876)

backgrounds in the museum catalogue, disembodied from any sort of context, as though the Bukharan Jewish culture they represent is static and "out-of-time."[15] In addition to the lack of historical context, little social context is provided. The display of ritual items is sparse, leaving the viewer with the sense that Bukharan Jews had little in common with Jews in other parts of the world. Likewise, the exhibit provides no information about the ways in which the culture of the Bukharan Jews might have resembled (or differed from) that of their Muslim neighbors. While the costumes on display are portrayed as "Bukharan Jewish," most of their features are, in fact, simply "Central Asian."

The Israel Museum's portrayal of Bukharan Jews echoes an image that appeared in the 1939 *Universal Jewish Encyclopedia*'s entry on "Bokhara" (see figure 7.1, "Bokharan Jewess and child"). The cap the woman wears in this illustration closely resembles those that were on display in the Israel Museum's 1967 exhibit. And, as in the museum exhibit, the woman's costume, jewelry, hairstyle, and *doyra* (tambourine) might be mistaken as typically "Bukharan Jewish." Yet, aside from the young boy's sidelocks, all the features shown in the painting are simply

Central Asian. Indeed, the etching "Women of Samarkand" (figure 7.2), which appeared in Eugene Schulyer's 1876 travelogue, highlights the strong resemblance between the costume and hairstyles of Samarkand's Muslim women and those of the city's Jewish women, represented in the previous image.

A similar portrayal that depicts Bukharan Jews as isolated from history, from their Muslim neighbors, and from Jews in other parts of the world reappeared in the New York Jewish Museum's exhibit "Facing West" in 1999. The display, drawn from the collection of the Russian Museum of Ethnography, consisted of objects that had belonged to non-Ashkenazi Jews of the Soviet Union: Bukharan Jews of Uzbekistan and Tajikistan, Mountain Jews of Azerbaijan and Dagestan, and Jews of Georgia. Each group's set of objects was displayed independently, giving the viewer the impression that the groups had no contact with each other. In addition, as with the 1967 Jerusalem exhibit, little visual or textual information provided information about existing connections between these groups and the world's other Jews, or between these groups and their non-Jewish neighbors.

The reviews of the exhibit and its accompanying catalogue testify to the strength of the impression the viewer receives of these groups as distinct and separate. One reviewer concludes that the Jews portrayed inhabited an "exotic landscape" and were so "ensconced" in their remote regions that "no one knew much about them" beyond the notion that they may have been "part of the 10 lost tribes of Israel."[16] Another reviewer notes that "those accustomed to thinking of the Jews as one people, united by a common culture" will be surprised to encounter the people of this exhibit and catalogue, who are so unique and whose customs are so distinct that they "might have dropped from the moon. Or perhaps . . . they really are the descendants of the Lost Ten Tribes of Israel."[17]

While these two exhibits tell us little about the Bukharan Jews themselves, they do tell us a lot about the way this particular group—as well as a great many other Jewish diaspora groups—is perceived in the popular Jewish imagination. The deep-rooted paradigm of the Jewish universe as divided into tribes, or *edot,* allows for accommodation, and even celebration, of the Jews' great cultural diversity. At the same time, it exoticizes these groups by isolating them in space and depicting them as "out-of-time." In contrast to this ontological depiction of Bukharan Jewishness, the historical analysis that follows presents the Bukharan Jewish *edah* as a generative category, developed in historical time and in conversation with others.

The Jews of Samarkand as "Bukharan Jews"

In the 1990s, when I first came into contact with Jews from Uzbekistan and Tajikistan, I was perplexed by the label *Bukharan Jews* that they used to refer to themselves. While it was not difficult to understand why those from the city of Bukhara used this label, I wondered about those from other cities in the region. Why did the Jews of Samarkand, for example, refer to themselves as Bukharan Jews?

The most straightforward answer to this question is that Samarkand had long been part of the Bukharan kingdom, and that by referring to themselves as "Bukharan," the Jews there invoked the collective memory of having belonged to that territory in the days prior to Russian domination of the area. As I continued my research, however, I encountered cases that confounded this explanation. In particular, I met a number of individuals who told me that their ancestors were from Iran, and others who told me that theirs were from Afghanistan; they claimed that their relatives had fled to Samarkand and settled there after encountering persecution in their home cities. Despite carrying the family memory of having come from elsewhere, these individuals nevertheless referred to themselves as "Bukharan Jews." Why they identified as such was particularly puzzling, given the timing of their ancestors' arrival in Samarkand.

Those who came from Meshed likely came with a group escaping an outburst of violence against the Jews in that city in 1839,[18] and those who fled from Kabul likely arrived with a group expelled in 1859.[19] Not long after these refugees resettled in Samarkand, the city was carved out of the Bukharan emirate and incorporated into Russian Turkestan. Still later, the city was incorporated into Uzbekistan, one of the republics of the Soviet Union. In the face of this movement and territorial flux, the identity marker *Bukharan Jew* emerged and remained the most salient. By contrast, I never heard Jews from Samarkand refer to themselves as "Samarkandi Jews." Nor have I ever heard people from Samarkand refer to themselves as "Kabuli Jews" or "Meshedi Jews" (even if they were aware that their forebears had come from one of these cities). If these terms had ever been invoked, their resonance was lost over time, and they fell into disuse. The story of how this occurred is told below.

Historical documents show that the existence of a community that identified itself as the "Bukharan Jewish *edah*" does not stretch back as long as the history of Jewish presence in Central Asia, or even as long as the history of the kingdom of Bukhara. Rather, Bukharan Jewish group identity emerged at the turn of the last century, and came to encompass the Jews in Samarkand (including those who had come from Meshed and Kabul), as well as Jews in other parts of Russian Turkestan. Rather than being a reflection of a long, static past confined to a single territory, the term emerged at the very moment in history when contact with other Jewish communities became most pronounced. It was in Jerusalem—as a result of encounters with Jews from other parts of the world—that those Jews who arrived from Bukhara, Samarkand, and other cities in Central Asia discovered and highlighted their commonality with one another and their distinctness from the other Jewish populations there.

In describing this process, I draw on the approach of Fredrik Barth, whose 1969 watershed publication "Ethnic Groups and Boundaries" offered a critique of the long-held notion that ethnic groups could be studied as independent units. The world, he writes, is not made up of "separate peoples each with a culture and each organized in a society which can legitimately be isolated for description as an island to itself."[20] Instead, ethnic identity emerges as a result of contact with others. Accordingly, Barth turned away from the widely accepted project of describing the attributes of ethnic groups and collecting and describing their material culture. In place, he proposed a model of analysis that emphasizes the process of ethnic group formation, maintenance, and change.

Anthropologist Charles Keyes further developed Barth's approach, asserting that ethnicity is articulated when it "serves to orient people in the pursuit of their interest vis-à-vis other people."[21] He claims that people emphasize distinct group identities in situations where material needs cannot be met and there is competition for resources. In such situations, opposing interest groups form. The lines that define and divide one group from the next, he contends, are cultural differences that are highlighted as a means for the groups to organize and mobilize themselves.

In the Bukharan Jewish case, there was indeed competition for financial resources—not, however, due to a shortage of life's basic necessities. Rather, amidst relative wealth, the competition was for resources that would allow for expression of group honor. The tasks of creating a plan for a residential neighborhood in Jerusalem, collecting money to fund its building, choosing a board of directors, and deciding what the neighborhood organization should be called all contributed toward the formation of a collective identity. One aspect of this process was the group's effort to define itself as separate from both the Ashkenazi and the Sephardi communities in Jerusalem. That project entailed detailing "who we are not." The second aspect of the process was solidifying a sense of "group-ness" or "we-ness" by defining "who we are," who is included within the group, what the group would be called, and determining its important characteristics. Only after years of negotiation did this "we" come to be defined as "The Bukharan Jews." A set of historical documents provides us with a window into both of these processes.[22]

Group Unity through a "Holy Committee"

In 1890, a number of Central Asian Jewish community leaders residing in Jerusalem composed an announcement to send to their friends and relatives back home.[23] They begin their missive by describing life in Jerusalem. The city is a lively place, they wrote, which is in the process of rejuvenation. Spearheading the efforts at revitalization are "our scattered brothers," who have come together in this city from various corners of the earth. They "understand their obligation" to "build up the ruins of Jerusalem," and have taken action. God has looked favorably upon them, having "made them successful in their endeavors: They have established societies and organizations. They have built beautiful homes, and synagogues for glorification and grandeur, and houses of study, and every kind of charity house needed."

The writers continue: "And what about us?" While these other groups "have opened their eyes and have improved their lot . . . we have not been stirred to move even one step forward." Lamenting their lack of progress in contributing to Jerusalem's revitalization, they list the various institutions established by Jerusalem's Ashkenazi Jews, as well as institutions built by the city's Sephardi Jews, and then ask, "Why should we have less than our brothers? Why should our lot be any worse than theirs?"

In the next section of their missive, they offer an explanation about why they are languishing in Jerusalem. It is not because they lack the resources, nor is it because there are not enough people to support their own building projects. Instead, they blame their lack of progress on the fact that they have not joined with one another to work together. There is "a division of hearts" and "a lack of order" among us, they explain: "We have no shepherd. We have no leader. Each person does as he sees fit. . . ."

Having outlined the problem, the writers then present their solution: "It is for this reason that we awoke and arose . . . and gathered together last Wednesday night." Here they reach the central purpose of their announcement: to make it known that they held a meeting to publicize what was decided there, and to state who had played a role in the deciding.

What was decided was "to establish a holy committee" tasked with overseeing the fundraising, planning, and building of a residential quarter in Jerusalem, replete with synagogues and schools to service it. Those who came together to form the committee included "our brothers who live here" as well as "our honorable brothers who are here [visiting from Central Asia] to celebrate the holiday of Shavuot." These two categories of attendees—those who made the permanent move from Central Asia, as well as those who were visitors—suggest that the planned neighborhood was envisioned as a home not only for those who would become permanent residents within it, but for the whole of the transnational community.

But just who is included in this community? The answer to this question, which gets to the heart of uncovering the contours of group identity, is found in the opening and closing lines of the document: the announcement is addressed to "the members of our *edah* living in a land which is not their own," and is signed, "from the Society of Lovers of Zion of the Holy Committee of Bukhara, Samarkand, Tashkent, and Environs." With this greeting and signature, the authors proclaim that they who are in the Holy Land who have come from Bukhara, Samarkand, Tashkent, and these cities' environs have come together to form a society in Jerusalem. They invite those who reside in those cities back in Central Asia to take part in this society, proclaiming that they all share the task of building a neighborhood for themselves in Jerusalem because they are all members of the same *edah.*

Much is at stake with their use of the term *edah* to refer to themselves, as is highlighted in another letter—also written to the Jewish communities in Central Asia—by Jerusalem's Sephardi leaders.

Fundraising and Group Identity

Just a few months after forming their "holy committee" and declaring themselves an *edah,* Central Asia's Jews launched a fundraising project intended to garner financial support for the building of their new neighborhood. The plan was to send an emissary to Central Asia on behalf of their organization, who would bring with him batches of the four plants necessary for ritual observance of the Sukkot holiday. He would distribute these items as gifts to members of Central Asia's Jewish communities. In turn, it was expected that the receivers would send charitable donations to support the neighborhood-building project in Jerusalem. However, when the Rishon LeTsion and other leaders in the Sephardi *kollel* received word of this plan, controversy erupted. Sephardi leaders in Ottoman Palestine composed a letter cautioning Jewish leaders in Central Asia not to donate money toward this project.[24] They write:

> We had the idea of honoring you by sending you carefully selected, splendid, praiseworthy citron fruits, palm branches, and myrtle using funds from our *kollel* [with the hopes that] you would make donations—each one of you according to his ability—and perhaps from this, the poor of our *kollel* would benefit.
>
> And after we had already agreed, and undertaken this great endeavor, and sent you authoritative letters [stating that] you should not buy citron fruits, palm branches, and myrtle from anyone except those people whom we ourselves have sent, we found out that the people of the cities of Bukhara . . . who are dwelling here . . . in Jerusalem . . . rose up, went out, and claimed that this great idea was their own [and that they had decided to implement it as a means to raise funds] to assist their own society that they founded here in Jerusalem.
>
> We warned them not to. . . .

For years, the Sephardi *kollel* had been sending emissaries to Central Asia, who had been successful in raising funds that were channeled back to their institutions in Ottoman Palestine. However, when Central Asia's

Jews decided to organize their own fundraising campaign in support of their own institutions, the leaders of the Sephardi *kollel* made what appears to be an audacious demand—insisting that the Jews in Central Asia had no right to contribute money toward the organization that their own family members and friends had established. They justify this position on the basis of two claims. First, "because we came up with this idea," they argue, and second, "because our *kollel* has over 5,000 poor people among it." After years of raising money and disbursing it, they have come to take responsibility for a great number of the city's poor, whom they cannot simply abandon. Continued funding is necessary to cover this budget item.

Perhaps the most potent claim on the money, though, is the argument that Jews from Central Asia do not constitute an *edah,* and therefore have no right to a financially independent organization. This position is not overtly articulated, but emerges from a number of interesting passages. The letter begins, "Shall we not begin by telling you that we are the leaders of the upstanding *edah* of the holy community of the Sephardim here in Jerusalem." Their use of the term *edah* to refer to themselves is deliberate and self-conscious, as is their reticence to use it to refer to others. They write, for example, "The poor and needy, the orphans, and widows, the modest Torah scholars and the people from Yemen are becoming more numerous everyday." Those from Yemen, in other words, are individuals rather than a collective; they are "the people from," rather than members of an *edah.* So, too, "the people of the cities of Bukhara" are described as individuals rather than as constituting an *edah.* While the Sephardi leaders label themselves members of an *edah,* which gives them legitimate claims to organize a *kollel* and raise funds on its behalf, those from Bukhara are not.

The two community announcements presented here highlight the first process in the formation of a collective identity: the Jews from Central Asia (Bukhara, Samarkand, Tashkent, and their environs) struggle to define themselves as separate and distinct both from the Ashkenazi and the Sephardi communities in Jerusalem. They have a clear sense of who they are not, and on this basis proclaim themselves an *edah,* using the very term to which the Sephardi community leaders attempt to retain exclusive rights.

The question of "who they are" has yet to be addressed.

Evolving Group Identity

As a window into the evolving process of naming and defining themselves, we turn to the Central Asians' "Society Regulations" that were printed in Ottoman Palestine between 1889 and 1911. In those years, the regulations were updated and reprinted a number of times. The changes in these documents serve as an excellent tool for tracing the evolution of the organization's name.

In 1891, the society founded by the Jews from Central Asia was named Hevrat Hovevei Tsion le-Vinyan Batim be'ad Anshei Bukhara ve-Samarkand ve-Tashkand ve-Agapeiha (The Society of Lovers of Zion to Build Houses for the People of Bukhara, Samarkand, Tashkent, and Their Outskirts).[25] A revised version of the regulations was printed in 1904. The name of the society as printed here was shorter and simpler: "The Society of Bukharia and Its Outskirts."[26]

What transpired in the organizational meetings attended by the society leaders between 1891 and 1904? One issue that must have been discussed was the question of how the group should present itself, and what label it should use to gain recognition and legitimacy. The benefit of the name chosen in 1891 was that it spelled out clearly who was represented in this newly founded society. Those from the cities Bukhara, Samarkand, Tashkent, or any of the neighboring cities and towns knew they were represented. The drawback was that the name was unwieldy and confusing, hardly encouraging others to perceive of them as a unified and distinct group.

To sharpen and tighten their collective identity, and to lend legitimacy to their group as an *edah*, rather than a collection of individuals from various cities and towns, the name had to be streamlined. By 1904 they had become "The Society of Bukharia and Its Outskirts."

Their singular identity was further emphasized in the Regulation Handbook of 1911 through the introduction of a graphic change.[27] In a clever innovation, the word *Bukhara* was printed in boldface, whereas the term *outskirts* appeared in smaller typeface. All those from outside Bukhara (such as those from Samarkand) were still represented. Yet, the reader's attention was drawn to the single term *Bukhara*, facilitating a crystallization of group identity. A singular term had become almost enough to represent all the Jews of Central Asia.

Just as the name of the society evolved, so, too, did the name of its neighborhood. When the Jews from Central Asia first founded their neighborhood in Jerusalem, they called it Rehovot (from the root *RHV*, meaning wide, spacious, extensive). This name was chosen as a specific reference to the sentence in Genesis that tells how Isaac dug a well and named it Rehovot, proclaiming that "God has extended himself to us and allowed us to be fruitful in the land."[28] In naming their own neighborhood Rehovot, the founders invoked many layers of imagery: their identification with Isaac who claimed land by building a well and sanctifying it by invoking God's name, their thankfulness to God for having extended Himself to them in the Land of Israel, and pride in their plan for a spacious neighborhood that would reflect the prosperity of their *edah*.[29]

Over the years, the name of the neighborhood changed to Rehovot ha-Bukharim (Streets of the Bukharans). With this new name, a different connotation of the word *rehovot* was emphasized. In addition to (or perhaps instead of) evoking the originally intended biblical imagery, the colloquial meaning of *rehovot*—simply as streets—was used. By 1910, "The Streets of the Bukharans" became the neighborhood title that was used on the society's official letterhead and seals.

Over time, the neighborhood's name continued to evolve. The word *rehovot* was totally dropped when the area became defined as Shkhunat ha-Bukharim (The Bukharans' Neighborhood), which is how it is popularly referred to today. The evolution of the neighborhood name from Rehovot, to Rehovot ha-Bukharim, to Shkhunat ha-Bukharim further strengthened the articulation of the inhabitants' collective identity. Practically speaking, the neighborhood was a place to live. But much more than that, it became a physical manifestation and marker of group identity.

Circulating Notions of Identity

Shlomo Baba Jon Pinhasov was born in Kabul in 1843, shortly after his parents settled there after fleeing from their homes in Meshed. As a young man, he left Kabul, again fleeing Jewish persecution. He resettled in Samarkand, where he spent much of his adult life. In 1893, when Pinhasov was fifty years old, he left Samarkand to travel to Jerusalem for the first time. He stayed there for three years, and then returned to

Samarkand. Subsequently, he traveled to Jerusalem on two other occasions, residing there between 1904 and 1906, and then from 1907 until
his death in 1928.[30]

How did Shlomo Baba Jon Pinhasov identify himself? As Meshedi?
Kabuli? Samarkandi? Jerushalmi? Bukhari? The answer, which we do
not have, was probably fluid and depended on the particular social and
geographical context in which he found himself. A few interesting notes
about his identity, however, can be found in one of the five books he
brought to print in Jerusalem: a dictionary of six languages.[31] Published
in 1908, the languages contained in the work, all set in Hebrew characters, included Persian, Hebrew, Russian, Arabic, Turkish, and French.[32]

In the frontispiece of the dictionary, the editor refers to himself as
"Shlomo, who is nicknamed Baba Jon Pinhasov, from the city of Samarkand, who is currently living in the holy city of Jerusalem." He did not
identify himself here as "Bukharan," nor did he identify the text's Persian
language as "Bukharit."[33] Yet, he announced in the dictionary's frontispiece: "This book is on sale at Mullah Yisrael Shaulov's [store], located
in Shkhunat ha-Bukharim [the Bukharans' Neighborhood]."[34] Baba Jon
Pinhasov's own identity may have been a shifting one, but nevertheless,
he recognized "Bukharan Jewish" as a category. He used the terminol-
ogy rather than contesting it by referring to the neighborhood as "Rehovot" or as "the neighborhood of Central Asian Jews in Jerusalem."
Perhaps this brief reference is an indicator of the role that the neighborhood itself—and its name—would come to play over time in fixing and
shaping a coherent ethnic label, "Bukharan Jewish," and its attendant
category.

The dictionary of six languages was widely circulated and Shlomo
Baba Jon Pinhasov's own mobility paralleled his books' mobility. His
books were printed in Jerusalem, but made their way to Central Asia.[35]
(In 1996, I bought a yellowed and brittle copy of the dictionary in Samarkand from a man who was selling all his books in preparation for
his move to the United States.) Like the community announcements
that were circulated between Palestine and Central Asia, this dictionary's movement points to the flow of discourse about Bukharan Jewish
identity and space.

While a solid group identity may have been born in conversation
with the Sephardi Jews in Jerusalem, it was not limited to this geographi-

cal place. Printed material, along with talk of the "Bukharan neighbor-hood," was disseminated in Central Asia via Jewish travelers, business-men, and fundraisers. In this way, the formation of a group identity that evolved in Ottoman Palestine came to stretch across oceans, to encompass the Jews from Central Asia living in Ottoman Palestine as well as those who remained in Central Asia, under a singular collective identity defined as Bukharan Jewry.

Today, museum exhibits, documentary films, and the popular press treat "Bukharan Jews" as a reified group with clear and persistent so-cial boundaries and with distinct, enduring cultural characteristics that came into existence independent of contact with others. Not unique to Bukharan Jews, this characterization draws on the *Edah* Paradigm, a compelling framework for conceptualizing diversity amid Jewish unity. Like the Center-Periphery Paradigm, however, it is a constructed one. Just as the terms *center* and *periphery* are neither stable nor sui generis, the various *edot* are not static units, descended intact from the biblical tribal groups. Rather, they are constructed and maintained through a dynamic process of unfolding relationships with others.

PART 4

Twentieth-Century Conversations

EIGHT

Local Jewish Forms

The cosmopolitan, global quality of the Bukharan Jewish community was short-lived. In the 1920s the Soviets dismantled the remaining vestige of the Bukharan emirate, cut through the old borders, carved new ones, and incorporated the region into the USSR. Where the emirate once stood, two new political entities were created: the Uzbek Soviet Socialist Republic and the Tajik Soviet Socialist Republic.

For the Jews of the region, this new geopolitical landscape meant a sudden severing of their international ties. Under Soviet rule, their movement became highly restricted, bringing an end to their participation in social, religious, and mercantile networks that had stretched between Central Asia, Europe, and Palestine. Those who remained in Central Asia were no longer able to travel out, and religious emissaries from abroad were no longer permitted to enter. Tight control on human traffic extended to the flow of information as well. Just as people were forbidden from crossing the borders, so, too, was the written word. Letters were monitored and censored, and religious texts printed elsewhere in the Jewish world were not permitted entry.

The severance of these transnational connections brought an abrupt end to the religious conversations in which Central Asia's Jews had been engaged in the nineteenth and early twentieth centuries. Furthermore, the communist assault on religion made it difficult to teach, discuss, or practice religion in any open, public forum. Bukharan Jews did continue to engage in Jewish practice and to maintain a strong sense of Jewish identity despite their isolation from Jewish communities in other parts of the world, and regardless of having to practice in relative secrecy. Yet, over the course of the next seventy years of Soviet rule, their religion took on a localized form. This characterization refers to two qualities: first, the idiosyncrasies that emerged and were elaborated upon as a result of Judaism's interactions with the particular non-Jewish world in which it was embedded. These forms became pronounced during the Soviet period because they were not tempered by interactions with Jewish communities outside the region. Second, the characterization of religious life as "localized" refers to the way in which Judaism was experienced in Central Asia during Soviet rule. As a result of going underground (to evade the authorities), people came to experience Judaism as intimately connected to local community life, with little sense of it as linked to an abstract, global religious system. Both these aspects of localization are addressed in this chapter. They set the stage for chapter 9, which returns to the Center-Periphery Paradigm to analyze encounters between Central Asia's Bukharan Jews and representatives of international Jewish organizations who arrived in the region when the Soviet Union dissolved.

Religion in Central Asia during the Soviet Period

When the Soviet Union formed, peoples of vastly different cultural backgrounds who populated a massive swath of varied social and geographical terrain, which stretched from Eastern Europe to the borders of China and Afghanistan, were incorporated into a single empire. A variety of policies were instituted in an effort to unite these disparate peoples and places into a single classless society, and to realize a vision of a "new, thoroughly rational *Homo Sovieticus*."[1] Among them were policies directed at the eradication of religion, which was viewed as a primitive vestige of the past and a regressive social force.

In Central Asia, campaigns were primarily targeted against Islam, the dominant religion in the region.[2] In some periods, antireligious policies were particularly harsh: religious courts and schools were shut down, prayer services in mosques were banned, and members of the clergy were denounced as "exploiters, criminals and corrupters of moral values."[3] In other periods, greater leniencies allowed for the practice and transmission of religion. For example, during World War II, when "Muslim support for the Soviet state became a matter of vital interest to the party,"[4] some religious educational institutions were opened and permitted to operate. Their numbers, however, were limited, and those that were allowed to function were monitored and closely supervised under the auspices of state-sponsored "Spiritual Directorates."[5]

While Jews constituted a tiny minority of the Central Asian population,[6] policies designed to bring about the demise of religion in the region were applied to them as well. Synagogues were closed and religious schools for children were banned, as were institutions for the training of clergy. Yet in spite of these official policies, Judaism—like Islam—remained an important social force in Soviet Central Asia. Parents had their sons ritually circumcised, couples married in religious ceremonies officiated by clergy, and religious idiom continued to inform rituals surrounding death and mourning. Most Bukharan Jews observed key Jewish holidays including Yom Kippur, Passover, and the Sabbath, and adhered to many aspects of *kashrut* (religious dietary practices) throughout the Soviet era.[7]

Social scientists who have written about Islam in the region have offered a variety of reasons to explain why and how Central Asians continued to practice their religion throughout the Soviet era, in spite of the "extraordinarily organized and profound" efforts to eradicate it.[8] These studies offer useful tools for understanding Judaism in Central Asia as well. Teresa Rakowska Harmstone, for example, explains the tenacity of Islam in Central Asia by highlighting the Soviets' laxity in enforcing antireligious policy in the region.[9] Michael Chlenov, likewise, explains that Central Asia and the Caucasus "were much less influenced by the state policy of atheism than were Russian and other Western parts of the Empire." As a result, a proportionally higher number of synagogues and religious schools were allowed to remain open, and Jewish life remained relatively active.[10]

In his book *Everyday Islam,* Sergei Poliakov offers a different approach to explain the tenacity of religious life in Central Asia. Writing at the end of the Soviet era, he notes that "the number of officially registered religious institutions does not constitute even one percent of the mosques and mazars that actually operate and regulate the Muslims' way of life."[11] Looking beyond policies and institutional life, his work focuses on "parallel Islam," a term he uses to refer to religious life that cannot be quantified or measured using official data. Instead, he offers an ethnographic description of the fabric of Central Asia society to illuminate the informal mechanisms through which religious life was perpetuated.

Poliakov explains that as a result of low levels of urbanization and industrialization in Central Asia, people had little incentive to leave their home villages and towns in search of employment, education, or high culture. Low levels of mobility were linked to the maintenance of strong, tightly knit extended kinship networks, which offered a resilient site for the transmission of religion outside of the institutional sphere. Likewise, the *mahalla*—loosely translated as a neighborhood or residential quarter—acted as a site for the practice and transmission of unofficial Islam. Operating as a religious parish, the *mahalla* and its neighborhood council "shapes public opinion, policing observation of norms of behavior derived from *sharia, adat,* and local practices . . . any violation of the *mahalla*'s way of doing things is inescapably followed by punishment in the form of social censure."[12] While the Soviets could exert control over official religious institutions, they had little control over the domestic and neighborhood domain, where "parallel Islam" continued to be practiced.

This situation closely mirrored that of the region's Jews. Like Central Asia's Muslims, they tended to marry and raise their children in the cities and towns where they were born. Low mobility rates coupled with low levels of intermarriage[13] yielded a high rate of marriage among Bukharan Jews who lived in the same city. Furthermore, because the Jewish population in each town and city never exceeded several thousand, over the course of several decades the ties between neighbors and friends came to overlap with kinship ties, creating tightly knit social networks. "We are all cousins here," people often answered in response to my questions about the relationships between them.[14] These kinship networks provided the means for perpetuating Judaism even in the face of weak institutional life. Likewise, every city and town in Uzbekistan and Tajikistan that was home to a substantial Bukharan Jewish population had a *mahalla* (residential quarter) where Jews concentrated, and which functioned as a center of Jewish communal life. While the Soviets were able to exert control over religious life in the institutional sphere, they had little control over religious expression among friends and kin in the informal sphere of the *mahalla*.

This chapter focuses on two aspects of Jewish life that were maintained via these informal channels throughout the Soviet era: *kashrut* and rituals related to life-cycle events (in particular, marriage and death). In addition, local understandings of the structure of Jewish identity and of the way in which it is transmitted from one generation to the next are discussed.

Kashrut

In the Spring of 1997, the Yitzhakov family made a long list of things they needed to do before Passover. I was living with them at that time, and participated in some of these preparatory tasks, including the purchase of meat for the holiday meals. What would have been a routine trip to the kosher butcher shop had I been home in the United States, in Samarkand was noteworthy enough for me to write about in a letter. "First, you have to get attuned to the rumors of the comings and goings of the *shohet* [ritual slaughterer] . . ." I began.

There were no kosher butcher shops in Samarkand. During the Soviet era, owning or operating such a store would have been forbidden. And in the midst of the great migration unfolding in the post-Soviet era, none had been opened. Buying kosher meat, then, involved identifying the ritual slaughterer's whereabouts. Recently, this had become complicated because the city's last *shohet* had left town a few months before. The closest one lived in Bukhara (a four-hour drive away) and traveled to Samarkand every so often to perform his work.

"Once you find out his approximate time of arrival to this city," I continued in my letter, "you have to figure out where he is shehting [slaughtering] and when." Meat was in high demand for the Passover meals, and people had to rely on word of mouth to find him, which "isn't always easy," I explained, "because he runs around the whole city. . . ." He would station himself in certain locales to give people the opportunity to bring their chickens (which they bought in the market or raised themselves) for him to slaughter. For beef, the *shohet* made arrangements with butchers, who would meet him in a designated spot and pay him to slaughter the cow they brought with them. He would mark the meat with his stamp, indicating that it was kosher, and the butchers would sell it. The slaughtering and selling often took place at the home

FIGURE 8.1
A Jewish ritual slaughter, performed in the home
of a Bukharan Jewish family, Samarkand, 1994
Courtesy of Alanna E. Cooper

of someone who would get a cut of the meat (literally) in exchange for hosting.

The definition of "keeping kosher" is largely agreed upon throughout the Jewish world. It involves consuming only food that is classified as kosher, which primarily refers to the flesh of permitted animals, killed and prepared in a ritually prescribed manner. In addition, keeping kosher involves the separation of meat and milk. This entails a restriction against consuming dairy and meat (or poultry) at the same meal. It also involves waiting a prescribed amount of time between eating them, and using separate kitchenware for each. While this broad definition is shared by most Jews regardless of where they live, variations in the culture of food preparation and consumption create differences in how these rules are understood and implemented.

In Uzbekistan, most of the Jews whom I met in the 1990s told me that they kept kosher, and that they had kept kosher during the Soviet era as well. When asked to identify what exactly they meant by "keeping kosher," I found differences between the answers they gave and those American Jews tend to offer. For example, American Jews might refer to whether the processed food they consume only includes items that bear a *hekhsher* (kosher certification). In Uzbekistan, where there were few processed food items on the market, and no infrastructure for regulating kosher certification, this sort of criteria for keeping kosher was largely irrelevant.

Like American Jews, Bukharan Jews often referred to practices related to the way in which they organized their kitchens, including the use of separate kitchenware for dairy and meat meals. However, with fewer products and appliances available in Uzbekistan than in the United States, many of the items to which American Jews might refer (such as separate sponges for meat and dairy, separate dish racks, and even separate sinks and dishwashers) were irrelevant.

Another difference relates to the processing of meat prior to consumption. Many women I met in Uzbekistan spoke about the practice they had learned from their mothers of salting and soaking meat prior to cooking it in order to drain it of blood. In contrast, few contemporary American Jews engage in this procedure or even know how to do it, as in recent decades the practice has been taken over by the kosher meatpacking factories.

Finally, Jews in Uzbekistan and Jews in the United States speak very differently about the act of purchasing kosher meat. In the United States, the training of ritual slaughterers and the certification of meat as kosher is publicly regulated, and most kosher meat on the market today is processed and packaged in large factories and distributed through impersonal channels. This means that when contemporary American Jews purchase kosher meat (whether in grocery stores or in kosher butcher shops) they do not know who the slaughterer was, and are mostly unaware of where the meat was processed.

In Samarkand, Jews experienced the purchase of kosher meat differently. In Soviet Central Asia, the process for certifying ritual slaughterers could not be institutionalized, meat could not be publicly certified as kosher, and kosher meat processing was not industrialized. This meant that individuals were deemed worthy of being slaughterers by their mentors through a quiet, private process. They qualified to serve as ritual slaughterers without public ceremony or pronouncement, and the meat they killed was deemed kosher through trust and informal social consensus. Furthermore, these ritual functionaries did not work in publicly established slaughterhouses or butcher shops. Rather, they surreptitiously conducted their work in roaming spots (including people's homes) within the confines of the Jewish *mahalla*, and people learned where and when kosher meat was being sold through word of mouth. Buying kosher meat, then, required engaging in a private communal landscape. It was this aspect to which people most often referred in my discussions with them about keeping kosher.

When I spoke with Nina, for example, about keeping kosher while growing up in Samarkand in the 1960s, she referred to her vivid memories of trips she took with her mother to buy meat. They would leave their home in the new city before daybreak, Nina told me, and take the bus to the Jewish *mahalla*. Their first stop would be the spot where the ritual slaughter had taken place that morning. Arriving early, they would get their choice of the best cut of meat. From there, they would walk to the bazaar—the large open market—located just outside the *mahalla*, where they bought produce. They would then return home, their arms heavy with their shopping bags filled with food for the week.

Unlike Nina, Berta grew up in the *mahalla*, where she lived with her husband and teenage daughter when I met her in the 1990s. When

I asked her if her family had kept kosher during the Soviet period, she responded, "Yes we did. We did not go to the bazaar to buy our meat." Likewise, in response to my question about keeping kosher in the post-Soviet era, she explained that most of the Jews in Samarkand's Jewish *mahalla* continue to keep kosher. "Yes they do," she answered. "There are only one or two [families in the *mahalla*] who buy meat from bazaar."

While "keeping kosher" means a variety of things, one of the most salient aspects for Nina, Berta, and others was related to the act of purchasing meat. The fact that Jewish ritual slaughtering was only done in the Jewish *mahalla* meant that the Jews living in that neighborhood stayed within Jewish space when they bought their meat, whereas Jews living in the "new city" traveled to the *mahalla* to buy their meat. By contrast, meat considered not fit for consumption was equated to that which belonged to the impersonal and undefined space of the open-air market. In this framework, keeping kosher was not experienced as an act of adherence to a global religious system or an abstract set of laws. Rather, it was an articulation and reinforcement of one's ties to the local Jewish community, and to the space that the community called home.

Memorial Services and Prayer

On a winter day in 1993, I awoke while it was still dark outside to accompany my host to morning prayers. I had just arrived in Bukhara the night before, and as we set out into the narrow, dimly lit streets of the Jewish *mahalla,* I wondered what I would find in the synagogue. We walked for just a few minutes, but after several twists and turns, and without street signs as guideposts, I quickly lost track of where we were, and was glad to have someone showing me the way. When we arrived, the small warm room was already filled with some twenty men. There was no space set aside for women here, but someone brought a chair and placed it in the vestibule for me.

From this spot, I was able to see into the sanctuary, and hear the man who stood at the reading table in the center of the room. He led a service that was familiar to me from my own synagogue attendance in the United States. The structure of the prayers followed the same basic pattern, and I recognized the Hebrew liturgy. Nevertheless, the accent, melodies, and cadence were thoroughly foreign, making it difficult for me to follow the service.

As I watched, I saw that some of the men in the sanctuary held books and used them to recite the prayers along with the leader. Most, however, did not. They sat comfortably in their seats, which were arranged in a U-shape around the room's perimeter, some leaning on the tables in front of them, most unengaged in the prayer. One man walked around the room offering tea, some sipped from their bowl-shaped cups, and others distracted themselves with small activities at their tables.

Although there was not much of a focal point of attention in this informal atmosphere, when the leader reached particular junctures in the service, the diffuse group suddenly joined together. They rose to their feet simultaneously. They answered *amen* in unison. And when the leader reached the central *shema* prayer, each man stopped whatever he was doing, covered his eyes, and joined the others, chanting together.

The men gathered in this synagogue had a deep and personal understanding of how the service unfolded, of what to expect, and how to behave. Yet this understanding was markedly different from the sort of knowledge imparted to me in the schools I had attended in the United States. In these frameworks, I had been taught to read the prayers, to understand their meanings, and to properly sing and chant the words. Most of the men in this synagogue, by contrast, had been unable to study religion in any institution. Rather than a formal knowledge of the prayer service, theirs was bodily, aesthetic, and communal.

This sort of knowledge can only be taught and learned through modeling, watching, and interacting. But in what sort of venue? The level of comfort and sense of givenness in the way this prayer service unfolded made it clear that those present must have been participating in services such as this one over the course of many years, even decades. Yet, this particular synagogue had only opened since the dissolution of the Soviet Union, two years earlier. Where, then, had they acquired their facility?

As is explained in the section that follows, the experience of prayer during the Soviet era had become intertwined with that of the *yushvo*. An inexorable part of Bukharan Jews' social life, this ritual of mourning and remembering is held primarily in the domestic sphere.

Yushvo Memorial Service

Among Bukharan Jews, the treatment of the deceased and the rites that surround the seven-day period of mourning (*shiva*) are carried out in much the same way as they are among most Jews around the world. Breaking from life's ordinary rhythm and social pattern, those closest to the deceased do not leave their homes during this period, do not change their clothes, go to work, shop, or prepare food for themselves. Neighbors, friends, and extended kin (who are not part of the closest circle of mourners) visit to offer comfort and to attend to the mourners' daily needs, preparing and serving them food, for example. Visits are also scheduled to coincide with the time of daily prayers so that mourners can recite the *kaddish* prayer amid the requisite quorum. Like Jews in most parts of the world, Bukharan Jews also mark the yearly anniversary of an individual's death. Each year, on that day, those who were closest to the deceased light a candle and recite the *kaddish* prayer. Among Bukharan Jews, the *yushvo*[15] (also referred to as *pominki,* or *azkara,*[16] depending on the geographical and historical context of the speaker) is added to these practices.

Whereas in the United States rituals of death and mourning are carried out as affairs that are relatively cut off from the everyday flow of life, among Bukharan Jews they are a common element of social life. The *yushvo,* in particular, is tightly woven into the fabric of daily living, and throughout my research I received many invitations to attend such events. Among approximately twenty in which I participated—some in Uzbekistan and others with immigrants in Israel and in the United States—was one in Samarkand, in Nina's home.

The date was February 18, 1997, which coincided with Adar 12, the day on the Hebrew calendar on which Nina's grandfather, Nerio, had passed away twenty-two years before. Although more than two decades had intervened, a *yushvo* was still held in his honor each year. This year, Nerio's son Ilya (who held primary responsibility for arranging the event) asked his niece Nina if she would hold it in her house.[17] She had agreed, and her home bustled with excitement throughout the day.

Crates of soft drinks, vodka, fruits, vegetables, and meat were brought in; food was prepared; and tables were arranged in a U-shape around the perimeter of the family's spacious living room. Ilya stood watch, orchestrating and organizing the activities. By the evening, Nina and Ilya's wife

FIGURE 8.2
Family gathered in their home at the conclusion of a *yushvo,* Bukhara, 1993
Photographer: Gregory Maniouk. Courtesy of Alanna E. Cooper

had completed setting the tables with small plates of raisins and sugar cubes, meant to "sweeten the sadness of loss," as well as with apples, oranges, and grapes, and platters of radishes and pickled tomatoes. Finally, pots of tea were dispersed.

The arrangement of the tables and chairs was typical for large social events, including those I attended among Muslims. Most striking, it echoed that found in Uzbekistan's synagogues, where the chairs and long tables were also arranged in a U-shape, with a single row reserved for community leaders and rabbis, who faced the rest of the room. Here in Nina's home, this row was set aside for the community dignitaries who would preside over the *yushvo.* In the synagogue, this prominent row of seats is generally broken in the center by the *aron kodesh* (holy ark) that holds the Torah. In Nina's home, there was no ark. However, in the spot where it would have been situated had this been a synagogue, a portrait of the deceased was hung.

In the late afternoon, just as the preparations were completed, the guests began to arrive. Family members, extended relatives, and community friends filed into the seats. This event, like the first synagogue service in which I had taken part in Bukhara in 1993, was primarily for men. The handful of women who did attend were seated toward the back of the room, at the tips of the "U."

The event began with *minha*, the afternoon prayer service. Throughout this portion of the *yushvo*, the guests participated, rising to their feet simultaneously and responding *amen* together at certain junctures in the service. But like the service I had observed in Bukhara, most were without prayer books, did not recite the words of the prayers, and relied on one of the men presiding over the *yushvo* to carry the prayers. Following this first portion of the evening, a series of activities took place: the recitation of sections from the Zohar, the *hashkava* (rest-in-peace prayer), toasts over vodka, speeches, and *ma'ariv* (the evening service) were interlaced with an elaborate meal, served in many courses.

In his doctoral dissertation on Bukharan Jewish customs as they were practiced in the nineteenth century, Baruch Moshavi's discussion of the *yushvo* sounds strikingly similar to this one, held in memory of Nerio.[18] He describes a well-orchestrated set of activities, which integrated prayer, remembrance, religious lessons, and feasting. The ceremony was held every evening during the first week after someone died, on the one-year anniversary after the individual's passing, and on that same date each subsequent year. In addition, during the entire first year of mourning, a *yushvo* was held each month on the day of the month that the person had passed away. For example, if a person had died on the fifteenth of the month, a *yushvo* was held in his or her honor on the fifteenth of each month during the entire first year of mourning. Not included in Moshavi's description is a practice that seems to have evolved during the Soviet era: throughout the first month of mourning, the ritual came to be held every week on the day that the person had passed away. For example, if a person had passed away on a Tuesday, a *yushvo* came to be held every Tuesday during the first month of mourning.

Across much of the Jewish world, prayer services are held in the home of the deceased's close family members during their first week of mourning. In his book *When a Jew Dies*, Samuel Heilman notes the psychological significance of bringing the prayer service into the home of the mourners (rather than having them attend the synagogue to recite the *kaddish* prayer during this period). He explains, "Some of the rabbis

. . . argued that by remaining indoors, the bereaved would be less likely to be 'diverted' from their mourning by the world's attractions and concerns. They . . . believed that a rushed return to this-worldly life would rob them of their need to weep and come to terms with their spiritual loss."[19] In Uzbekistan, the practice of bringing the prayer service into the home of the mourners also served an important communal function.

Although the Soviets restricted prayer in the synagogue, they did little to monitor or ban rituals of mourning that took place in the domestic sphere. In the event that a particular *yushvo* was subject to surveillance, its religious components could be easily concealed. Prayer served to structure the event, but the elaborate meal and toasts to the deceased did so as well. In addition, most of the attendees did not hold prayer books, making their religious activity difficult to detect. Finally, the officiating leaders often used the *yushvo* as a forum to deliver religious instructions and teachings about an upcoming Jewish holiday, or to express ideas about the weekly Torah portion. However, these aspects could also be omitted in the eulogies for the deceased that addressed their attributes and accomplishments, which need not have been construed as religious.

In all my discussions about the *yushvo,* no one ever intimated that aspects of the service were consciously used as strategies to conceal those components which the Soviets might classify as "religious." Yet the complex weave of prayer and feasting, mourning and worshiping, and domestic activities and ritual generally reserved for the synagogue was a source of its resilience. Soviet authorities could close down synagogues, but they could not stop family members from remembering their loved ones. As a result, despite restrictions placed on institutional religion, the tradition of communal prayer was perpetuated. On account of one individual's death, family members and neighborhood friends gathered to pray together some twenty times during the course of one year. Multiply twenty by the number of deaths in a community per year, and add to that sum the annual services held for individuals who had passed away even decades before. The total number of death rites, ironically, yielded a vibrant and active prayer community.

My own participation in these *yushvo* services provided important context for making sense of the familial and informal quality of the synagogue service I attended during my first trip to Bukhara in 1993. Many of the men gathered at that service may not have been able to recite the prayers on their own, or understand their meaning. Likewise, they may not have related to their prayer experience as a fulfillment of the religious obligation, prescribed in Jewish legal codes and rabbinic texts. Yet, prayer was a regular part of life, and these men knew what to do when they came together for that purpose. They learned this primarily through the *yushvo*, amid family, friends, food, toasts, and reflections on the lives of those who had died. In this setting, the experience of prayer became deeply connected to the memories of particular individuals, and to domestic family space.

Weddings

Throughout the Soviet era, Central Asia's Jews—like their Muslim neighbors—celebrated their weddings in several stages, each designated by a separate event. The festivities generally began with the exchange of sweets between the family of the bride and groom to signify their engagement. Parties designed to solidify relationships between the two kin networks were then held, and a number of events were arranged to prepare the bride and groom for the wedding. This string of celebratory affairs culminated with the wedding ceremony itself: the civil ceremony, which was implemented during the Soviet era, and the religious ceremony referred to as *qiddush* by Jews and as *nikoh* by Muslims.[20]

This section describes two events in the long procession of Jewish wedding festivities: the *qosh-chinon* (removal of the brow), which belongs to the process of preparing the bride for the wedding, and the *qiddush*. Unlike the preceding discussions about prayer and about keeping kosher, in this section the term *localized* is not used to refer to the way in which Judaism was experienced as intimately linked to local community life. Rather, the emphasis here is on the ways in which the practices of Bukharan Jews were shaped in response to local cultural, social, political, and economic circumstances.

THE *QIDDUSH*

In 1993, at the end of her senior year of high school, Anna married Amnon. Both were immigrants from Uzbekistan. Anna had arrived in the United States two years before, and Amnon had come as a child in the

1970s. I, along with Anna's other teachers at Torah Academy High School in New York, were among the very few attendees at the wedding who were not Bukharan Jewish immigrants.

The event was held in a nondescript American synagogue. In this setting, the chiffon and flowers that festooned the hall were unremarkable, as was Anna's white gown and Amnon's suit. Yet these typical American trappings belied the features of the event that were to follow. When the ceremony got under way, I took a seat, pulled out a pen and my small notebook, and furiously began to record those aspects that were foreign to me, and which I assumed to be "Central Asian." Though I had not yet taken my first trip to the region, by the end of the ceremony I believed I had a clear picture of the way Bukharan Jews celebrated their weddings prior to their great migration. I learned later that I could not have been more wrong.

A festive air prevailed in the hall as the guests arrived, the women bedecked in shiny dresses and the men in suits and colorful ties. They filled the sanctuary in a slow, loud, disorderly manner until a man in a tuxedo—the master of ceremonies—ascended the podium and called the crowd to order. Once the guests took their seats, he welcomed everyone and announced that the ceremony was about to begin. In a loud, dramatic voice of a game-show host, he asked that the members of the audience turn around in their seats to face the back of the room. *Now let us warmly acknowledge the families of the bride and groom!* A curtain was lifted to reveal a small crowd of smiling aunts, uncles, brothers, sisters, and grandparents, and the audience applauded with exuberance. As the curtain was lowered, a keyboard player, who was situated at the front of the room near the *huppah* (wedding canopy), began to play, and the atmosphere grew more boisterous. Family members emerged from behind the curtain one by one, and the master of ceremonies announced the name of each, as well as their relationship to the bride or groom. The audience responded with applause as each individual proceeded down the aisle. Finally, some forty had gathered at the front of the room, all hovering around the *huppah*, freely milling about and chatting with one another.

When the religious segment of the ceremony was about to begin, an American rabbi took over from the master of ceremonies, and asked all those present to become quiet. The noise level dropped slightly, but informality prevailed, as a slow crescendo of noise came from the audience and from those surrounding the *huppah*. Other than the carnival atmosphere, this next part of the ceremony resembled all the other Jewish weddings I had seen: it included the reading of the *ketubah* (marriage document), the chanting of the blessings, and the formula the groom was directed to recite. Finally—like other Jewish weddings—a glass was placed under the groom's foot and he broke it, bringing the ceremony to an end.

In the winter following Anna and Amnon's wedding, I took my first trip to Uzbekistan. During that month of research, I was invited to many *yushvo* mourning services, and was surprised by the ubiquitous nature of the ritual. By contrast, I found no Jewish weddings to attend. In the midst of mass migration, as people watched their community and neighborhood life crumble, few were interested in starting new families. The idea of marriage in Central Asia at that moment in history was not only existentially unsettling, but it also posed a pragmatic challenge. In contemplating the possibility of marrying off their children, parents had to consider the fact that the in-laws might resettle somewhere far away and take the children with them. Nineteen-year-old Dima, for example, pined for Lena, often speaking of his desire to marry her. Dima's older sister, however, had already immigrated to Israel, which is where his own parents planned to resettle. In the meantime, Lena and her parents were waiting to receive immigration documents from the United States. Neither set of parents would consider allowing their children to marry.

That is not to say that none of Uzbekistan's Jews married in the 1990s. Indeed, during subsequent trips to Uzbekistan, I did learn about a number of Bukharan Jewish weddings and managed to obtain invitations to attend a few parties. Unlike the *yushvo* ritual, however, these were few and far between. In addition, many were held privately and quietly. Among the string of events held in conjunction with each wedding, the *qiddush* was the most closed of all. While a lively, loud, and open atmosphere prevailed at Anna and Amnon's *qiddush* ceremony in New York, in Uzbekistan these events were small, private, quiet affairs where outsiders were most unwelcome. I was lucky to have discovered a single one to attend.

In the summer of 1994 I spent a few weeks in Samarkand with a small film crew, collecting footage for a documentary on Bukharan

Jews.[21] Sasha, a young local Bukharan Jew who served as an assistant to the crew, learned of a wedding scheduled to take place while we were there, and secured permission for us to attend.

We arrived at the groom's house in the late afternoon, while family members were working in the courtyard to set up tables, string lights, and arrange the sound system. Over the next couple of hours, we watched the courtyard grow crowded as the guests trickled in and milled about. At dusk, the loud bellowing call of the *karnai* horn was sounded, indicating the arrival of the bride and groom. The guests rushed outside to greet them and encircled the pair, singing and dancing. The groom carried the bride around a bonfire situated at the threshold of the home.[22] Once the couple entered the courtyard and took their seats, food was served, vodka was poured, music played, and the guests celebrated.

After hours of eating, dancing, and drinking had passed, the marriage ceremony had yet to take place. Close to midnight, the guests began to say good-bye and started leaving. The musicians packed and left. The tables were cleared and dismantled. The colorful padded blankets were taken off the benches, folded, and stacked. The courtyard was now empty and the small film crew and I found ourselves alone among the closest family members of the bride and groom. The rabbi who would conduct the ceremony was scheduled to arrive at any moment, so we waited, standing apart from the wedding party, quietly speaking among ourselves. Sasha explained that the groom had been divorced from his first wife only a few months previously, and that the bride was Russian, and not Jewish. Sasha did not know either one of them well, but in his opinion the couple made an unlikely pair. Intermarriage among Bukharan Jews in Central Asia was rare, but he suspected that this was not a love match. Rather, he conjectured, the bride was somehow using the groom—who was planning to emigrate shortly—to help her get to America. It was highly unusual for individuals who were not among the family's closest circle to attend the *qiddush* ceremony, Sasha explained. The bride's parents, however, were not Jewish, and did not know any better, which is why we had not been asked to leave.

At one o'clock in the morning, when the rabbi finally arrived, he walked across the courtyard and entered the house. The small wedding party trailed behind him, and quietly gathered in the room where the *qiddush* would take place. A few elements of the short ceremony were familiar to me: the signing of the *ketubah,* the blessings chanted by the rabbi, and the formula recited by the groom. Other elements differed slightly from the mostly Ashkenazi Jewish weddings I had attended in the past: rather than a freestanding structure, the *huppah* was a prayer shawl held above the bride and groom by those present. And rather than breaking a glass at the end of the ceremony, the groom stomped on a plate.

A few of the practices I found utterly foreign. As the bride and groom took their positions under the prayer shawl, those assembled raised their hands overhead, and stretched their fingers open. Sasha whispered to me to do the same, and we all kept this posture throughout the ceremony. Meanwhile, the mother of the bride and the mother of the groom each took a needle and thread in hand, and positioned themselves behind the couple, the groom's mother behind her son, and the bride's mother behind her daughter. Throughout the ceremony, the mothers stitched their needles through the fabric of their children's clothing. Because the threads were not knotted at the end, they pulled through freely. Finally, the couple stood throughout the ceremony with their clothing open; the bride's dress unzipped, and the groom's shirt unbuttoned and belt buckle open.

When I asked about these elements of the wedding, I learned that they were typical. Bukharan Jews in Uzbekistan generally held their wedding ceremonies quietly, very late at night, and with only a very small group present. In addition, the outstretched arms, the needle through the clothing of the bride and groom, and the couple's open clothing were standard practices. Bukharan Jewish weddings held during the pre-Soviet era, however, were different. They did not take place late at night or in a secretive manner. Rather, they were typically held at dusk, following *minha* (the afternoon prayer service). The *qiddush* was conducted among many guests, and a festive party followed.[23]

There were, however, occasions when weddings held during the pre-Soviet era did not follow this pattern. Such was the case when there was a suspicion that a relative or community member harbored some ill will toward the family of the bride or groom. In these cases, energies were focused on contending with the possibility that an enemy might cast a spell upon the groom, rendering him impotent so that the marriage might never be consummated. When this sort of fear arose, the pre-Soviet ceremony—like the ceremony I had witnessed—would be held quietly, privately, and late at night.[24] And in cases where the fear was acute, two elderly women would pull threads through the clothing of the bride and groom during the *qiddush,* and all those present would be instructed to hold their hands overhead and stretch out their fingers.[25]

Sometime during the Soviet era, these practices—previously carried out only in unusual circumstances—became standard. In the process of this shift, the language Bukharan Jews used to explain them also changed. Baruch Moshavi's informants, who offered descriptions of weddings as they were held prior to the Soviet era, referred to these actions as warding off the groom's impotence, his loss of vigor, and the possibility of his becoming *kashur* (tied). By contrast, Bukharan Jewish men and women who discussed the topic of *qiddush* with me in the 1990s did not refer to the groom's sexuality. Rather, they addressed the fear that someone present might be concealing their true thoughts, wishes, or intentions. Some did allude to the notion that such a person might wish ill upon the couple and attempt to "cast a spell." More often, though, people suggested that the bride and groom opened their clothing during the ceremony so that luck would easily come upon them; the guests' hands should be outstretched so that the couple's life together would be "open"; and the threads should be unknotted so that things for them would be "free" and "easy."

The distinction between the nineteenth-century language and the language developed during Soviet rule points to the ways in which situational concerns work to structure ritual elements. Likewise, the difference between the quiet, closed wedding I witnessed in Uzbekistan (the form of which seems to have been a holdover from the Soviet era) and Anna and Amnon's boisterous and open wedding in the United States points to the ways in which local circumstances shape practice.

In Soviet Central Asia, where members of the Bukharan Jewish community in each city and town were all able to trace some sort of kinship relationship to everyone else, all were involved in some way in each other's business. In this social context, where there was no anonymity and little room to escape the watchful gaze of community and family, the possibilities for gossip and feuds were high, and the consequences severe. It is not surprising, then, that an atmosphere of fear and danger might surround the ceremony in which the bride and groom—and their two respective families—were joined.

FIGURE 8.3
Celebration after civil wedding ceremony, Samarkand, 1992
Photographer: Misha Heifitz. Courtesy of Alanna E. Cooper

During the Soviet era, this sort of fear became more pronounced and concrete as civil authorities attempted to supplant the religious ceremony with a civil one. "Palaces of Culture" were erected for the civil registration of life-cycle events (including marriage and the birth of a child). These buildings also served as social halls to house parties held in conjunction with civil ceremonies, and Soviet authorities scripted rituals for these occasions.[26] Jews, like their Muslim neighbors, incorporated the civil ceremony (referred to as ZAGS)[27] into the long string of events surrounding their weddings. Yet the ZAGS never came to replace the religious wedding. Frustrated by the local population's "traditionalism," the authorities looked for ways to eradicate the religious ceremony. In 1967, one ethnographer writing for the establishment explained, "The fact that the civil registration has become common in the Uzbek SSR, becoming a constituent event of the traditional wedding, is a great achievement. But it could become still more important and supplant the *nikoh*."[28]

The Jews' response to these social policies and attitudes was to go underground with their religious ceremonies. Even then, the fear of surveillance and suspicion that someone present might be posing or harboring secrets was pervasive. The outstretched hands, the unknotted threads, the open clothing—once linked to anxieties about the groom's sexual potency—turned into measures to ward off the ill will of those whose loyalties might be misplaced.

For Bukharan Jewish immigrants in their new homes, the concerns are markedly different. In the United States and Israel, where old community ties have been ruptured as a result of splintering migration patterns, the net of social relationships has been pulled across wide areas and stretched thin. In this context, people's worries do not stem from the consequences of thickly intertwined relationships, which can often put relatives at odds with one another. Nor are they situated in fears associated with evading the civil authorities. Instead, worries are linked to the loss of the powerful social safety nets that had been in place prior to immigration. Weddings, then, become an opportunity to bring together relatives who may no longer be in close contact. Likewise, they serve as a rare opportunity to introduce the families of the bride and groom, who may not know each other at all. The game-show style, in which the master of ceremonies introduces each family member, allows the guests to become acquainted with the new kin network of which they are now a part.

THE QOSH-CHINON

In the spring of 1997, nineteen-year-old Irina had her facial hair manicured for the first time. Her eyebrows were shaped, the hair between them removed, the sides of her face cleaned of their dark wisps, and the strands above her upper lip plucked. This depilation and beautification was done a few days prior to her *qiddush* ceremony, in the presence of a large gathering of women friends and relatives, at a festive party replete with music, food, and dancing. Irina and her groom—twenty-one-year-old Yisrael—were born and raised in Bukhara. Their families, who had known each other for many years, were shortly moving to Israel, and the parents had encouraged the couple to marry prior to their migration.

I arrived at the home of the bride's parents in the late morning. Only a few elderly women were there, gathered in the courtyard. I chatted with them while the food was being distributed on the tables and the

FIGURE 8.4
Qosh-chinon performed on a Bukharan Jewish bride, Samarkand, 1994
Courtesy of Alanna E. Cooper

keyboard player arranged his equipment. Some played the *doyra*[29] and sang. In the meantime, the couple was at a government building, where their civil marriage ceremony was taking place. Upon its conclusion, the bride and her women friends and relatives who had been present at the ZAGS made their way to her parents' home. When other women in the *mahalla* heard the music and fanfare announcing the bride's arrival, they made their way to the family courtyard as well.

A total of some eighty guests assembled, mostly women, with a few close male relatives. Food was served, music played, and the guests danced. Irina's father spoke into the microphone. "We are here to celebrate the creation of a new family. We wish the bride and groom much happiness and a long life together." Trays with tiny glasses of sugary tea were passed around. "This is so their lives together will be sweet," a guest explained while handing me a glass.

After several hours of festivities, Irina left the courtyard, went into the house, and took off the Western-style white wedding gown she had donned earlier that day for the ZAGS ceremony. She emerged in a bright dress made from a colorful silk material known as Uzbekistan's "national textile." This change seemed to signify that Irina was leaving behind the Soviet-imposed segment of her wedding in preparation for a ritual that had been in place among the local population long before the arrival of the Russians. Irina made her way to a seat set in the middle of the courtyard, ushered by women family members. The music grew louder and the cosmetician, hired for the event, approached her. The other women crowded around, while the men who were present milled about the periphery of the courtyard.

The cosmetician wrapped a scarf around Irina's head, patted her face with powder, and pulled out a string. She moved back and forth, twisting the string and pulling it to pluck her facial hairs. While she worked, Irina's women relatives took turns standing behind her. One by one they held the bride's head, gave her a blessing, and then placed a few bills in her scarf, which were later turned over to the cosmetician as payment for her services. A few men, too, including Irina's father and her groom, took turns holding the bride's head. When the process was complete, Irina was handed a mirror, a scarf was draped over her, and she was given a few private moments to look at herself.

A variety of approaches can be taken to understand the purpose and meaning of this event. Baruch Moshavi explains that the *qosh-chinon*—as conducted in the pre-Soviet era—was followed by the bride's immersion in the *mikveh*. The proximity and order of the events suggest that the bride's hair depilation may have been linked to the cleaning of her body before her immersion in the ritual waters.

Another approach situates the practice in its local context. Jews in Central Asia—like their Muslim neighbors—often have thick, dark hair apparent on the upper lip and between the eyebrows. Jewish girls, like their Muslim counterparts, are taught that they must not manicure their facial hair until they become women. Within the local symbol system—which cuts across religious communities—this hair serves as a mark of girlhood, whereas a smooth, clean face serves as a mark of womanhood. The passage from one life stage to the next is understood to occur through marriage. Among Jews, the *qosh-chinon* ceremony, held just a few days before the *qiddush,* publicly inscribes this status transition on the body.

This rich cluster of local symbols is even more complex when it is understood in relationship to status transitions associated with mourning. During the entire year after the loss of a close relative, many of the Bukharan Jewish women I met in Uzbekistan (as well as many immigrants) refrained from buying new clothing, from putting on makeup, from getting their hair cut, and from having their facial hair removed. At the end of the year, these women would mark their coming out of mourning by organizing a party called *sogh-buroron*.[30] At two such events I attended, the friends and relatives of the women coming out of mourning joined them in their respective homes. The hostess of each (who was coming out of mourning) served a meal, and the guests delivered speeches and toasts, similar to the *yushvo* (though without the prayer services). In addition, the hostess sat down with a cosmetician, surrounded by her guests, who gathered to watch as she had her facial hair manicured. In this moving ceremony, the woman undergoes a physical change, as she is ushered out of her status as a mourner. Likewise, hosting the event signifies her return to aspects of her social role from which she had taken a hiatus. In a succinct expression of this transformation, one woman toasted her friend whose year of mourning had ended, exclaiming, "We welcome her back!"

In this complex of symbols, unruly hair does not belong to the world of girlhood alone. More generally, it belongs to those who are at the margins of society, either because they are not yet adult, or because they are in mourning and temporarily take leave of their regular social roles. Upon marriage, girls become women and enter the adult social world. Likewise, adult women who finish their year of mourning return to their regular roles and are subjected to the social world's taming norms. For both, the manicuring of facial hair signifies this transition.

Among Jews in other parts of the world, the *qosh-chinon* (like the *sogh-buroron*) might be classified as an idiosyncratic ritual, in that it is carried out by Jews in this particular geographic region alone. Likewise, the practice of holding religious wedding ceremonies quietly, late at night, with open clothing, outstretched hands, and unknotted threads, is particular to Jewish life in this region. In these rituals, what separates Bukharan Jews from other Jews is precisely that which connects them to the society and culture in which they lived. Developed in the local context, they shed light on the ties that bound the Jews to the Soviet, Turko-Persian Muslim society and culture of which they were a part.

Transmission of Identity

In 1998, nineteen-year-old Dima left Samarkand and moved to Israel. Shortly after he arrived, he met Nadya, who had also immigrated without her family. They fell in love, moved in together, and within a year Nadya gave birth to a baby boy.

She herself was born and raised in Russia, considered herself Russian (as opposed to Jewish), and aside from her one Jewish grandparent, had little if any connection to Jewish religion and culture. Although Dima's parents had always assumed he would marry someone Bukharan Jewish and that he would have a Bukharan Jewish wedding, they accepted the new course his life had taken. His mother, Dora, traveled from her home in Samarkand to spend several weeks with the couple in Israel after the baby's birth.

Shortly after arriving in the country, Dora called and invited me to her grandson's circumcision. I took the trip to Or Yehuda (from Jerusalem, where I was living) to visit with the family and attend the event. It was held in a small rented hall, a multicourse dinner was served, and

Dima and Nadya's friends danced to popular Israel and Russian music. In the middle of the party, a Bukharan Jewish rabbi arrived, performed the circumcision ceremony, said a few words of congratulations, and left. I was puzzled by the affair. Because Israeli civil law as well as *halakhah* (religious law) stipulate that Judaism is transmitted matrilineally, I wondered about the circumstances under which the rabbi had agreed to perform circumcision, and was curious about how the family members viewed the baby's identity.

Dora told me that when the rabbi was hired to conduct the circumcision, he had asked no questions about the baby's parents' identity. As for herself, Dora understood the baby to be Jewish. *I know the Israeli government does not view him as Jewish.* But as far as she was concerned, he was. *His father is Jewish; he is Jewish too,* she told me. Dora's view of Jewish identity transmission, which was shaped by cultural norms prevalent in Soviet Central Asia, not only runs counter to Israeli state law, but runs counter to notions that have prevailed (until recently)[31] in almost every part of the Jewish world.

Structure of Jewish Identity in Soviet Central Asia

Although Soviet policies were devised to eradicate Judaism as a religion, Jewishness as a cultural or ethnic identity was legitimized, marked, and in some periods and regions even celebrated. Jews were defined as one of the Soviet Union's myriad ethnic groups labeled as "nationalities." Like members of all other Soviet nationality groups, they were viewed as belonging to an objectively defined, ontological social category, and Jewishness was understood to be a biologically transmitted identity that could neither be chosen nor suppressed.

Within this system, Jewish identity was inscribed as an individual's "nationality" on his or her civil documents regardless of the republic in which he or she resided. Jews who were citizens of Uzbekistan were not classified as "Uzbeks" by nationality. Rather, they were classified as "Jews," like Jews who resided in all other republics of the Soviet Union. Likewise, Ukrainians who lived in Uzbekistan, for example, were considered citizens of Uzbekistan, but Ukrainian by nationality.[32]

As this system of classification became entrenched, Bukharan Jews came to view their religious identity (as Jews) and their civil identity (as Jews) as one and the same. This conception of identity came to be so taken for granted that when I told people that I was American, many assumed this meant I was not Jewish, and were incredulous to learn that I could be both.

In a particularly interesting conversation, Yura—a Bukharan Jewish man whom I met in Samarkand in 1997—explained what he believed to be the difference between the way American Jews and Bukharan Jews understand the structure of Jewish identity. "According to your faith," Yura explained to me, "you are Jewish. But according to your passport, you are a citizen of America. So when you are at home, you are a Jew. But when you go on the street, you think that you are just a citizen of America." The structure of identity among Bukharan Jews, Yura explained, "is not like that." He continued, "Among us, at home you are a Jew and on the street you are a Jew. . . . in every situation you are a Jew."

In this statement, Yura noted a distinction between my state-assigned identity (American), and my identity as derived from belonging to a religious community (Jewish). He distinguishes this from the way in which identity is structured among Bukharan Jews. Their Jewish identity as defined by the state is experienced as one and the same as their identity derived from their belonging to a religious community.

Transmission of Jewish Identity in Soviet Central Asia

The internal passport of all Soviet citizens defined and inscribed their personal identity, and included the individual's "name, time and place of birth, authorized domicile," as well as his or her "nationality," which was calculated through the parents.[33] In cases of mixed parentage, authorities were instructed to give preference to the nationality of the child's mother.[34] In Central Asia, however, the unofficial rules differed. In this region, where the majority of the population is Muslim, religious identity is transmitted patrilineally. The patriline is also given preference in residence patterns. When a woman married, she generally went to live in her husband's courtyard with his family. Her children, therefore, would grow up in their father's house, governed by the rules of their father's kin. Children, in this sense, belonged to their father's family rather than their mother's. Not surprisingly, Central Asians' Soviet-ascribed nationality (such as Uzbek and Tajik) was also understood to be transmitted through the father's line. Although calculating nationality through the father was not instituted as official policy in Central Asia, it did become the prevailing norm.

Bukharan Jews also accepted the notion that nationality is transmitted patrilineally. Hence, they understood a child's Jewish national identity—as assigned by the State—to be derived from the child's father's Jewish identity. For Bukharan Jews, this meant that an individual who was the child of a Jewish father and a non-Jewish mother was classified as "Jewish," according to his or her nationality. This method of reckoning national identity came to overlap with the way in which Jews reckoned the transmission of their religious identity. The fact that their Muslim neighbors traced their religious identity through the patriline reinforced this conception of identity transmission.

When Dora welcomed her grandson into the world, she understood his identity through the prism of the Soviet system and the norms prevalent among the dominant population in Uzbekistan. And so, despite the fact that she was in Israel and she knew that the religious and civil authorities there did not recognize the newborn as Jewish, she viewed him as Jewish regardless of his mother's non-Jewish status.

Jewishness and Bukharan Jewishness

Bukharan Jews' understandings of their Jewish identity were also shaped by their experience of separation from Jews in other parts of the world during the Soviet period. In Israel and the United States, Bukharan Jews are regarded as one "brand" of Jews within a multiethnic Jewish world. Museum exhibits, folk festivals, cookbooks, films, and popular magazines highlight the "ethnic" qualities of this group: their special music, dance, cuisine, language, and dress. Indeed, in late nineteenth-century Ottoman Palestine, Central Asia's Jews also emphasized their ethnic distinctiveness as a means to justify the building of their own neighborhood, schools, and printing press in Jerusalem.[35]

During the Soviet era, however, contacts between Bukharan Jews in Central Asia and other Jewish groups were severed. Confined in Central Asia, they began to compare themselves to the only other Jews they knew: local Ashkenazi Jews, most of whom arrived in Central Asia during World War II, after escaping or being evacuated out of their homes in Eastern Europe.[36] Unlike themselves, these Jews tended to be structurally and culturally assimilated into Uzbekistan's Russian population.

In comparing themselves to Ashkenazi Jews, Central Asia's Bukharan Jews did not distinguish themselves by pointing to particular ethnic customs or traditions. Rather, they tended to characterize themselves as "real Jews," because they continued to practice Judaism and to strongly identify as Jews throughout the Soviet era, whereas Ashkenazi Jews—the Central Asian Jews say—are not *chistiye evrei;* that is, they are not pure Jews. Indeed, one Central Asian Jewish teenager told me that growing up she had always thought that the literal translation of "Ashkenazi Jew" was "half-Jew."

This distinction between Central Asia's Bukharan Jews and Ashkenazi Jews is clearly expressed in the low rates of intermarriage between them.[37] It is also articulated in Uzbekistan's Jewish cemeteries, where Ashkenazi Jews are buried in a separate section. While I was touring the Jewish cemetery in Bukhara in 1998, one man explained to me that just as people who commit suicide are buried separately, so, too, are Ashkenazi Jews. Indeed, religious prescriptions stipulate that individuals who have broken in some way with the community can only be buried along the margins of the Jewish cemetery. According to this explanation, Ashkenazi Jews and Bukharan Jews are not regarded as separate but equal Jewish ethnic groups. Rather, Ashkenazi Jews are classified as a distinct group by virtue of the fact that they have *broken with* that which is viewed as the "normative" Jewish community.

These notions about the contours of Jewish identity, like their localized versions of Jewish ritual, developed in the context of Bukharan Jews' separation from Jewish communities in other parts of the world. When the Soviet Union dissolved in 1991, these ideas and practices underwent dramatic change. The next chapter explores how.

NINE

International Jewish Organizations Encounter Local Jewish Community Life

When the Soviet Union dissolved, emigration restrictions lifted and the Jews of Central Asia (like those in the rest of the Soviet Union) began leaving en masse. By 1993, the first time I visited Uzbekistan, the Bukharan Jewish population, which had numbered approximately 35,000 in 1989, had already been reduced to about half that size. In Tajikistan, the rate of emigration was even more dramatic. Following civil war there, the Bukharan Jewish population was reduced from approximately 15,000 to 2,000.[1]

As immigrants from the USSR began pouring into Israel and the United States, the exuberance that had fueled the Struggle for Soviet Jewry movement was redirected. Whereas Israeli and American Jews had worked to aid Jewish *refuseniks* during the Soviet era, their energies and monies were now rechanneled toward assisting them in their resettlement process. This project had two dimensions. It involved helping the immigrants adjust to their new lives by working with them on language learning, professional retraining, and navigating bureaucracies. It also involved providing them with a formal Jewish education, which had been denied to them under Soviet rule. Here we return to the story of Torah Academy with which this book opened.

Torah Academy was founded by ultra-Orthodox Ashkenazi Jews in order to instill the "basic bedrock of belief" in students who had come to the United States supposedly "devoid of everything and anything Jewish."[2] In its effort to reconnect Bukharan Jews to their religious roots and to the Jewish People, Torah Academy was not alone. Many other institutions with similar goals, including schools, synagogue programs, youth groups, and summer camps, were established in the cities and towns where Soviet émigrés—Bukharan Jewish among them—were resettling.

Such institutions were also set up in areas of the former Soviet Union where Jews still remained. Taking advantage of new religious freedoms and possibilities for unrestricted travel into the newly independent states, many nonprofit Jewish organizations established operations in situ to teach those who had not yet immigrated (or who had no plans to immigrate). In Uzbekistan, these organizations included the Jewish Agency for Israel (Zionist), Bnei Akiva (religious Zionist), Chabad-Lubavitch (ultra-Orthodox), the Joint Distribution Committee (nonsectarian welfare), and Midrash Sephardi. Although these organizations differ widely in their ideological views about Judaism and Jewish Peoplehood, their work in Uzbekistan has been driven by a common desire to reunite Jews who had long been disconnected from the Jewish world.

What was the nature of the interactions between representatives of these international Jewish organizations and the local Jewish population? And what sort of impact did they have on local Jewish understandings and practices? Thus far, we have explored two historical encounters between Central Asia's Jews and Jewish emissaries from other parts of the world, one facilitated by Yosef Maman in the late eighteenth century, and the other by Shlomo Lev Eliezerov on the heels of Russian colonialism at the end of the nineteenth century. With the dissolution of the Soviet Union, I was presented with an opportunity that simply had not been available to me in the study of these previous encounters: I was able to watch this one unfold.

Traveling between Uzbekistan, Israel, and the United States, I collected information about the emissary organizations through discussions with those who worked in their headquarters (in the United States and Israel) as well as with those who were stationed in Uzbekistan, where they worked directly with local Bukharan Jews. In addition to conducting formal interviews and holding informal conversations with these emissaries, I also observed and took part in their classes, seminars, religious rituals, and holiday events. Looking at the work of these organizations from the local perspective, I discussed with Bukharan Jews themselves their impressions of the emissaries, their organizations, their work, and the changes they had initiated.

Just as the ethnographic approach differed from the research methods I had used to study previous encounters, so, too, the sorts of questions and issues addressed here differ. Whereas the eighteenth-century reunion was analyzed from a historiographic perspective, and the nineteenth-century one focused on contestation between local and global forms of religious institutional authority, this chapter draws on discussions I had with common people about their ideas, understandings, and feelings about the changes in which they were taking part at this very dramatic juncture in history. These conversations, which gave me insight into individuals' perceptions of their own experiences, form the basis of the intimate and personal accounts that follow.

The chapter is divided into two sections. The first explores the structure of two emissary organizations that established outfits in Uzbekistan after the Soviet Union dissolved, the people who worked in them, their goals, and their methods of teaching. The second explores how the locals responded to these encounters.

A final preliminary note: the sorts of interactions that unfolded between the locals and the emissary organizations differed in each city. In Bukhara, for example, Midrash Sephardi played a dominant role, while the influence of Chabad-Lubavitch was almost nonexistent. In Samarkand, on the other hand, Chabad-Lubavitch continued to have a strong presence from the turn of the last century (with the arrival of Shlomo Lev Eliezerov) through the Soviet era, and its influence was strengthened further after the dissolution of the Soviet Union. To provide an intimate picture of the impact that emissary organizations had upon local understandings of Judaism, I have chosen to focus here on one particular city.

Analysis of events in Samarkand at the turn of the last century (in chapter 7) drew attention to the ways in which traditional and modern aspects of community life intersected. This legacy has remained a powerful one. In the 1990s, when I conducted my research, the Jewish *mahalla* was still well populated, considered a Jewish space, and understood to have a historical connection to the traditional Jewish community that lived there in the pre-tsarist era. At the same time, Jewish life in the new city was also vibrant. There was a synagogue in both the new city and the old city, Jewish classes were held in each area, and people traveled freely between them. It was in Samarkand—where the new and the old exist side by side—that I found conversations about Judaism to be the most complex and interesting, and these form the basis of this chapter.

Emissary Organizations and the Unraveling of Jewish Identity

Since the dissolution of the Soviet Union, Central Asia's Jews' localized understandings of their Jewish identity have been thrown wide open, and have been subjected to the disembedding forces of globalization. This rupture of the tight link between place and identity is first and foremost due to massive emigration. Within a decade after the flood of migration began, almost all of Central Asia's Bukharan Jews had left their homes, having moved primarily to the United States and to Israel. Now family groups and communities that were once tightly knit and grounded in a common space are scattered and dispersed from one another.[3]

For those who remained behind, occupying the same homes and neighborhoods they had prior to the dissolution of the USSR, the link between place and identity has also come undone.[4] With kinship ties and friendships stretched across oceans, their sense of "home" has been torn asunder. Through letters, telephone calls, and visits, those left behind remain in close touch with their friends and family members who have immigrated. No longer sealed off from contact with the wider Jewish world, their long-held ideas of what it means to be Jewish and what it means to be "Bukharan Jewish" are challenged by what goes on abroad. More immediate, however, are the challenges posed by Jewish emissaries who come to Uzbekistan from abroad in an effort to reshape the locals' understanding of their Jewishness.

The discussion that follows focuses on the Jewish Agency for Israel and Chabad-Lubavitch, two organizations that have had a particularly strong presence in Samarkand. It addresses these groups' efforts to introduce abstract and global definitions of Judaism into a system of highly localized understandings.

Jewish Agency for Israel

In the weeks before Passover (1997), 2,600 boxes of matza shipped from Moscow made their way to Samarkand. Two days before the holiday, with well over 1,000 boxes still remaining in the synagogue (where they were being sold), it appeared that someone had grossly overestimated the amount that Samarkand's Jews would consume. Perhaps the carefully kept transaction log would allow for a more accurate estimate the following year.

One of the Chabad-Lubavitch emissaries who had overseen the shipment and delivery of the matza told me about this log, suggesting that it might provide me with an accurate account of Samarkand's Jewish population. With the exception of the few families who still made matza in their homes (as they had done during the Soviet era, when factory-manufactured matza could not be sold or purchased),[5] Samarkand's Jews could only obtain this ritual holiday food in the synagogue. This meant that the name of every person in the city who purchased matza was recorded in the log, alongside the number of boxes that each person bought for his or her household.

I spent a sunny afternoon in the synagogue courtyard going over the list with the man conducting the sales. With no copying machine on hand, he carefully read each handwritten line with me, which I then recorded into my own notebook. A total of 257 Bukharan Jews had bought 864 boxes, and a total of 144 Ashkenazi Jews had bought 375 boxes. Could a correlation be drawn between these numbers and the number of Jews in the city?

A few days later, I went to discuss with Mikhael Chulpayev what I had learned in the synagogue, guessing he might offer a different perspective on the matter. Posters and Israeli flags were tacked on the walls of the one-story structure where he works; these items advertise his organization as a Zionist institution, meant to strengthen the local Jews' connections to the State of Israel. The kitchen sink in one of the classrooms, and the tub in the bathroom offer evidence that the property had only recently been renovated from what had been a home. It now serves as the offices of the Jewish Agency for Israel. Indeed, the institution over which Mikhael presides had been established in Samarkand only a few years earlier, and its geographical coordinates carry no historical significance for the Jewish community.

Likewise, Mikhael himself has no background in communal leadership. Only a few years before he came to sit behind his large, shiny wood desk, he worked in the Jewish Agency building as a maintenance man. His quick ascent to his current position was facilitated by his diligent

study of Hebrew (which he now speaks fluently) and his friendly disposition. More significant though, Mikhael's move from Jewish Agency
plumber to general manager was made possible by the high level of turn-
over in the institution's staff. As one of the organization's central purposes is to assist and encourage people to move to Israel, it is no surprise
that its employees, participants, and leaders are constantly leaving, and
positions always need to be filled. Finally, Mikhael's career trajectory
is testimony to the openness of the Jewish Agency. There is no clear
distinction between those who belong and those who do not, between
who is a leader and who is not. If there is an inner, elite core, it is a fleeting one, constantly in flux. These organizational qualities serve as apt
metaphors for the type of communal life the Jewish Agency has created:
one that is fluid and open, where boundaries that separate who is "in"
from who is "out" are not clearly defined.

As general manager, Mikhael is well aware of the goings-on in Jewish Samarkand, and I was curious to hear what he thought about the
numbers I had collected a few days earlier. *Do you think this data is helpful in estimating Samarkand's Jewish population?* I asked, showing him
the roster of matza purchasers compiled at the nearby synagogue. He
responded with an adamant "no," explaining that this list did not include
anyone who did not observe the holiday. Nor did it include anyone who
did not identify as a Jew.

How would one go about finding Jews who do not identify as Jews? I
asked him. *And if they don't identify as Jews,* I wondered out loud, *should
they be included at all?* These were complicated questions, to which Mikhael did not directly respond. Instead, he got up from his desk, walked
across the room, and unlocked a small safe. *This,* he told me as he removed a thin notebook with a soft cover, *will be much more helpful for
you.*

Flipping through the book, he arrived at the page on which an in-
termediate total had been recorded: it listed the names of 450 Bukharan
Jews and 350 Ashkenazi Jews. These numbers, though, still did not tell
the whole story—Mikhael was quick to point out—because the Jewish
Agency's population accounting was in flux, as always. On the one hand,
the names of those people who had emigrated in the past few weeks had
yet to be crossed out. On the other hand, the names of 300 people were
listed on forms that had recently been collected, but had yet to be entered

in the book. Most significant, though, was that there were still people who had not filled out data forms at all.[6]

"How will you find these people?" I asked him. *It won't be difficult to locate the Bukharan Jews,* Mikhael answered. As a Bukharan Jew who was born in Samarkand (as were his parents and grandparents), he was well connected to the city's tight-knit Bukharan Jewish network, and would have little trouble finding the individuals among them who had not yet filled out the forms. It was the Ashkenazi Jews—particularly those who did not identify—who posed a much more difficult problem, as the quality of their Jewishness is highly elusive. Some of them do not have "Jew" listed on their official documents, do not participate in any sort of Jewish communal activities, do not think of themselves as Jews, and have parents who do not consider themselves to be Jews. For Mikhael, however, these many obstacles posed no deterrent. As the local Jewish Agency representative, he viewed the task of identifying these people as one of his very raisons d'être, a first step toward strengthening their sense of belonging to the Jewish People, heightening their awareness of their connection to the State of Israel, and ultimately increasing the rate of migration to Israel. But who exactly are they?

THE LAW OF RETURN

The individuals listed in Mikhael's notebook are people who matter in the accounting of the Jewish Agency for Israel: those who are included in Israel's Law of Return. The earliest form of this law, which serves as the basis of Israel's immigration policy, was articulated in Israel's Declaration of Independence. In accord with its defining characteristic as a politically legitimate homeland for Jews wherever they reside, the new state was proclaimed to be "open to Jewish immigration, and for the ingathering of exiles."

In 1950, the Israeli parliament gave this statement legislative authority with its enactment of the Law of Return, which states that "Every Jew has the right to immigrate to the country."[7] In an impassioned speech, Prime Minister David Ben-Gurion declared that this legal clause was no mere civil creation. While it was necessary to pass such a law for bureaucratic reasons, in fact, it was simply an articulation of a natural truth. By naming it the Law of Return, the intention was to express the undeniable "historical bond between the fatherland and the nation." All Jews, Ben-Gurion explained, are foreigners when they are outside of Israel, and all have the right to "return home." This right, he continued, is a fundamental one. It "preceded the state of Israel" and upon it, the state was built.[8] In this framework, where the bonds between the land and the people were characterized as authentic, natural, and transparent, no definition of Jew was offered.

But to whom, exactly, does this "right of return" belong? And what happens when an individual demands citizenship on the basis of his or her Jewish identity, but there is no consensus that he or she is Jewish? Not many years would pass before this question would call for a well-defined response. The first and most famous such case to arise was that of Oswald Rufeisen. Born in Poland to Jewish parents, he converted to Catholicism during World War II, and was later ordained as Brother Daniel. In 1958, at the age of thirty-six, he arrived in Israel and applied for citizenship under the Law of Return, based on his understanding of himself as a Jew by nationality (separate from his religious identity as a Catholic). The government denied his application and Rufeisen filed a suit.

This case, as well as subsequent others, generated significant controversy surrounding the question of "who is a Jew," and led to discussion about who, exactly, is included in the Law of Return.[9] As a result of such debates, an amendment was ultimately added to the law in 1970, which answered these questions. The status *Jew* was defined in accordance with *halakhah* (religious law) as a person who "was born of a Jewish mother or has become converted to Judaism and who is not a member of another religion." It was clear to the authors of the amendment that this narrow definition of the term *Jew* would introduce a new set of difficulties. For example, in the late 1960s, there was a slight ease in migration restrictions from the USSR, and the rate of migration from there to Israel rose. Given the high rates of intermarriage, pressing questions arose about the sorts of rights carried by these migrants' non-Jewish family members. The status of a Jewish man's non-Jewish wife, for example, had to be considered. Should the right of automatic citizenship be extended to her so that she could accompany her husband? And what about their children? Anticipating these questions, and others like them, a second clause was added to the 1970 amendment, extending the Law of Return to include anyone with a Jewish parent (mother or father), a Jewish grandparent (from either side), or a Jewish spouse.[10] Drafted primarily to solve a technical problem rather than to promote an ideological position, this legislation created a paradoxical new class of citizens: those whom the state did not recognize as Jews religiously, yet who were defined as "returnees" to the Jewish homeland.

The result in Samarkand is that a great number of those who appear on Mikhael's roster are not officially recognized as Jewish by the State of Israel, nor do many of them think of themselves as Jewish. All, however, are invested with the right to become citizens of Israel without having to go through a process of naturalization. The Jewish Agency has built a massive infrastructure to find these people, create a sense of community among them, heighten their connection to Israel, and encourage them to resettle there.

ORGANIZATIONAL STRUCTURE

In working toward these goals, Mikhael's office in Samarkand is just one branch of a transnational body. Established by the World Zionist Organization in 1929, the Jewish Agency for Palestine served as an organizational framework for Jews residing outside of Palestine to "work on behalf of the Jewish National Home."[11] When the State of Israel was established in 1948, the organization's name was changed to the Jewish Agency for Israel. Aspects of its mission were redefined, but it remained a nongovernmental organization, dedicated to supporting the State of Israel primarily by education and fundraising among Jews who lived outside the country, encouraging Jewish immigration to Israel, and assisting in the resettlement of new immigrants.

In the late 1980s, as the Soviet Union teetered on the brink of collapse, the Jewish Agency for Israel's Department of Immigration and Absorption turned its attention toward the Jewish population residing there. As emigration restrictions were lifted, and the tremendous possibility for attracting Jews to move from the USSR to Israel became apparent, the Unit for the Commonwealth of Independent States was established. Through its headquarters in Israel, staff members were recruited to work in four mission offices that were overseen and coordinated by this central office: the Russia/Belarus Mission, the Ukraine/Moldova Mission, the South Caucasus Mission, and finally, the Central Asian Mission, which is most relevant to our story.

The Central Asian Mission office was established in Tashkent (Uzbekistan's capital). Israelis hired by the Jewish Agency in Jerusalem were sent there as *shlihim* (emissaries) to work for periods of one to two years.[12] These employees occupied four positions, each with a distinct portfolio. These same positions were replicated in each of the other three mission offices: the immigration coordinator (referred to as the *aliyah*[13] coordinator) was charged with organizing and running information seminars to educate people about who was entitled to the right of return, about the migration process, and to facilitate the move for those who opted to take advantage of this right. The youth programmer was charged with overseeing and organizing informal educational programs, summer camps, and social activities for children and teenagers. Some of these activities are Israel-oriented, and others are intended simply as fun, social events. The education coordinator oversees the Hebrew language program. Finally, the general manager supervises and coordinates all these activities. Together, the *shlihim* who occupy these four positions in Tashkent manage all Jewish Agency programs in the city. The scope of their responsibilities, however, is much more expansive, in that they also oversee the activities in each of the twelve Central Asian branch offices (of which Samarkand is one).[14]

To facilitate the smooth functioning of the various programs in the branch offices, each *shaliah* (emissary) in Tashkent has a counterpart in each of the branch offices. As general manager of Samarkand's Jewish Agency office, Mikhael is well acquainted with his colleagues who occupy this same position in the other branches, because the general manager in Tashkent often gathers these individuals together for retreats and seminars. Such events are meant to standardize and coordinate the work of the various Jewish Agency offices. In addition, they foster a sense of community, connecting the manager of each branch office to a large network of people who are all working toward the same goals. On occasion, the managers of the various branches of the Central Asian Mission also meet together with the managers of the Russia/Belarus Mission, the Ukraine/Moldova Mission, and the South Caucasus Mission, tying them into an even larger community.

Similar networks are created and nurtured among individuals who occupy other sorts of positions. The education coordinator in Tashkent, for example, convenes regular meetings of the education coordinators and teachers in the various branch offices. At seminars and retreats, these individuals discuss the contours of their classes (numbers of students, their levels, and pedagogical challenges). In addition, they study Hebrew together under the direction of Tashkent's education coordinator. On occasion, the Hebrew teachers in Central Asia's branch offices are flown to Israel for large seminars where they meet and study with their counterparts who are scattered across the former Soviet Union.

Through this organizational structure, individuals who work at the local level (such as those in the Samarkand branch office) regularly come together with others through nodes of activity facilitated by the mission office (in Tashkent), by the regional coordinators (in the Unit for the Commonwealth of Independent States), and finally by the headquarters office in Israel, the central address that ties them to the work being done by the Jewish Agency across the globe. The nurturing of these ties provides individuals who work at the local level (such as those in the Samarkand branch office) with an awareness of the place they occupy in a much larger network that stretches across national boundaries.

The sense of belonging to a transnational social and organizational body is also fostered by the multiple ways through which people can become involved as Jewish Agency leaders. An individual need not be a Jewish Agency employee nor have an official title to participate in regional or transnational conferences. In Hebrew classes, for example, outstanding students, who are identified as potential future teachers, are often invited to attend language seminars. With trips and accommodations paid for, and many opportunities for socializing, such invitations are viewed as honors and are generally coveted. Likewise, youth coordinators in each city work to identify individuals who regularly attend their programs and who are particularly dedicated, energetic participants. Invitations are often extended to such individuals to participate in conferences that hook them into a large network of other youth.

In addition to fostering these transnational networks, Jewish Agency employees also work to create and nurture a sense of community at the local level. Branch offices organize holiday celebrations, social events, and enrichment classes. In Samarkand, a buzz about these lively activities has spread by word of mouth. Though the events may have originally been intended to reach those who are included in the Law of Return, such a broadly defined "group" has made it relatively easy for others to join as well. For example, Natasha, whose mother is Jewish, is considered to be Jewish by the State of Israel, and she holds the "Right of Return." Her father, however, is Russian and not Jewish. Natasha herself has "Russian" printed on her identity documents, does not think of herself as Jewish, and has never set foot in a Jewish institution. But when she heard about the activities of the Jewish Agency from a friend, she was interested in attending one to see if she might enjoy it. She convinced her good friend, Luba—who has no one Jewish in her family tree—to come with her. They were both welcome, had a good time, and returned for other events. Luba has since begun to learn Hebrew and has even become a group leader for some of the office's children's activities.

It is difficult to get an accurate picture of just how many people who attend Jewish Agency events are Jewish (according to the State of Israel), how many are not Jewish but are still included in the Law of Return, and how many are not even included in the Law of Return. This difficulty stems in part from the fact that the Jewish Agency has no membership dues or mailing lists, making it unclear who should or should not be counted as a participant. Confounding this difficulty, against the backdrop of tremendous emigration, the configuration of people who attend Jewish Agency events is constantly in flux. In addition to people emigrating, groups are constantly reconfigured, as Jewish Agency employees work hard to keep their numbers of participants up. Efforts to reach further and further into the pool of those who might be interested in attending events are generally well rewarded. As one man explained, "Plenty of Jews may be leaving, but new ones appear every day."

With those caveats in mind, and based on data gathered at a variety of Jewish Agency events held in Samarkand in 1997, I estimated that roughly 60 percent of those who attended Jewish Agency events at that time were Jews according to the definition of the State of Israel,[15] and 40 percent were not. Among those who are not considered Jewish by the state, the large majority have some Jewish connection (either a Jewish father, Jewish grandparent, or Jewish spouse), but a small minority, like Luba, have no Jewish familial connection at all.

People attend Jewish Agency events for a variety of reasons. Some are aligned with the organization's mission in that they are interested in socializing with other Jews, connecting to their Jewish heritage, and learning about Israel. Many, like Natasha, however, participate in events simply because they are fun. At dances, at the weekly youth club, and in some of the classes (including martial arts and drawing), doses of Zionist teachings and nationalist ideology are weak, if not totally absent. Youth coordinators facilitate a lively, light atmosphere through group games, puzzles, and competitions, which provide many opportunities for young men and women to meet, form relationships, and enjoy each other's company. With few movie theaters, pubs, and cafes open in the evenings in post-Soviet Samarkand, there are not many other opportunities for socializing, and the Jewish Agency activities provide a welcome outlet. As one young man involved in coordinating youth activities explained in response to my question about the attraction of Jewish Agency events, "Things here [at the Jewish Agency] are interesting. There are seminars. All kinds of them: in Tashkent, in Alma Ata. It's fun to travel, to go hear what people are talking about. And the Jewish Agency here [in Samarkand] has a lot of parties. . . . People come—one time, two times, three times, and that's how it is. Everyone becomes friends."

Other reasons people attend Jewish Agency events are related to their desire to move to Israel, some for nationalist reasons, but most for pragmatic ones. In Uzbekistan, the difficult transition from communism gave rise to a depressed and unstable economy, a weak health care system, a bankrupt system of education, mistrust of the new government, and very little social security. Many individuals are simply looking for a better life someplace else, and believe Israel might provide it.

For those included in the Law of Return and who plan to move to Israel with hope for a better life, the Jewish Agency offers a vehicle for acculturation even before they set foot in the country, through Hebrew language classes and courses on Israeli culture. For those who are not included in the Law of Return, attending activities at the Jewish Agency may open up opportunities to become included. I was told about Lily, for example, who is a Hebrew teacher for the Jewish Agency and is active in several programs, although she has no Jews in her family, and is not included in the Law of Return. She would, however, like to move to

Israel and hopes that through her involvement she will meet someone Jewish to marry, who might help her attain this dream.

IMPACT OF THE JEWISH AGENCY FOR ISRAEL ON SAMARKAND'S BUKHARAN JEWS

Before the dissolution of the Soviet Union, there was a strong overlap among Bukharan Jews' social networks, kinship networks, place of residence, religious community, and individuals' self-identity as "Bukharan Jew" (which also carried the meaning of "real Jew"). As a result of the Jewish Agency's activities in Samarkand, aspects of that organic relationship have been ruptured. Holiday celebrations, Hebrew classes, and youth activities bring Bukharan Jews together with other individuals, most of whom share the "Right of Return," but whose group boundaries are fluid and relatively ill-defined. This reconfiguration of social networks has occurred against the backdrop of massive emigration, which has obviated the possibility of retreating into old community ties.

As a result, for Samarkand's Bukharan Jews, the boundary that once so clearly separated those who are Jewish from those who are not has been blurred. Several Bukharan Jewish young adults told me that since the Jewish Agency has become active in Samarkand, students with whom they had gone to school for years, who had never identified themselves as Jewish, suddenly began claiming themselves to be Jews. Ruben, for example, explained:

> When I was growing up, I thought I was the only Jew in my class and the kids used to tease me and beat me because of it. Now, years later, I found out that there were other Jewish kids in my class, but they never said then that they were Jewish. One girl's father is Tatar and her mother is Jewish. She always said she was Tatar, but now she wants to go to Israel so she says that she is Jewish.

More disorienting than the emergence of Jews who denied their Jewish identity during the Soviet era are those individuals who claim to be included in the "Law of Return," but who appear to have no Jewish kin at all. Luba, for example, has raised difficult questions about identity and community for those who have become acquainted with her through her involvement in Jewish Agency activities. In her early twenties, she is known among her peers as someone whose mother is Armenian and whose father is Uzbek (according to the nationality written on their passports). Recently, though, she has expressed a desire to move to Israel, and has begun to claim that she has a Jewish grandmother who lives there.

Gavriel, a young Bukharan Jew who is active in Jewish Agency activities, is certain that Luba has no grandmother in Israel. He says that Luba began participating in Jewish Agency events because she found them interesting and fun. Through her participation, Gavriel claims, she heard that the standard of living is better in Israel, and that life is easier there. Therefore, she fabricated a Jewish grandmother in Israel in an effort to legitimize her intense participation in Jewish Agency programs, hoping that through some connection, friendship, or romance, she will be able to find a way to move there herself.

While Gavriel is confident that Luba is not Jewish, there are many others who participate irregularly in Jewish Agency events whom Gavriel does not know well. He has also participated in many seminars attended by youth from cities all over Central Asia, as well as some attended by youth from all over the former Soviet Union. In such settings, where contact is not contextualized in terms of community, family, or shared history, Gavriel—like the others—has found that he now has no way of knowing who is Jewish and who is not. The questions surrounding Luba's status as a Jew (or non-Jew), then, are more than just questions about her. Although people such as Luba (who may have no Jewish kin at all) are a small minority of Jewish Agency participants, they are symptoms of the disorientation that has suddenly come to surround aspects of identity that were once clear and taken for granted.

These new questions about Jewish identity do not only touch the youth, and are not only relevant for those who are intimately involved with the Jewish Agency. Nina's confusion about the Jewish (or non-Jewish) status of her neighbor, Olga, illustrates the pervasive nature of these questions.

Olga and her twenty-nine-year-old daughter, Rita, would both like to move to Israel. With no documented Jewish family members, however, they are not included in the Law of Return, and have no way to get there, except through (apparent) scheming. One possibility is to find a Jewish man for Rita to marry. In this endeavor, Olga has attempted to enlist the help of Nina, a Bukharan Jew, who was born and raised in Samarkand (as were her parents).

Although Nina's social network consists primarily of her relatives, in-laws, and other Bukharan Jewish friends, she lives in the new city on a small street with non-Jewish neighbors with whom she is friendly. Olga and Rita are among them. Having agreed to make some inquiries regarding the search for a Jewish husband for Rita, Nina turned to me, wondering if I might have met anyone at the Jewish Agency who would be interested. Her question was tentative, though, and ended with a slight giggle. "Never mind," she quickly retracted, explaining that this search for a Jewish husband really would not matter if Olga was able to prove that she is Jewish after all.

Nina has lived near her for many years, yet Olga never made any mention of Jewish ancestry until quite recently, when she started to claim Jewish roots. As a small child—Olga's story goes—her mother passed away. Her father, left a widower, soon remarried. Raised by her non-Jewish father and non-Jewish stepmother, Olga only recently re-called being told that her biological mother was Jewish. However, she has no way to prove her Jewish identity because her mother's identifica-tion documents were lost during the war. Nevertheless, Olga has gone to the Jewish Agency branch office in Samarkand to fill out a form to register herself (and her daughter Rita) as "Jewish." With no proof of her status as a Jew, the office will not process her papers for the purposes of immigration. However, the general manager did agree to pass along her name to the local representative of the Joint Distribution Com-mittee (an international Jewish welfare organization that offers aid to needy Jews).

Passover began about a week after Nina told me this story. In prep-aration for the holiday, Nina thoroughly cleaned her house to get rid of all bread and other leavened products, in accordance with religious prescriptions. Early one morning—in the midst of the eight-day-long holiday—Olga came around, letting herself into the house while Nina was still asleep. When Nina awoke, she found an Easter cake on her table, with a holiday note from Olga.

Do you see what Olga brought over here? Nina asked me, pointing to the now sullied table, which she had cleaned thoroughly for Passover a few days before. *She is so stupid! She is Jewish, and should know bet-ter,* Nina exclaimed. Under the impression that Nina did not consider Olga Jewish, her remark surprised me. *But I thought she isn't Jewish,* I answered, perplexed. In response to my confusion, Nina explained that the Joint Distribution Committee had sent Olga a package of food just before Passover, as part of their holiday charity drive. For Nina, this delivery served as an indicator of Olga's Jewishness. *So you think she is Jewish?* I asked, in an effort to clarify. At this point, she changed her mind again, deciding that Olga is just posing as a Jew in an effort to get to Israel. *She does everything a Russian does. I don't believe she is Jewish.*

For Nina, the indicators of an individual's Jewishness (or non-Jewishness) were once all aligned. That was in the Soviet days, when those who were Jewish used to eat together, mourn together, pray together, live together, and marry one another. Since the breakup of the Soviet Union, the Jewish Agency for Israel (among other organizations) has contributed to the severing of those intertwined and overlapping relationships by gathering together those who were previously unrelated and by creating a variety of frames through which an individual's Jewish (or non-Jewish) status might be detected. Now Nina has a series of fractured reference points for defining whether or not Olga is a Jew. As a result, a more general confusion about who belongs and who does not abounds, as do difficult questions about the nature of the bonds that join those who do.

Chabad-Lubavitch

Chabad-Lubavitch, an ultra-Orthodox Hasidic movement, is known for its work across the globe in towns and cities with relatively small Jewish populations and weak religious infrastructures.[16] As Jewish missionaries, their work is aimed at strengthening religious practice and belief among other Jews. One man summarized: "What we're really after is that people should realize that we have to lead our lives according to the Torah. This is what has kept the Jews together for so long."[17]

Shneur Zalman gave birth to the movement in late eighteenth-century Eastern Europe, where its population headquarters and center of religious influence remained until World War II. At that time, the sixth Lubavitcher Rebbe (spiritual leader), along with many of his followers who had managed to survive the war, relocated to New York. In 1994, the seventh Lubavitcher Rebbe, Menachem Mendel Schneerson, died, leaving behind no successor.

FIGURE 9.1
Chabad Emissary with Bukharan Jewish students, Samarkand, 1993
Photographer: Gregory Maniouk. Courtesy of Alanna E. Cooper

Although Chabad-Lubavitch emissaries have always been entrepreneurial and independent (largely responsible for their own fundraising), in the years following the death of Menachem Mendel Schneerson they experienced an even greater degree of decentralization in their work. The movement continued to flourish and even grow, taking advantage of the opportunities for work presented by the dissolution of the Soviet Union. However, in the absence of their charismatic leader, the organizational infrastructure linking Chabad-Lubavitch emissaries in any particular city or town to those working elsewhere in the region was weak, if nonexistent.

In Samarkand, this meant that in contrast to the situation of the Jewish Agency employees there, whose positions were well defined within the highly centralized larger organization, Chabad-Lubavitch emissaries had no structured chain of authority or infrastructure to govern their activities or decisions. It is no coincidence, then, that the most self-confident, independent, adored (and sometimes loathed) emissaries whom I met while in Uzbekistan were Lubavitchers, whereas the Jewish Agency em-

ployees whom I met were mostly competent, nice, and hard-working—
but just that.

In their roles, Jewish Agency employees depend on the infrastructure
of the organization to guide their actions and support their positions,
whereas Lubavitcher emissaries (for whom the term *employee* would be
inappropriate) depend on their own personal capabilities and wit. For this
reason, the following discussion about the work of Chabad-Lubavitch in
Samarkand is structured around depictions of individual personalities.

EMANUEL SHIMUNOV[18]

Seated at the head table where he was leading a memorial service I attended in Samarkand in 1994, Emanuel Shimunov stood out as different
from all the other men in the room. His black hat, black coat, starched
white shirt, and untrimmed beard marked him as Chabad-Lubavitch,
and I assumed that he had come from the Lubavitch headquarters in
Crown Heights, New York, to do missionary work in Samarkand. When
he began to lead the prayers, though, his accent, register, and melody
all signaled Central Asian. Was he Bukharan in the garb of Lubavitch?
Or was he Lubavitch, trained in Bukharan cantillation? A local? Or an
emissary?

In fact, Emanuel Shimunov is both. He was born and raised in Samarkand, where he attended an underground religious school from the
time he was a small child. His teachers had been students of Chabad-
Lubavitchers who had fled to Central Asia from Eastern Europe during
World War II. They had also been students (or the students of students)
of Shlomo Lev Eliezerov, the Chabad emissary from Hebron who had
spurred the 1904 slaughtering controversy in Samarkand. Although
Eliezerov had left the city many decades before, his spiritual legacy remained powerful. His students continued to identify as "Chabad" and
to pass this identity on to their students.

In the late 1960s, when Emanuel Shimunov began his studies, one of
his teachers was Shlomo Haye Niyazov, who was just a teenager himself
at the time. Niyazov had not directly studied with Eliezerov. However,
his own father and teacher had. In 1979, when the younger and older
Niyazovs immigrated to New York,[19] Emanuel Shimunov, who was eighteen at the time, remained behind.

According to his own account, Emanuel Shimunov was the last religious leader in the city after the departure of Shlomo Haye Niyazov. "I was left alone here," he told me—"just the heavens and the earth [and me]." This story of leadership succession offers one explanation of how Emanuel Shimunov came to be identified as the city's chief rabbi. Elaborating in Samarkand's Jewish newspaper, he explained, "Without me, it would not be possible to carry out a single religious ceremony, a wedding, a circumcision, or a memorial service."[20] Indeed, Emanuel Shimunov did come to occupy a very powerful position in the city. In addition to filling a critical role as religious functionary, he organized summer camps, schools, adult education courses, youth enrichment, and community-wide holiday parties, coordinating, hiring, managing, and overseeing budgets for all these programs.

His rise to this leadership role, however, may not have been due to the fact that he remained the only religious leader in the city after Shlomo Haye Niyazov had left. I met and was told about other religious leaders—some elderly and some contemporaries of Emanuel Shimunov—who had also studied underground during the Soviet era, and who continued to live in Samarkand through the 1980s and 1990s. Another explanation for Shimunov's rise to power involves the relationships he formed with people outside Samarkand, both with wealthy financiers and with other powerful Lubavitch leaders, including the Rebbe himself.

Raphael Shamsiyev was one figure who helped to facilitate such relationships. He had grown up in Uzbekistan, and like Emanuel Shimunov had studied religion underground with the students of Shlomo Lev Eliezerov. In the 1970s, he moved to Israel. But when the Soviet Union dissolved, he returned to Uzbekistan to help build Samarkand's religious institutions, backed by funding from Lev Leviev, a diamond merchant billionaire and fellow Bukharan Jew.[21] Once in Samarkand, Shamsiyev worked with Shimunov to build a religious school for the city's Jewish children.

Shimunov's rise to his position of leadership was also aided by his personal interactions with the Chabad-Lubavitch Rebbe; the movement's charismatic leader. Assisted by his connections with other Chabad leaders, Shimunov traveled to New York in 1991, where he met the Rebbe. Upon returning home, an article in *Shofar* described his encounter: "The

Rebbe asked me about Samarkand and the problems that we have in our community. He told me to go back and to do all that I thought [was necessary]. The Rebbe blessed me. I continually feel the clasp of the Almighty and of the Lubavitcher Rebbe."[22] Shimunov's meeting infused him with spiritual energy, and the photograph that accompanied the newspaper article, which was testimony to his intimate contact with this beloved leader, must have enhanced his prestige in the eyes of the locals. In addition, Shimunov's international connections with the Lubavitch movement aided him in securing funds for various projects, and helped him to bring Lubavitch emissaries from Israel and the United States to Samarkand to serve as teachers, act as ritual slaughterers, and help run a summer camp.

I met Shimunov in Uzbekistan in 1994, at which time he was very active in Samarkand. By the time I returned to Samarkand in 1997, he had moved to Tashkent, where he lived for about a year before immigrating to Queens, New York. While living in Tashkent, he visited Samarkand approximately once a week to monitor his programs there, though he had basically left them in the hands of Osher Karnowsky, a nineteen-year-old emissary from London.

CHABAD-LUBAVITCH PROGRAMS IN SAMARKAND, 1997

The Jewish day school that Emanuel Shimunov and Raphael Shamsiyev had opened in the early 1990s had closed by 1996 because most of the school's Bukharan Jewish students had emigrated. Nevertheless, with the help of funding from Lev Leviev, a number of educational programs continued to function in the city. These included a religious program for men held every weekday morning in the *mahalla* synagogue. Participants recited the morning prayers together and attended classes taught by a few locals and by Lubavitch emissaries. The men who were enrolled in the program came on a daily basis, and were paid a stipend based on their attendance.[23] For women, a similar but less intense program was held two afternoons a week. The fifty participants gathered together in two separate groups; one met in the Bukharan Jewish cultural center in the *mahalla*, and the other in the synagogue in the new city.[24]

In addition to classes, funding was used toward maintaining the *mikveh* (ritual bath) in Samarkand, and to cover expenses incurred for the celebration of holidays: a community-wide party and feast on Purim, for example, and subsidized matza on Passover. Finally, Lev Leviev's funding allowed for the very presence of the emissaries in Samarkand, the ramifications of which are difficult to outline. It is impossible to draw up a formal list of the duties and responsibilities of the emissaries. Much of their work was not done according to a prescribed schedule and each emissary created his[25] own "position" and set of jobs tailored to his own capabilities, strengths, and interests.

When Osher arrived in Samarkand from London in 1996, he was eighteen years old. He came to work as a *shaliah* with friends who had already been living in the city for a year, had learned Russian, had built strong working relationships with local personalities, and knew how to get things done there. Osher, on the other hand, did not know any of the local languages, and as a newcomer he did not know the people in the town, how to get around, or how things ran. But Osher is quick, driven, and carries himself with confidence. Within a year, he learned the language, the people, the pace, and the politics of Samarkand.

Shortly before I met Osher in 1997, his friends had returned home. He recruited two other friends (one from London and the other from New York) to join him. He had trouble, however, securing cash to pay for his friends' airline tickets. For Osher, this financial technicality presented a minimal obstacle. He convinced them that if they paid for their own flights, he would be able to work out a deal with Emanuel Shimunov to cover their expenses once they arrived, which is exactly what happened.

One program that had been running during Osher's first year in Samarkand was a school for boys that met for a few hours every day. Each morning, the boys would pray with the older men in the synagogue. Afterwards, they would have recess and then convene in the synagogue classroom. When class ended, they would have lunch together, which was prepared in the synagogue kitchen by a cook.

Osher put his friends in charge of taking care of the boys. They went to services early each morning to help them pray, watched over them during recess, taught them, and supervised lunch, which included making sure the students made the proper blessings before and after eating. Osher oversaw the program. Each week he worked out a menu with the cook and made sure that she had the necessary products (which involved shopping at the bazaar and buying meat in the *mahalla*). When she emigrated, he hired a new cook. He dealt with parents interested in enrolling their children, oversaw attendance, looked over exams, and disbursed funds to students who met the minimum requirements.

In addition to monitoring this (and other) educational programs, Osher facilitated services in the new-city synagogue on Sabbath mornings. He generally chanted the Torah portion each week and either led services or made sure someone else was present to lead them. Shortly before Passover, he arranged for a large shipment of matza to Samarkand from Moscow. In honor of Purim, he organized (among other events) a party that was held in the synagogue in the *mahalla*. He posted invitations, hired a cook, bought the food and liquor, hired a band, and recruited people to help him set up chairs and tables for the event, which was attended by about 150 people of all ages.

Outside the religious sphere, Osher played an important financial role. He was the liaison between Emanuel Shimunov and the students who received significant stipends for the classes in which they were enrolled. He also paid the salaries of cooks, drivers, and synagogue caretakers. People knew of his access to liquid cash and some came to him begging for charity or with requests to borrow money. Dealing in both U.S. dollars and local currency, Osher also played the role of "money changer."

With the help of his access to money, his religious knowledge, and his self-confidence, Osher engendered the respect and trust of many. People not only came to ask him for financial assistance, but also for personal and religious counseling that often touched on the most intimate areas of their lives.

None of this work was in Osher's "job description." He had no manager watching to see that he fulfilled any duties. He had no specific term of service to fill, no set salary or allowance (all was negotiable with Emanuel Shimunov), no set hours of work, and no set vacation time. He decided when to work, how hard to work, and what kinds of projects to initiate. His relationships with Shimunov and with the friends whom he recruited to help him were not based on a contract or preset agreement. They were dynamic, worked out as they went along, depending on how circumstances changed and presented themselves.

IMPACT OF CHABAD-LUBAVITCH ON
SAMARKAND'S BUKHARAN JEWS

For the Jewish Agency, ideological platforms were developed to support the organizational infrastructure and de facto policies. For Chabad-Lubavitch, which has a weak infrastructure and policies that are not institutionalized, the ideological platform stands alone. For the Jewish Agency, there are no clear answers to questions, including the following: Is there a Jewish People? If there is, what is the nature of their bonds? What is Jewish history? And how should holidays be celebrated? For Chabad-Lubavitch, there are real answers to these questions, found in texts that are understood to be authentic, true, and timeless. The Rebbe eloquently explained:

> The essential element which unites our "dispersed and scattered people" and makes it "one people" throughout its dispersion and regardless of time, is the Torah and the Mitzvoth [religious commandments], the Jewish way of life which has remained basically the same throughout the ages and in all places.[26]

This means that in classes run by Lubavitch emissaries, unlike those run by the Jewish Agency, Judaism is taught rather than discussed or pondered. Classes for women, for example, focus on practical *halakhah* related to keeping kosher, to use of the *mikveh,* and to holiday observance. In the men's classes emphasis is placed on attendance at daily morning prayers; much of class time is spent reading the weekly portion from the Torah as a devotional act.

In the boys' classes, emphasis is placed on having students learn to do Jewish things. Shmulie, an emissary from the United States and one of Osher's two friends, summarized his teaching goals as follows: "Most important is that they learn to make *brachas* [blessings] on their food. Other things that are important are *benching* [blessing after meals], *davening* [praying], and [wearing a] *yarmulke* [and] *tzitzis* [the four-cornered garment that men and boys wear under their shirts]."

In Chabad-Lubavitch classes, unlike Jewish Agency classes, the students learn the "right" and "authentic" way to practice Judaism, which they are encouraged to follow. Likewise, emissaries of Chabad-Lubavitch have very precise understandings of "who is Jew," based on *halakhah.* Although rates of intermarriage among Bukharan Jews are low, the rare questions that arise about identity transmission as a result of the marriage between a Jew and non-Jew draw attention to the way in which the emissaries' views are at odds with local conceptions. Grisha, for example, a man whose father is a Bukharan Jew and whose mother is Tatar, grew up practicing Judaism and believing himself to be Jewish. In the late 1990s, a year after his father died, he went to the synagogue to say *kaddish* in his father's memory. A Lubavitch emissary, however, would not permit him to take an active role in the service, explaining that he is not Jewish according to *halakhah*. As Grisha grew up in the Soviet era, his understanding of his Jewish identity was one and the same as that of his community, of the neighboring Muslims, and of the Soviet authorities. With the arrival of Chabad-Lubavitch, this integrated sense of Jewishness has became undone.

By presenting Jewish law as an abstract, transcendent, and enduring system, Chabad-Lubavitch has contributed toward the rupturing of the once intertwined relationship between the religious practices, social organization, and community space of the city's Bukharan Jews. In the religious classes organized by Chabad, women are taught how to properly salt meat (to drain it of blood) before cooking it. Many of the women told me that they had learned how to do this ritual act by watching their mothers or grandmothers, and expressed surprise to find out that what they had learned mimetically in the home was often not "correct." There were certain details of law they never knew, such as how much time may elapse between the moment of slaughter and the moment the salting process is begun, and how much time (minimum and maximum) the meat must be soaked in water. There were other details—they learned—that their mothers and grandmothers had added that were superfluous. One day after a class on meat-salting, Nina reflected:

> My mother-in-law was very religious and very strict with the laws. She would not use the same hand to put the salt on the meat as the one she used to take the meat out of the water. One time my mother-in-law saw my mother not following this [she used the same hand for both] and she yelled at her, "You are an old woman! How is it that you do not know how to do this properly?"
>
> When I think about this today, I feel very sad that my mother-in-law spoke to my mother like this, especially since it was all nonsense [there is no prohibition against using the same hand for both tasks]. They lived in the *mahalla* for 150 years and they did things all wrong.

While Nina describes the past as a time when people "did things all wrong," fifty-seven-year-old Uri describes it as a time when people remained faithful to Judaism, even if they may not have followed all the religious details. Referring to the emissaries, he says:

> For some reason, they think that over these seventy years [of communism] we have gotten so bad. But it's not so. Maybe we weren't always so religious, but for us religion was always stored away in our hearts.... Those [emissaries] who come here, they think they have to help us. But there's been no change here these seventy years with our faith in God, and our faith in religion.

Elaborating on Uri's approach, middle-aged Raya describes the ways in which people practiced Judaism throughout the Soviet era. She characterizes the past as a time when people did not know the reasons behind their religious actions:

> My grandfather[27] had seven children. Each of those children had four or five children. So on Passover, fifty people would get together. Our uncles would read the *haggadah*, but we didn't understand [what they were reading]. They would hold up the matza and say, "This is the bread of our poverty, whoever is hungry come and eat." ... But they would say it in our language, "*ho lahmo anyo* ... [she sings]" and we didn't understand it. Our grandfather would read [a section] and we grandchildren would answer, "*dayenu*," and laugh. We didn't know what it meant. My grandfather didn't know either.

Despite the fact that her family members did not know why they did what they did, Raya praises their continued religious observance. Nevertheless, she also points out that there were many details of proper religious observance that they simply did not know:

> It was important that the women knew about *mikveh* and they immersed themselves ... [but they] didn't know ... what kind of *mikveh* [how it should be built according to religious law]. They also didn't know how many days were allowed and how many days were not allowed.[28] They didn't know about *bedikot* [examinations].[29] But they did know that when a woman was like that [in *niddah*],[30] it [sexual intimacy] is not allowed. And they knew that after that [period of *niddah*], one has to wash [by immersing in the ritual bath]. More than that—they didn't know.

For Raya, the arrival of Lubavitch emissaries was the event that demarcated the past from the present. She explains that it was their arrival that brought about the change from practicing religion without knowing why or how, to practicing properly, with a full understanding of the underlying reasons. Raya attributes the importance of Lubavitch influence to the books they brought with them:

> In 1990, the guys [Lubavitch emissaries] started to come from Israel with books. My daughters started to go to [Lubavitch] school. . . . They started to learn: how many minutes, what kind of salt, for what and why. The girls would come home . . . and I would ask them exactly [how to do it] by the law. Then they brought books [home]. [Among them] there was a translation of the Passover *haggadah*.

When I asked if she was surprised to learn these things, Raya responded:

> We did it already! We did it. It's just that we did not understand [why]: Mother said, mother did it this way, and I do it this way too. Why? Because in the Torah it's written that way? Because there is *halakhah*? This we didn't know! What is *halakhah*? What is *Shulhan Aruch*? We didn't know. Now we know.

Here Raya articulates the difference between learning from books and learning from grandmothers. Knowledge transmitted orally ("mother said this") and mimetically ("mother did this") is grounded in an intimate social context. It is local and provincial. Knowledge transmitted through texts is shared across vast spans of time and space and is abstract and universal. The reference Raya makes to learning Jewish law from her daughters is powerful because it indicates a rupture in the system of knowledge transmission. When religious law and observance are thought of as universal, the younger generation can just as easily teach "tradition" as they can receive it. So, too, young foreign emissaries can serve as teachers to locals who are as old as their parents and grandparents.

Navigating between Chabad-Lubavitch and the Jewish Agency in Samarkand: Case Study

Chabad-Lubavitch, like the Jewish Agency for Israel, has contributed toward the rupturing of the once intertwined relationship between religious practice, community, and local space for Samarkand's Bukharan Jews. The Jewish Agency has done so by undoing the link between local space and Jewish identity. Chabad-Lubavitch, on the other hand, has done so by presenting Jewish law as an abstract and universal system, divorced from (and sometimes at odds with) mimetically received tradition.

For Samarkand's Bukharan Jews, the pervasive influence of these emissary organizations has posed a complex problem. In the popularized account of Yosef Maman's eighteenth-century encounter with the locals, the emissary reforms the locals from their errant ways. In contrast, the Bukharan Jews I met were engaged in the difficult task of coming to terms with changes introduced by the emissaries (and by the new era of religious freedom) without simply discarding the views about Judaism and Jewishness they carried with them from the past.

Focusing on the issue of identity, Nina struggles to reach an understanding of her neighbor Olga's status. Is she Jewish or not? Likewise, Ruben works to reorient his view of his classmates who he always believed were not Jewish, but who now claim that they are. And focusing on the issue of practice, Raya, Nina, and Uri look for ways to navigate between the new religious rubrics introduced by the Lubavitch emissaries and their old views of religion that were shaped by their experience living Jewishly under communism. Nina laments having done things "wrong." Uri characterizes religion as something that can be carried in the heart and need not be practiced. And Raya describes the past as a time of innocence when they practiced without knowing why.

The effort to rethink Judaism is further complicated by the fact that the approaches of Chabad-Lubavitch and the Jewish Agency are not only in conflict with local versions. In significant ways they are also at odds with one another. Yet, despite the stark differences between the organizations, the two work together on many projects in Samarkand. In part, their cooperation is simply a means for each to stretch their respective financial resources. Rather than each organizing a separate carnival for Purim, for example, they pool resources and work together. Their cooperation is also related to the dwindling Jewish population in the city. The two organizations have to share their participants because there are not a lot to go around. Finally, their cooperation is related to the fact that despite the organizations' formal ideological differences, emissaries often cross boundaries in terms of their own convictions and loyalties. Mikhael, for example, was general manager of the Jewish Agency, but was also sympathetic to the work of Chabad-Lubavitch. In addition, the Jewish Agency regularly sends young adult volunteers to work with youth in Samarkand (and other parts of the former USSR) for two-month periods. Many of these short-term emissaries are recruited through Bnei Akiva, a religious Zionist youth organization. Though they strongly identify with the Jewish Agency's Zionist ideology, their religious orientation is closer to that of Chabad-Lubavitch. For example, the short-term emissaries who worked for the Jewish Agency in Samarkand when I was there would not eat at Jewish Agency–sponsored programs because the food was not kosher. Likewise, they sometimes chose to participate in and help to organize holiday events sponsored by Chabad-Lubavitch. For example, they helped plan the religiously oriented feast the Lubavitch emissaries sponsored in the *mahalla* for the holiday of Purim, rather than the Purim disco sponsored by the Jewish Agency. As a result of the organizations' fluidity at the managerial level, Bukharan Jews themselves have little or no loyalty to one organization over another.

The ways in which Rivka, a Bukharan Jew in her early twenties, participated in both organizations illustrates the freedom with which individuals move between organizations. Her efforts to navigate between them and to integrate their approaches to Judaism with what she knows from her past are narrated below. This case study is based on two formal interviews I conducted with her in 1997, along with many informal discussions.

Rivka's story of how she became involved with both Chabad-Lubavitch and the Jewish Agency begins in 1992. She had just finished high school in Samarkand and went with her mother to visit her aunts, uncles, and cousins in Israel. They stayed for a few months, during which time Rivka attended a religious boarding school.

Shortly after she returned to Samarkand, Rikva's father (who attended daily prayer services) approached Emanuel Shimunov to ask if he might have any employment opportunities for Rivka. "He told Emanuel that I had learned Hebrew [in Israel] and that I knew how to type. . . . So he hired me to work in the synagogue as a secretary." Soon, Shimunov asked Rivka to teach a few religious classes. "I had about thirty students," Rivka told me, "and I taught them Torah, history, traditions, and Hebrew." For teaching material, she drew on the lessons she had learned as a student in the religious boarding school she had attended in Israel, and she enriched her knowledge through study with several Bnei Akiva emissaries in Samarkand who worked for the Jewish Agency but who had strong religious backgrounds themselves.

Over time, Rikva became involved in running other programs with Shimunov. After her first year of teaching in his school, she helped him organize a summer camp. One year, she worked with two young Lubavitch women who came from New York to work in Shimunov's camp. Another summer, she helped organize the camp together with a woman who had been sent from Israel by the Jewish Agency. Rivka explained, "She was not religious, and she wanted to make the camp more like they do it in Israel. But she worked well with Emanuel."

Through her involvement in Chabad-Lubavitch, Rivka came into direct contact with the movement's teachings, ideas, and influence. This exposure, however, in no way limited her access to the Jewish Agency, and she did, in fact, become heavily involved in their programs as well. She worked as a Hebrew teacher for them, and through this involvement also became active in their youth programming. Over the years, she received (and accepted) eight invitations to participate in Jewish Agency regional seminars—several to enrich her skills as a youth leader, and others to enhance her skills as a Hebrew teacher.

When Rivka recalls what life was like for her in the past—before the Soviet Union dissolved, before she attended the religious boarding school in Israel, and before the emissary organizations arrived in Samarkand— she focuses on the difficulties she encountered being stigmatized as a Jew.

Growing up in the new city, she did not live near any other Jewish families, and was the only Jewish student in her class (or so she believed at the time). Occasionally, Rivka felt like an outsider, and she recalled one particularly acute fifth-grade experience of being stigmatized. Participating in a popular activity of creating memory books with the other girls in her class, she exchanged notebooks with one of her friends. Thumbing through to see what others had written, she came across the question, "Who do you like in the class?" and read the responses. "I saw that a few kids wrote that they don't like me because I am a Jew." Rivka told me:

> I came home and I cried a lot. . . . How is this [that they don't like me]? What is this? In what way am I different? I have the same two eyes, ears, feet, and hands. It's just that I'm a Jew and that's it. In what way am I different?

In recent years, Rikva has learned that some of these same girls are actually Jewish themselves. At that time, they had "Russian" written on their passports and they hid their Jewish identity. Now they have started to advertise their Jewishness because they are trying to get to Israel so that they can get ahead financially.

While Rivka feels anger and hurt looking back at this incident, when she reminisces about her childhood memories of religious observance at home, it is with great fondness:

> I knew about Passover. We celebrated it every year and I really loved it: getting the house in order before the holiday. But it was not like I know and do today—[Today we clean] all the walls, corners, shelves, and chairs [in preparation for the holiday]. We didn't know [then] that we had to do all that. But what we did do was paint the whole house white so it would look nice. My mother would do the whole thing—even the ceiling—and we [kids] would help her.

For Rivka, what distinguishes the past from the present is not only the difference in the way her family practiced the rituals. Like Raya, she also defines the past as a time when her family practiced the tradition that they had received, without understanding why they did what they did. In contrast, the present is the time in which they "now know":

> Then, I did not know the reason. I did not know why [we celebrated Passover]. They [my parents] did not know why either. . . . Dad had a book. . . . He would read it [at the *seder*], but he did not know what [he was reading] and I didn't know either.

Rivka also distinguishes between a time "before," when they celebrated holidays together as a whole family, from "now," the years since her family members have emigrated and scattered. In her words:

> Then we would sit all together, waiting . . . for Dad to read [the *haggadah*] and the whole family would be together, and we would drink a lot and laugh and eat a lot. Now it's not like that anymore, like it was in my childhood. We are older now and the whole family is [scattered]—one here and one there, but Passover then was something really special that I really remember well as one of the nicest things from my childhood.

Rivka's nostalgia for "being together" in the past also ran through her description of Yom Kippur:

I knew about Yom Kippur; that we had to fast, but I didn't know the reason why. I would go to school on Yom Kippur. We would all go. . . . It was forbidden [by government law] for us not to go, but I would not eat anything. . . . When I would get home from school, mom would put the food on the gas to warm it up and we would quickly go out to the synagogue to hear the [blowing of the] *shofar*.

Everyone would be in white clothes. . . . There would be many, many people there, and I would wait for the time that they would sound the *shofar*. Then we would walk home. I loved that—we would all be walking together and looking at the sky and there would be a lot of stars and we would get home and eat after the fast.

In Rivka's description, the sweetness of her memories is connected to the sense that her family's observance in days gone by was innocent and naive. This view is related in part to the fact that she is remembering through the eyes of a child, and in part to the fact that her memories are of the days before her relatives and siblings had emigrated. Additionally, the feeling of innocence is related to the fact that her family's observance was not based on what they had learned in an impersonal manner divorced from their social context, such as by reading books.

Shabbat [then] was not like we observe it now. Shabbat was like this: my mother would not do laundry on Shabbat or cook, but we would watch TV and turn on lights and sometimes turn on the gas on Shabbat to warm up food. I guess my mother didn't know that these things were forbidden.

Rather, it was based on what they had learned mimetically, in the domestic sphere:

These things were passed down orally. There was no book to read where it was written, "This is allowed" and "This is forbidden." They would know [what to do] from the grandmothers who would say, "This is forbidden," and they would not explain why.

Like children, they did what was always done, without knowing—or caring to know—the reasons why. In those days, it was easy for Rivka to accept the practices her parents and grandparents taught her, even those that seemed contradictory. For example, at home she only ate kosher food. In school, however, she ate the food that was served, even though it was not kosher. "I didn't know why there were certain foods I did not eat at home, but I did eat at school." When she would ask about this inconsistency, her parents would tell her, "That's the way it has to be." Rivka accepted this. "That [explanation] was enough," she told me. "I believed in my parents. If they said this is the way it has to be . . . I trusted them."

In contrast to the religious teachings from Rivka's past, to which she felt organically connected, she has not easily accepted the lessons imparted by emissaries who come from the outside, and who use books rather than mimetically transmitted tradition to justify their teachings. One evening, while I was eating dinner in the synagogue with one of the Lubavitch emissaries, Rivka approached us with the book of the Torah in her hand. She had been reading the weekly portion and had a question about practices surrounding the term *tameh* (ritual impurity). Linking the passage she was reading with what she had learned in a Chabad women's class she had recently attended, which dealt with the topic of *niddah,* she asked why a woman is considered impure while she is menstruating.

The young Lubavitch emissary responded with a tautological answer. *Because this is what is written in the Torah. Whatever is written in the Torah is what we do.* He elaborated by posing a rhetorical question, *Why don't we kill?* He answered: *Some people might say that we don't kill because killing is immoral. But we do not do things on account of the fact that we ourselves believe that they are moral, or immoral. But because that is what the Torah tells us to do.*

Frustrated with this answer, Rivka explained that she wanted to understand the reasons behind the laws: *I don't want to just follow things without thinking!* she exclaimed; *God gave me a brain so that I should use it!* While her adamant response was shaped by many factors, one was related to her participation in both of Samarkand's emissary organizations. Chabad emissaries have worked to spread the Rebbe's message that the Jews are united as a single, enduring people through observance of the Torah, but this teaching is at serious odds with the messages of the Jewish Agency. Bereft of a single, grounded religious authority, Rivka now has the sense that it is her prerogative to stitch together her own version of Judaism. "I cannot say that I am secular," she tells me, "but I can also not say that I am religious." Most significant is her conclusion, "And I do not think this is a problem." For Rivka, what is most important now about being Jewish is that she takes the opportunity to choose her own path, to create a relationship to religion that feels meaningful and authentic. Both emissary groups have had a large impact in changing the way that Rikva thinks about Judaism and understands her own Jewish identity. Neither, however, has done so without the participation of Rivka herself, who continues to navigate between multiple understandings of Judaism and Jewish Peoplehood.

The Center-Periphery Paradigm presented in the popular account of the Maman story suggests that the Jews of Bukhara accepted the teachings of the eighteenth-century emissary, discarded their errant local practices, and were thereby returned to the stage of Jewish history. In Nissim Tagger's version of this same story, there is no such trajectory. Instead, it was the sustained engagement between the locals and the emissary—regardless of the precise outcome—that bound them and reaffirmed their relationship. Two hundred years later, the story continues. Central Asia's Jews carry their local version of Judaism together with their history of connection to global Judaism. Not surprisingly, therefore, their attitudes toward the emissaries in post-Soviet Samarkand are ambivalent and fraught with contestation. Many have embraced the new religious knowledge, ways of identifying, and practices that the emissaries and their organizations have imparted. Yet, this acceptance has not been total. Rather, it has occurred alongside the effort to reach new understandings of religion and self. By virtue of this very engagement and struggle, the ties between the Jews of Bukhara and the rest of the Jewish world are cultivated and maintained.

TEN

Varieties of
Bukharan Jewishness

Whereas the previous chapter focused on the ways that Judaism and Jewish identity are being debated in the post-Soviet era, this chapter returns to the *Edah* Paradigm to explore current debates surrounding Bukharan Jewish identity. In this analysis, our gaze shifts away from Central Asia to explore the experiences of those who left the Bukharan Jewish heartland. In Central Asia, the most hotly contested questions of identity surrounded questions of Jewishness. In Israel and the United States—the countries with the largest Bukharan Jewish populations today—questions about what exactly it means to be "Bukharan Jewish" are up for serious debate.

At the turn of the last century, shortly after the Bukharan residential quarter had been established, far-flung Bukharan Jews still constituted a single transnational community. Over the course of three generations of Soviet rule, however, the ties that had bound those who occupied distant locales frayed, and in some cases even dissolved. Their historical experiences differed so greatly that much of the cultural resemblance between those who had remained in Central Asia and those whose parents and grandparents had emigrated decades before was lost.

At the dawn of the twenty-first century, all of this has changed. The opening of the Soviet Union's borders in the late 1980s, and the USSR's ultimate demise in 1991, coincided with the rise of the Internet, cheap international flights, and improved communications technology. Combined, these factors have created a host of situations in which individuals, who had developed very different ideas about what it means to be

"Bukharan Jewish," have come into intense contact with each other. In the shared social landscape they now occupy, they are working to renew common understandings of what Bukharan Jewishness is all about. This is achieved, however, not without great deliberation.

This chapter sets the stage for understanding these negotiations through a discussion about the range of Bukharan Jewish migration experiences that unfolded over the past century. The macro social forces that gave rise to these migrations, as well as personal and intimate portraits of individuals who were affected by them, explain the variety of views circulating today about what it means to be a Bukharan Jew.

Migration at the Turn of the Last Century

Intensification of relationships between Jews in Central Asia and those in Europe and Ottoman Palestine precipitated a small wave of emigration, which lasted from the 1890s to the 1920s. Among those who relocated during this period were merchants traveling back and forth between their Central Asian homes and Europe. When the Soviets solidified their borders in the 1920s and made it difficult to travel in and out of their newly incorporated Central Asian territories, many of these merchants simply remained in Moscow, Paris, London, and the other urban centers where they found themselves. They probably numbered 1,000 at most and little information about them (or their descendants) has been collected.

Others moved to Palestine during this period, drawn by a religious calling to settle in the Holy Land. This group of no more than 2,000 individuals was active in establishing and building the Bukharan residential quarter in Jerusalem.[1] During World War I, the Ottoman army requisitioned the buildings of the Bukharan neighborhood for its own use, and many who lived there and had taken an active role in building it moved out.[2] As in the case of those Bukharan Jews who settled in Europe during this period, little information has been collected about what became of these individuals once they left this initial point of settlement and moved out of their ethnic enclave. Likewise, my process of locating their descendants to interview them was not straightforward.

Bukharan Jews who left their Central Asian homes in recent years have gathered together in immigrant institutions and neighborhoods and are easy to locate. In contrast, descendants of immigrants who came at the turn of the last century blend into the diverse social landscapes in which they live. I generally found them by stumbling upon them, rather than by seeking them out. As I went about my daily life—riding a bus, sitting in a library, socializing at a dinner party—when I told people about my research project, someone would occasionally mention that they had a friend who was Bukharan Jewish, or even that they themselves were Bukharan Jewish.

Leora was one such person. I met her while living in Israel at a dinner party hosted by a friend. I told her about the work I was doing, and to my surprise, she told me that she had Bukharan Jewish ancestors. She did not know much about her family, but she did have a cousin (who also happened to be named Leora) who was writing a family history and compiling a family tree. She gave me her cousin's phone number; I called, introduced myself, and we arranged a time to meet.

My visit to Leora Gevirtzman's home took me far away from my regular research sites, which in the United States was primarily in Queens, New York, and in Israel was primarily in the depressed neighborhoods of South Tel Aviv: both areas where Bukharan Jewish immigrants clustered. Leora lived with her husband and four children in a well-manicured village in Gush Etzion, where most of the residents are religious, nationalist, Ashkenazi Jews.

In her kitchen, over coffee, Leora unfolded the family tree that she had carefully drawn across several pages. The tree, she explained, was of her father's side alone. Her mother is an Ashkenazi Jew who was born and grew up in Canada. "That would be a totally separate project," she said, referring to the possibility of one day tracing her mother's family origins.

Leora's father was born in Israel, as were his parents and grandparents. Their ancestors, though, were all born in Central Asia. Many among them were noteworthy leaders, including Yosef Maman, whose biographies have been popularized both in Bukharan Jewish folk histories and in the popular press. One family ancestor was Shlomo Musayev, Leora's great-great-grandfather, who is well known both in Zionist lore and in Bukharan Jewish history as the founder of the Bukharan Quarter in Jerusalem. Indeed, I had seen his signature on several of the letters I had studied while researching the nineteenth-century history of Bukharan Jews.

Leora had not consulted the archives that I had, but she had drawn much of her information from the same books I had used in my research.

In addition, she had collected family stories through discussions with her relatives, as well as from a book that her grandfather had self-published.[3] Although our interests in Bukharan Jewish history overlapped, Leora astutely pointed out that her efforts—unlike my own—were not for academic ends. Her purpose, she explained, was so that the younger generation, herself included, "will know where they are from." Her hope was to complete the family tree and then to organize a family reunion, which would include Bukharan food, as well as a tour of the Bukharan Quarter in Jerusalem.

The Bukharan Quarter offered a tangible connection to her ancestry. As a child, she told me, she had made a trip to the neighborhood once a year prior to the High Holidays. Together with her cousins, aunts, uncles, and grandparents, she would visit the synagogues and school buildings that her forebears had built and populated. She stated that she found little in common with the people who currently reside there, few of whom are Bukharan Jews. Those who were Bukharan Jews had arrived in recent years, and Leora did not identify with them either. "We got to know the Bukharans [there] a little," she explained, choosing words that expressed a distance between herself and them ("the Bukharans"). "But it was like another world for us."

Indeed, she has no personal relationships with any immigrants who grew up in Central Asia during the Soviet period. "I don't have any connection to them," she told me. "I don't know any of them." For Leora, who considers herself "half-Bukharan," this aspect of her identity is a "family thing" rather than a sense that she and these new immigrants belong to a common Bukharan Jewish *edah*.

Over the years, I have met several other descendants of Jews who emigrated from Central Asia at the turn of the last century. Many have family trees that trace their lineage to pious, learned, and wealthy ancestors who are well known in the annals of Bukharan Jewish history. They express pride in this aspect of their identity, but do not have a preference for marrying others like them, and generally blend into the broader American or Israeli social landscapes in which they find themselves. Some may refer to themselves as Bukharan Jews, while others identify themselves simply as "descendants of Bukharan Jews."

For Leora and others like her, whose ancestors arrived at the turn of the last century, to be Bukharan Jewish signifies being connected to a family heritage. So too, Bukharan Jewishness is about having a personal tie to the building of the State of Israel. In Leora's case, this connection is particularly pronounced, as her forebear, Shlomo Musayev, played a pivotal role in establishing the Bukharan Quarter, one of Jerusalem's first modern building projects. Yet even those who do not claim Shlomo Musayev as an ancestor—but who live in Israel or feel closely connected to Israel—tend to point to the nineteenth-century residential quarter as a defining feature of their Bukharan Jewishness. Although the neighborhood nearly lacks a living Bukharan Jewish presence today, it is referred to as a concrete monument and solid testimony to the group's historical existence and accomplishments.

Migration in the 1920s and 1930s

A second small wave of migration began in the 1920s as a result of the economic depression faced by Central Asia's inhabitants after the region's incorporation into the Soviet Union. In 1928, Stalin implemented his first five-year economic plan. Intended to spark commercial growth and productivity, industrialization and collectivization resulted instead in widespread poverty and famine. By 1932, an estimated 60,000 refugees had illegally crossed the border into Afghanistan to escape poverty.[4] Among them were a few thousand Jews, some of whom were fleeing from starvation and others from the Soviets' restrictions on religion.[5]

In 1932, Afghanistan sealed its border with the USSR, and Iran became a popular destination for Central Asians fleeing the Soviets. While residing in these two countries, many Jewish refugees made efforts to acquire certificates of immigration from the British government to allow them to enter Palestine.[6] Those who were not successful worked to rebuild their lives in the host countries where they resided, often with the assistance of the long-established local Jewish communities. In 1948, when the State of Israel was created and migration into the country became legal, the Jewish population of Afghanistan, with very few exceptions, left for Israel.[7] Included among them were some 2,000 Bukharan Jews.[8] Rahel Karayof was one of them.

I met Rahel in 1996 in the depressed neighborhood in South Tel Aviv where she lived; the area was home to several thousand residents, a large proportion of whom were Bukharan Jewish immigrants. Rahel ran the weekly meetings of the Bukharan Jewish women's club there, and I quickly identified her as the group leader the first time I entered the small auditorium where thirty or so women were gathered. In her early sixties, she stood facing the group of her contemporaries, in command of the space. Unlike the other women, who were wearing loose flowery dresses and colorful headscarves characteristic of Central Asian immigrants, Rahel wore a practical dress and a small round cap—typical garb for a religious Israeli woman, whose origins could have been anywhere.

That evening—like every other Tuesday night—Rahel moderated the women's sharing of information about family milestones, imparted lessons about religious holidays and the weekly Torah portion, led the women in Central Asian song and dance, and made announcements about upcoming events sponsored by Bukharan Jewish community organizations. Most of the participants in the club had arrived in Israel since the dissolution of the Soviet Union in 1991. A few others had come in the 1970s when there was a slight ease in migration restrictions from the USSR. These immigrants from the 1970s viewed themselves as "old-timers" in comparison to those who had come in the 1990s. Rahel, however—who had arrived in Israel in 1951, just after the State was founded—called them all "newcomers."

Also unlike the others, Rahel was not born in the Bukharan emirate. Her mother, Zilpo, was born there, but fled as a young woman.[9] Many years later, when Zilpo was older, married, and a mother of five children, she became famous among her family members and neighbors for her great skills as a storyteller. In Zilpo's repertoire of biblical stories, rabbinic legends, and family lore, an oft-told tale was her narrative of leaving Bukhara.

Zilpo, the youngest of many children, was born in 1916. A *bat zekunim* (daughter of her parents' old age), she lost her mother when she was a child. Distraught after his wife's death, Zilpo's father found himself unable to care for his young daughter. David, one of his older, married sons, agreed to take in his younger sister and raise her.

David—Rahel told me—was a deeply religious man, who worked as a ritual slaughterer and a religion teacher. He taught his young sister Zilpo how to pray and told her rabbinic legends, which she remembered and retold over the course of her life. In 1924, when the Bukharan emirate—where their family had lived for countless generations—was dismantled and incorporated into the Soviet Union, life became quite difficult for David. The Soviets implemented harsh antireligious policies, and by 1932, when he was no longer able to escape the eyes of the communists, he fled.

After a harrowing illegal journey across dangerous terrain, David arrived in Afghanistan. There he settled in Kabul among a small but growing community of Jewish refugees from Bukhara. After some time, he secured documents for his wife and young son to join him and arranged for Zilpo to accompany them. Given little time to prepare, she packed a few things and rushed away, without having the chance to say good-bye to her father or her sisters.

After a long, difficult trip, Zilpo, her sister-in-law, and the young boy were smuggled across the border and arrived safely in Kabul. Only upon her arrival did the young and naive Zilpo realize that she was never to return home. She longed for her sisters, who remained in Bukhara. She lamented having left her mother behind in the cemetery in Bukhara without having paid a final visit, and she yearned to see her father again. Although the man whom she would later marry, and the children they would raise together, provided her solace, she never overcame the sudden rupture that left her bereft of her home and all she had left behind. Rahel grew up hearing her mother's stories of loss. And I, in turn, heard them from Rahel, as though she, too, had suffered the loss of her family and home in Bukhara.

Rahel's father—like her Uncle David—was a devout man who fled from the Soviets across the border. Three years after arriving in Afghanistan, he and Zilpo married. Together they built a home and raised five children, but their lives in Afghanistan were forever temporary, a fleeting state sandwiched between a mourned past and an idyllic future. Though Rahel's father found himself physically surrounded by the sights and smells of Kabul, in his imagination—she told me—he continued to walk the streets of Bukhara. He would gather his children around him to describe the courtyard of the home in which he grew up, the path that led from his home to the synagogue, the architectural details of the synagogue, and the Labi Hawz open plaza that surrounded the city's reservoir where men would drink their afternoon tea and children would come to play on long, hot summer afternoons.

In Kabul, his suitcases were like furniture. Rather than unpacking them and tucking them away, he was "forever sitting on his bags," Rahel told me, waiting for the moment that he might be granted permission to move to the Holy Land. It was not until 1948, when the State of Israel was established and migration into the country was legalized, that this became possible. He, his wife, and his children (the adolescent Rahel among them) left Afghanistan and resettled in Tel Aviv.

There, Rahel married a man who was also from Bukhara, and who had a similar migration story. They raised three children together, who were adults by the time I met them. Rahel and her husband often spoke with one another in a Persian language (which they referred to as Bukharit). To their children, however, none of whom took much of an interest in their family history, they spoke in Hebrew.

Moshe, their eldest, married a woman whose parents had immigrated from Yemen. Matti was single and living with his parents. He was often home during the evenings I spent with his mother, but showed little interest in the folktales and family stories his mother told me, and rarely paid attention to our conversations. And Ilana, who was married to a man whose family had immigrated from Morocco, was frustrated by her mother's involvement with the recently arrived Bukharan immigrants. She blamed them for her mother's intense interest in all things Bukharan: her Bukharan cooking, her use of Bukharit to communicate, the songs she sang with prominent Bukharan Jewish musicians who occasionally gathered in her home, her talk of visiting Bukhara one day, the Bukharan folk festivals she attended, and the Bukharan garb which she donned on celebratory occasions.

Ilana told me that at her own son's bar mitzvah, the family put on Bukharan robes and danced to traditional Bukharan music, even though she herself was uncomfortable with this ethnic display. "Sure, the traditions are very nice . . . and my roots are important," she explained, "but I am different than they are. I am a *sabarit* [native-born Israeli]."

Her mother Rahel is no *sabarit*. Although she is a proud Israeli citizen, she has not left her Bukharan past behind. The past to which she clings, however, is a complex one because she longs not for the place where she was born and raised, but rather for her parents' lost home, a place she has never seen.

Like Leora (the descendant of Shlomo Musayev), Rahel was not born in Bukhara, nor has she ever traveled there. However, the families of these two women emigrated under very different circumstances. Shlomo Musayev left because he yearned to live in Jerusalem, and he realized his dream of playing a role in building the city. In contrast, Rahel's parents' relationship to Bukhara was cut short and left unresolved. They were born when the area was under tsarist rule, during the Bukharan Jews' "golden era" of travel, trade, wealth, cosmopolitanism, and great religious freedom. All this changed when the region came under Soviet rule, and they were forced to flee in the midst of famine, poverty, and religious persecution. They bade Bukhara good-bye not only because they were going to live far away, but because Bukhara as they had known it had ceased to exist. Rahel is still trying to conjure up that place through music, singing, stories, and food among friends, at family celebrations, and at the Women's Club social evenings over which she presides. She romanticizes the past, and works to preserve it through the glorification of Bukharan Jewish culture and identity.

Migration in the 1970s

Throughout most of the Soviet period, emigration from the USSR was nearly impossible. In the 1970s, however, when the restrictions were slightly relaxed, many Soviet Jews took advantage of the opportunity to leave. Included among their numbers were several thousand from Uzbekistan and Tajikistan.[10] While most of them moved to Israel, a small minority went elsewhere.[11] Regardless of where they settled, Bukharan Jews who emigrated during this period tended to strongly identify with Judaism and were religiously oriented.[12] Included among them were many dissidents.

Shlomo Haye Niyazov was one of them, remaining steadfast in his commitment to practice and teach Judaism, even in the face of Soviet surveillance. Together with his father, he worked stealthily, teaching religion, running prayer services, and officiating at life-cycle rituals. Always working undercover, Niyazov and his father were still unable to evade the authorities who followed their "each and every step" until they were eventually caught. Under a Jewish pseudonym, an "A. Davidov" (apparently a KGB accomplice) published an article about father and son in *Leninskii Put'* ("Lenin's Way"), the Russian-language daily, which circulated in their hometown, Samarkand.[13]

The piece enumerated the Niyazovs' illegal activities, including "brainwashing" youngsters, performing religious circumcisions, officiating at Jewish weddings, and overseeing religious divorce proceedings. They "strictly observe the law of Moses," penned A. Davidov, but "never the laws of our country." All this, the article continued, is not out of religious conviction, but as part of a calculated and convoluted scheme to get rich (through the support of religious benefactors in the United States). In a final, ominous statement, the author concluded by suggesting that the Niyazovs be given the opportunity to study the laws of the Soviet Union: more specifically, the criminal code, which—A. Davidov explains—calls for their imprisonment, for "they deserve it."

Within weeks of the article's publication, twenty-five-year-old Shlomo Haye Niyazov fled to the United States with his parents, wife, and children. Over time, he adjusted to his life in New York, but never forgot the article published in "Lenin's Way." He established a home, a new synagogue, and published his own book, where he reprinted the article. Here, in *Misirut Nefesh shel Yehudei Bukhara*, it is he—not A. Davidov—who has the last word.

Literally translated, the book's title means "The Soul Sacrifice of the Bukharan Jews." But this translation does not do the words justice. Figuratively, *misirut nefesh* or "soul sacrifice" means the giving over of one's entire self, showing readiness to sacrifice one's very life in the face of great danger, in order to practice Judaism and transmit it to the next generation. The work is a collection of stories about Shlomo Haye Niyazov's role models who worked tirelessly to preserve Judaism in the Soviet Union despite terrible persecution, not for money or honor, but for the pursuit of what is true and right, to carry out the will of God.

Niyazov's book came into my hands in 1993, the year I was teaching at Torah Academy in Queens. I had just begun to search for information to become acquainted with my students' backgrounds. *Read this*, suggested a Bukharan Jewish teacher who gave it to me, *and you will learn who the Bukharan Jews are.* At that time, there was little written material available about the Bukharan Jews' experiences during the Soviet era, and I was grateful for the resource. Nevertheless, I found it perplexing.

While I kept it in the section of my bookshelf devoted to Bukharan Jewish history and culture, the book's spine stuck out as different, suggesting that it may be misclassified. Popular wisdom teaches us that one "cannot judge a book by its cover." Yet, a cover should not be ignored, because it communicates—with the immediacy of the visual and the tactile—its purpose and for whom the book is intended. In the case of Shlomo Haye Niyazov's work, the brown faux-leather binding, with its Hebrew golden-lettered title, has much to say. Its rich texture, devoid of any image, exudes a seriousness of purpose, announcing itself as a book of tradition and truth, the sort of book that a devout Jew would refer to as a *sefer*. In Hebrew, this word, *sefer*, simply means "book." But when an English speaker uses the term, invoking the holy language, he indicates that the work belongs to the same Great Library as the books of Torah and its commentaries, the Mishnah, the Talmud, the codes of Jewish Laws, the works of religious philosophers and mystical thinkers, and the books of psalms and prayers.

Niyazov's *sefer*, with its dark cover, seemed to belong on the shelves of a *beit midrash* (house of religious study), not alongside my other Bukharan Jewish books with their pictures of colorful Central Asian costumes, feasts, musical instruments, and architectural edifices. Based on the black-and-white photo on the front page of the work, Niyazov himself appears to belong in a *beit midrash* as well. Rather than posing in a velvet Central Asian robe and an embroidered cap or karakul hat, his outfit consists of a black fedora and a simple white button-down shirt without a tie. This is a portrait of an ultra-Orthodox Jew. Minus the color, the ethnic performance, the customs and cuisine peculiar to this people, what exactly does it mean that he is a Bukharan Jew?

I arranged to interview Shlomo Haye Niyazov, hoping to gain insight into his own understanding of Bukharan Jewishness, as well as to gather information to fill out the biography he presents in his work, which includes only the sketchiest details. He was born in 1953, studied religion covertly, was certified by his teachers as a religious functionary, was threatened by the KGB, emigrated shortly thereafter, and settled in Brooklyn, New York.

His life story opened many questions that I hoped he would answer in an interview. How did he study and how did he teach without religious texts (which were banned by the Soviets)? What did it mean to be "certified" or "ordained" in an environment where religious institutional life was prohibited? How did he motivate his students to study when facing persecution and great danger?

And then about his Bukharan Jewishness: how does this aspect of his identity fit in with his Jewishness? Does he believe that it is important to preserve and transmit Bukharan Jewishness in America? Does he teach "Bukharan Jewishness" to his students in the United States? And if so, what does this mean, and how does he go about it?

On three separate occasions, I visited him in his cramped jewelry shop in midtown Manhattan. Gentle, slight of frame, and soft-spoken, Shlomo Haye Niyazov was difficult to engage. Each time we met, he seated me across from him, between us a row of glass showcases stuffed with plastic bins that were overflowing with semiprecious stones in sandwich bags. Behind me, I could see into the workroom, a tiny space filled with two heavily worn, pockmarked workbenches. A man sat hunched over each one, working amid scattered silver chains, tiny links, pliers, and colorful jewels.

I tried to ease into our conversations by addressing the immediate surroundings.

"How long have you owned this shop?" I asked.

"A long time," he answered.

"Oh. How many years?"

"Many. . . ."

He trailed off, picked a package off the display case, emptied its contents, and examined them. I tried again.

"Did you learn the trade here or in Uzbekistan before you came?"

"Here. There," he said vaguely, then picked up a slip of paper and jotted down a few notes to himself. I fumbled through my papers, waiting for his attention.

While Shlomo Haye Niyazov was reluctant to offer any information about his jewelry business, when he discussed gems as a spiritual metaphor, his disposition shifted. Speaking immigrant English at a fast clip, and fully focused, he told a story of his father's father Eliyahu Mani:

During World War II, many Ashkenazi Jews fled from their homes in Eastern Europe to Uzbekistan. Seeing that they came to Samarkand destitute and with no social safety network, Grandfather Eliyahu Mani brought many of them into his home. When a typhus epidemic swept through Samarkand, his generosity was not challenged. Although illness ravaged the city, killing many, Eliyahu Mani took in many sick refugees and attended to their ailments, encouraging other Bukharan Jews to do the same. "Go to the streets. They are filled with diamonds!" he would preach. The diamonds of which he spoke were, of course, not material objects, but people, impoverished and ill, each, nevertheless, a fellow Jew, a jewel. Eventually, Eliyahu Mani himself fell ill and succumbed to the sickness, dying at a young age. Shlomo Haye Niyazov, his grandson, never met him, but he was strongly influenced by his actions as well as his teachings.

How did Eliyahu Mani teach Judaism under the Soviets? With whom had he studied and who were his students? In response to these questions, Shlomo Hai Niyazov put aside his notepapers and strings of gems. He looked down toward the floor, locked his hands behind his back, and began to pace as he told me the story of transmission.

In the often-cited *Ethics of the Fathers,* the "chain of transmission" outlines the history of the passing down of the Torah to each successive generation. There, the narrative begins with Moses himself: "Moses received the Torah from God at Sinai. He transmitted it to Joshua, Joshua to the elders, the elders to the prophets, the prophets to the members of the Great Assembly," and so the tradition is passed down, from generation to generation, in an uninterrupted line. Shlomo Haye Niyazov chose to begin his story a mere century ago, but with the understanding that his starting point is just one link that holds the history of the entire chain that preceded it.

Rabbi Shlomo Lev Eliezerov arrived in Bukhara. Until that moment in history, Shlomo Haye Niyazov explained, the Jews of the area had remained steadfast in their religious piety throughout the generations. However, they would not have had the strength to withstand the difficult trials and tribulations that the Soviets were soon to impose upon them, had they not been infused with the mystical and moral teachings of Hasidism.

Shlomo Lev Eliezerov, a disciple of Chabad-Lubavitch, was one of the vehicles through which Hasidism arrived in Bukhara. This was the same man who had come to Central Asia from Hebron, bringing the 1904 meat-slaughtering controversy with him.[14] This dispute, however, held no place in Shlomo Haye Niyazov's narrative. Instead, he focused

on Eliezerov as a teacher who, at the turn of the last century, attracted
many Bukharan Jewish students to his classes on the mystical texts, including the Tanya and the Zohar. Among the students who imbibed his
teachings were those who would rise to become key leaders in the 1920s,
1930s, and 1940s, working to maintain religious practice in Uzbekistan
during Stalin's rule, a period of great oppression. Eliyahu Mani was one
of these students, who in turn passed down the lessons to his son David,
and David, in turn, passed them down to his son, Shlomo Haye himself. Holding fast to their trust in God, the value of *misirut nefesh,* and
the belief in the absolute authority of the religious tradition, these men
transmitted Judaism from one generation to the next.

One synagogue in Samarkand was permitted to function throughout the Soviet era. Built in the 1880s[15] on a small alley in the Jewish
quarter, the Kaniso-i Gumbaz (Domed Synagogue), with its detailed
wood lattice work and its pale-blue painted walls, was the city's officially
sanctioned synagogue. Permitting this single public place of Jewish worship in Samarkand to remain open was part of the Soviets' effort to con-
strain (and eventually eliminate) Judaism by allowing it, while keeping
it controlled and under strict surveillance.

Judaism in Samarkand, however, was not successfully contained
in this single space. The city's Jews would gather together secretly to
run daily prayer services in private homes. Many of these prayer groups
were presided over by elderly men who served as religious functionaries,
leaders, and teachers: Daniel Shakarov, Yosef Alayev, and Eliyahu Mani,
all students of Shlomo Lev Eliezerov. These men also taught Judaism
in homes across the city, studying among small groups. School-aged
students dressed in their red scarves would walk through the streets, as
though going to attend a *komsomol*[16] meeting. When they arrived, they
would put aside their communist trappings and gather together to learn
from their religious teachers.

Shlomo Haye Niyazov studied in this manner, and later ran a large
school that functioned the same way. "I would teach ten kids and each
of those ten had ten students that they taught. . . . That's how it was."
During the years just prior to his emigration, more than one hundred
students belonged to these study circles.

When he emigrated in 1979, Shlomo Haye Niyazov appointed one
of his own students, Emanuel Shimunov (discussed in chapter 9), to

take over his position as "principal" of the underground school. In a conversation with Shimunov,[17] he explained to me: "There was fear from the Communists, from the KGB. So it wasn't advertised that we had a yeshiva. Rather, the students would learn in houses, ten here and ten there. Even the parents did not know where their own children were headed [when they left home]."

After the Soviet era ended, Emanuel Shimunov remained a powerful and influential rabbi in Samarkand, still closely connected to his intellectual and spiritual Hasidic roots. In the late 1990s, when I was doing fieldwork in Samarkand, he was receiving money from Chabad-Lubavitch sources in New York and Israel, which he used to fund a school and summer camp for youngsters, as well as classes for adults.

In the meantime, Shlomo Haye Niyazov had resettled in New York. Although most of New York's Bukharan Jewish immigrants clustered in Queens, he and his family moved to Brooklyn to be close to the residence of the spiritual leader of Chabad-Lubavitch. In Brooklyn, where the doors of the synagogues and study houses were always open, Niyazov was free to come and go as he pleased, and was relieved from the surveillance and threats that had followed him in his hometown. Nevertheless, he found himself uncomfortable in a new way. He missed the aesthetic and style of prayer particular to Bukharan Jews, to which he was accustomed, and felt like an outsider in Brooklyn's established religious institutions. Nor was he alone. He learned that other Bukharan Jews who were scattered in various places across Brooklyn felt the same. Taking on a leadership role again, he gathered together Brooklyn's Bukharan Jewish immigrants and went searching for a space they might call their own.

He found an old Ashekanzi synagogue with rows of seats that were mostly empty on Saturday mornings. He approached the rabbi who presided over the dying congregation: "You have space but no people," he pointed out the obvious, "and we have people but no space." *Let us come fill your hall*—he suggested—*We will rent the space if we can structure a prayer service with which we are accustomed.* A deal was struck, and Shlomo Haye Niyazov became the rabbi of the congregation.

Since then, the congregation has bought its own space, over which Shlomo Haye Niyazov continues to preside. In addition to his role as rabbi, he holds classes, records lectures, and organizes religious programming for youth. In describing his work with the Bukharan Jewish community in New York today, he shrugs his shoulders and explains, "Whatever we are trying [to do] is not enough." A businessman—he tells me—would never say, "I have one dollar and that is enough." So too, five kilos of gold may become heavy, and a difficult load to carry. But if someone says to you, "I'll give you five more," *are you going to take it?* he asked me. *Sure you are!* With a bright smile, he answered his own question.

I never found out how Shlomo Haye Niyazov learned the profession that he practices in his cramped shop in Manhattan's diamond district. But it was clearly his grandfather who inspired him to become a jeweler of the spiritual sort. Niyazov carries the weight of gold on his shoulders, following the lessons of his grandfather who taught him to go out to the streets and collect that which is precious, the hearts and souls of his people.

Today, Shlomo Haye Niyazov is among the elder Bukharan rabbis in New York, not only in terms of his age, but also in terms of the length of time that he has been in service of the Bukharan Jewish immigrant community. For his life's work, he was recently honored by the major umbrella organization, The Bukharan Jewish Congress, for his "visionary leadership and ongoing dedication" to the Bukharan Jewish community in Brooklyn and beyond.

Although Niyazov's extreme religious devotion and his leadership capabilities set him apart from most, his life story nevertheless illuminates several key aspects of the Bukharan Jewish experience. In describing their group's unique characteristics, Bukharan Jews often highlight their continued commitment to Judaism throughout the Soviet era. In particular, they tend to invoke this defining feature when comparing themselves to other Soviet Jews. Like the other Jews who emigrated from the Soviet Union in the 1970s (and later in the 1990s), Bukharan Jews were educated in the Soviet system and speak Russian.[18] For this reason, Americans and Israelis often lump them together. *But we are not Russian Jews,* they emphasize. Unlike many of "them," Bukharan Jews point to their own very low rates of intermarriage and their continued observance of *kashrut* and key Jewish holidays throughout the Soviet era, despite persecution. In this context, "Bukharan Jewish" simply means "committed Jewish."

In the context of migration, though, Bukharan Jewish has come to mean something very different. When Shlomo Haye Niyazov moved to Brooklyn and was surrounded by religious Jews, it was his Central Asianness that suddenly became salient, and he set about looking for that familiar feeling of his synagogue back home. Others search for such familiarity in their cuisine, in the marketplace, or in forms of entertainment. For them—as for Shlomo Haye Niyazov—to be Bukharan means to be Jewish and to be Central Asian.

Migration in the 1990s

Unlike the migration of the 1970s, which involved a small segment of the Bukharan Jewish population, in the years following the disintegration of the Soviet Union almost all of those living in Tajikistan and Uzbekistan packed up their homes and left. Whereas they numbered 50,000 in 1989,[19] today the Bukharan Jewish population in Tajikistan numbers some 100, and in Uzbekistan, less than 1,000 remain. With this population displacement, one of the Jewish world's longest chapters of diaspora history has come to a close.

Several reasons account for their exodus, including economic instability, the rise of Uzbek nationalism, and a fear of Muslim fundamentalism.[20] Perhaps the most complex cause is their tight-knit kinship system.[21] When migration restrictions were eased in 1989 and the first Bukharan Jews packed their belongings and left, irreparable fissures appeared in the tight weave of overlapping relationships. Like a heavy wind that begins to dislodge a sturdy tree from the ground, the leaving of the first critical mass initiated the dramatic rupture that would follow. When a man left with his wife, for example, her sister might soon follow, then that sister's parents-in-law, then those in-laws' siblings, those siblings' children, and so the chain of migration continued. By the first time I visited Uzbekistan in 1993, everyone I met had a child, parent, sibling, or cousin in the United States or Israel.

Those who remained behind watched as the homes of their friends, relatives, and neighbors were sold off, one by one, to Uzbek and Tajik families. Mazal Tsionov commented, "It's terrible what has happened in Bukhara over the last few years. It used to be that only Jews lived here [in this neighborhood]. . . . People would bring out benches and sit on the streets and talk. Now people don't know where they'll be tomorrow." Likewise, fifteen-year-old Nelya told me nostalgically of the days when she and her friends would roam freely through the narrow streets of Samarkand's Jewish *mahalla*. Now their movements were more circumscribed as they found themselves living among outsiders in a neighborhood that no longer belonged to them.

This is what happened to twenty-nine-year-old Dina. Today, she lives with her husband in a tidy one-bedroom apartment in Queens, New York. A vase filled with silk flowers sits on their dining room table, a poster of the Manhattan skyline hangs in the kitchen, and framed portraits from their wedding hang on the living room wall. One day Dina and Alex hope to buy a place of their own, and to have children to fill it. But in the meantime, they are settled where they are.

Much has changed since I met Dina in 1997, when she did not know what place to call home. At that time, I was in the midst of collecting information for my doctoral dissertation, she was fifteen, and we stumbled into a relationship through a set of unexpected circumstances which I describe below. In the decade and a half that has elapsed since then, we have stayed in touch through email and visits in several settings across the globe—in Israel, Uzbekistan, and the United States.

Dina's story of travel in search of a place to call home is particularly appropriate for this section, which addresses the contemporary trials of Bukharan Jews: the dislodging of their millennia-long history in Central Asia and the rupture of their intimate relationship between identity and place. But it is also my own story, as a traveling ethnographer in an interconnected global research setting; where fieldwork is no longer about traveling to a remote locale, collecting data there, and then returning home to analyze and write it up. When ethnographic research occurs in a fluid and fractured setting, the researcher's work easily bleeds into her personal life, as her world and the world of her informants collide. The line between the ethnographer–informant relationship on the one hand, and friendship on the other, can become blurry indeed.

In 1997, I was living in Israel and planning an upcoming research trip to Uzbekistan. In preparing, I had made contact with Midrash Sephardi in the Old City of Jerusalem. This institution was founded in 1980 to address the religious needs of Sephardi communities, scattered across the globe and labeled as "neglected": those that do not have their own rabbis or Jewish schools, and lack access to kosher food and religious texts. Included among Midrash Sephardi's list of such communities are Bogotá, Bombay, Zagreb, Istanbul, Hong Kong, and Bukhara.[22]

To learn about Midrash Sephardi's work in Bukhara, and to connect with the people active in running the programs there, I made an appointment to meet with one of the institution's rabbis and directors. In our very brief meeting, Samuel Kassin—a round and animated middle-aged man—rushed through a description of Midrash Sephardi's main projects in Bukhara: administering a religious elementary school and high school there, and recruiting local religious leadership. Talented and motivated young men who have completed their studies in Midrash Sephardi's high school are identified for further training. They are brought from Bukhara to Jerusalem, where they live and study in Midrash Sephardi's headquarters, and are then sent back to Bukhara to serve as religious functionaries, and in some cases to help teach and administer the Midrash Sephardi school there.

I jotted all of this down, but had no time to ask questions as Samuel Kassin rushed around his office, gathering together his jacket, his cell phone, and scattered papers. *Can't talk now,* he juggled his belongings as he scrambled out of the office with me trailing behind. He was on his way to Ben Gurion International airport to meet twenty youth who were arriving for a study-abroad program. *If you come along for the ride, I'll tell you more. . . .*

I took him up on the offer and hopped in the car. On the way, he told me that I was about to take part in a historic event, as it was the first time Midrash Sephardi was bringing a group of young students from Bukhara to study religion in Israel. The initiative was modeled after "Na'aleh,"[23] a program sponsored by the Jewish Agency for Israel, which brings students to Israel for a year of study with the hope they will learn Hebrew, become acclimated to the country, and ultimately set down roots, become citizens, and encourage their families to join them. Na'aleh occurs within a nonreligious framework, and is primarily targeted toward Ashkenazi Jewish youth from Russia. Midrash Sephardi initiated their new program in an effort to further the institution's religious cause alongside their Zionist one, specifically for the non-Ashkenazi Jewish populations of the former Soviet Union. As we zipped along the highway, Kassin continued: Midrash Sephardi had bought airline tickets for the youngsters who were about to arrive in the country on condition that they each agree to study in a religious boarding school. However, arrangements with boarding schools had yet to be made. Despite the rush and the disorganization, *ha'kol y'hiyeh b'seder,* everything would be fine, he remarked with an excited giggle.

Looking dazed as they exited from the airport, the young teenagers from Bukhara were gathered up and shepherded onto a chartered bus. Samuel Kassin instructed me to join them. *You can take care of the girls,* he winked, and then disappeared, busily conferring with the other Midrash Sephardi administrators. Among them were a number of young men who had been studying in Midrash Sephardi's Jerusalem school for several months, and who knew the newly arrived youth from back home in Bukhara. These young men were assigned the role of "counselors": to help make the youngsters comfortable, particularly in their first days in the country when they would be staying in the Midrash Sephardi dorms (before being placed in the boarding schools where they would spend the year). In the male world of Midrash Sephardi, where no women are to be found (aside from the one who answered phones in the office), arrangements had not been made to tend to the needs of the five adolescent girls among the group of newcomers. At Samuel Kassin's sudden suggestion, I unexpectedly found myself in that role. And that is how I met Dina.

In the traditional city of Bukhara, families tend to keep their daughters close to home, and it is highly unusual for girls to be sent on "study-abroad" programs. The girls who had come on this program, though, all had aunts, uncles, and grandparents already living in Israel, and their own parents were preparing to immigrate within a few months or less. They sent their daughters ahead so that they might start learning Hebrew and getting acclimated in the new country.

Dina's story, though, was different. Her parents still lived in Bukhara and they had no plans to leave. Not that the subject of immigration was not on their minds. Indeed, it was. In fact, it was a constant cause of debate in her home, and a source of great tension between her mother— who was one of eight siblings—and her father, who was an only child.

In the early 1990s, in the months after Uzbekistan became independent, Dina's aunts and uncles (her mother's siblings) began to leave. One by one, they gathered their belongings, sold their homes, and emigrated. Some went to Israel and some to the United States. Dina sensed her mother's increasing loneliness with each passing Jewish holiday. Fewer and fewer relatives remained with whom to celebrate, until at last their family was the only one among the extended kin group that remained behind. Dina's mother cried often, and became depressed. Not only because she missed her parents, her siblings, and her nieces and nephews, but also because she knew her four children had no future in Uzbekistan. With the Jewish community emptying out, who would be left for them to marry? And with nationalism and antisemitism on the rise, what sort of lives could they build there, anyway?

But none of this concerned Dina's grandmother—her father's mother—with whom the family lived. She was an elderly widow, a powerful controlling personality, and set in her ways. She had worked hard her whole life, had bought and rebuilt the house in which she now lived, and was uninterested in moving to a new home or a new country. Dina's father, Simha, who occupied the role of arbiter between his mother's insistence to stay and his wife's pleas to leave, remained steadfastly loyal to his mother. In Central Asia's patrilocal and patriarchal society, the stance Simha took is not an uncommon one. There, when a couple marries, the groom remains in the house where he grew up, and his bride follows him. In his parents' house, where the couple raise their children and make their home, the bonds of filial piety tend to take precedence over the ties of marriage.

Although the tug-of-war that Dina's mother and grandmother were playing for Simha's loyalty made sense in this cultural context, the arguments were nevertheless unpleasant, and Dina wanted to escape. Like her mother, Dina believed that she and her siblings had no future in Uzbekistan. So, too, she understood her mother's situation of powerlessness. "I was the oldest [child]" she told me, reflecting back years later, "and I thought maybe I could [be the one to] make a change in the family." When Midrash Sephardi publicized its new all-expenses-paid study-abroad program, she saw this as the opportunity she had been looking for. Strong-willed and driven, she planned to improve her Hebrew, learn to navigate Israel, and send for her siblings soon enough. She hoped her parents would eventually come as well. Yet, in spite of Dina's independent streak and her sharp wits, she was still only fifteen. She became homesick almost as soon as she arrived in Israel, and her plan did not unfold as she had hoped it would.

During their first few days in the country, Dina and the other young-sters were bright-eyed and excited about their new adventure. They all stayed in the Midrash Sephardi dorms, they ate their meals together, and toured Jerusalem together. Tending to their needs was me (who took a special interest in learning about the lives they had left behind in Bukhara) as well as the young men whom they knew from home.

This changed, though, when the handful of girls was separated from the boys with whom they had arrived, taken out of Midrash Sephardi's small, warm dormitory life, and placed in an ultra-Orthodox boarding school in Bnei Brak, where the teachers and counselors did not know them or understand their language. The school was run on a low budget, accommodations were less than adequate, the student-to-staff ratio was high, and the new girls were given little attention and no emotional sup-port to help them settle into their new lives.

Dina, the most outspoken of the bunch, and the only one whose parents were not on their way to the country, called me, crying, at every brief opportunity she was given to use the phone. After many telephone conversations, and after I paid a few visits to the school's campus in Bnei Brak, I conferred with Midrash Sephardi administrators about releasing Dina from the boarding school. We packed her belongings into a little bag, left the campus, and traveled together to her relatives' homes to see if any of them might agree to take her in. We went to her mother's siblings in Yehud, and to her grandmother's sister in Tel Aviv. All were recent immigrants, crowded into small apartments, working long hours, barely making enough to feed their own children. No one was willing to take their niece on as a responsibility. Lonely and homeless, Dina spent a few nights on a mattress on the floor of my apartment.

Not more than two months after she had arrived in Israel, Dina was on a plane back to Uzbekistan. I helped her book the ticket, and bought one for myself on the same flight. There, among the many people whom I interviewed and spent time with during this research stint, were the family members of all the Midrash Sephardi youth whom I had got-ten to know in Israel. Among them, of course, were Dina's parents, her grandmother, and her siblings, who lived together in a large house that wrapped around a courtyard in Bukhara's Jewish quarter.

Dina moved back into the bedroom that she shared with her sisters, and she reenrolled in the Bukhara branch of the Midrash Sephardi high school where she had been a student before leaving for Israel. She was, however, still unsettled. The dynamic in her small class was dramatically different now that four of her friends were living in Israel. Outside the walls of the school, the Jewish quarter also continued to empty of her friends, relatives, and neighbors. As the Jews moved out, Uzbeks and Tajiks (local Muslims) moved in. Dina—like all those who were left behind—felt increasingly like a stranger in the neighborhood she used to call home.

Although she was a straight-A student, when she finished her studies and graduated from the Jewish school, Dina did not enroll in a local university, nor did she seek employment. *No use investing in life in Uzbekistan,* Dina thought, as she continued to wait for her grandmother and father to give into the great tidal wave of emigration that had left her and her siblings behind, like a few scattered pebbles on a sandy beach. Though she was physically still on Central Asian soil, her heart was already abroad, where she knew that a degree from Bukhara's university was worth little, and whatever earnings she would make in the local currency were hardly worth the effort. So she remained at Midrash Sephardi, a small international Jewish island, now in the role of teacher.

Finally, late in the fall of 1999, her waiting ended. The family received news from the U.S. immigration agency handling their case that their entry visas could no longer be renewed. They had been issued years ago, and an aunt of Dina's who lived in New York had paid an annual fee to keep them active. This would soon not be possible. If the family did not leave within the next few months, their opportunity would be lost.

Dina's mother hired a lawyer and began making preparations to divorce her husband and take her children to the United States. At that moment, when Dina's mother became resolute about leaving, it so happened that her mother-in-law, who was now close to eighty, had begun to lose some of her mental faculties. She ceased to hold her ground, and Simha agreed to leave with his wife and children, taking his mother with them.

The seven of them landed in New York in December 1999, at the turn of the millennium. Ready to finally embark on her new life, Dina felt the timing was appropriate. Nevertheless, the family's arrival during the dead of winter brought the logistical problem of finding a vacant apartment in the midst of America's holiday season, when no one was moving anywhere. Dina's mother's sisters each offered their help, but none was able to host all seven newcomers. The family members then scattered among the four aunts. Dina went to live with the aunt in Brooklyn. Dina's parents, grandmother, and youngest brother went to live with one aunt in Queens. And Dina's two sisters also separated, each moving in with different aunts (also in Queens). "We split up and spread out," Dina told me. She was speaking about her immediate family's experiences, but also seemed to be addressing the experiences of all the families from her hometown who were now scattered and dispersed across cities and continents.

I visited Dina that summer, several months after their arrival. She was working in a bakery, studying English, and getting ready to enroll in a local university. Her family had finally found a place to live. From their sprawling house and courtyard in Bukhara, the seven of them had crowded into a modest one-bedroom apartment.

Dina did not stay there for long. Less than two years after she arrived in the country, she met the young man who would become her husband. They were both students at a university in Queens, where many Bukharan Jewish immigrants have enrolled. They took note of each other in the hallways. "I knew he was Bukharian," Dina told me; "He has the look." But she never considered engaging him in conversation. She had planned to date traditionally, which meant that her parents (or a matchmaker of their choosing) would select her suitors, and that she would only go out with a young man after his parents and her own had met and formally agreed to allow the pair to get to know one another. While they would have the opportunity to go out for dinner, to a movie, or to a park, their comings and goings would be closely monitored, with the clear understanding that the purpose of such encounters was solely to determine if they were suited for marriage.

When Alex began flirting with her by asking for her class notes and offering her rides home, she shied away from his advances. "I am not that type," she would say. He was from the same cultural universe as she, and understood what that meant. His family, however, had emigrated when he was still a boy. Having grown up in the United States, he did not feel as strongly bound to the cultural norms of Central Asia. "You are too old-fashioned," he joked with her. "We are in America now."

Dina was caught between the old world and the new. In Bukhara, she had learned that courtship was a family affair, governed by rules that did not allow for the indulgence of passion. In this system, the "dating" period was primarily for the families to determine whether they were suited to become in-laws. While in America, where romantic love is celebrated, she came to understand that both courtship and marriage belong first and foremost to the couple themselves.

Making a subtle allowance for this cataclysmic shift in orientation, Dina gave in to a few brief furtive meetings with Alex. Never swaying far, though, she demanded that if they were to continue to get to know one another it would have to be done properly. Complying, Alex had his parents pay a formal visit to her parents to request permission for them to date.

Two months later, after a series of closely monitored excursions, Alex's parents presented Dina's parents with a basket of sweets, signifying a proposal for marriage. Dina's parents responded by inviting Alex's family to a celebratory dinner. With that, the couple was formally engaged. They married soon thereafter, and moved into his parents' home, as they would have done if they were still living in Central Asia. This living arrangement was a way to save money, and Dina insisted that once she graduated and found a job, they would rent a place of their own. Life in the same house as her in-laws, she feared, would recreate the harsh dynamic between wife, husband, and mother-in-law that she had witnessed growing up. *We are in America now,* she reminded Alex.

As though to emphasize this point, two large photographs of the couple hang on the living-room wall of the tidy one-bedroom apartment in which they now live. If this living room had been in Central Asia, two very different sorts of portraits would have occupied this same space on the wall: one of the family matriarch, and the other of the patriarch. Here in New York, though, the pictures in their massive gilded frames are of her in her white bridal gown, and him in his black tuxedo.

They stand alone. No parents, in-laws, grandparents, or siblings are around them. Or so it seems. A visitor can be fooled by these pictures, which appear to pay homage to the strength of the marriage bond itself, but which hover here like question marks in Dina and Alex's apartment.

The invitation to their wedding asked guests to take part in their "celebration of love," and the romance of couplehood was given much attention that evening. But the parents of the bride and groom stood by awkwardly, not sure of what to do when the bridal pair performed an elaborate, choreographed dance amid soft blue lights and a theatrical mist emitted from a dry-ice smoke machine. Many elderly relatives ignored all this romantic staging, offering toasts to the family, rather than to the couple, that they should come together again in a year to celebrate the circumcision of Dina and Alex's firstborn son.

Today, several years later, these blessings have still not been realized. And the choreographed dance of love has become fraught with difficulties. After much trouble conceiving, and extensive medical intervention, there are still no children. "Alanna, you can't understand what it's really like," Dina tells me, knowing full well that I, myself, had been through years of infertility treatment before my daughters were born. Coping with it as a Bukharan Jew, though, is a wholly different experience. "You Americans have easier ways of dealing with this sort of thing," she says.

When Dina came to visit me in Cambridge, Massachusetts, a few years ago, she noted that my husband and I live far from my parents, siblings, in-laws, and other kin. She remarked that I have much less social support than she has as a Bukharan Jew in Queens; there is no one to help me when my husband is out of town, or when my children are home from daycare due to illness. At the same time, she understood that this arrangement translates into a great deal of freedom from the sort of prying and prodding that she experiences, from kin members who feel that her reproductive life is just as much their business as hers. She wondered out loud what her infertility experience would be like if she lived far from her relatives and in-laws.

But it is not only nosy relatives to which she was referring when she compared the "American" way of coping with infertility to the Bukharan way. *You Americans,* she told me, have the possibility of adoption. *For us, Bukharans, this is not really an option.* The bonds of kinship and group identity are simply too strong. An adopted child would forever be an ostracized outsider among them: "He would never be accepted, and no one would allow their daughter to marry him." Dina herself knows only one person who is adopted; a boy who was the seventh child born to his biological mother. Taking pity on her childless sister, the mother gave the baby away, to be raised by his aunt and uncle. This is the only sort of adoption that would be accepted among the Bukharans, Dina explained, one that remained in the family. As the oldest sibling, Dina holds out no hope for such an arrangement.

Of all the difficulties associated with infertility among Bukharan Jews, perhaps the most difficult to contend with are the shadows cast by the folktales, stories, and halakhic discussions about what happens to a woman who is unable to conceive after ten years of marriage. The couple must divorce, so that the man may father children and continue his patriline.

Late at night, after Alex has gone to sleep, Dina and I stay up talking at her dining-room table, under the gaze of their wedding portraits. She wonders if her own marriage will end this way a few years from now. Are these tales from the old world relevant in the new one? Can marriage exist outside of the kinship network that was so powerful in Central Asia? Just how resilient are the ties of love that bind a couple together here in America?

For Dina, to be a Bukharan Jew is about having lived through upheaval and dispersion. It is about making a new home in the face of dramatic rupture between history, identity, and the past. So, too, to be a Bukharan Jew is to be a part of a large, tight-knit community and to navigate the difficult line between the rules and cultural norms brought from Central Asia and the ideals presented to them as new Americans.

Leora, Rahel, Shlomo Haye, and Dina have had different experiences as Bukharan Jews, each shaped in part by their individual characters and respective personal life trajectories. Each has also been shaped by the larger social forces to which they have been exposed: Leora, as the descendant of a Bukharan Jew who helped to found the Bukharan Jewish quarter, Rahel as the descendant of refugees from Bukhara to Afghanistan and later Israel, Shlomo Haye as a Soviet dissident, and Dina as a recent migrant who left Central Asia in the midst of massive community upheaval.

Although each one of them carries their own particular views, experiences, and inheritances, in the post-Soviet, interconnected world in which they now live, none is isolated from the others. Encounters with Bukharan Jews—some with experiences very different from their own—have challenged their ideas about what Bukharan Jewishness is all about.

ELEVEN

Negotiating Authenticity
and Identity: Bukharan Jews
Encounter Each Other and the Self

Having explored the experiences of Bukharan Jews who emigrated (or whose ancestors emigrated) from Central Asia during four different eras, and under four very different sets of circumstances, we return here to a critical examination of the *Edah* Paradigm. This conceptual framework is used as a vehicle to contend with cultural difference within the Jewish world. With strong parallels to the biblical portrayal of ancient Israelite tribes, it allows for a great range of diversity among the Jewish People by legitimizing and celebrating the unique histories and traditions of various diaspora groups (characterized as *edot*, the plural of *edah*), while maintaining a view of the Jews as a common, united people.

The paradigm hinges on the notion that like other *edot*, the Bukharan Jewish *edah* has its own unique history, a well-defined territory that came to be thought of as their diaspora homeland, and a clear set of traditions and character traits. In this model, variations *between* the *edot* are presented and understood to be ordered, predictable, and even sacred, rather than random or idiosyncratic. For this reason, regional differences and historical change *within* each particular *edah* tend to be flattened in exchange for an image of a static, culturally isolated group. Along these lines, museum exhibits, documentary films, and folk festivals present Bukharan Jews as a reified community; these venues gloss over the very same cultural and historical differences among them that were carefully developed in the previous chapter.

What this means for Bukharan Jews' understandings of themselves is complex. Through intimate, firsthand knowledge, Bukharan Jews are acutely aware of the great historical and cultural diversity that exists among them. Yet, they are simultaneously exposed to the same images presented to a wider Jewish public and have internalized this view, at least to some extent. These two sources of knowledge—the intimate, on the one hand, and the public, on the other—often generate contradictory messages.

This chapter is about two sorts of conceptual negotiations that surround Bukharan Jews' own efforts to understand and define this aspect of their identity. The first consists of debates between various individuals, each with different sorts of historical experiences, about what Bukharan Jewishness is, and who has the authority to decide. The second is the individual's complicated effort to navigate between a view of himself or herself as belonging to a reified, clearly defined *edah,* alongside the understanding of the category's dynamic and slippery nature.

Encounters

It used to be that anthropologists would travel to discrete and bounded sites called "the field," stay there, do research, and then return home. As an anthropologist studying Bukharan Jews in the 1990s, my experience was very different.[1] Massive emigration, which splintered apart family and community groups, has meant that there is no longer a "homeland" or single place where they might be studied. Over the course of my traveling fieldwork, which took me to far-flung sites in the United States, Israel, and Uzbekistan, I found that just as there is no single place that might be considered "home" to the Bukharan Jews, so, too, there is no model "Bukharan Jew."

The life stories of Leora, Rahel, Shlomo Haye, and Dina presented in the previous chapter are an effort to capture the multiplicity of understandings of what being Bukharan Jewish is all about. This sort of presentation, however, only tells a part of the story, for in this portrayal, each individual occupies his or her own separate frame. In reality, immigrants from the various waves do not occupy discrete places. Rather, they pass through shared spaces. Just as I, the anthropologist, came into contact with a wide array of Bukharan Jews, so, too, they came into contact with one another in a variety of forums, described below.

INSTITUTIONAL LIFE

Bukharan Jewish institutional life is one important area of encounter.
In the 1990s, mass migration from the former Soviet Union put a strain
on social service aid agencies already in place to help new immigrants,
such as the Ministry of Absorption in Israel, and nongovernmental organizations in the United States, such as the New York Association for
New Americans and the Hebrew Immigrant Aid Society. In response,
Bukharan Jews who had left Central Asia in decades past (or whose parents or grandparents had) took an interest in the fate of those who were
newly arriving; they poured funds and energies into organizing schools,
newspapers, elderly centers, synagogues, and Internet sites to provide
them with tools to successfully adapt to their new homes. In Tel Aviv,
for example, old-timer Bukharan Jews set up soup kitchens to cater
specifically to the needs of impoverished Bukharan Jewish immigrants.
Likewise, long-time resident Bukharan Jews in New York established
Jewish youth clubs to provide a healthy, drug-free atmosphere for newcomer Bukharan Jewish youth to socialize with their peers.

Among communal leaders, there is disagreement about whether
serving these immigrants within a specifically Bukharan Jewish framework is a means to an end, or an end in itself; whether the ultimate aim
is to preserve Bukharan Jewish identity and culture, or simply to use
it as a bridge to ease the immigrants' integration into wider society.
Regardless, there is general consensus among nonprofit aid workers in
both the United States and Israel that the most successful way to ease
the immigrants' transition to their new homes is to offer social services
in a Bukharan Jewish context.

Such services tend to be organized and run by individuals who are
themselves Bukharan Jews, but who had immigrated in previous waves
(or at the very beginning of the most recent wave).[2] They are generally
funded by these same Bukharan Jews, who often leverage their financial contributions to involve other governmental and nongovernmental
organizations.

One such modest organization was Moreshet Yahadut Bukhara (The
Heritage of Bukharan Jews), founded in the early 1990s in the Shapira
neighborhood of South Tel Aviv. Among other activities, this organization supported a Bukharan Jewish theater troupe, a soup kitchen, and

a Bukharan Jewish women's club (the one over which Rahel presided, as described in the previous chapter). The founder of this organization, Eli Aminov, is a politician who represented his district on the Tel Aviv City Council.[3]

Aminov's constituency consisted primarily of Shapira's large Bukharan Jewish population, mostly immigrants who have arrived since 1990. Aminov, too, is a Bukharan Jew. Unlike most of Shapira's residents, however, he was born in Israel and is the descendant of immigrants who left Bukhara in the 1920s. Likewise, his advisors, administrators, and secretaries are all second- or third-generation Bukharan Jewish immigrants.

An organization considerably older than Moreshet Yahadut Bukhara and which has had a much larger impact on the Bukharan Jewish social landscape is the Bukharan Jewish Center, located in Queens, New York. This organization, founded in 1953 as a social club and charity foundation, was originally named The Bokharan Jewish Aid Society.[4] At that time, the Bukharan Jewish population in New York numbered only some twenty families.[5] Most had come to New York from Central Asia via Israel, and had founded the Aid Society to raise money to support fellow Bukharan Jews who were in need in Israel.[6]

In the early 1960s, the Bokharan Jewish Aid Society gave up its largest project, handing over the Aminoff Home for the Aged to the Israeli government. The organization was renamed "The Bokharan Jewish Association," and its fundraising efforts were channeled toward creating a "Bokharan Jewish Community Center" in Queens, meant to serve the Bukharan Jewish families residing in New York, whose numbers had increased to about one hundred by that time.[7]

In the 1970s, when emigration restrictions from the former Soviet Union were slightly relaxed, a new wave of Bukharan Jewish immigrants arrived in New York.[8] In response, the "old-timers" revamped their programs to serve the needs of these new immigrants, and invested in a new building.[9] Among those who were active at that time was Hanan Benjamini, who was born in 1917, left Samarkand in 1922, and moved to pre-State Israel. Later in life he left Israel and resettled in the United States, where he played a pivotal role in managing what came to be known as the Bukharan Jewish Community Center.[10] When the Soviet Union dissolved and Bukharan Jews began to pour into New York, Benjamini continued his aid work. In 1998, when I conducted a needs-assessment study of the Bukharan Jewish population in Queens,[11] I was urged to speak to Benjamini because he was considered to be an elderly, respected leader with a broad, long-range view of New York's Bukharan Jewish institutional life. Among other projects, he had been involved in establishing a loan society, organizing a burial society, arranging language courses for new immigrants to learn English, coordinating a soup kitchen, and recruiting religious leadership to serve the community.

Today, Hanan Benjamini is no longer alive, but the projects in which he was so involved for thirty years continue to thrive. The modest building that had housed the Bukharan Jewish Community Center was torn down and a new building was opened in its place in 2005. At a cost of several million dollars, the impressive structure now stands five stories tall, and houses meeting rooms and classrooms, offices, two party halls, and three sanctuaries that can accommodate up to 1,000 worshipers.[12] Those who use the services of the community center are primarily Bukharan Jews who have immigrated since the dissolution of the Soviet Union. Many (though not all) of those who fund, administer, and preside over the center, however, are old-timers who came in previous waves of migration.

Perhaps most noteworthy of all Bukharan Jewish organizations is the Bukharan Jewish World Congress, which serves as a worldwide umbrella organization for Bukharan Jewish communal institutions scattered across the globe. This organizing body was founded in 1996 in an effort "to create local community centers" and to "unite [the] disconnected hearths of Bukharian Jewish life."[13] Today branches of the Congress exist in Israel, Austria, Russia, Canada, and the United States.

The Bukharan Jewish North American Congress, which oversees the functioning of more than fifty religious and cultural organizations, was launched in 1999. The colorful, oversized, 384-page book, published in celebration of its founding, charts the Congress's history and documents the organization's founding event with transcripts of the speeches delivered by over fifty delegates to the convocation. It contains biographical notes on the Congress's committee chairs, minutes from planning meetings, congratulatory letters written by public officials, information on Bukharan Jewish communities scattered across North America, and hundreds of photo collages documenting the life of the Congress and its various organizations.

This book's title offers a strong and succinct statement of the Congress's purpose. Written in large letters, it is printed in the center of the hefty volume, surrounded by an array of thumbnail photos of Bukharan Jews. Amid the young and old, women and men, dark- and fair-skinned, the title proclaims, "The Congress United Us." Indeed, this was the central message of the event itself, which served as a forum for delegates and visitors from Bukharan Jewish organizations who emigrated from Central Asia in different migration waves, and who traveled from their new homes in places scattered across the United States and Canada[14] to come together, meet each other, share their ideas and experiences, and articulate their belonging to a common group as well as share their vision for its future.

The organizations described above—Moreshet Yahadut Bukhara in Tel Aviv, the Bukharan Jewish Community Center in New York, and the North American Congress—are just three examples of institutional frameworks that serve as meeting grounds for individuals who all identify as "Bukharan Jews," but who have had varied migration histories and exposure to a range of cultural and social influences.

FAMILY REUNIONS

Another forum in which Bukharan Jews from different waves of immigration intersect is at family reunions, such as the one that Leora Gevirtzman imagined she might plan when we met in her home in Israel to discuss her family tree (see chapter 10). The Issacharoff family successfully organized such a reunion, which was held in Israel in the summer of 1998. I learned about the event through Yitzhak Abramov, a middle-aged man whom I had met while doing research in Samarkand in 1997, and with whom I reconnected in Israel shortly after he immigrated. He told me about the reunion he had attended in Jerusalem, which had been organized in honor of the arrival of the family matriarch, Malko, in Jerusalem one hundred years earlier.

At the time of her migration, Malko was an elderly woman. Some of her children moved to Jerusalem with her, and others remained in Central Asia, creating branches of a family tree that came to reside in several locales. Those who organized the reunion were from the branch that had been living in Israel since the late nineteenth century, whereas

Yitzhak Abramov, a great-great-grandson of Malko, was from a branch that had remained in Central Asia. Despite the generations and varied experiences that separated Yitzhak and the reunion organizers, they came together, along with some five hundred others, to celebrate their common family history. Together they visited the Bukharan quarter and cemeteries where their ancestors were buried, and attended a reception. Name tags were distributed, and people introduced themselves to one another, each reporting when they (or their ancestors) had arrived in Israel. "A year, ten years, twenty years, sixty years, eighty years they have been living here," Yitzhak told me. Each participant was also given a book that had been prepared by the old-time Israeli family members who had organized the reunion. The book, *Issacharoff: A Tale of a Family*,[15] contains a massive family tree with biographical data for the more than one thousand individuals included in the diagram, as well as photographs and life stories of many family members.

While the Issacharoff family reunion was carefully planned and orchestrated, memorial services for the deceased[16] provide a forum through which family members come together in an ad hoc fashion. In Central Asia these rituals were generally local affairs, where family members and friends living in the same city would get together to mourn and remember. As a result of the splintering migration patterns of these community and family groups, memorial services held today now serve as a forum for them to reconnect. In addition, they have become a venue for Bukharan Jews who immigrated during various waves to activate family ties that had long been dormant.

For example, I attended a memorial service with Rahel Karayof[17] that marked thirty days after the passing of her aunt.[18] I expected that the others in attendance would be old-timers (like Rahel, who had been living in Israel since the 1950s), so I was taken aback when I saw Aron Tsionov, whom I knew from my recent trips to Bukhara. My surprise was in part because I had not realized that he had emigrated. More disorienting, though, was the collision of two areas of my research. I kept separate file folders for my research in Uzbekistan and my research in Israel, tended to use different languages in each site, and generally imagined the two as separate. Yet Aron and Rahel were, in fact, related, and here at this memorial service their lives intersected, as did those of the others present, some of whom had arrived in Israel in the 1950s, some in the 1970s, and others—like Aron—in the 1990s.

TOURISM

Travel and tourism is a third forum in which the lives of Bukharan Jews from different waves of immigration intersect. When the Soviet Union dissolved, many of the restrictions placed on tourists visiting Uzbekistan were lifted. Additionally, flights into the area became less expensive and more frequent. Bukharan Jews who had left their homes in the 1970s, and who had not been able to return since then, took advantage of these new travel opportunities and came to visit family members whom they had left behind. Uzbekistan also became a popular destination for individuals who were not born in Central Asia (but whose parents and grandparents were) as a means to connect to their roots.

In addition to traveling to visit the homes they left behind (or that their ancestors had left behind), some Bukharan Jews who emigrated in previous decades return to Uzbekistan to serve as teachers and community leaders in the Jewish institutions that have been established in the post-Soviet era. These institutions are primarily funded and administered by Jewish organizations in Israel and the United States. For example, Bukharan Jews who immigrated to Israel in the 1970s as children, and who were trained to serve as religious functionaries at Midrash Sephardi's Jerusalem headquarters, return to Uzbekistan to serve as administrators and teachers in the high school and adult education programs that Midrash Sephardi runs there.

PUBLIC DISCOURSE

Public discourse is another forum in which Bukharan Jews with varied migration histories encounter one another. Among the films, newspaper articles, books, museum exhibits, websites, and folklore festivals, some are produced, written, and sponsored by Bukharan Jews themselves, while others are produced by filmmakers, journalists, historians, photographers, and museum curators who are not Bukharan Jews. Regardless, they send out messages to the general public as well as to those who identify as Bukharan Jews, and are available for the consumption of both.

FIGURE 11.1
Portrait of a Bukharan Jewish meal, staged in Tel Aviv, 1997
Courtesy of Nelli Sheffer

These media present a range of images about the nature of Bukharan Jewish culture and identity. The images fall into three broad categories. First, Bukharan Jews had a unique, rich, and colorful culture in Central Asia. Now that their history in the region has come to a close, that culture is in danger of being lost, so efforts must be made to preserve it. Second, Bukharan Jews faced much hardship in their efforts to remain loyal to Jewish traditions. During much of their history they were far away from the world's Jewish religious centers, and during the Soviet period they were subject to great oppression. In spite of these difficulties, they were successful in upholding the religion and maintaining their identity as Jews through their great devotion and commitment to the religion. Third, Bukharan Jews had an enduring commitment to the Jewish People and to the national homeland in Israel. The Bukharan Quarter in Jerusalem is one important manifestation of this commitment.

Each of these messages highlights a different aspect of Bukharan Jewishness, which in some ways stand in opposition to one another. Nevertheless, together they lend an aura of facticity to the category of Bukharan Jews. Use of the term in writing, performance, and display solidifies and maintains the notion that it has a stable, definable referent.

NEGOTIATING BUKHARAN JEWISHNESS: CLAIMING AUTHENTICITY

Charles Lindholm's book *Culture and Authenticity* aptly illustrates that in their yearning for belonging and authenticity, "people strongly identify themselves as members of various national-ethnic-racial-tribal-religious collectives" that are "felt to be real, essential, and vital" and that provide participants with "meaning, unity, and a surpassing sense of belonging."[19] While the anthropologist might highlight the ways in which "such collective identities are historically constructed, internally complex, and inevitably divided," such evidence "does not make them any less real and compelling to those who belong to them."[20] This is most certainly true in the case of Bukharan Jews. But it is also true that they—like the anthropologist—regularly come face to face with the complexity and blurriness of the very category itself. In their travels, in the immigrant institutions in which they take part, in the family reunions they attend, and in public discourse, individuals who identify as Bukharan Jews cannot help but engage with others who also identify as Bukharan Jews, but who have very different ideas about what this means. Such encounters make it nearly impossible to avoid difficult questions related to the nature of the group's authenticity: Who and what is representative of "Bukharan Jewish" and who is authorized to decide these questions? Most poignantly, if the answers are so unclear, is this category legitimate at all?

Earlier in this book I presented a historical discussion about the way in which the term *Bukharan Jew* and its attendant category came into existence in late nineteenth-century Jerusalem.[21] This explanation, pieced together through analysis of letters and community announcements, offered a detached social history, rather than a story I heard from Bukharan Jews themselves.

Also interested in individuals' conceptions of their own identity, I turned to them to learn the ways they understand and discuss the category. How do people speak about their own sense of what it means to be a Bukharan Jew? When and how do they believe the group came into existence? And what do they see as the salient characteristics of Bukharan Jewishness? In the process of asking these questions, I found that the very features that some view as defining and essential may be derided and even dismissed by others.

David grew up in Samarkand and moved to Israel as a teenager, which is where I met him in 1997, a few years after he had immigrated. In a discussion about why he refers to himself as a "Bukharan Jew" given that he was not born in the city of Bukhara, he invoked a familiar story: Long ago, the emir of Bukhara brought ten families from Persia to serve as craftsmen in his court. David's ancestors were among this group. "Over the years," David continued, "these families had children, and these children had children," and they spread across the region. Despite having resettled in Samarkand, he explained, his ancestors participated in the Bukharan Jews' defining event, and for this reason they carry this status wherever they go.

David is just the sort of person who Roza believes is mistaken in calling himself a Bukharan Jew. I met her in 1997 at a meeting of the Bukharan Jewish Women's Club in South Tel Aviv. Sitting next to me and watching me take notes, she leaned over to ask what I was doing. When I told her that I was gathering information for a book on Bukharan Jews, she advised, "Most of the women here are not Bukharan Jews. If you want to know about Bukharan Jews, come to my house. I can tell you all about them. I know because I am a Bukharan Jew. I am from the city Bukhara. These other women are mostly from other cities: Samarkand, Margalan, Kokand, Fergana. They aren't the real Bukharan Jews. The real ones stayed in their own city [Bukhara] and did not leave."

For Yosef, on the other hand, the point of origin is irrelevant with regard to people like David and Roza, who are recent immigrants from Central Asia. I met him in Israel in 1997, and we discussed the book I was writing. When I explained that I had conducted many interviews with new immigrants to Israel, Yosef frowned. He himself is an elderly man who was born in Dushanbe, Tajikistan's capital, and immigrated to Israel when he was a young child. "If you want to see the true Bukharans, then you should speak to those who came to Israel in the 1930s." Unlike the new immigrants, whom he described as "Bukharans, but not really Bukharans," these old-timers, Yosef remarked, were Zionists who came to pre-State Israel to build up the state. He and his family were involved in funding and administering organizations that serve the new Bukharan Jewish immigrants, and he clearly felt connected to them. Yet, as I packed up my notebook and said good-bye, he left me with this parting piece of advice: "Regarding those who just came recently—don't waste your time!"

Unlike Yosef, those individuals who were still living in Uzbekistan in the 1990s often emphasized that Bukharan Jews like themselves, who were born in Central Asia and who grew up there, are the authentic ones. In this framework, Yosef is viewed as Israeli and "not really Bukharan." This was the approach of forty-year-old Luda, whom I met in Samarkand in 1997. She was born there, as were her parents and grandparents. She has a cousin who left Samarkand in 1969 to move to Israel. Before immigrating her cousin gave birth to a son, and some time after she had resettled she gave birth to another son. "There is only five years' difference in age between the son [who was born in Israel] and his brother," Luda pointed out. "But his face looks different. Maybe it is because the sun in Israel is different because it is closer to the equator. Seriously, I saw a difference. He knows the Bukharan language, but his character is different and his ideas are different, even though he is from the same parents. Just totally different. Honestly. Even if you compare photographs of the boys from when they were each four years old, you can see that he is totally different."

For Luda, to be a Bukharan Jew means to be born in Central Asia. This idea was echoed in a discussion I had with Chana, who immigrated to Israel from Dushanbe in 1991 when she was in her twenties. In describing a cousin who was born in Israel to parents who were from Central Asia, Chana said, "She does not look Bukharan." I questioned her, "Why not? Her parents are Bukharan." Chana answered by pointing to her daughter who was playing in the living room where we were talking. "She was born here and she doesn't look Bukharan." Fumbling for an explanation, she suggested that it may be "because of the food," or because of the "people that her mother was looking at when she was pregnant." Whatever the explanation, to her it was clear that children who are not "of Bukhara" are not truly Bukharan.

Debates

When individuals such as David, Roza, Yosef, Luda, and Chana, who all identify as Bukharan Jews but who carry very different ideas about what this means, come together, contestation often ensues. Such debates are carried out in public discourse, in the institutional sphere, and in private arenas. So, too, they are carried out in the most intimate recesses of the self, as individuals question whether they themselves belong to the category "Bukharan Jew" and if so, what exactly this means.

PUBLIC DISCOURSE

While the existence of "the Bukharan Jews" is taken for granted in titles of books and newspapers, the defining features of the group are often questioned within these same works. For example, in *Shofar,* the newspaper published by the Bukharan Jewish Cultural Center in Samarkand, an article appeared in 1998 titled "Why Are We Bukharan Jews?" The piece began with the statement, "Strange question, isn't it?"[22] A question was also used as the title of an article that appeared in 1998 in the Bukharan Jewish Israeli newspaper, *Bukharskaya Gazeta:* "If We Bukharan Jews are not Sephardim, then who are we?"[23]

In his self-published book *The Bukharan Jews,* Yu Datkhaev argues that the term did not originate when the emir of Bukhara brought ten families from Persia to his court (as David suggested, above). Rather, the term came into use in the context of the Jews' diaspora *from* Bukhara in the fourteenth century when the conqueror Tamerlane "sent several hundred Jewish families [from the city Bukhara] to help rebuild the city Samarkand."[24]

Many remained in Samarkand, but others scattered across the region. Despite their dispersion, they never forgot their origins. "They did not become known as 'Samarkand Jews,' 'Tashkent Jews,' 'Khudzhand Jews' or 'Hissar Jews,'" Datkhaev argues. Rather, they retained strong connections to their origins, calling themselves "Bukharan Jews."

Datkhaev then goes on to criticize those who use general terms such as "native Jews," "local Jews," or "Central Asian Jews" in place of the designation *Bukharan Jews*. Pointing his finger at the Jews of Samarkand and Tashkent, he claims it is primarily they who are guilty of avoiding the term *Bukharan Jew*. The reason, he contends, is that they consider themselves to be "elite" and wish to dissociate themselves from the Jews who remained in the city Bukhara, whom they consider to be "much lower."[25] He continues, berating them, "Whether you like it or not, dear brothers from Tashkent and Samarkand, the term 'Bukharan Jew' is the historically correct name for our ethnic group."[26]

Author Pinhas Niyazov disagrees, responding to Datkhaev's point with a rebuttal. In his article "How and Why the Jews of Central Asia Came to Be Called Bukharan Jews,"[27] he points out that some (like Datkhaev) argue that the vague term *Central Asian Jews* is inappropriate because it obscures the group's common point of origin. Arguing with this approach, Niyazov stresses that the Jews who are scattered across Central Asia do not live—nor did they ever live—"in one Bukhara." It is, therefore, more accurate to call them by the more inclusive name "Central Asian Jews."

Given the expansive nature of the term, Niyazov notes that it might lead some to the mistaken impression that it does not refer to a "concrete Jewish ethnic group." But if it is not common origins that bind them together, what is it? Niyazov himself is unsure. He is, however, clearly attuned to the implications of the following question: If we are not sure what binds us, and if the term we use to refer to "us" is one that is overly inclusive and vague, then how can we be sure that we are, in fact, a "concrete Jewish ethnic group"?[28] He responds to the question with an unwavering commitment to group identity. Instead of calling into question the existence of the *edah*, he pleads for further research and investigation: "The time has come to study our roots in a thorough fashion in order that we can clearly understand who we are and what lies ahead of us."

CONVERSATIONS IN THE INSTITUTIONAL SPHERE

While spending time at the Moreshet Yahadut Bukhara office in South Tel Aviv in 1997, I witnessed an interesting conversation about language, held between a number of individuals, all of whom identified as Bukharan Jews. In the midst of their multilingual discussion, they disagreed about which language should be spoken among them and which language form was most emblematic of their group.

The administrators who preside over Moreshet Yahadut Bukhara came to Israel in the 1930s as children (or were born to parents who had left Soviet Central Asia at that time). Having grown up in Israel, their primary language is Hebrew. They tend to speak a Persian language (which they generally refer to as Bukharit)[29] but not fluently, as they learned it by overhearing their parents or grandparents speak it between themselves, often to hide secrets from the children. By contrast, the immigrants who have arrived since the dissolution of the Soviet Union tend to come knowing little if any Hebrew. Instead, their primary languages are Russian (as they grew up in the Soviet Union, attending Russian-speaking schools) and Bukharit.

Although the old-timers and the newcomers both identify as Bukharan Jews, they find it difficult to communicate with one another. Even in cases in which old-timers do have some facility in Bukharit, most speak a version that is different from that of the newcomers. The Bukharit with which they are familiar was influenced by Dari (the Persian variant they heard when many of them resided in Afghanistan). By contrast, the newcomers who remained in Uzbekistan and Tajikistan for an additional two generations speak a Bukharit that is closer to Tajik (the Persian variant spoken in Tajikistan and among a large minority in Uzbekistan). Additionally, over the course of the Soviet era, the newcomers' version of Bukharit absorbed many Russian words.

These language differences cause practical difficulties when new immigrants try to explain their needs to the caseworkers at Moreshet Yahadut Bukhara. Beyond the pragmatic, language differences also pose obstacles to people's efforts to create a sense of commonality and of belonging to a single group. This difficulty came to the fore in a 1997 meeting of folk artists, held in the South Tel Aviv office of Moreshet Yahadut Bukhara. The organization had invited a group of Bukharan Jewish musicians and dancers who reside in New York to visit and perform in Israel as part of an effort to create a sense of unity amid the splintered Bukharan Jewish world. When these New York–based performers (who are recent immigrants) came together with a group of Israel-based performers (who are also new immigrants) and their Israeli sponsors in the Moreshet Yahadut Bukhara office (who are old-timers), there was much confusion and disagreement about which language they should employ.

When Rafael, editor-in-chief of *Most* (a Bukharan Jewish newspaper published in New York),[30] addressed the group, he began by saying, "I do not know Hebrew, so I will speak in Russian." He then went on to explain (in Russian) that his goal as editor of *Most* (which means "bridge" in Russian, and which was billed as an "international" paper) was to unite the various Bukharan Jewish communities scattered across the globe. Barely able to finish this sentiment, he was interrupted by others who chided him: "We are speaking Bukharit here," they said.

Bukharit was presumably the language that drew all of them together: newcomers and old-timers, Israelis and U.S. citizens alike. However, when Eli Aminov, the director of Moreshet Yahadut Bukhara, was asked to record a message that would be aired on a radio show for Bukharan Jewish immigrants in New York, he fumbled. Born in Israel, he grew up hearing his family members speak a version of Bukharit that was influenced by the language they heard during the years they dwelled in Afghanistan. Yet, unable to adequately speak the language himself, he asked one of the recent immigrant musicians to dictate a statement. Aminov unsuccessfully attempted to repeat the words. *Can you slow down and repeat?* he asked the musician. As he did so, Aminov quickly jotted down his words. He did not write them in Cyrillic (as a recent immigrant would have done). Rather, he transliterated them into Hebrew characters. *OK, I've got it,* Aminov said, and motioned to have the tape recorder turned on. Working off his notes, he became flustered again, stopped, and motioned for the tape recorder to be turned off.

"This is Bukhari-Tajiki!" he exclaimed. "It's not the Bukharan [language] that I know!" Laughter ensued, and people shifted in their seats uncomfortably, but with much good humor. Aminov practiced out loud again, while being corrected and encouraged along the way. The tape recorder was once again turned on. Again, he fumbled. This time, though, the recorder was left running and Aminov simply switched into Hebrew, stating, "I hope all the Bukharan Jews who are listening to this in the United States will come to Israel soon—for a visit or for good— and that a new generation of Bukharan Jewish performers will flourish here." He concluded this short, Israel-centered Hebrew speech (which

246

few Bukharan Jewish immigrants in New York would understand) with a message in Bukharit: *Khush omaded ba Yisroel.* Anyone (regardless of whether their Bukharit was more influenced by Tajik or by Dari) could understand his simple sentiment: "You are all welcome in Israel!" Yet the statement contributed little to the project of creating a sense of commonality among the world's scattered Bukharan Jews.

PRIVATE CONVERSATION

The question hovering over the performers' meeting was whether there is a shared Bukharan Jewish culture, and if so, how differences might be bridged. In a conversation between Soffa and her granddaughter, the definition of who is a Bukharan Jew was up for debate.

Soffa was born in Uzbekistan and immigrated to Israel in 1972. I met her at the weekly Bukharan Jewish Women's Club meeting in Tel Aviv, and one evening visited her at home. After spending some time talking with me, she left the room. Her teenage granddaughter (her daughter's daughter) sat down near me, watched me jot down a few notes, and asked what I was doing. When I told Ronit that I was collecting information about Bukharan Jews, she made a face of disapproval and said that she "hates Bukharans." She went on to tell me that there are a lot of Bukharan Jews at her school who are new immigrants to Israel, and she wants nothing to do with them. She dissociates herself by claiming her father's Ashkenazi identity as her own.

Ronit's seven-year-old cousin (another one of Soffa's grandchildren) overheard our conversation and reacted, "You are Bukharan!" He repeated this several times and each time she denied it. Listening in, Soffa became upset. She came back into the room and responded to Ronit by deriding Ashkenazi Jews. Unlike Bukharan Jews, Soffa proclaimed, Ashkenazi Jews do not know how to show honor or respect. "Well, I am not like that!" Ronit responded. To which Soffa retorted, "Anyway, whatever the mother is, that is what the child is. It doesn't matter what you [as an individual] *want.* You are what your mother is [which in this case is Bukharan]." In this conversation, Soffa and Ronit debate how Bukharan Jewishness is transmitted, whether one can choose (or suppress) one's Bukharan Jewishness, and whether this identity carries certain inalienable qualities.

PERSONAL NEGOTIATIONS

In the public sphere as well as in private talk, the designation *Bukharan Jews* is used as though it refers to an objective group, defined by commonly agreed-upon social boundaries and cultural characteristics. At the same time, through intimate, firsthand knowledge, Bukharan Jews are acutely aware of the great historical and cultural diversity that exists among them, as well as of the fact that the geographical coordinates of their diaspora homeland(s) are shifting and ill-defined.

What are the implications of these different messages on individuals' personal understandings of self? How does the individual who identifies as a Bukharan Jew negotiate between the notion that he or she belongs to a concrete Jewish ethnic group (or *edah*) and an awareness that the contours of this group are debated and unclear?

When I first began conducting research among Bukharan Jews, I found myself confused when one person provided me with information about the group that contradicted what another said. More confusing still was when an individual would say something about her own Bukharan Jewishness, and then turn the around the next day—or even in the next sentence—and contradict what he or she had just said.

Yet, over time it became clear that I need not regard such inconsistencies as obstacles to my research, but rather as symptoms and indicators of a complex past and contemporary situation. With this understanding, I became attuned to the discrepancies I encountered, and embraced them as keys to locating the ways in which long-range macro historical processes influence individuals' understandings of themselves and how they negotiated their sense of belonging, alongside the doubts raised by their personal encounters and life histories. The vignettes below provide windows into these personal struggles.

Tamir

Born and raised in the United States, as an adult Tamir moved to Israel, which is where I met him in 1998. We did not meet in the ethnic enclaves of South Tel Aviv, where I conducted much of my ethnographic research. Rather—similar to the way I met Leora Gevirtzman[31]—I was going about my usual business when a friend suggested I get in touch with a friend of hers, who was a Bukharan Jew.

We arranged to meet at his office, and went for lunch to talk about his background and family history. Tamir's grandparents left Central Asia in the 1920s and immigrated to Israel, where Tamir's father was raised and married. Later in life, Tamir's father resettled in the United States, where he raised his children.

Growing up, Tamir knew he was Bukharan Jewish, and it was primarily his family members who shaped his ideas about what this meant. "My family—my father and his siblings—wake up at five or six in the morning and they start working and they can't relax." Because of their industrious nature, Tamir understood Bukharan Jews to be "hard-working people." Tamir's conception of Bukharan Jewishness was also influenced by the stories his grandfather often told about his ancestors' wealth and his own lavish childhood house, which was built around a beautiful courtyard.

In the 1990s, Tamir's long-held perceptions of Bukharan Jewishness were called into question. Vacationing at a popular Israeli beach destination, he happened to meet a few Bukharan Jews who—unlike himself—were recent immigrants. Tamir was surprised, he told me, by how lazy they seemed. Tamir's understanding of Bukharan Jews was also confused during a trip to Uzbekistan he had taken a few months before we met. He visited a few Bukharan Jewish homes, which—he explained—were neither lavish nor beautiful. Not at all like the way he had imagined them (based on his grandfather's stories), they were mostly in a state of disrepair and the people who lived in them appeared poor. "I was suddenly embarrassed," he confessed, that his traveling companion knew he himself was a Bukharan Jew.

In our discussion, Tamir did not take into account the fact that standards of luxury in contemporary Israel are quite different from what standards of luxury were in Central Asia at the beginning of the twentieth century. And in discussing his view of the Bukharan Jewish work ethic, he did not take into account the historical changes that had transpired since his own grandparents immigrated in the 1920s. During that period, when Jewish businesses were booming and Jews were encouraged to take part in long-distance trade, the work ethnic was very different than it was in the tightly controlled socialist Soviet system.

Rather than explaining or accounting for the differences between his own family and the Bukharan Jews whom he had recently met, Tamir was disturbed to learn that the qualities he believed to be essential features of Bukharan Jewishness were absent among those Jews who were born and raised in Bukhara. These challenges to his long-held notions left him wondering about the true nature of his own Bukharan Jewishness, and whether he should publicize this aspect of his identity. Based on his understandings of the *edah* culled from his father's family members who immigrated in the 1930s, he is proud to present himself as a Bukharan Jew. But he also worries that people may view his Bukharan Jewishness as connected to the recent immigrants, and make assumptions about him that are not true.

Marik

In 1997, on the last day of a research trip in Uzbekistan, I received a visit from Marik Fazilov, director of Samarkand's Bukharan Jewish Cultural Center, who came to interview me for an article to be published in *Shofar,* the local Jewish newspaper. He asked about my research project and a few other details about my background, and then turned to his main issue of interest. What—he wanted to know—had I learned about Bukharan Jews during my sojourn in Samarkand?

Searching for a summary statement, I did a quick mental scan through my field notes, and paused for a long moment. I had no easy answer for Marik, because what I had learned was that it was much more difficult to characterize Bukharan Jews and their culture than I had ever anticipated.

It had been four years since I had worked at Torah Academy, the high school for Bukharan Jews in Queens, New York, where I had begun my fieldwork. Now, sitting in front of Marik, after having been engaged in a multisited research project among Bukharan Jews in Samarkand, Bukhara, New York, and Tel Aviv, I realized I still had not found a simple way to describe them. Indeed, the more I traveled about the Bukharan Jewish world, which had undergone unprecedented change since the Soviet Union dissolved, the more their complex culture eluded me. So, I told Marik the one thing I had learned of which I was quite certain: that the Bukharan Jews and their culture are in a state of great flux.

He was clearly disappointed with my answer. *Is that what you came all the way to Uzbekistan to learn?* he wanted to know. He then lamented the fact that there were no ethnographies that systematically describe Bukharan Jewish cuisine, costume, and customs, and wondered why I had not focused my energies on such a task.

I explained, "I have been to Bukharan Jewish weddings in New York, Tel Aviv, and Bukhara. Finding each different from the next, how could I write a singular ethnographic description?" He cut in, with a comment that again conveyed his view of "Bukharan Jews" as an objective and stable category: "Look," he said, "the Bukharan Jews in the United States aren't really Bukharan Jews. Just because someone says he is a Bukharan Jew doesn't mean that he is one."

Yet, when our conversation switched to a discussion about Marik's own identity, he wavered. While recounting his family history, he told me that his great-grandparents were immigrants to Bukhara, who had been born in Iran. "So, are you really a Bukharan Jew?" I asked. He hesitated, then answered, "Because we are all called 'Bukharan Jews,' people think that we are all from the city Bukhara—which, of course, is not true." He continued, "The name 'Bukharan Jew' is a problematic one." He followed up by explaining that the term *Bukharan Jew* is, in fact, not an "objective" one. He is a Bukharan Jew—he said—because this is how he and his family view themselves.

The Bukharan Jewish *edah* is a powerful construct that informs the way people think about themselves. Yet at the same time, Marik—like most others—is aware of the shifting reality in which they live that does not lend itself to clearly defined categories.

Rahel

In addition to the question of social boundaries (Who is an authentic Bukharan Jew? Who belongs to the category and who does not?) that I discussed with Marik and Tamir, questions surrounding the nature of Bukharan Jewish content are also pressing: What qualities characterize language, ritual, costume, and cuisine as Bukharan Jewish? A discussion about *sogh-buroron,* a women's ritual linked to the process of coming out of mourning, illustrates the difficulties involved in addressing these questions.

Sixty-year-old Rahel Karayof, whose parents left Bukhara in the 1930s and immigrated to Israel via Afghanistan,[32] invited me to attend a *sogh-buroron* with her (in December 1996). The event was to be held in the Shapira neighborhood of Tel Aviv, at the home of her friend Tamara, who was coming out of mourning one year after her father had passed away. It would be attended by women friends and relatives, and would include lunch, speeches in honor and in memory of the deceased, and finally, the manicuring of Tamara's facial hair.

As we walked together to Tamara's house, Rahel explained to me that Bukharan Jewish immigrants who arrived in Israel in the 1970s (like Tamara) tended to keep the *sogh-buroron* tradition throughout the Soviet era, and when they immigrated to Israel, they brought this custom with them. Rahel also told me that the situation is different among the newly arriving immigrants. Exposed to one more generation of Soviet influence, she explained, many of these immigrants from the 1990s have lost some of their customs, including that of the *sogh-buroron*.

Which group would Rahel say is to be praised? The 1970s immigrants who held onto the custom? Or the 1990s immigrants who lost it? The answer is complex and unclear. The *sogh-buroron,* Rahel told me, is not prescribed by Jewish law. Rather—she continued—it is a ritual that Jews adopted from the neighboring Muslims. She went on: According to Jewish mourning laws, men do not shave and women do not cut their hair for the first month after a close relative dies. In Central Asia, the Jews picked up the local Muslims' more stringent mourning observance, abstaining from haircuts and facial hair removal for a whole year after a close relative dies. The *sogh-buroron* ritual, she concluded, originated to mark the end of this year of mourning.

Rahel and I were among the first few guests to arrive at Tamara's house. While the few women present prepared food platters in the kitchen, Rahel spoke with them, assuming the tone of a religious mentor, the position she occupied as leader of the weekly women's club meetings. She explained the origins of the ritual in which these women were about to take part. *The sogh-buroron comes from the custom of not cutting our hair for a full year of mourning.* Her hands resting firmly on the kitchen counter in front of her, she continued: *But this custom belongs to the non-Jews,* she advised the women. *It is not our own.* Then she stopped and paused, as though deliberating with herself. When she began to speak again, her tone suddenly changed as did her message. With pride, she pointed out that Bukharan Jewish women tenaciously held on to their customs over the course of their long diaspora history. And with a note of sadness, she worried out loud that the generation being raised in Israel today will not continue to practice the *sogh-buroron* ritual, and will forget their other Bukharan Jewish traditions as well.

This speech lasted only a few brief moments, and then the women turned back to their food preparation. Yet, Rahel's fleeting statements were laden with all the tensions surrounding the question of the place Bukharan Jews occupy within the broader Jewish universe. She exposed Bukharan Jews as having strayed from "normative" Judaism, but almost within the very same breath, she invoked the *Edah* Paradigm, highlighting the unique attributes of the age-old Bukharan Jewish diaspora group, and the importance of preserving them.

While Rahel, like Tamir, Marik, and so many others, negotiates questions about what Bukharan Jewishness is really about, the *Edah* Paradigm continues to ground her, offering a clear and unchallenged relationship between community ("The Bukharan Jews"), place ("Bukhara"), language ("Bukharit"), history (a discrete shared history of diaspora), and culture. In this case, the *sogh-buroron* serves as referent for the Bukharan Jewish *edah*. In other cases, it is Bukharan Jewish cookbooks, museum exhibits, newspapers, social organizations, folk festivals, or musical performances.

This book has shown that the category *Bukharan Jews* is neither natural nor ontological. Nevertheless, it is a powerful construct, having been built—literally—more than a century ago as part of a glorious building project: the neighborhood that was first called Rehovot and which later came to be known as Shkhunat ha-Bukharim. But even one hundred years ago, this identity construction was not new but rested upon a strong foundation. The ancient biblical portrayal of twelve Jewish tribes, each with unique attributes, is a powerful image that allows for cultural diversity within a unified peoplehood.

At the same time, complex boundary shifts, migrations within the broad region, and many waves of immigration under very different sorts of circumstances call into question who and what is a true representative of the *edah*. In the post-Soviet era, when encounters between various sorts of Bukharan Jews have become intense, this challenge has become impossible to evade. Yet struggles to define this paradigm-of-belonging continue, and through these very efforts the category remains resilient.

TWELVE

Jewish History
as a Conversation

Representing Two Paradigms-of-Belonging

In the winter of 1997, two large-scale Bukharan Jewish celebrations were held in Tel Aviv in celebration of Hanukkah. This holiday marks the Jews' second-century BCE victory over Greek cultural, spiritual, and national subjugation. Its central message is that with courage and commitment, group identity, autonomy, and faith can be maintained even in the face of a powerful adversary. Two Bukharan Jewish organizations used the opportunity to publicize this lesson, so relevant for Bukharan Jews, by each sponsoring a holiday festival. Attending both, I was surprised by the great difference between the flavor and style of each. Yet, analyzed together, they offer a powerful vehicle for summarizing the Center-Periphery Paradigm and the *Edah* Paradigm, and offer a clear illustration of how these two paradigms-of-belonging are articulated and transmitted.

The first such event was sponsored by Moreshet Yahadut Bukhara (The Heritage of Bukharan Jews), a nonprofit organization based in South Tel Aviv, founded and run by politician Eli Aminov, who represents his district on the Tel Aviv City Council.[1] His organization's Hanukkah festival centered around a display and celebration of material and performance culture, supposedly representative of the Bukharan Jewish *edah*.

In the theater's entry hall, attendees were greeted by a museum-like exhibit, consisting of objects imported from Central Asia. Old copper utensils, heavy jewelry, small pieces of ornately carved wooden furniture, silk robes, colorful hats, and delicate musical instruments were displayed against bright hand-embroidered hangings that lined the walls. This colorful display continued in the auditorium. The back of the stage was lined with massive Central Asian wall hangings, and the event's master of ceremonies was outfitted in a large bright silk robe. The evening's program included several dance performances, musical numbers, a few comic acts, and several speeches.

Among the speakers, the most prominent was Zevulun Hammer, then the State of Israel's Minister of Education and Culture. He emphasized that Bukharan Jews have distinct values, culture, and traditions that should be celebrated: "The Bukharans are a wonderful and special *edah*," he said, and then without depicting their precise attributes, he described his deep respect for the group because "they keep their ways, and they hold on to their heritage and their art," much like the Jews in ancient Greece who refused to betray their cultural uniqueness. Drawing a lesson from this group that might be applied to Israeli society at large, Hammer continued, "We have all come to Israel with our own culture and our own traditions. We should not lose them. We are like a mosaic, each person coming with his own heritage and donating it to the country."

This celebration of the unique cultural attributes of Bukharan Jews in particular, and the multiethnic nature of the Jewish People more generally, was given no attention at the second Hanukkah event. Likewise, the term *edah* was little used. This festival was sponsored by Hazon Avner,[2] a nonprofit religious organization founded by a prominent Bukharan Jewish philanthropist, Lev Leviev,[3] who had ties both to Chabad-Lubavitch and to Israel's religious Sephardi political party, Shas. At this event, neither the theater's entry hall nor the auditorium was decorated. A stark backdrop hung on the stage on which the name of the sponsoring organization was printed in simple bold lettering. Unlike at the previous event where most of the speakers and performers were dressed in colorful "ethnic" garb, here the speakers (almost all male) were dressed in generic religious garb: black suits, white shirts with no ties, and black hats.

The most prominent speaker at this event was a member of Israel's National Parliament. Instead of occupying a cultural role like Zevulun Hammer, however, Bukharan Jew Raphael Pinhasi belongs to the religious party Shas. He downplayed Bukharan Jewish cultural uniqueness and emphasized, instead, the group's religious tenacity. He began by asking, "What is Hanukkah [and why] . . . do we celebrate the holiday?" Answering his own question, he described the Jewish experience under Greek rule:

> During Greek times, they did not want us to keep the Torah. . . . They is-
> sued edicts proclaiming that the Jews not keep [the religious laws pertain-
> ing to] Shabbat, *milah* [religious circumcision], or *taharat ha-mishpaha*
> [family purity]. . . . A Jew who kept the *mitsvot* [religious commandments]
> was killed.

Drawing a parallel between the religious oppression suffered by the Jews in ancient Judea and the recent situation of Bukharan Jews in the Soviet Union, Pinhasi exclaimed, "The Bukharan Jews kept their Judaism even behind the iron curtain. In secret. They did not forget about Torah and *mitsvot* and they demonstrated great religious devotion."

The distinction between Moreshet Yahadut Bukhara's emphasis on the Bukharan Jews' cultural attributes and Hazon Avner's emphasis on their religious attributes is most clearly highlighted in a comparison of two dance acts performed at the respective events. At the Hazon Avner festival, the male members of a Bukharan Jewish family dance troupe dressed in generic ultra-Orthodox garb: white shirts, long black coats, and black hats. The act was set to Eastern European klezmer music and the choreography was meant to mimic—in caricature fashion—move-ments of Hasidic Jews engaged in prayer. At the climax of the dance, the brothers lined up in order of height, one in back of the other, with their profiles facing the audience. Each boy extended his arms, placing them on the waist of the brother standing in front of him, with the smallest boy at the front of the line. His hands were extended toward his father, who stood facing him. Reaching toward the lineup of his sons, the father held a large book in his hands, and gestured toward them as though to say, "I give the tradition to you, my sons, to carry it on."

At the Moreshet Yahadut Bukhara event, a little girl who looked to be about the same age and size as the young boy in the other venue took center stage at a highpoint in the dance performance. She was bedecked in bright "ethnic" clothing from head to toe, and the spotlight focused on her as she twirled and pulsed, moving to the sounds and rhythm of Central Asian music. When she finished and the audience's excited applause died down, one of the speakers commended her performance, lauding the "continuing generation" for "taking the tradition into their hands."

The messages of these Hanukkah events, encapsulated by the dances, clearly articulate two paradigms-of-belonging, which are powerful tools for conceptualizing a global Judaism and the Jewish People. With regard to Central Asia's Jews in particular, they address where and how this group fits onto the Jewish world stage. In the wake of the Soviet Union's dissolution, and in the midst of massive emigration, these are urgent questions for Central Asia's Jews themselves, as they search for a solid sense of identity and belonging in the midst of great flux. So, too, they are pressing questions for other Jews who face new encounters with those from Central Asia, who had long been out of the touch with the rest of the Jewish world. While these encounters draw attention to that which Bukharan Jews and other Jews hold in common, they also highlight the wide cultural, religious, and social divides that set the group off as distinct and separate. In short, the post-Soviet reunion of Central Asia's Jews with other segments of the Jewish world challenges the extent to which Jews can be thought of as a single people and Judaism can be considered a single religion.

The *Edah* Paradigm, as articulated at the Moreshet Yahadut Bukhara event, addresses this problem by categorizing Jews—who have had wide and varied diaspora experiences—as groups with distinct geographical boundaries, histories, and cultures. In addition to defining these groups as *edot*, the paradigm legitimizes their particular histories and celebrates their cultural differences. With its origins in the biblical narrative, this construct treats the Jewish People as having been divided into tribal units since their inception, each with their own essential qualities, familial bonds, and God-given territorial homelands. Within this paradigm, cultural difference neither corrupts nor calls into question the unitary nature of Jewish Peoplehood, but rather is understood to be a defining feature of it.

The Center-Periphery Paradigm, by contrast, with its focus on religious difference rather than on culture, treats Jews as bound through a common, authentic religion, rather than as a colorful mosaic. In this depiction, diaspora groups have either remained connected and true to authentic Judaism, or have diverged from it. In the former case, they are praised for their conformity to "normative" standards, and in the latter, they are chastised for their deviation. At the Hazon Avner Hanukkah event, it is no surprise that the Bukharan Jewish dancers are dressed in black and white, rather than in colorful Central Asian garb, and that their acceptance of "tradition" is depicted as knowledge transmitted through text (in the form of a book) rather than as a cultural form (such as a dance), which is transmitted mimetically. Nor is it coincidence that at the Hazon Avner event, the figure depicted as taking tradition into his hands was a young boy attached to a chain of other boys and men, whereas at the Moreshet Yahadut Bukhara event, the figure depicted as taking tradition into her hands was a girl, dancing solo. The former emphasizes Jewish religious authority, characterized as global, institutional, uniform, textual, and masculine by nature. In contrast, the latter emphasizes Jewish cultural tradition, characterized as local, domestic, unique (even isolated), and feminine by nature.

Toward a Processual Definition of Judaism and Jewish Peoplehood

For audience members, these two persuasive paradigms-of-belonging are imbued with an aura of truth because they are articulated in the context of dramatic public staging, each in a large hall, in the presence of hundreds of audience members, and with the rhetorical force of speeches delivered by Israel's government officials. Just as significant to the performative nature of these events is the fact that the messages they convey do not stand alone. Rather than being isolated representations, the structure of Judaism and the Jewish world portrayed at these two events fits into conceptions that are deeply rooted and widespread.

Using a historical and ethnographic approach, this book has shown the multiple, thickly layered ways in which the two paradigms-of-belonging are invoked to depict the relationship between Bukharan Jews and the wider Jewish world. But they are not mere depictions. It is not enough to point out that "center," "periphery," and "*edah*" are social constructions rather than essential, enduring categories. For regardless of their status, they are continually enacted and come to fruition through this very process of dynamic engagement.

The larger implication, then, is that the broad categories of *Judaism* and *Jewish Peoplehood* (which the two paradigms-of-belonging are designed to normalize) are likewise articulated and maintained through ongoing engagement between center(s) and peripheries (both defined de facto) and between the *edot* (which are constructed and maintained in conversation with others).

This book has focused on three levels on which these dynamic interactions take place. The first is the meta-level, through an investigation of the ways in which memory of the past is shaped through conversation and contestation. The second is the level of religious and community institutions and leaders, through an analysis of public debate surrounding Jewish law and practice. And the final level at which the engagement between center and periphery was examined was in the intimate sphere, through an analysis of the ways in which debates surrounding how these categories ought to be defined have an impact upon individuals' conceptions of self. Encounters between Bukharan Jews and representatives of international Jewish organizations have stirred up great ambivalence. Bukharan Jews living in Uzbekistan in the 1990s neither fully accepted nor fully rejected the teachings and authority of the various organizations that claimed to represent "normative" Judaism. Warily, they worked to incorporate their own understandings and practices of Judaism (as they existed prior to the post-Soviet encounter) with the new ideas to which they were being exposed.

The effort to reach alignment between "center" and "periphery" is an ongoing, dynamic project in all of its dimensions: on the meta-plane, in the institutional sphere, and in the innermost, intimate conversations of the self. So, too, is the study of Jewish history, religion, and culture, which takes into account both global and local forms. Such an approach requires research that simultaneously crosscuts historical eras, and includes areas of the Jewish world that are diverse and often far-flung. This effort should not be mistaken for comparative study. It is not about isolating slices of history and drawing parallels between them. Nor is it about identifying discrete communities in order to analyze the differences and commonalities between their practices, beliefs, and texts. Rather, this approach to understanding the relationships between Judaism in its global and local forms calls for a dynamic investigation of the very interactions, or "conversations," that serve to construct, maintain, or alter them.

JEWISH HISTORY AS A CONVERSATION

Jewish History as a Conversation

Traditionally, Jewish historians took it for granted that there was a single entity called "The Jewish People," a normative religion called "Judaism," and that a singular narrative could be told of their past. As the constructed, contingent, and imagined nature of national-ethnic-racial-tribal-religious collectives has gained widespread acceptance in the social sciences, Jewish Studies scholars have responded in kind. The once taken-for-granted assumptions that there is a Judaism and a Jewish People, and that each possesses an enduring essence and authentic form, have gone by the wayside. Indeed, scholarship in recent years has focused on the particularities of Jewish experiences, and on the ways in which these experiences must be understood in their local and temporal contexts. Attention has been increasingly devoted to the study of interactions between Jews and their non-Jewish neighbors and the ways in which these relationships have shaped and enriched the various forms of Jewish life that have emerged. This approach—which blurs the distinction between Jewish and non-Jewish worlds, rather than focusing on Jews as a socially isolated and distinct group—has given rise to fundamental and practical questions about where the boundaries of Jewish Studies lie: What sorts of topics belong in Jewish Studies journals, at Jewish Studies conferences, and in Jewish Studies departments? And what approaches should be taken to answer these questions? Perhaps most poignant, and most challenging, though, are questions of definition: Is there a Jewish People at all? A Jewish history? A single Judaism?

Rather than totally discarding these categories, some scholars have worked to find a "middle ground" that incorporates both a unitary and fractured approach, to show that it is possible to talk about "Judaism," "Jewish People," and "Jewish History" while simultaneously recognizing the multiplicity of these categories. Two interesting metaphors have emerged from this project. One is that of Michael Meyer, who proposes that Jewish history might be imagined as a rope. Such a rope, he explains, "contains many and diverse material and spiritual strands," each of which runs only "for some portion of its entire length." There is, then, no single segment of the rope that contains exactly the same strands as any other. Nevertheless, "the overlap is so great that each remains bound up with the others."[4]

Also looking for a way to describe a Jewish past that possesses "historical continuity," on the one hand, but "remain[s] unfettered by attachment to a single constant," on the other, Robert Seltzer offers the metaphor of a tapestry. He describes "an immense weaving of multiple dimensions of culture and event, intellectuality and folk." Such a tapestry, he continues, is "made up of interconnected threads of many colors," some of which "run through almost the whole" while some "are threads that hang loose, were snipped off, or morphed into a different form."[5]

In Seltzer's tapestry, as in Meyer's rope, the various strands represent Jewish attributes, texts, ideas, beliefs, material artifacts, practices, and events, which woven together form something tangible. While both these metaphorical objects are useful for thinking about Jewish history as simultaneously unified and multiple, I would like to suggest that they approach the issue from the backside. Neither the rope nor the tapestry offers a head-on representation of Jewish history. Instead, they are representations of the *artifacts* of the Jews' common experience. They are, in other words, metaphors that help us to visualize the *products* or the *results* of a shared history. But they do not help us in the task of imagining the commonality itself. Anthropologist Fredrik Barth explains: the "sharing of a common culture" (which includes texts, beliefs, and experiences) is not the "definitional characteristic" of a group.[6] That is to say, individuals do not constitute a group because they share a common culture. Instead, they share a common culture because they are a group.

What is it, then, that defines the group? To answer this question, let us turn to a different metaphor. Rather than viewing Jewish history as a material object, I propose moving beyond the tangible to an image that cannot be visualized in concrete form. In place of highlighting the stuff of culture, this image brings social relationships into sharp relief.

What if Jewish history is understood as a set of encounters, or a conversation? I do not refer here to the spoken words alone, which can be simply represented by a transcript. But rather, I refer to a conversation in all of its dimensions, replete with pauses, gestures, intonations, glances, and even silences. Nor do I refer to the sort of conversation that occurs in a discrete locale and has a clear beginning and end, like a simple business transaction, or a court proceeding. Rather, I refer to a conversation that is embedded in long-standing relationships, where the start is difficult to define and there is no final statement, because discussions begun in one generation spill over into the next. This is an invested conversation. It is one fraught with emotion; sometimes understanding, love, and empathy, sometimes judgment, jealousy, and betrayal. It is one where friendly, familial, and neighborly discussions bleed into business exchanges, marriage contracts, and negotiations of authority.

As this conversation unfolds across great distances and historical eras, every given moment carries each preceding moment with it. Laden with historical baggage, it becomes so intimately connected to each party's sense of who they are in the world, that abandoning it becomes almost unthinkable.

This is the approach that I have taken here, in this study of Central Asia's Jews and their relationships with the wider Jewish world. Judaism, I contend, is a single religion, and the Jewish people are a single people. Not because these are natural, sui generis categories, which are singular in their essence. But rather, because they are enacted as such. Through representations of the Center-Periphery Paradigm and the *Edah* Paradigm, and through engaging and acting upon these representations, Bukharan Jews—de facto—have remained part of the Jewish People, and connected to Judaism. More generally, it is through these same engagements that Jewish Peoplehood and Judaism as a global religion have been maintained. These interrelated processes have been neither straightforward nor simple. They have unfolded through relations of fellowship and power, of camaraderie and authority, of identification and distance. Through efforts to incorporate and to erase local Jewish practices, ideas and leadership structures, they have worked to rein in diaspora's margins. Not, however, without struggle and cost.

NOTES

Preface

1. There was also a large population of Ashkenazi Jews, most of whom had arrived during World War II. See Yaacov Ro'i, "The Religious Life of the Bukharan Jewish Community in Soviet Central Asia after World War II," in *Bukharan Jews in the 20th Century: History, Experience and Narration,* ed. Ingeborg Baldauf, Moshe Gammer, and Thomas Loy (Wiesbaden: Reichert-Verlag, 2008), 57. See also Baruch Gur, *Daf Matsav Mispar 4: Uzbekistan* [Situation Paper Number 4: Uzbekistan] (Jerusalem: Jewish Agency for Israel, Unit for the Commonwealth of Independent States and Eastern Europe, 1993); and *Situation Paper Number 6: The Jewish Population of the Former Soviet Union, An Empirical Analysis as of Mid-1993* (Jerusalem: Jewish Agency for Israel, Unit for the Commonwealth of Independent States and Eastern Europe, 1993).

2. Sergio DellaPergola, "World Jewish Population 2002," in *American Jewish Year Book* 102 (New York, 2002).

3. In 1962, on the eve of the Algerian Revolution. Lloyd Cabot Briggs, *No More For Ever* (Cambridge, Mass.: The Peabody Museum, 1964).

4. Barbara Myerhoff, *Number Our Days* (New York: Dutton, 1978).

5. Irene Awret, *Days of Honey: The Tunisian Boyhood of Rafael Uzan* (New York: Schocken Books, 1984).

6. Jack Kugelmass and Jonathan Boyarin, trans. and eds., *From a Ruined Garden: The Memory Books of Polish Jewry* (New York: Schocken Books, 1983).

7. Joelle Bahloul, *The Architecture of Memory: A Jewish-Muslim Household in Colonial Algeria* (New York: Cambridge University Press, 1996).

8. Used, for example, as the title of Part Two in David Biale, *Cultures of the Jews: A New History* (New York: Schocken Books, 2002).

9. See, for example, Murray Jay Rosman, *How Jewish Is Jewish History?* (Oxford: The Littman Library of Jewish Civilization, 2007), and Michael Satlow, *Creating Judaism: History, Tradition, Practice* (New York: Columbia University Press, 2006).

10. Frank Korom, "Reconciling the Local and the Global: The Ritual of Shi'i Islam in Trinidad," *Journal of Ritual Studies* 13, no. 1 (Summer 1999): 22.

1. First Encounter

1. Agudat Israel of America is a communal organization that represents most sectors of ultra-Orthodox Jews in the United States.

2. Susan Berfield, "Heritage 101: High School Eases Teens' Culture Shock," *New York Newsday, Queens Sunday Section,* January 3, 1985, 5.

3. In 1989 the population of Ashkenazi Jews in Uzbekistan was an estimated 60,000, with most of them concentrated in the republic's capital city, Tashkent. Baruch Gur, "Daf Matsav Mispar 4: Uzbekistan" [Report Number 4: Uzbekistan] (Jerusalem: Jewish Agency for Israel, Unit for the Commonwealth of Independent States and Eastern Europe, August, 1993), 4.

4. Bronislaw Malinowski, *The Sexual Life of Savages in North-Western Melanesia* (New York: H. Liveright, 1929), 5.

2. Writing Bukharan Jewish History

1. Michael Zand, "Bukharan Jews," in *Encyclopedia Iranica,* vol. III, ed. Ehsan Yar-Shater (London: Routledge & Kegan Paul, 1990), 531.

2. Transoxiana was bound in the south by the Persian province of Khorasan and by the Amu Darya (in ancient times called the Oxus River) and in the north by the Syr Darya (in ancient times called the Jaxartes River).

3. Seymour Becker, *Russia's Protectorates in Central Asia: Bukhara and Khiva, 1865–1924* (Cambridge, Mass.: Harvard University Press, 1968), 4–5.

4. At the end of the eighteenth century, Kokand was formed in the Fergana Valley region (having become independent of the Bukharan kingdom).

5. The city of Bukhara was the capital of the Bukharan kingdom.

6. Robert L. Canfield and School of American Research, eds., *Turko-Persia in Historical Perspective* (Cambridge: Cambridge University Press, 1991), 12.

7. Becker, *Russia's Protectorates in Central Asia,* 4.

8. Becker, "National Consciousness and the Politics of the Bukhara People's Conciliar Republic," in *The Nationality Question in Soviet Central Asia,* ed. Edward Allworth (New York: Praeger, 1973), 159.

9. Eugene Schuyler, *Turkistan: Notes of a Journey in Russian Turkistan, Kokand, Bukhara and Kuldja,* ed. Geoffrey Wheeler (New York: F. A. Praeger, 1966), 53–54.

10. Ibid.

11. Sergei Abashin, "The Transformation of Ethnic Identity in Central Asia: A Case Study of the Uzbeks and Tajiks," *Russian Regional Perspectives Journal* 1, no. 2 (2003): accessed 2010, http://www.iiss.org/programmes/russia-and-eurasia/russian-regional-perspectives-journal/rrp-volume-1-issue-2/the-transformation-of-ethnic-identity-in-central-asia/; Becker, "National Consciousness and Politics of the Bukhara People's Conciliar Republic," 160.

12. Schuyler, *Turkistan.*

13. Becker, "National Consciousness and the Politics of the Bukhara People's Conciliar Republic," 160.

14. Robert L. Canfield and School of American Research, eds., *Turko-Persia in Historical Perspective* (Cambridge: Cambridge University Press, 1991), 12.

15. Yitzhak Ben-Zvi, *The Exiled and the Redeemed* (Philadelphia: Jewish Publication Society of America, 1957), 80–84.

16. Bernard Lewis, *The Jews of Islam* (Princeton, N.J.: Princeton University Press, 1984), 20–21; Harvey E. Goldberg, ed., *Sephardi and Middle Eastern Jewries: History and Culture in the Modern Era* (Bloomington: Indiana University Press, 1996), 3.

17. These prohibitions are cited in M. M. Abramov, *Bukharskie Evrei v Samarkande (1843–1917)* [Bukharan Jews in Samarkand (1843–1917)] (Samarkand: Samarkand Bukharan Jewish Cultural Center, 1993), 6–7; Becker, *Russia's Protectorates in Central Asia*, 86–87; Kate Fitz Gibbon and Andrew Hale, *Ikat: Silks of Central Asia* (London: Laurence King Publishing, 1997), 103; Ephraim Neumark, *Masa be-Eretz ha-Kedem: Surya, Kurdistan, Aram-Naharayim, Paras ve-Asya ha-Merkazit* [Journey to the Land of the Orient: Syria, Kurdistan, Mesopotamia, Persia, and Central Asia], ed. Avraham Ya'ari (Jerusalem: Ha-Ahim Levin Epstein, 1947), 102; Ben-Zvi, *The Exiled and the Redeemed*, 86–87.

18. The term *khomlo*, which means Jewish religious schoolhouse (the equivalent of the Yiddish term *heder*), is a contraction of the words *khona'i mullo*, which literally means house of the rabbi. See Thomas Loy's footnote, "Reflection on the Memoirs of Mordekhay Bachayev," in *Bukharan Jews in the 20th Century: History, Experience and Narration*, ed. Baldauf, Gammer, and Loy, 130.

19. For further discussion, see Sergei Poliakov, *Everyday Islam: Religion and Tradition in Rural Central Asia*, ed. Martha Brill Olcott (Armonk, N.Y.: M. E. Sharpe, 1992).

20. In 1979, only 6 percent of the married Uzbeks living in Uzbekistan's capital city, Tashkent, had married non-Uzbeks. See Ju. V Arutjunian, *Uzbekistan, Stolichnye Zhiteli* [Uzbekistan: Inhabitants of the Capital] (Moscow: Russian Academy of Sciences, Institute of Ethnology and Anthropology, 1996), 186.

21. Survey data indicate that in 1991, a total of 39 percent of Uzbeks living in Tashkent spoke Russian either with some difficulty or with great difficulty, and 5 percent did not speak Russian at all. See ibid., 89.

22. According to Mordechai Altshuler, in 1962, some 8 percent of Central Asian Jews in Tashkent, Uzbekistan's capital and largest city, were married to non-Jews. Presumably this number was lower in the region's less cosmopolitan cities. See Mordechai Altshuler, "Some Statistics on Mixed Marriages among Soviet Jews," *Bulletin on Soviet and East European Jewish Affairs* 6 (1970): 30–32.

23. Literally, "Eastern Jews." The meaning of this term, its development, and its political and social connotations are analyzed in Harvey E. Goldberg and Chen Bram, "Sephardi/Mizrahi/Arab-Jews: Reflections on Critical Sociology and the Study of Middle Eastern Jewries within the Context of Israeli Society," *Studies in Contemporary Jewry* 22 (2007): 227–56.

24. Between the eighth and tenth centuries, Baghdad, which was the capital of the powerful Abbasid caliphate, was also an influential center of the Jewish world. When the Abbasid caliphate foundered around 950, the widespread influence of Baghdad's Jewish communal institutions also waned. For an excellent overview of this history, see Robert Brody, *The Geonim of Babylonia and the Shaping of Medieval Jewish Culture* (New Haven, Conn.: Yale University Press, 1998).

25. Zand, "Bukharan Jews," 532.

26. Ibid., 533.

27. Jacob Rader Marcus, *The Jew in the Medieval World: A Source Book, 315–1791* (New York: Meridian Books, 1960), 187 (my italics).

28. Zand, "Bukhara," in *Encyclopedia Judaica Yearbook* (Jerusalem: Encyclopaedia Judaica, 1975), 183; Vera Basch Moreen, *In Queen Esther's Garden: An Anthology of Judeo-Persian Literature* (New Haven, Conn.: Yale University Press, 2000); Walter Fischel, "The Leaders of the Jews of Bokhara," in *Jewish Leaders: 1750–1940*, ed. Leo Jung (Jerusalem: Boys Town Jerusalem Publishers, 1964), 536–38.

29. Zand, "Bukhara," 183–84.

30. Fischel, "The Leaders of the Jews of Bokhara," 538–39.

31. Ibid.

32. Ben-Zvi, *The Exiled and the Redeemed*, 75–76; Zand, "Bukhara," 184.

33. Yosef Hayim Yerushalmi, *Zakhor: Jewish History and Jewish Memory* (Seattle: University of Washington Press, 1996), xxxiii.

34. Ismar Schorsch, introduction to Heinrich Graetz, *The Structure of Jewish History, and Other Essays*, trans. Ismar Schorsch (New York: Jewish Theological Seminary of America, 1975), 4.

35. Louis Jacobs, *A Concise Companion to the Jewish Religion* (Oxford: Oxford University Press, 1999), 118.

36. Ibid.

37. Michael A. Meyer, ed., *Ideas of Jewish History* (New York: Behrman House, 1974), 5.

38. Robert Seltzer, "Jewish History after the End of Ideology," in *At the Cutting Edge of Jewish Studies*, ed. Gershon Hundert (1999), http://www.arts.mcgill.ca/programs/jewish/30yrs/index.html.

39. Jonathan Frankel and Steven J. Zipperstein, eds., *Assimilation and Community: The Jews in Nineteenth-Century Europe* (Cambridge: Cambridge University Press, 1992), 2.

40. Graetz and Schorsch, *The Structure of Jewish History*; Seltzer, "Jewish History after the End of Ideology"; Meyer, *Ideas of Jewish History*, 28–36.

41. Meyer, *Ideas of Jewish History*, 31.

42. As quoted in Meyer, *Ideas of Jewish History*, 239–40.

43. As quoted in Meyer, *Ideas of Jewish History*, 265.

44. Seltzer, "Jewish History after the End of Ideology."

45. See note 23 regarding the term *Mizrahi*. In this case, I am referring to those Jews in the post-Geonic era who were neither of Sephardi nor Ashkenazi origin.

46. Todd Endelman, "In Defense of Jewish Social History," *Jewish Social Studies* 7, no. 3 (2001): 57.

47. Seltzer, "Jewish History after the End of Ideology."

48. David Biale, ed., *Cultures of the Jews*, xxix.

49. Ibid., xxiv.

50. I have adopted these terms used from Joan Scott, who employs them in her discussion of the categories male and female in "Gender: A Useful Category of Historical Analysis," *The American Historical Review* 91, no. 5 (1986): 1053–75. Peripheries of the Jewish world have qualities that might be considered "feminine" whereas centers have qualities that might be regarded as "masculine." While it is not within the scope of this book, I hope to provide an analysis of this matrix in the future.

3. An Emissary from the Holy Land in Central Asia

1. A. Z. Idelsohn published an earlier version that is rarely cited. It is addressed in the next chapter.

2. Avraham Ya'ari, *Sifrei Yehudei Bukhara* [The Books of the Jews of Bukhara] (Jerusalem: Kiryat Sefer, 1942), 1.

3. Yitzhak Ben Zvi, *Nidhei Yisrael* [The Remnants of Israel] (Tel Aviv: N. Tverski, 1952/53).

4. Yitzhak Ben-Zvi, *The Exiled and the Redeemed* (Philadelphia: Jewish Publication Society of America, 1957).

5. Perry Bialor, "Rebuilding their World: Bukharan Jews in the United States," *The World and I* (March 1995): 228–39; Tirza Yuval, "The Last Celebration," *Eretz Magazine* (Winter 1993): 18–34; "The Jews of the Caucasus, Central Asia," *The Chicago Sentinel*, March 21, 1994, 13–15.

6. David D'Beth Hillel, *The Travels of R'David D'Beth Hillel from Jerusalem through Arabia, Koordistan, Part of Persia and India to Madras* (Madras, 1828). It is also reprinted in Walter Fischel's 1973 edited version of the diary, *Unknown Jews in Unknown Lands: The Travels of Rabbi D'Beth Hillel (1824–1832)* (New York: KTAV Publishing House, 1973).

7. Fischel presents D'Beth Hillel's biographical information in *Unknown Jews.* Some details, however, are missing.

8. For a more detailed discussion of his travelogue, see Alanna Cooper, "India's Jewish Geography as Described by Nineteenth-Century Jewish Traveler David D'Beth Hillel," *Journal of Indo-Judaic Studies* 7-8 (2004): 25–35.

9. D'Beth Hillel, *The Travels of R'David D'Beth Hillel,* 67–69.

10. Ibid.

11. Joseph Wolff, *Researches and Missionary Labors among the Jews, Mohammedans and other Sects* (London: James Nisbet & Co., 1835), vii.

12. Ibid., 134.

13. Ibid., 134–35.

14. Ibid.

15. Avraham Ya'ari edited this account of Ephraim Neumark's travels, and published it as *Masa be-Eretz ha-Kedem: Surya, Kurdistan, Aram-Naharayim Paras ye-Asya ha-Merkazit* [Journey to the Land of the Orient: Syria, Kurdistan, Mesopotamia, Persia and Central Asia] (Jerusalem: Ha-Ahim Levin Epstein, 1947).

16. Neumark, *Journey to the Land of the Orient,* 103.

17. Ibid.

18. Ibid.

19. Ibid., 103–104.

20. Elkan Adler, "The Persian Jews: Their Books and Their Ritual," *Jewish Quarterly Review* 10 (1898): 584.

21. Ibid., 591.

22. Ibid., 597.

23. Ibid., 594.

24. For an extensive list of other religious texts owned by Bukharan Jews prior to Maman's arrival, see Giora Fuzailov's article "Li-she'elat Matsavam ha'Ruhani shel Yehudei Bukhara Erev Hagaato shel Hakham Yosef Maman" [Regarding the Spiritual

Situation of the Bukharan Jews on the Eve of Yosef Maman's Arrival], *AB"A: Ktav et le-Heker ve-Limud Yehudei Iran, Bukhara, ve-Afganistan* [Journal for the Research and Study of the Jews of Iran, Bukhara, and Afghanistan] (Winter 2007): 7–12.

25. Adler, "The Persian Jews," 587.

26. The Hebrew term *Sephardi* literally means "of Spain." Sephardi liturgy refers to the style of prayer that originated among the Jewish communities on the Iberian Peninsula in the Middle Ages, and which continued to be used by those Jews (and their descendants) who were expelled from there at the end of the fifteenth century and who relocated to parts of the Ottoman Empire and the new world.

27. Adler, "The Persian Jews," 602.

28. *Ktav espanioli.*

29. Shimon Hakham, ed., *Sefer Zekher Tsadik* [Memory of a Righteous One] (Jerusalem: Sh. Weinfeld, 1948), 161.

30. Ibid.

31. D'Beth Hillel, *The Travels of R'David D'Beth Hillel,* 67–69.

32. Wolff, *Researches and Missionary Labors among the Jews, Mohammedans and other Sects,* 134.

33. Several years after Adler returned from his trip, he changed his story. In the revised version, his facts more closely align with those of the others. See "Bokhara" in *The Jewish Encyclopedia,* vol. B, ed. Isadore Singer (New York: Ktav Publishing House, Inc., 1901). Here, the name of the emissary appears as Yosef instead of Abraham, and he dates Maman's arrival to "the end of the eighteenth century" (296). Adler's changes were likely influenced by his reading of the others. His rewriting of history foreshadows what is to come—a preference for relying on written rather than oral evidence, and a tendency to whitewash over the discrepancies in favor of a consistent, coherent narrative.

34. Ya'ari, *The Books of the Jews of Bukhara,* 2.

35. Ibid., 2, fn. 1.

36. Ibid.

37. Neumark, *Journey to the Land of the Orient.*

38. Avraham Ya'ari, ed., *Sefer Masa Teiman* [Journey to Yemen] (Jerusalem: Epstein, 1945).

39. David Biale, *Cultures of the Jews,* xxiv.

40. Michael A. Meyer, *Ideas of Jewish History,* 289.

41. Uri Ram, "Zionist Historiography and the Invention of Modern Jewish Nationhood: The Case of Ben Zion Dinur," *History and Memory* 7, no. 1 (1995): 91–124.

42. See Avraham Ya'ari, *Zikhronot Erets Yisrael: Me'ah ve-Esrim Pirkei Zikhronot me-Hayei ha-Yishuv ba-Arets me-ha-Me'ah ha-Shva-Esreh ve-ad Yameinu* [Land of Israel Memoirs: One-Hundred-Twenty Memoir Chapters, about Life in the Land from the Seventh Century until Today] (Jerusalem: ha-Mahlaka le-Inyenei ha-No'ar shel ha-Histadrut ha-Tsiyonit, 1946/1947); and Avraham Ya'ari, *Igrot Erets Yisrael: She-Katvu ha-Yehudim ha-Yoshvim ba-Arets La-Aheihem she-ba-Golah mi-'Yeme Galut Bavel ve-ad Shivat Tsiyon she-be-Yameinu* [Letters from the Land of Israel: Written by Jews Residing in the Land to their Brethren in the Diaspora, from the Days of the Babylonian Exile until the Ingathering of the Exiles in Our Own Days] (Ramat Gan, Israel: Masadah, 1971).

43. Avraham Ya'ari, *Shluhei Erets Yisrael: Toldot ha-Shlihut me-ha-Arets la-Gola me-Hurban Bayit Sheni ad ha-Me'ah ha-Tesha-Esreh* [Emissaries of the Land of Israel: The History of Emissary Work from the Land of Israel to the Diaspora, from the Destruction of the Second Temple until the Nineteenth Century] (Jerusalem: Mosad HaRav Kuk, 1977), xi.

44. Ibid.

45. Ya'ari, *The Books of the Jews of Bukhara*, 1.

46. Ya'ari, *Emissaries of the Land of Israel*, 1.

47. Ibid., 1.

48. Between the time that he fled Tetuan and the time that he set out on his travels east.

49. Leah Abramowitz, "Faded Glory: Leah Abramowitz Pays a Visit to the Decaying Bukharan Quarter," *Jerusalem Post Magazine*, April 27, 1979, 12.

50. E. K. Meiendorf, *Voyage d'Orenbourg a Boukhara, fait en 1820: à travers les steppes qui s'étendent à l'Est de la Mer d'Aral et au-delà de l'Ancien Jaxartes* [Orenbourg Voyage to Bukhara, Taken in 1820: By Way of the Steppes of the Eastern Sea of Aral and Ancient Jakarta], trans. M. Pander (Paris: Librarie Orientale de Dondey-Dupré père et fils, 1826), 174–75.

51. Ibid.

52. Walter Fischel, "The Leaders of the Jews of Bokhara," 538–39.

4. Revisiting the Story of the Emissary from the Holy Land

1. A. Z. Idelsohn, "Yehudei Bukhara" [The Jews of Bukhara], *Mizrah u-Ma'arav* 1 (1920): 317–26.

2. Idelsohn's interpretation is supported by a family legend recorded in a memoir by Aryeh Fuzailov, who writes that his forebear, Rabbi Yosef Chacha, left his home in Iraq and traveled to Bukhara in the late eighteenth century. Furthermore, he writes that at about the same time, Rabbi Yosef Ma'aravi, who was born in Tetuan and who had moved to Safed, traveled to Bukhara. According to Fuzailov, these two Yosefs—who were both to become leaders in Bukhara—crossed paths during their journeys to Bukhara. *Me-Arayot Gavéru: Bukhara, Samarkand, Yerushalayim* [Stronger than Lions: Bukhara, Samarkand, Jerusalem] (self-published, Israel: Aryeh Fuzailov, 1995).

3. Idelsohn, "The Jews of Bukhara," 319.

4. For explanation of the term *Mizrahi Jews*, see chapter 2, note 23.

5. Avraham Elmaliah, "Te'udatenu" [Our Mission], *Mizrah u-Ma'arav* 1 (1920), 2.

6. Avraham Ya'ari, *Sifrei Yehudei Bukhara* [The Books of the Jews of Bukhara] (Jerusalem: Kiryat Sefer, 1942), 2, fn. 1.

7. Nissim Tagger, *Toldot Yehudei Bukhara: be-Bukhara u-ve-Yisrael* [The History of the Jews of Bukhara in Bukhara and in Israel from the Year 600 CE to 1970] (Tel Aviv, n.p., 1970).

8. The Hebrew appears on the top half of each page. The "Bukharit" (a dialect scholars often refer to as Judeo-Tajik) is written in Hebrew characters. It appears on the bottom half of each page.

9. Tagger, *The History of the Jews of Bukhara in Bukhara and in Israel*, 4.

10. Ibid., 62.

11. Ibid., 6.

12. Ibid., 53.

13. *Hakham,* which literally means "wise man," is an honorific title, often interchangeable with the term *rabbi.*

14. Plural of *hakham.*

15. Ibid., 52–53.

16. Elkan Adler, "The Persian Jews: Their Books and Their Ritual," *Jewish Quarterly Review* 10 (1898): 602.

17. Tagger, *The History of the Jews of Bukhara in Bukhara and in Israel,* 53.

18. Ibid., 54.

19. Ibid., 62.

20. Avraham Ya'ari, *The Books of the Jews of Bukhara,* 2, fn. 1.

21. Terms referenced in David Herman, *Basic Elements of Narrative* (Chichester, U.K.: Wiley-Blackwell, 2009).

5. Russian Colonialism and Central Asian Jewish Routes

1. Seymour Becker, *Russia's Protectorates in Central Asia: Bukhara and Khiva, 1865–1924* (Cambridge, Mass.: Harvard University Press, 1968), 25–36.

2. Elizabeth E. Bacon, *Central Asians under Russian Rule: A Study in Culture Change* (Ithaca, N.Y.: Cornell University Press, 1966), 106.

3. Becker, *Russia's Protectorates in Central Asia,* 74–75.

4. Ibid., 90.

5. Bacon, *Central Asians under Russian Rule,* 108.

6. Michael Rywkin, *Moscow's Muslim Challenge: Soviet Central Asia,* rev. ed. (Armonk, N.Y.: M. E. Sharpe, 1990), 15.

7. Becker, *Russia's Protectorates in Central Asia,* 128.

8. Bacon, *Central Asians under Russian Rule,* 108.

9. Yitzhak Ben-Zvi, *The Exiled and the Redeemed* (Philadelphia: Jewish Publication Society of America, 1957).

10. As jewelers, smiths, distillers, tailors, shoemakers, and hairdressers. See Ya. I. Kalantarov, "Sredneaziatskiye Yevrei" [The Central Asian Jews], in *Narody Mira* [Peoples of the World], vol. 2, *Narody Sredney Azii I Kazakhstana* [The Peoples of Central Asia and Kazakhstan] (Moscow: Institute of Ethnography, 1963); Kate Fitz Gibbon and Andrew Hale, *Ikat: Silks of Central Asia—The Guido Goldman Collection* (London: Laurence King Publishing, 1997), 181.

11. Alexander Burnes, a British army officer who visited Bukhara in 1832, noted that the Jews in Bukhara were "chiefly employed in dyeing cloth" (Alexander Burnes, "Description of Bokhara," *Journal and Proceeding of the Asiatic Society of Bengal* 2 [1833]: 228). Likewise, Franz von Schwarz, who lived in Tashkent from 1874 to 1890, remarked, "Nearly all the dyers, especially the dyers of silk, are Jews" (as noted by Elkan Adler, "Bokhara" in *The Jewish Encyclopedia,* 294). The Jews were particularly known for their dye work with indigo. Traveler Annette Meakin observed, "you can generally tell a Hebrew from a Sart by the purple stain on his hands" (Annette M. B. Meakin, *In Russian Turkestan: A Garden of Asia and its People* [New York: Scribner, 1915], 176). The profession was so popularly associated with Jews that the Tajik phrase "to go to the Jew" came to mean "to give material to be dyed blue" (Michael Zand, "Yahadut Bukhara ve-Khibush Asya ha-Tikhona bi-Yedei ha-Rusim" [Bukharan

Jewry and the Russian Conquest of Central Asia], *Pe'amim: Studies in the Cultural Heritage of Oriental Jewry* 35 [1988]: 59). In her book on Central Asian textiles, Fitz Gibbon explains that the Jews' role as dyers was linked to their low social status, as the work was thought to be polluting (Fitz Gibbon and Hale, *Ikat: Silks of Central Asia—The Guido Goldman Collection*, 181). Kalantarov, on the other hand, calls it an "honored craft" that was said to "have been inherited from their ancestors in Persia and . . . handed down from father to son" (Kalantarov, "Sredneaziatskiye Yevrei").

    12. Ibid., 181.

    13. Dov B. Yaroshevski, "Al Ma'amadam ha-Mishpati shel Yehudei Asya ha-Tikhona" [On the Legal Status of the Jews of Central Asia], *Pe'amim: Studies in the Cultural Heritage of Oriental Jewry* 35 (1988): 84.

    14. Zand, "Bukharan Jewry and the Russian Conquest of Central Asia," 61–62; Becker, *Russia's Protectorates in Central Asia*, 164–66.

    15. Meakin, *In Russian Turkestan*, 178.

    16. Eugene Schuyler, *Turkistan: Notes of a Journey in Russian Turkistan, Kokand, Bukhara and Kuldja*, ed. Geoffrey Wheeler (New York: F. A. Praeger, 1966), 259.

    17. Elkan Nathan Adler, *Jews in Many Lands* (Philadelphia: The Jewish Publication Society of America, 1905), 219.

    18. O. Olufsen, *The Emir of Bokhara and His Country: Journeys and Studies in Bokhara (with a Chapter on My Voyage on the Amu Darya to Khiva)* (Copenhagen, Gyldendal: Nordisk forlag, 1911), 297.

    19. Ephraim Neumark, *Journey to the Land of the Orient*, 109.

    20. Schuyler, *Turkistan*, 259.

    21. Olufsen, *The Emir of Bokhara and His Country*, 297.

    22. Neumark, *Journey to the Land of the Orient*, 104.

    23. Binyamin Ben-David, "Natan Davidoff: Yazam Kalkali mi-Turkestan ha-Rusit 1896–1923" [Natan Davidoff: An Economic Entrepreneur from Russian Turkestan, 1896–1923], *Pe'amim: Studies in the Cultural Heritage of Oriental Jewry* 35 (1988): 110.

    24. Ibid., 111.

    25. Albert Kaganovitch, "Shlomo Tagger: Rav Rashi li-Yehudei Bukhara be-Turkestan" [Shlomo Tagger: Chief Rabbi of the Jews of Bukhara in Turketsan], *Pe'amim: Studies in the Cultural Heritage of Oriental Jewry* 79 (1999): 46, fn. 32.

    26. Henry Lansdell, *Russian Central Asia, Including Kuldja, Bokhara, Khiva and Merv* (Boston: Houghton, Mifflin and Co., 1885), 446–48.

    27. See note 18 in chapter 2.

    28. Kaganovitch, "The Education of Bukharan Jews in Turkestan Province: 1865–1917," *Irano-Judaica* 5 (2003): 203.

    29. Ibid., 207.

    30. Father of author Nissim Tagger.

    31. Nissim Tagger, *Toldot Yehudei Bukharah: be-Bukharah u-ve-Yisrael* (Part II), 20.

    32. Ibid., 25–26, 70.

    33. Yu. I. Datkhaev, *The Bukharan Jews: A Short Chronicle and Reflections* (New York: Autograph Publishing House, 1995), 26; Shlomo-Haye Niyazov, *Mesirut Nefesh shel Yehudei Bukhara* [Self-Sacrifice of the Bukharan Jews] (New York: Empire Press, 1985), 31; Tagger, *The History of the Jews of Bukhara in Bukhara and in Israel* [Part II],

19. I was also told versions of this story by several Bukharan Jews in Uzbekistan and in Israel.

34. Becker, *Russia's Protectorates in Central Asia: Bukhara and Khiva, 1865–1924,* 3.

35. As told to me by communal leader Aron Tsionov, Bukhara, 1997.

36. Becker, *Russia's Protectorates in Central Asia: Bukhara and Khiva, 1865–1924,* 119–21.

37. Ibid., 112.

38. Ibid., 133.

39. A critical biography is offered in chapter 6.

40. Yehuda ha-Kohen Rabin, *Zarah Kochav mi-Ya'akov* [A Star Shone Forth from Ya'akov: The Holy Ways of Our Bukharan Rabbis] (Jerusalem: Yitzhak ha-Kohen Rabin, 1989), 42.

41. The title *Rishon LeTsion* literally means "First of Zion."

42. Rabin, *A Star Shone Forth from Ya'akov,* 48.

43. Ibid., 63.

44. Ibid., 64.

45. Michael Signer, ed., *The Itinerary of Benjamin of Tudela: Travels in the Middle Ages* (New York: Nightingale Resources, 2005).

46. Walter Fischel, "Secret Jews of Persia: A Century-Old Marrano Community in Asia," *Commentary,* January 1949, 31; Zand, "Bukhara," 184; Aryeh Fuzailov, *Me-Arayot Gavéru: Bukhara, Samarkand, Yerushalayim,* 58.

47. Yefim Yakubov, "The 'Declaration of Native Jews'—The Final Legislative Act Induced by the 'Bukharan Jewish Question,'" in *Bukharan Jews in the 20th Century: History, Experience and Narration,* ed. Baldauf, Gammer, and Loy, 11–21.

48. Tagger, *The History of the Jews of Bukhara in Bukhara and in Israel;* Menachem Eshel, *Galerya: Dmuyot shel Rashei Yahadut Bukhara* [Gallery: Portraits of the Leaders of the Jews of Bukhara] (Tel Aviv: Bet ha-Tarbut li-Yehudei Bukhara be-Yisrael, 1965), 165.

49. Issacharoff Family, *Issacharoff: A Tale of a Family* (Haifa: Issacharoff Family, 1997). For information about the reunion, see chapter 11.

50. Tagger, *The History of the Jews of Bukhara in Bukhara and in Israel* (Part II), 20.

6. A Matter of Meat

1. Yosef Hayim Yerushalmi, *Zakhor: Jewish History and Jewish Memory,* 17.

2. The biographical sketch of Pinhas ha-Gadol provided here was gleaned from the work written by his great-grandson, Yehuda ha-Kohen Rabin, *Zarah Kochav mi-Ya'akov.*

3. Yehuda ha-Kohen Rabin.

4. Yehuda ha-Kohen Rabin, *Zarah Kochav mi-Ya'akov* [A Star Shone Forth from Ya'akov: The Holy Ways of Our Bukharan Rabbis] (Jerusalem: Yitzhak ha-Kohen Rabin, 1989), 42.

5. Yitzhak Hayim ha-Kohen to religious leaders in Samarkand, date unknown. The original letter was written in Judeo-Tajik. It appears in Hebrew translation in Rabin, *A Star Shone Forth from Ya'akov,* 47. My translation into English is from the Hebrew.

6. Ibid.

7. Notes on Yosef Khojenov's biography can be found in Tagger, *The History of the Jews of Bukhara in Bukhara and in Israel from the Year 600 CE to 1970* (Part II), 80–81; in Eshel, *Gallery: Portraits of the Leaders of the Jews of Bukhara*, 84–91; and in Shlomo Hayim Asherov, *Mi-Samarkand ad Petah Tikva: Zikhronot ma'apil Bukhari* [From Samarkand to Petach Tikva: Memoirs of a Bukharan Immigrant] (Tel Aviv: Brit Yotsei Bukhara, 1977), 41–53.

8. The same Neumark discussed in chapter 2.

9. Ephraim Neumark, *Journey to the Land of the Orient: Syria, Kurdistan, Mesopotamia, Persia and Central Asia*, 105.

10. Yehoshua Ben-Arieh, *Jerusalem in the Nineteenth Century: The Old City* (Jerusalem: Yad Yitzhak Ben Zvi, 1986), 186.

11. Giora Fuzailov addresses this leadership-succession crisis in his article "The System of Succession in the Bukharan Rabbinate 1790–1917," *Shvut: Studies in the History and Culture of the Jews of Russia and Eastern Europe* 8, no. 14 (1999): 36–57. He attributes the conflict primarily to Hizikiya's young age at the time of his father's death. Without dismissing this as a possible cause, the presentation here focuses on geopolitical factors.

12. Jewish leaders in Bukhara to Rishon LeTsion, Ya'akov Shaul Elyashar, 1897, Ya'akov Shaul Elyashar archive, ARC 4°1271, 555, Department of Archives, The National Library of Israel.

13. *Encyclopedia Judaica*, first ed., s.v. "Rishon Le-Zion."

14. Ben-Arieh, *Jerusalem in the Nineteenth Century*, 289.

15. Moshe Ma'oz, "Changes in the Position of the Jewish Communities of Palestine and Syria in the Mid-Nineteenth Century," in *Studies on Palestine during the Ottoman Period*, ed. Moshe Ma'oz (Jerusalem: Magnes Press, 1975), 151.

16. Proclamation of the Rishon LeTsion, Ya'akov Shaul Elyashar, 1901, as it appears in Rabin, *A Star Shone Forth from Ya'akov*, 81.

17. According to the 1866 Montefiore census, the Jewish population in Ottoman Palestine in 1866 was "close to 13,100" (personal correspondence with the research team of the Montefiore Censuses Digitization Project, June 2011).

18. This biography of Shlomo Lev Eliezerov was woven together from information presented in the following works: Shalom Dov-Ber Levin, *Toldot ChaBa"D be-Eretz ha-Kodesh ba-Shanim Tav-Kuf-Lamed-Zayin—Tav-Shin-Yod* [History of Chabad in the Holy Land: 1777–1950] (Brooklyn: Kehot Publication Society, 1988), 151–60; Avraham Rabin, "Shluhei Eretz-Yisrael be-Bukhara Tav-Resh-Mem-Alef— Tav-Resh-Ayin-Dalet" [Emissaries from the Land of Israel to Bukhara, 1881–1914], *Pe'amim: Studies in the Cultural Heritage of Oriental Jewry* 35 (1988), 139–55; Tagger, *History of the Jews of Bukhara*, 75; and Rabin, *A Star Shone Forth from Ya'akov*, 168–73.

19. Chabad-Lubavitch is one branch of Hasidism, a Jewish movement founded in eighteenth-century Eastern Europe, which popularized Jewish mystical teachings and emphasizes spiritual connection to the Divine through contemplative and joyful devotion. Shalom Dov-Ber Levin dates the foundation of the Chabad community in Hebron to 1820. Levin, *History of Chabad in the Holy Land*, 33. According to the 1866 Montefiore census, in 1866 there were approximately 284 Sephardi Jews and 228 Ashkenazi (all Chabad) Jews living in Hebron. This data, soon to be available online, was provided in a personal correspondence with the research team of the Montefiore Censuses Digitization Project, June 2011.

20. For an extensive discussion on emissary work, see Avraham Yaʻari, *Emissaries of the Land of Israel*. For a brief overview, see *Encyclopedia Judaica*, first ed., s.v. "Sheluhei Erez Yisrael."

21. For a list of his communal accomplishments, see Levin, *History of Chabad in the Holy Land*, 151.

22. Ibid., 52

23. Shlomo Lev Eliezerov, Yosef Hayim ha-Kohen, and Avraham Filosof to Rishon LeTsion, Yaʻakov Shaul Elyashar, 1884, Yaʻakov Shaul Elyashar archive, ARC 4° 1271, 164, Department of Archives, The National Library of Israel. Excerpts of this letter are printed in Rabin, "Emissaries from the Land of Israel to Bukhara," 139–55.

24. Levin, *History of Chabad in the Holy Land*, 155.

25. The Rishon LeTsion (in the position of *Hakham Bashi*) was responsible for presenting the Jewish communal poll tax to the Ottoman authorities. With this responsibility came the role of appointing and supervising the emissaries who were sent abroad to collect funds. One portion of the money collected was used to pay the poll tax. Another portion was used to support Jewish communal life in Ottoman Palestine. The Rishon LeTsion oversaw this distribution. See Ben Arieh, *Jerusalem in the Nineteenth Century*, 290.

26. Levin believes this was actually his third period of emissary work. See Levin, *History of Chabad in the Holy Land*, 152–55.

27. I have been unable to locate this letter, a document that Shlomo Lev Eliezerov refers to in his own writings.

28. Shlomo Lev Eliezerov to Rishon LeTsion Yaʻakov Shaul Elyashar, 1898; Yaʻakov Shaul Elyashar archive, ARC 4° 1271, 555, Department of Archives, The National Library of Israel. Unless indicated otherwise, all quotations in this section are from this source.

29. Levin, *History of Chabad in the Holy Land*.

30. Although they had adopted many Sephardi practices as a result of their long-standing interactions with the Sephardi world.

31. For further discussion, see Jeremiah J. Berman, *Shehitah: A Study in the Cultural and Social Life of the Jewish People* (New York: Bloch Publishing Co., 1941).

32. Isadore Twersky, "The Shulhan ʼAruk: Enduring Code of Jewish Law," *Judaism* 16, no. 2 (1967): 148.

33. Ibid., 145–47.

34. Ibid., 148–49.

35. H. J. Zimmels, *Ashkenazim and Sephardim: Their Relations, Differences and Problems as Reflected in the Rabbinical Responsa* (London: Oxford University Press, 1958), 57.

36. Ibid., 57–58.

37. Shlomo Lev Eliezerov, terms of service, 1899, Yaʻakov Shaul Elyashar archive, ARC 4° 1271, Department of Archives, The National Library of Israel.

38. Ibid.

39. This is the man to whom Yitzhak Hayim ha-Kohen addressed his letter regarding the remarriage of Zhora Kandin to the woman who had admitted to an adulterous affair.

40. Albert Kaganovitch, "Shlomo Tagger: Rav Rashi li-Yehudei Bukhara be-Turkestan [Shlomo Tagger: Chief Rabbi of the Jews of Bukhara in Turketsan], *Peʻamim: Studies in the Cultural Heritage of Oriental Jewry* 35 (1999): 42.

41. Whose biographical sketch was presented in the previous chapter. Not to be confused with Hizkiya ha-Kohen Rabin, Rabbi in Bukhara.

42. Kaganovitch, "Shlomo Tagger," 41.

43. Shlomo Tagger to Rishon LeTsion, Ya'akov Shaul Elyashar, 1902, Ya'akov Shaul Elyashar archive, ARC 4° 1271, 555, Department of Archives, The National Library of Israel.

44. Laws of separation between husband and wife during times when the wife is considered to be in a state of ritual impurity.

45. According to rabbinic literature, a woman must remove all barriers before she immerses in the ritual bath (such as dirt below her fingernails, bandages, and knots in her hair) so that the waters will touch every part of her body.

46. Shlomo Tagger to Hizkiya ha-Kohen Rabin, 1906; Rabin, *A Star Shone Forth from Ya'akov*, 114–16.

47. Shlomo Tagger to Rishon LeTsion, Ya'akov Shaul Elyashar, 1903. Ya'akov Shaul Elyashar archive, ARC 4° 1271, 555, Department of Archives, The National Library of Israel.

48. Shlomo Tagger to Rishon LeTsion, Ya'akov Shaul Elyashar, 1903, Ya'akov Shaul Elyashar archive, ARC 4° 1271, 555, Department of Archives, The National Library of Israel.

49. According to Nissim Tagger, Yosef Khojenov did not die until 1924. Tagger, *History of the Bukharan Jews* (Part II), 81.

50. Samarkand community leaders to Rishon LeTsion, Ya'akov Shaul Elyashar, 1904, Ya'akov Shaul Elyashar archive, ARC 4° 1271, 555, Department of Archives, The National Library of Israel.

51. The letter written by Samarkand's leaders is written on one large page that is folded in half. Their letter appears on the first half and Shlomo Tagger's letter appears on the second half.

52. Avraham Ya'ari, *Sifrei Yehudei Bukhara*, 1.

7. Building a Neighborhood and Constructing Bukharan Jewish Identity

1. The term *edah* is defined in the Alkalai Hebrew/English dictionary as "community" and "congregation." Unlike the term *kehillah* (also translated as "community" or "congregation," but which comes from the root *kahal,* meaning "to gather or to assemble together"), *edah* has a connotation of sacred bonds, group memory, and primordial ties. See for example, Leviticus 19:2, which speaks of *adat b'nei Yisrael* (the *edah* of the children of Israel). Yet, this complex term also carries connotations of separatism and factionalism. See, for example, Numbers 16:5, which speaks of the rebellious group *adat Korah.*

2. In some instances, the term *edah* is used to refer to groups other than Jewish diaspora groups. For example, the term *ha-edah ha-haredit* denotes a segment of ultra-Orthodox Jewry in Israel, and carries no ethnic connotation. For further discussion, see Virginia Dominguez, *People as Subject, People as Object* (Madison: University of Wisconsin Press, 1989).

3. Joshua 13–21.

4. Genesis 49, Deuteronomy 33.

5. Exodus 28.

276 NOTES TO PAGES 121–129

6. Isadore Twersky, *A Maimonides Reader* (Springfield, N.J.: Behrman House Inc., 1972), 35.

7. Oreh Hayim, 90:4.

8. See Magen Avraham commentary on Shulhan Aruch, Oreh Hayim.

9. Yitzhak Ben-Zvi, *The Exiled and the Redeemed* (Philadelphia: Jewish Publication Society of America, 1957), vi.

10. Yisrael Aharoni and Nelli Sheffer, *Ha-Mitbah shel Kur ha-Hitukh* [The Melting Pot Kitchen] (Tel Aviv: Mishkal Hotsa'ah Le-or, 1998).

11. The fifteenth-century religious scholar Rabbi David ben Zimra proclaimed the Jews of Ethiopia to be descendants of the tribe of Dan. Drawing on this ruling, Chief Sephardi Rabbi Ovadia Yosef declared them Jews in 1973, and encouraged their migration to Israel.

12. For a full description and history of this group, see Hillel Halkin, *Across the Sabbath River* (New York: Houghton Mifflin, 2002).

13. I thank Harvey Goldberg for pointing out that use of the term *tribe* to refer to the Jews of Ethiopia and Manipur is related to "questions surrounding their status as Jews" that have arisen on account of their disconnection from the rest of the Jewish world for much of their history. In these cases, "biblical history is mobilized" to assert that their connection to "Judaism" is an ancient one (personal correspondence, February 2010).

14. Moze'on Yisrael, *Bokhara* (Jerusalem: Israel Museum, 1967).

15. A term used by Johannes Fabian in his book *Time and the Other: How Anthropology Makes Its Object* (New York: Columbia University Press, 1983).

16. Grace Glueck, "Design Review: When Russia Uncovered Exotic Jewish Cultures," *The New York Times,* August 6, 1999, Section E, Part 2, 44.

17. John D. Klier, "Facing West: Oriental Jews of Central Asia and the Caucasus: Review," *The Historian* 62, no. 4 (June 2000): 932–33.

18. Walter Fischel, "Secret Jews of Persia: A Century-Old Marrano Community in Asia," *Commentary,* January 1949, 31; Michael Zand, "Bukhara," in *Encyclopedia Judaica Yearbook,* 184.

19. Giora Fuzailov, *Mi-Bukhara li-Yerushalayim: Aliyatam ve-Hityashvutam shel Yehudei Bukhara be-Erets Yisrael 628–708 (1868–1948)* [From Bukhara to Jerusalem: Immigration and Settlement of Bukharan Jews in the Land of Israel (1868–1948)] (Jerusalem: Misgav Yerushalayim, 1995), 58.

20. Fredrik Barth, *Ethnic Groups and Boundaries* (Boston: Little Brown, 1969), 11.

21. Charles F. Keyes, "The Dialectics of Ethnic Change," in *Ethnic Change,* ed. Charles F. Keyes (Seattle: University of Washington Press, 1981).

22. These documents were written in Hebrew, which may indicate that they were meant to be read by other Jews residing in Ottoman Palestine (not only those from Central Asia). It may also be an indication of a growing trend toward the use of Hebrew among the Jews of Central Asia, due to intense contact with Ottoman Palestine. All translations are my own.

23. Announcement from the Society of Lovers of Zion of the Holy Community of Bukhara, Samarkand, Tashkent, and Environs, to "Members of our *edah* living in a land that is not their own," leaflet, 1890, Israel National Library. To see a reproduction of this document, consult Dror Wahrman, *Ha-Bukharim u-Shkhunatam*

bi-Yerushalayim [The Bukharans and their Neighborhood] (Jerusalem: Yad Yitzchak Ben Zvi, 1991), 20.

24. See announcement signed by Rishon LeTsion Ya'akov Shaul Elyashar, and Rafael Meir Panizil, 1890, in Yehudah ha-Kohen Rabin, *A Star Shone Forth from Ya'akov*, 44–47.

25. "Regulations of the Society of Lovers of Zion to Build Houses for the People of Bukhara, Samarkand, Tashkent, and Their Outskirts," pamphlet, 1891, Israel National Library. A reproduction of the pamphlet cover appears in Giora Fuzailov, *Yahudut Bukhara: Gdoleha u-Minhageha* [The Jews of Bukhara: Their Leaders and Traditions] (Jerusalem: Misrad ha-Hinukh ve-ha-Tarbut, 1993), 21.

26. "Regulations of the Society Bukharia and Its Outskirts in Jerusalem," leaflet, 1904, Israel National Library. A reproduction of this leaflet appears in Giora Fuzailov, *The Jews of Bukhara*, 167.

27. "Regulations of The Society of the Treasured Holy Community Bukhara and Its Outskirts in Jerusalem." A reproduction of the leaflet cover appears in Giora Fuzailov, *The Jews of Bukhara*, 238.

28. Genesis 26:22.

29. Fuzailov, *From Bukhara to Jerusalem*, 94.

30. Ya'akov Pinhasi, "*Avotay u-Veit Avi: Masoret Mishpaha ve-Zikhronot*" [My Forefathers and Ancestors: Family Tradition and Memoirs], in *Asarah Sipurei-Am mi-Bukhara* [Ten Folk Tales from Bukhara], ed. Dov Noi (Jerusalem: ha-Merkaz le-Heker ha-Folklor, 1978): 12–36.

31. Shlomo Baba Jon Pinhasov, *Sefer Milim Shisha* [Dictionary of Six Languages] (Jerusalem: Shlomo Baba Jon Pinhasov, 1908).

32. In the second edition, published in 1911, he substituted Spanish as the sixth language in place of French. For further information about the dictionary, see Pinhasi, "My Forefathers and Ancestors," 23–24, fn. 19, 20; and M. M. Abramov, "O Slavarye na Shesti Yazikakh" [About the Dictionary of Six Languages], *Shofar*, June 1992, 2.

33. Unlike Shlomo Baba Jon Pinhasov's work, dictionaries and translations published by Bukharan Jews since the 1970s tend to refer to their language as "Bukharian" or "Bukharit" rather than Persian.

34. A photocopy of this dictionary's frontispiece appears in Giora Fuzailov, *The Jews of Bukhara*, 138.

35. For information about the book's circulation, see M. M. Abramov, "O Slavarye na Shesti Yezikakh." Here, Abramov writes that 20,000 copies of the book were published. This total seems very high to me.

8. Local Jewish Forms

1. Maria Elisabeth Louw, *Everyday Islam in Post-Soviet Central Asia* (London: Routledge, 2007), 3.

2. In 1979, Muslims constituted 84.2 percent of the population in Uzbekistan and 85.5 percent of the population in Tajikistan. See Teresa Rakowska-Harmstone, "Islam and Nationalism: Central Asia and Kazakhstan under Soviet Rule," *Central Asian Survey* 20 (1983): 13.

3. Ibid., 29.

4. Ibid., 32.

5. Ibid., 33.

6. In 1979, Jews constituted 0.6 percent of Uzbekistan's population, and 0.4 percent of Tajikistan's population. Ibid., 13.

7. For data on religious institutions and religious observance during the Soviet era, see Yaacov Ro'i, "The Religious Life of the Bukharan Jewish Community in Soviet Central Asia after World War II," in *Bukharan Jews in the 20th Century: History, Experience and Narration,* ed. Baldauf, Gammer, and Loy.

8. Louw, *Everyday Islam in Post-Soviet Central Asia,* 3.

9. Rakowska-Harmstone, "Islam and Nationalism," 55.

10. Michael Chlenov, *Oriental Jewish Groups in the Former Soviet Union: Modern Trends of Development* (University of Cincinnati, Department of Judaism Studies: 1998), 11.

11. Sergei Poliakov, *Everyday Islam: Religion and Tradition in Rural Central Asia,* ed. Martha Brill Olcott (Armonk, N.Y.: M. E. Sharpe, 1992).

12. Ibid., 77–78.

13. According to Mordechai Altshuler, in 1962 only some 8 percent of Bukharan Jews in Tashkent (Uzbekistan's capital, and one of the Central Asia's most cosmopolitan cities) were married to non-Jews. Presumably this number was much lower in Samarkand and Bukhara. See Mordechai Altshuler, "Some Statistics on Mixed Marriages among Soviet Jews," *Bulletin on Soviet and East European Jewish Affairs* 6 (1970): 30–32.

14. For further details, see Alanna Cooper, "Looking Out for One's Identity: Central Asian Jews in the Wake of Communism," in *New Jewish Identities: Contemporary Europe and Beyond,* ed. Zvi Gitelman (Budapest: Central European Press, 2003), 189–210.

15. A Judeo-Tajik term, derived from the Hebrew *yeshiva.* See Baruch Moshavi, "Customs and Folklore of Nineteenth Century Bukharian Jews in Central Asia" (Ph.D. diss., Yeshiva University, 1974), 240.

16. *Pominki* is a Russian term (meaning funeral repast) adopted during the colonial era. *Azkara* is a Hebrew term (meaning remembrance or commemoration), often used among Bukharan Jewish immigrants in Israel. Occasionally, the Yiddish term *yahrzeit* is used among Bukharan Jewish immigrants who have adopted the term from Ashkenazi Jews.

17. During the Soviet era, this would have been unusual. Memorial meals were generally organized by the deceased's son or grandson, and held in his home. Most likely this would have also been the home where the deceased had lived, as homes were passed as inheritances from father to son. Since the USSR's dissolution, however, this all has changed. Now scattered, sons and grandsons are often no longer able to host memorial services in the homes where their parents and grandparents once lived, and accommodations are made. For a variety of reasons Ilya could not hold the event in his home, nor could any other male descendants of Nerio. For further details, see Alanna E. Cooper, "Rituals of Mourning among Central Asia's Bukharan Jews: Remembering the Past to Address the Present," in *Revisioning Ritual: Jewish Traditions in Transition,* ed. Simon Bronner (Oxford: The Littman Library of Jewish Civilization, 2010), 290–314.

18. Moshavi, "Customs and Folklore of Nineteenth Century Bukharian Jews," 213–70.

19. Samuel C. Heilman, "When a Jew Dies: The Ethnography of a Bereaved Son" (Berkeley: University of California Press, 2001), 125.

20. For information about how Muslims celebrated weddings during the Soviet era, see N. P. Lobacheva, "Wedding Rites in the Uzbek SSR," *Central Asian Review* 15 (1967): 290–99. For information about how they are celebrated in the post-Soviet era, see Deniz Kandiyoti and Nadira Azimova, "The Communal and the Sacred: Women's Worlds of Ritual in Uzbekistan," *Journal of the Royal Anthropological Institute* 10 (2004): 327–49; and Asli Baykal, "Surviving the Post-Soviet Transition: Changing Family and Community Relations in Urban Uzbekistan" (Ph.D. diss., Boston University, 2007).

21. As far as I know, this film was never produced. I hold copies of the raw footage.

22. This practice is common among Jews and Muslims. I was told that its origins are "from Zoroastrian times" (prior to Islam's introduction to the region).

23. Moshavi, "Customs and Folklore of Nineteenth Century Bukharian Jews," 185.

24. Ibid., 155–56, 170–71.

25. Ibid., 185.

26. Lobacheva, "Wedding Rites in the Uzbek SSR."

27. ZAGS is an acronym for [*Otdel*] *Zapisyi Aktov Grazhdanskogo Sostoyaniya* (Department of Registration of Civil Acts), the government bureau where marriages are registered.

28. Lobacheva, "Wedding Rites in the Uzbek SSR," 296–97.

29. Central Asian tambourine.

30. This term translates as "to bring out of mourning, safely and in good health." *Sogh* is a Turkic loan word that means "in good health." *Buroron* comes from the verb *burovurdan,* which means "to take out" or "to bring out." I thank Max Malkiel for this explanation.

31. In 1983, the Reform movement in the United States issued the first official religious ruling calling for the acceptance of Jewish patrilineal descent. The Orthodox movement in the United States still accepts only matrilineal descent. Likewise, the Conservative movement accepts only matrilineal descent; however, it allows for some flexibility.

32. For a discussion on Soviet nationalities policy, see Yuri Slezkine, "The USSR as a Communal Apartment or How a Socialist State Promoted Ethnic Particularism," *Slavic Review* 53 (1994): 414–52.

33. Ibid., 444.

34. Mordechai Altshuler, *Soviet Jewry since the Second World War: Population and Social Structure* (New York: Greenwood Press, 1987), 16.

35. In response to pressure exerted on Jerusalem's Central Asian Jews to donate money to the existing Sephardi institutions, rather than channeling funding into their own private community organizations. See chapter 7.

36. According to demographic statistics gathered by the Jewish Agency for Israel, the population of Ashkenazi Jews in Uzbekistan in 1989 numbered 60,000, concentrated in Uzbekistan's most populous cities. Most lived in Tashkent. See Baruch Gur, "Report Number 6: The Jewish Population of the Former Soviet Union: An Empirical

Analysis as of Mid-1993," Jerusalem: Jewish Agency for Israel, Unit for the CIS and Eastern Europe, 1993. In Samarkand there were 7,000 Ashkenazi Jews in 1979. See M. Zubin in "Yehudei Mehoz Samarkand bi-Shnat 1979—Skira Statistit" [The Jews of Samarkand in the Year 1979—A Statistical Survey], *Pe'amim: Studies in the Cultural Heritage of Oriental Jewry* 35 (1988): 170–77. Fewer lived in Bukhara (personal communications with Ashkenazi and Central Asian Jewish residents in Bukhara, and with local Jewish community leaders, 1997).

37. Although official statistics on intermarriage between Central Asian Jews and Ashkenazi Jews are unavailable, during the course of five months of ethnographic research in Samarkand, I learned of six cases of Central Asian Jews in Samarkand who had married non-Jews and only two cases of Central Asian Jews in Samarkand who had married Ashkenazi Jews.

9. International Jewish Organizations Encounter Local Jewish Community Life

1. See Baruch Gur, "Situation Paper No. 6: The Jewish Population of the Former Soviet Union: An Empirical Analysis as of Mid-1993," Jerusalem: Jewish Agency for Israel, Unit for the CIS and Eastern Europe, 1993, 12–13.

2. See chapter 1.

3. For a detailed discussion on migration patterns, which splintered kin networks, see Alanna Cooper, "Negotiating Identity in the Context of Diaspora, Dispersion and Reunion" (Ph.D. diss., Boston University, 2000). This topic is addressed in chapter 11, "Post Soviet Emigration and Dispersion of Community," 277–90.

4. Use of the present tense here refers specifically to the 1990s, the period during which I conducted research in Uzbekistan.

5. For more information on the baking of matza during the Soviet period, see Ya'akov Ro'i, "The Religious Life of the Bukharan Jewish Community in Soviet Central Asia after World War II," in *Bukharan Jews in the 20th Century: History, Experience and Narration,* ed. Baldauf, Gammer, and Loy, 69.

6. In Mikhael's estimation, a total of four hundred Bukharan Jews and two thousand Ashkenazi Jews had yet to be accounted for.

7. With certain exceptions, such as "when the Minister of the Interior has reasons to believe that the applicant is acting against the Jewish people, or is likely to endanger public health or the security of the state." S. Zalman Abramov, *Perpetual Dilemma: Jewish Religion in the Jewish State* (Rutherford, N.J.: Fairleigh Dickinson University Press, 1976), 285.

8. Akiva Orr, *The UnJewish State* (London: Ithaca Press, 1983), 28–29.

9. For a detailed summary of these debates, see "Who Is a Jew?" in Abramov, *Perpetual Dilemma,* 270–320.

10. Ibid., 309. It also included anyone whose spouse had a Jewish parent or grandparent.

11. Ibid., 113.

12. Many of them had been born in the former Soviet Union, but emigrated as youth in the 1970s. This background gave them language facility in Russian, which they could use to speak with the locals, as well as full proficiency in Hebrew, which they could use to communicate Israeli culture and represent Israeli society.

13. The Hebrew term *aliyah,* which literally means "ascent" or "going up," conveys the notion that Jewish migration to Israel is not only a right but also a privilege.

14. The twelve branch offices included eight in Uzbekistan (Samarkand, Bukhara, Termes, Fergana, Kokand, Andizhan, Namangan, and Shakhrisabs), one in Tajikistan (Dushanbe, the capital city), one in Kazakhstan (Alma Ata, the capital city), one in Kyrgyzstan (Bishkek, the capital city), and one in Turkmenistan (Ashkabad, the capital city). Information as reported to me in 1997 by employees of the Jewish Agency for Israel who were stationed in Tashkent at that time.

15. This includes individuals with two Jewish parents, in addition to individuals whose mothers are Jewish, but whose fathers are not.

16. "Chabad" is a system of religious thought. Lubavitch is the town in Eastern Europe in which Chabad philosophy and theology first flourished. Today, the two terms are often used interchangeably. The "Chabad" discussed here is the same as introduced in chapter 7.

17. William Shaffir, *Life in a Religious Community: The Lubavitcher Chassidim in Montreal* (Toronto: Holt, Rinehart & Winston, 1974), 154.

18. Information for this section was gathered from several personal interactions with Emanuel Shimunov in Samarkand (in 1994 and 1997), an interview with him in his home in Queens, N.Y., in 1997, discussions with other Samarkandians, and from articles in Samarkand's local Jewish newspapers, including R. Yureva, "Vremya Dobrikh Nachinani" [A Time of Good Beginnings], *Shofar,* February 1992, 3, and F. Markielov, "Krupnim Planom: Blagasloveniye" [A True Blessing], *Shofar,* October 1992, 3.

19. Shlomo Haye Niyazov's biography and the story of his emigration are related in chapter 9.

20. Markielov, *A True Blessing,* 3.

21. Leviev himself is a Bukharan Jew, born in Tashkent. His parents and grandparents, however, were Samarkandians who had been influenced by Shlomo Lev Eliezerov and identified as Lubavitchers. For more information on him and his family, see Zev Chafets, "The Missionary Mogul," *New York Times Magazine,* September 16, 2007.

22. Markielov, *A True Blessing.*

23. U.S.$50 per month. The average monthly salary among most of the people I met in Uzbekistan was less than U.S.$20 per month.

24. The women were paid a stipend of U.S.$8 a month.

25. Some young women did serve as Lubavitch emissaries for short periods of time. However, they were specifically sent to help run summer programs. The other Lubavitch emissaries who came for a year or longer, and who served in broader roles, were all men.

26. Quotation of the Chabad Rebbe, Menachem Mendel Schneerson, as published by Shaffir, *Life in a Religious Community,* 66.

27. Father's father.

28. She is referring to the periods of time when physical intimacy between husband and wife is allowed and not allowed.

29. A woman's self-examinations to check for menstrual blood or spotting.

30. State of ritual impurity related to menstruation.

10. Varieties of Bukharan Jewishness

1. Some 1,500 Bukharan Jews lived in Ottoman Palestine in 1914. See Albert Kaganovitch, "The Bukharan Jewish Diaspora at the Beginning of the 21st Century," in *Bukharan Jews in the 20th Century: History, Experience and Narration*, ed. Baldauf, Gammer, and Loy, 111.

2. Dror Wahrman, *Ha-Bukharim u-Shkhunatam bi-Yerushalayim* [The Bukharans and their Neighborhood] (Jerusalem: Yad Yitzchak Ben Zvi, 1991).

3. With the help of editor Yehudit Rotem, *Mipninim Mikhrah: Zikhronot le-Veit Ben David* [A Price above Rubies: Memoirs of the Ben David Family] (Jerusalem: Ben David Family, 1986).

4. Sara Koplik, "The Demise of Afghanistan's Jewish Community and the Soviet Refugee Crisis (1932–1936)," *Iranian Studies* 36 (2003): 356.

5. Sara Koplik, "The Experiences of Bukharan Jews outside the Soviet Union in the 1930s and 1940s," in *Bukharan Jews in the 20th Century: History, Experience and Narration*, ed. Baldauf, Gammer, and Loy, 92–94. Kaganovitch, "The Bukharan Jewish Diaspora," 111. For a personal refugee account, see Shulamit Tilayov, *Shirat Shulamit* [The Poetry of Shulamit] (Tel Aviv: Brit Yotsei Bukhara, 1981).

6. See Shlomo Hayim Asherov, *Mi-Samarkand ad Petah Tikva: Zikhronot ma'apil Bukhari* [From Samarkand to Petach Tikva: Memoirs of a Bukharan Immigrant] (Tel Aviv: Brit Yotsei Bukharah, 1977); and Koplik, "The Experiences of Bukharan Jews."

7. Koplik, "The Experiences of Bukharan Jews," 107.

8. Koplik, "The Demise of Afghanistan's Jewish Community," 361.

9. Rahel related to me these details of her biography and family history over the course of many conversations we held in 1996 and 1997, mostly in her home.

10. Mark Tolts, "The Demographic Profile of the Bukharan Jews in the Late Soviet Period," in *Bukharan Jews in the 20th Century: History, Experience and Narration*, ed. Baldauf, Gammer, and Loy, 78.

11. Only 13 percent of the Jews who emigrated from Central Asia in the 1970s did not resettle in Israel. See Zvi Gitelman, "The Quality of Life in Israel and the United States," in *New Lives: The Adjustment of Soviet Jewish Immigrants in the United States and Israel*, ed. Rita Simon (Washington, D.C.: Lexington Books, 1985), 51.

12. Ibid., 52.

13. The article is reprinted in Shlomo-Haye Niyazov, *Mesirut Nefesh shel Yehudei Bukhara* [Self-Sacrifice of the Bukharan Jews] (New York: Empire Press, 1985), 133.

14. Discussed in chapter 7.

15. M. M. Abramov, *Bukharskie Evrei v Samarkande (1843–1917)* [Bukharan Jews in Samarkand (1843–1917)] (Samarkand: Samarkand Bukharan Jewish Cultural Center, 1993), 28.

16. Abreviation for *Kommunisticheskiy Soyuz Molodyozhi*, Soviet Communist Youth.

17. In his home in Queens, N.Y., 1997.

18. While most continued to speak their native language at home, they learned Russian in school, and by the 1970s spoke it fluently (with the exception of some elderly).

19. Baruch Gur, "Situation Paper Number 6: The Jewish Population of the Former Soviet Union: An Empirical Analysis as of Mid-1993" (Jerusalem: Jewish Agency for Israel, Unit for the CIS and Eastern Europe, 1993), 12–13.

20. For a more detailed analysis, see Alanna E. Cooper, "Where Have all the Jews Gone? Mass Migration and Uzbekistan's Independence," in *The Divergence of Judaism and Islam: Interdependence, Modernity and Political Turmoil*, ed. Michael Laskier and Yaacov Lev (Gainesville: University Press of Florida, 2011), 99–124.

21. As described in chapter 8.

22. Midrash Sephardi does not treat the term *Sephardi* literally. Rather than referring only to those Jews who are "of Spain," the institution employs the term in its most expansive sense, to refer to Jews who are not "Ashkenazi" (of Eastern European descent).

23. An acronym for *No'ar 'Olim Lifnei Horim* (Youth Arriving before Their Parents). For more information about the program see: http://www.naale.org.il/show.php ?id=7&lang=eng.

11. Negotiating Authenticity and Identity

1. James Clifford describes a general shift in attention in recent decades from the study of "roots" to the study of "routes" (patterns of migration, travel, movement, translocal connections, and global networks). James Clifford, *Routes: Travel and Translation in the Late Twentieth Century* (Cambridge, Mass.: Harvard University Press, 1997).

2. In the late 1980s, as the Soviet Union was teetering on the brink of collapse, just as migration restrictions began to ease.

3. In the late 1990s, during the time of my research.

4. Rebekah Ziona Mendelson, "The Bokharan Jewish Community of New York City" (M.A. thesis, Columbia University, 1964), 118.

5. Ibid., 89–95.

6. Mendelson writes, "The main goal of the society was to raise funds to help less fortunate Bokharans in Israel. Members felt that this charity was the responsibility for all members of the origin-group who had accumulated enough capital to establish themselves in the United States." The society supported three projects: the Aminoff Home for Aged in Israel, the purchase of two ambulances in Israel, and a scholarship for a Bukharan Israeli student to study at Hebrew University. Ibid., 119–20.

7. Ibid., 125–27.

8. The number of Bukharan Jews in New York in the 1970s and early 1980s is not readily available. According to a memorandum issued by the Queens Borough President's office, the population of Bukharan Jews in Queens had increased to approximately 5,000 individuals by 1987.

9. According to lay leader Hanan Benjamini, the community purchased its "new home" in 1976, located in Forest Hills, Queens (personal communication, December 1998).

10. Biographical information was collected from Hanan Benjamini himself during an interview I held with him in Queens, N.Y., in December 1998.

11. Alanna E. Cooper and Jacob B. Ukeles, "Service Needs of the Bukharan Population of the New York Area," Jewish Community Relations Council of New York, Metropolitan Council on Jewish Poverty, UJA-Federation of NY, August 1999, accessed in July 2012, http://www.bjpa.org/Publications/details.cfm? Publication ID=11676.

12. Boris Kandov and Arkadiy Yakubov, *The Congress United Us* (New York: Congress of Bukharian Jews in USA and Canada, 2005), 236–59.

13. Ibid., 9.

14. Including Toronto, New York, Boston, Philadelphia, Cleveland, Seattle, Phoenix, Denver, Atlanta, Los Angeles, and San Diego.

15. Published by the Issacharoff Family (Haifa, 1997).

16. *Yushvo.* Discussed in chapter 8.

17. She was born in Afghanistan, and had arrived in Israel as a teenager in 1951. Notes on her life history appear in chapter 10.

18. Her mother's sister.

19. Charles Lindholm, *Culture and Authenticity* (Malden, Mass.: Blackwell Publishing, 2008).

20. Ibid., 143.

21. Chapter 7.

22. Marik Fazilov, "Pochemu My 'Bukharskie' Yevrei" [Why Are We "Bukharan" Jews?], *Shofar,* March 1998, 16.

23. David Achildiyev, "Yesli My Bukharskiye Yevrei Ne Yavlayemsa Sefardami, to Kto Zhe My?" [If We Bukharan Jews Are Not Sephardi, Then Who Are We?], *Bukharskaya Gazeta,* June 1998.

24. Yu. I. Datkhayev, *The Bukharan Jews,* 30.

25. Presumably because they were distant from the seat of Russian colonial expansion, and were exposed to Western influences later, and in smaller doses.

26. Ibid., 58.

27. Pinhas Niyazov, "Kak i Pochemu Yevrei Srednei Azii Stali Nazivatsa Bukharskimi Yevreymai" [How and Why the Jews of Central Asia Came to Be Called Bukharan Jews], *Bukharskaya Gazeta,* October 1997.

28. Ibid., 16.

29. Scholars generally refer to this language as Judeo-Tajik. When speaking among themselves, Bukharan Jews from Tashkent tend to use Russian more often than Bukharit, whereas those from Bukhara tend to use Bukharit more often.

30. He later became editor-in-chief of the *Bukharian Times,* also based in New York.

31. See chapter 10.

32. Her biography is presented in the previous chapter.

12. Jewish History as a Conversation

1. Discussed in chapter 11.

2. *Hazon Avner* (which literally means "Avner's Vision") was founded by Lev Leviev in memory of his father, Avner Leviev.

3. As addressed in chapter 8.

4. Michael A. Meyer, ed., *Ideas of Jewish History* (New York: Behrman House, 1974), 40–41.

5. Robert Seltzer, "Jewish History after the End of Ideology," in *At the Cutting Edge of Jewish Studies,* ed. Gershon Hundert (1999), http://www.arts.mcgill.ca/programs/jewish/30yrs/index.html.

6. Fredrik Barth, *Ethnic Groups and Boundaries* (Boston: Little Brown, 1969), 11.

BIBLIOGRAPHY

Abashin, Sergei. "The Transformation of Ethnic Identity in Central Asia: A Case Study of the Uzbeks and Tajiks." *Russian Regional Perspectives Journal* 1, no. 2 (2003), http://www.iiss.org/programmes/russia-and-eurasia/russian-regional-perspectives-journal/rrp-volume-1-issue-2/the-transformation-of-ethnic-identity-in-central-asia/.

Abramov, M. M. *Bukharskie Yevrei v Samarkande (1843–1917)* [Bukharan Jews in Samarkand (1843–1917)]. Samarkand: Samarkand Bukharan Jewish Cultural Center, 1993.

———. "O Slovarye na Shesti Yazikakh" [On the Dictionary of Six Languages]. *Shofar*, June 1992.

Abramov, S. Zalman. *Perpetual Dilemma*. Rutherford, N.J.: Fairleigh Dickinson University Press, 1976.

Abramowitz, Leah. "Faded Glory: Leah Abramowitz Pays a Visit to the Decaying Bukharan Quarter." *Jerusalem Post Magazine*, April 27, 1979.

Achildiyev, David. *"Yesli My Bukharskiye Yevrei Ne Yavlayemsa Sefardami, to Kto Zhe My?"* [If We Bukharan Jews Are Not Sephardi, Then Who Are We?]. *Bukharskaya Gazeta*, June 1998.

Adler, Elkan. "Bokhara." In *The Jewish Encyclopedia,* edited by Isidore Singer and Cyrus Adler. Vol. B, 292–96. New York: Funk & Wagnalls Company, 1901.

———. *Jews in Many Lands*. Philadelphia: The Jewish Publication Society of America, 1905.

———. "The Persian Jews: Their Books and Their Ritual." *The Jewish Quarterly Review* 10, no. 4 (July 1898): 584–625.

Aharoni, Yisrael, and Nelli Sheffer. *Ha-Mitbah shel Kur ha-Hitukh* [The Melting Pot Kitchen]. Tel Aviv: Mishkal Hotsa'ah le-Or, 1998.

Altshuler, Mordechai. "Bukhara." In *Encyclopaedia Judaica,* 1470–74. Jerusalem: Keter Publishing House, 1972.

———. "Some Statistics on Mixed Marriages among Soviet Jews." *Bulletin on Soviet and East European Jewish Affairs* 6 (1970): 30–32.

———. *Soviet Jewry since the Second World War: Population and Social Structure*. New York: Greenwood Press, 1987.

Arutjunian, Ju V. *Uzbekistan, Stolichnye Zhiteli* [Uzbekistan: Inhabitants of the Capital]. Moscow: Institut etnologii i antropologii im. N.N. Miklukho-Maklaya [Institute of Ethnology and Anthropology], 1996.

Asherov, Shlomo Hayim, Michael Zand, M. Benayahu, and Eli Asherov. *Mi-Samarkand ad Petah Tikva: Zikhronot ma'apil Bukhari* [From Samarkand to Petah Tikva: Memoirs of a Bukharan Immigrant]. Tel Aviv: Brit Yotsei Bukhara, 1977.

Awret, Irene. *Days of Honey: The Tunisian Boyhood of Rafael Uzan.* New York: Schocken Books, 1984.

Bacon, Elizabeth E. *Central Asians under Russian Rule: A Study in Culture Change.* Ithaca, N.Y.: Cornell University Press, 1966.

Bahloul, Joëlle. *Architecture of Memory: A Jewish-Muslim Household in Colonial Algeria, 1937–1962.* New York: Cambridge University Press, 1996.

Barth, Fredrik, ed. *Ethnic Groups and Boundaries: The Social Organization of Culture Difference.* Boston: Little, Brown, 1969.

Baykal, Asli. "Surviving the Post-Soviet Transition: Changing Family and Community Relations in Urban Uzbekistan." Ph.D. diss., Boston University, 2007.

Becker, Seymour. "National Consciousness and the Politics of the Bukhara People's Conciliar Republic." In *The Nationality Question in Soviet Central Asia,* edited by Edward Allworth, 159–67. New York: Praeger, 1973.

———. *Russia's Protectorates in Central Asia: Bukhara and Khiva, 1865–1924.* Cambridge, Mass.: Harvard University Press, 1968.

Ben-Arieh, Yehoshua. *Jerusalem in the Nineteenth Century: The Old City.* Jerusalem: Yad Itzhak Ben Zvi, 1984.

———. "The Population of the Large Towns in Palestine during the First Eighty Years of the Nineteenth Century, according to Western Sources." In *Studies on Palestine during the Ottoman Period,* edited by Moshe Ma'oz, 49–69. Jerusalem: Magnes Press, 1957.

Ben-David, Binyamin. "Natan Davidoff: Yazam Kalkali mi-Turkestan ha-Rusit 1896–1923" [Natan Davidoff: An Economic Entrepreneur from Russian Turkestan, 1896–1923]. *Pe'amim: Studies in the Cultural Heritage of Oriental Jewry* 35 (1988): 102–20.

Benyaminov, Meyer R. *Bukharian Jews.* Union City, New Jersey: Gross Brothers Printing Company, 1992.

Ben-Zvi, Yitzhak. "The Jews of Bukhara." In *The Exiled and the Redeemed,* edited by Itzhak Ben-Zvi, 67–100. Philadelphia: Jewish Publication Society of America, 1957.

———. *Nidhei Yisrael* [The Remnants of Israel]. Tel Aviv: N. Tverski, 1952/53.

Berfield, Susan. "Heritage 101: High School Eases Teens' Culture Shock." *New York Newsday, Queens Sunday Section,* January 3, 1993: 1, 5.

Berg, Hetty. *Facing West: Oriental Jews of Central Asia and the Caucasus.* Zwolle, Netherlands: Waanders, 1997.

Berman, Jeremiah J. *Shehitah: A Study in the Cultural and Social Life of the Jewish People.* New York: Bloch Publishing Co., 1941.

Biale, David, ed. *Cultures of the Jews: A New History.* New York: Schocken Books, 2002.

Bialor, Perry. "Rebuilding Their World: Bukharan Jews in the United States." *The World and I,* March 1995, 228–39.

Bilu, Yoram. *Without Bounds: The Life and Death of Rabbi Ya'aqov Wazana.* Detroit: Wayne State University Press, 2000.

Brauer, Erich, and Raphael Patai. *The Jews of Kurdistan.* Detroit: Wayne State University Press, 1993.

Briggs, Lloyd Cabot, and Norina Lami Guède. *No More for Ever: A Saharan Jewish Town.* Cambridge, Mass.: The Peabody Museum, 1964.

Brody, Robert. *The Geonim of Babylonia and the Shaping of Medieval Jewish Culture.* New Haven, Conn.: Yale University Press, 1998.

Burnes, Alexander. "Description of Bokhara." *Journal and Proceedings of the Asiatic Society of Bengal* 2 (1833): 224–39.

Burton, Audrey. "Bukharan Jews: Ancient and Modern." *Transactions of the Jewish Historical Society of England* 34 (1997): 43–68.

Canfield, Robert L., ed. *Turko-Persia in Historical Perspective.* Cambridge: Cambridge University Press, 1991.

Chafets, Zev. The Missionary Mogul. *New York Times Magazine,* September 16, 2007. http://www.nytimes.com/2007/09/16/magazine/16Leviev-t.html.

The Chicago Sentinel, "The Jews of the Caucasus, Central Asia," April 21, 1994, 13–15.

Chlenov, Michael. *Oriental Jewish Groups in the Former Soviet Union: Modern Trends of Development.* Cincinnati: Department of Judaic Studies, University of Cincinnati, 1998.

Clifford, James. *Routes: Trends and Translation in the Late Twentieth Century.* Cambridge, Mass.: Harvard University Press, 1997.

Cooper, Alanna E. "Feasting, Memorializing, Praying and Remaining Jewish in the Soviet Union: The Case of the Bukharan Jews." In *Jewish Life after the USSR,* edited by Zvi Y. Gitelman, Musya Glants, and Marshall I. Goldman, 141–51. Bloomington: Indiana University Press, 2003.

———. "India's Jewish Geography as Described by Nineteenth-Century Jewish Traveler David D'Beth Hillel." *Journal of Indo-Judaic Studies* 7–8 (2004): 25–35.

———. "Looking Out for One's Identity: Central Asian Jews in the Wake of Communism." In *New Jewish Identities: Contemporary Europe and Beyond,* edited by Zvi Gitelman, Barry Kosman, and Andras Kovacs, 189–210. Budapest: Central European University Press, 2003.

———. "Rituals in Flux: Courtship and Marriage among Bukharan Jews." In *Bukharan Jews in the 20th Century: History, Experience and Narration,* edited by Ingeborg Baldauf, Moshe Gammer, and Thomas Loy, 187–208. Wiesbaden: Reichert-Verlag, 2008.

———. "Rituals of Mourning among Central Asia's Bukharan Jews: Remembering the Past to Address the Present." In *Revisioning Ritual: Jewish Traditions in Transition,* edited by Simon Bronner, 290–314. Oxford: The Littman Library of Jewish Civilization, 2011.

———. "Where Have All the Jews Gone? Mass Migration and Uzbekistan's Independence." In *The Divergence of Judaism and Islam: Interdependence, Modernity and Political Turmoil,* edited by Michael Laskier and Ya'akov Lev, 199–224. Gainesville: University Press of Florida, 2011.

———, and Jacob B. Ukeles. "Service Needs of the Bukharan Population of the New York Area." Jewish Community Relations Council of New York, Metropolitan Council on Jewish Poverty, UJA-Federation of NY. August 1999.

Datkhaev, Yu I. *The Bukharan Jews: A Short Chronicle and Reflections* [O Bukharskikh Yevreiyakh: Kratkie Ocherki i Razmyshleniya]. New York: Autograph Publishing House, 1995.

———. *O Bukharskikh Yevreiyakh* [About the Bukharan Jews]. Dushanbe, Tajikistan: MPP Simurg, 1992.

D'Beth Hillel, David. *The Travels of R' David D'Beth Hillel from Jerusalem through Arabia, Koordistan, Part of Persia and India to Madras.* Madras: 1828.

DellaPergola, Sergio. *World Jewish Population.* New York: American Jewish Year Book, 2002.

Dinur, Ben Zion. "Israel in the Diaspora." In *Ideas of Jewish History,* edited by Michael A. Meyer, 286–98. New York: Behrman House, Inc., 1974.

Dominguez, Virginia. *People as Subject, People as Object.* Madison: University of Wisconsin Press, 1989.

Elazar, Daniel, and Alysa M. Dortort. *Understanding the Jewish Agency.* Jerusalem: Jerusalem Center for Public Affairs, 1985.

Elmaliah, Avraham. "Te'udatenu" [Our Mission]. *Mizrah u-Ma'arav* 1 (1920): 1–7.

Endelman, Todd. "In Defense of Jewish Social History." *Jewish Social Studies* 7, no. 3 (2001): 52–67.

Eshel, Menachem. *Galerya: Dmuyot shel Rashei Yahadut Bukhara* [Gallery: Portraits of the Leaders of the Jews of Bukhara]. Tel Aviv: Bet ha-Tarbut li-Yehudei Bukhara be-Yisrael, 1965.

Fabian, Johannes. *Time and the Other: How Anthropology Makes Its Object.* New York: Columbia University Press, 1983.

Fazilov, Marik. "Pochemu My 'Bukharskie' Yevrei" [Why Are We "Bukharan" Jews?]. *Shofar,* March 1998, 1.

Fischel, Walter J. "The Leaders of the Jews of Bokhara." In *Jewish Leaders: 1750–1940,* edited by Leo Jung, 535–47. Jerusalem: Boys Town Jerusalem Publishers, 1964.

———. Secret Jews of Persia: A Century-Old Marrano Community in Asia. *Commentary,* January 1949: 28–33.

———, and David D'Beth Hillel. *Unknown Jews in Unknown Lands: The Travels of Rabbi D'Beth Hillel (1824–1832).* New York: KTAV Publishing House, 1971.

Fitz Gibbon, Kate, and Andrew Hale. *Ikat: Silks of Central Asia (the Guido Goldman Collection).* London: Laurence King Publishing, 1997.

Frankel, Jonathan. "Assimilation and the Jews in Nineteenth-Century Europe: Towards a New Historiography." In *Assimilation and Community: The Jews in Nineteenth-Century Europe,* edited by Jonathan Frankel and Steven J. Zipperstein, 1–37. Cambridge: Cambridge University Press, 1992.

Fuzailov, Aryeh. *Me-Arayot Gavéru: Bukhara, Samarkand, Yerushalayim* [Stronger Than Lions: Bukhara, Samarkand, Jerusalem]. Israel: Aryeh Fuzailov, 1995.

Fuzailov, Giora. "Li-she'elat Matsavam ha-Ruhani shel Yehudei Bukhara Erev Hagaato shel Hakham Yosef Maman" [Regarding the Spiritual Condition of the Bukharan Jews on the Eve of Yosef Maman's Arrival]. *AB''A: Ktav et le-Heker ve-Limud Yehudei Iran, Bukhara, ve-Afganistan* (Journal for the Research and Study of the Jews of Iran, Bukhara, and Afghanistan) (Winter 2007): 7–11.

———. *Mi-Bukharah li-Yerushalayim: Aliyatam ve-Hityashvutam shel Yehudei Bukhara be-Erets Yisrael 628–708 (1868–1948)* [Immigration and Settlement of Bukharan Jews in Eretz Israel (1868–1948)]. Jerusalem: Misgav Yerushalayim, 1995.

———. "The System of Succession in the Bukharan Rabbinate 1790–1917." *Shvut: Studies in the History and Culture of the Jews of Russia and Eastern Europe* 8, no. 14 (1999): 36–57.

———. *Yahudut Bukhara: Gdoleha u-Minhageha* [The Jews of Bukhara: Their Leaders and Traditions]. Jerusalem: Misrad ha-Hinukh ve-ha-Tarbut, 1993.

Gitelman, Zvi. "The Quality of Life in Israel and the United States." In *New Lives: The Adjustment of Soviet Jewish Immigrants in the United States and Israel,* edited by Rita Simon, 47–68. Washington, D.C.: Lexington Books, 1985.

Gitelman, Zvi Y., Barry A. Kosmin, and András Kovács, eds. *New Jewish Identities: Contemporary Europe and Beyond.* Budapest: Central European University Press, 2003.

Glueck, Grace. "Design Review: When Russia Uncovered Exotic Jewish Cultures." *The New York Times,* August 6, 1999, Section E, Part 2, 44.

Goldberg, Harvey E. *Jewish Life in Muslim Libya: Rivals & Relatives.* Chicago: University of Chicago Press, 1990; Berkeley: University of California Press, 2003.

———. *Sephardi and Middle Eastern Jewries: History and Culture in the Modern Era.* Bloomington: Indiana University Press, 1996.

Goldberg, Harvey E., and Chen Bram. "Sephardi/Mizrahi/Arab Jews: Anthropological Reflections on Critical Sociology in Israel and the Study of Middle Eastern Jewries within the Context of Israeli Society." *Studies in Contemporary Jewry* 22 (2007): 227–56.

Gorenberg, Gershom. "Samarkand." *Hadassah Magazine* (May 1993): 32–35.

Graetz, Heinrich. 1846. *The Structure of Jewish History, and Other Essays.* New York: Jewish Theological Seminary of America, 1975.

Gur, Baruch. *Daf Matsav Mispar 4: Uzbekistan* [Situation Paper Number 4: Uzbekistan]. Jerusalem: Jewish Agency for Israel, Unit for the Commonwealth of Independent States and Eastern Europe, 1993.

———. *Situation Paper Number 6: The Jewish Population of the Former Soviet Union, An Empirical Analysis as of Mid-1993.* Jerusalem: Jewish Agency for Israel, Unit for the Commonwealth of Independent States and Eastern Europe, 1993.

Hakham, Shimon, ed. *Sefer Zekher Tsadik* [Memory of a Righteous One]. Reprint of 1894 edition. Jerusalem: Sh. Weinfeld, 1948.

Halkin, Hillel. *Across the Sabbath River.* New York: Houghton, Mifflin and Company, 2002.

Heilman, Samuel C. *When a Jew Dies: The Ethnography of a Bereaved Son.* Berkeley: University of California Press, 2001.

Herman, David. *Basic Elements of Narrative.* Chichester, U.K.: Wiley-Blackwell, 2009.

Hopkirk, Peter. *The Great Game: The Struggle for Empire in Central Asia.* New York: Kodansha International, 1992.

Idelsohn, A. Z. "Yehudei Bukhara" [The Jews of Bukhara]. *Mizrah u-Ma'arav* 1 (1920): 317–26.

Issacharoff Family. *Issacharoff: A Tale of a Family.* Haifa: Issacharoff Family, 1997.

Jacobs, Louis. *The Jewish Religion: A Companion.* Oxford: Oxford University Press, 1995.

Kaganovitch, Albert. "The Bukharan Jewish Diaspora at the Beginning of the 21st Century." In *Bukharan Jews in the 20th Century: History, Experience and Narration,* edited by Ingeborg Baldauf, Moshe Gammer, and Thomas Loy, 111–116. Wiesbaden: Reichert-Verlag, 2008.

——. "The Education of Bukharan Jews in Turkestan Province: 1865–1917." *Irano-Judaica* V (2003): 202–213.

——. "The Legal and Political Situation of the Chalah—the Muslim Jews in Russian Turkestan, 1865–1917." *Shvut: Studies in the History and Culture of the Jews of Russia and Eastern Europe* 6, no. 22 (1997): 57–78.

——. "Shlomo Tagger: Rav Rashi li-Yehudei Bukhara be-Turkestan" [Shlomo Tagger: Chief Rabbi of the Jews of Bukhara in Turkestan]. *Pe'amim: Studies in the Cultural Heritage of Oriental Jewry* 35 (1999): 41–55.

Kalantarov, Ya I. "*Sredneaziatskiye Yevrei*" [The Central Asian Jews]. In *Narody Mira* [Peoples of the World], Vol. 2, Narody Sredney Azii i Kazakhstana [The Peoples of Central Asia and Kazakhstan], 610–30. Moscow: Institute of Ethnography, 1963.

Kandiyoti, Deniz, and Nadira Azimova. "The Communal and the Sacred: Women's Worlds of Ritual in Uzbekistan." *Journal of the Royal Anthropological Institute* 10 (2004): 327–49.

Kandov, Boris, and Arkadiy Yakubov. *The Congress United Us.* New York: Congress of Bukharian Jews in the USA and Canada, 2005.

Keyes, Charles F. "The Dialectics of Ethnic Change." In *Ethnic Change,* edited by Charles F. Keyes, 4–30. Seattle: University of Washington Press, 1981.

Khanykov, N. *Bokhara: Its Amir and Its People.* Translated by Clement Joseph Philip De Bode. London: J. Madden, 1845.

Klier, John D. "Facing West: Oriental Jews of Central Asia and the Caucasus: Review." *The Historian* 62, no. 4 (June 2000): 932–33.

Koplik, Sara. "The Demise of Afghanistan's Jewish Community and the Soviet Refugee Crisis (1932–1936)." *Iranian Studies* 36, no. 3 (2003): 353–79.

——. "The Experience of Bukharan Jews outside the Soviet Union in the 1930s and 1940s." In *Bukharan Jews in the 20th Century: History, Experience and Narration,* edited by Ingeborg Baldauf, Moshe Gammer, and Thomas Loy, 91–109. Wiesbaden: Reichert-Verlag, 2008.

Korom, Frank. "Reconciling the Local and the Global: The Ritual of Shi'i Islam in Trinidad." *Journal of Ritual Studies* 13:1 (1999): 21–36.

Kugelmass, Jack, and Jonathan Boyarin. *From a Ruined Garden: The Memorial Books of Polish Jewry.* New York: Schocken Books, 1983.

Lansdell, Henry. *Russian Central Asia, Including Kuldja, Bokhara, Khiva and Merv.* Boston: Houghton, Mifflin and Company, 1885.

Levin, Shalom Dov-Ber. *Toldot ChaBa"D be-Eretz ha-Kodesh ba-Shanim Tav-Kuf-Lamed-Zayin—Tav-Shin-Yod* [History of Chabad in the Holy Land: 1777–1950]. Brooklyn: Kehot Publication Society, 1988.

——. *Toldot ChaBa"D be-Rusya ha-Sovyetit ba-Shanim Tav-Resh-Ayin-Het—Tav-Shin-Yod* [History of Chabad in the USSR: 1917–1989]. Brooklyn: Kehot Publication Society, 1989.

Lewis, Bernard. *The Jews of Islam.* Princeton, N.J.: Princeton University Press, 1984.

Lindholm, Charles. *Culture and Authenticity.* Malden, Mass.: Blackwell, 2008.

Lobacheva, N. P. "Wedding Rites in the Uzbek SSR," *Central Asian Review* 15 (1967): 290–99.

Louw, Maria Elisabeth. *Everyday Islam in Post-Soviet Central Asia.* New York: Routledge, 2007.

Loy, Thomas. "Reflection on the Memoirs of Mordekhay Bachayev." In *Bukharan Jews in the 20th Century: History, Experience and Narration,* edited by Ingeborg Baldauf, Moshe Gammer, and Thomas Loy, 127–44. Wiesbaden: Reichert-Verlag, 2008.

Malinowski, Bronislaw. *The Sexual Life of Savages in North-Western Melanesia.* New York: H. Liveright, 1929.

Marcus, Jacob Rader. *The Jew in the Medieval World: A Source Book.* New York: Meridian Books, 1960.

Markielov, F. "Krupnim Planom: Blagasloveniye" [A True Blessing]. *Shofar,* October 1992, 3.

Meakin, Annette M. B. *In Russian Turkestan: A Garden of Asia and Its People.* New York: Scribner, 1915.

Meiendorf, E. K. *Voyage d'Orenbourg à Boukhara, fait en 1820: à travers les steppes qui s'étendent à l'Est de la Mer d'Aral et au-delà de l'Ancien Jaxartes.* Translated by Christian Heinrich Pander. Paris: Librairie Orientale de Dondey-Dupré père et fils, 1826.

Mendelson, Rebekah Ziona. "The Bokharan Jewish Community of New York City." Master's thesis, Columbia University, 1964.

Meyer, Michael A., ed. *Ideas of Jewish History.* New York: Behrman House, 1974.

Moreen, Vera Basch. *In Queen Esther's Garden: An Anthology of Judeo-Persian Literature.* New Haven, Conn.: Yale University Press, 2000.

Moshavi, Baruch. "Customs and Folklore of Nineteenth-Century Bukharian Jews in Central Asia: Birth, Engagement, Marriage, Mourning and Others." Ph.D. diss., Yeshiva University, 1974.

———. "R' Yosef Ben Moshe Maman Shaliah Tsfat be-Bukhara" [Rabbi Yosef the Son of Moshe Maman, Emissary of Tsfat in Bukhara]. *Talpiyot* 9 (1970): 873–86.

Moze'on Yisrael. *Bokhara: Ta'arukha* [Bokhara: Exhibit]. Jerusalem: Israel Museum, 1967.

Myerhoff, Barbara G. *Number Our Days.* New York: Dutton, 1978.

Neumark, Ephraim. *Masa be-Eretz ha-Kedem: Surya, Kurdistan, Aram-Naharayim, Paras ve-Asya ha-Merkazit* [Journey to the Land of the Orient: Syria, Kurdistan, Mesopotamia, Persia, and Central Asia], edited by Avraham Ya'ari. Jerusalem: Ha-Ahim Levin Epstein, 1947.

Niyazov, Pinhas. "Kak i Pochemu Yevrei Srednei Azii Stali Nazivatsa Bukharskimi Yevreymai" [How and Why the Jews of Central Asia Came to Be Called Bukharan Jews]. *Bukharskaya Gazeta* (October 1997): 16.

Niyazov, Shlomo Haye. *Mesirut Nefesh shel Yehudei Bukhara* [Self-Sacrifice of the Bukharan Jews]. New York: Empire Press, 1985.

Olufsen, O. *The Emir of Bokhara and His Country: Journeys and Studies in Bokhara.* London: Heinemann, 1911.

Orr, Akiva. *UnJewish State: The Politics of Jewish Identity in Israel.* London: Ithaca Press, 1983.

Pinhasi, Ya'akov. "Avotay u-Veit Avi: Masoret Mishpaha ve-Zikhronot" [My Forefathers and Ancestors: Family Tradition and Memoirs]. In *Asara Sipurei-Am mi-Bukhara* [Ten Folktales from Bukhara], edited by Dov Noy, 12–36. Jerusalem: Ha-Merkaz le-Heker ha-Folklor, 1978.

Pinhasov, Shlomo Baba Jon. *Sefer Milim Shisha* [Dictionary of Six Languages]. Jeru-
    salem: Shlomo Baba Jon Pinhasov, 1908.
Poliakov, Sergei Petrovich. *Everyday Islam: Religion and Tradition in Rural Central
    Asia,* edited by Martha Brill Olcott. Armonk, N.Y.: M. E. Sharpe, 1992.
Rabin, Avraham. "Shluhei Eretz-Yisrael be-Bukhara Tav-Resh-Mem-Alef—Tav-Resh-
    Ayin-Dalet" [Emissaries from the Land of Israel to Bukhara, 1881–1914]. *Pe'amim:
    Studies in the Cultural Heritage of Oriental Jewry* 35 (1988): 139–55.
Rabin, Yehuda ha-Kohen. *Zarah Kochav mi-Ya'akov* [A Star Shone Forth from Ya'akov:
    The History and the Holy Ways of Bukharan Rabbis]. Jerusalem: Yitzhak ha-
    Kohen Rabin, 1989.
Rakowska-Harmstone, Teresa. "Islam and Nationalism: Central Asia and Kazakhstan
    under Soviet Rule." *Central Asian Survey* 2 (1983): 7–87.
Ram, Uri. "Zionist Historiography and the Invention of Modern Jewish Nationhood:
    The Case of Ben Zion Dinur." *History & Memory* 7, no. 1 (1995): 91–124.
Ro'i, Yaacov. "The Religious Life of the Bukharan Jewish Community in Soviet
    Central Asia after World War II." In *Bukharan Jews in the 20th Century: History,
    Experience and Narration,* edited by Ingeborg Baldauf, Moshe Gammer, and
    Thomas Loy, 57–75. Wiesbaden: Reichert-Verlag, 2008.
Rosman, Murray Jay. *How Jewish Is Jewish History?* Oxford: The Littman Library of
    Jewish Civilization, 2007.
Rotem, Yehudit. *Mipninim Mikhrah: Zikhronot le-Veit Ben David* [A Price above
    Rubies: Memoirs of the Ben David Family]. Jerusalem: Ben David Family, 1986.
Rywkin, Michael. *Moscow's Muslim Challenge: Soviet Central Asia.* Armonk, N.Y.:
    M. E. Sharpe, 1990.
Sanders, Gabriel. "Life on the Fringes: Peering into the Hidden Cultures of Asia
    (Review of Facing West Exhibit)." *The Forward,* August 20, 1998.
Sapir, Ya'akov. *Sefer Masa Teiman* [Journey to Yemen], edited by Avraham Ya'ari.
    Jerusalem: Epstein, 1945.
Satlow, Michael. *Creating Judaism: History, Tradition, Practice.* New York: Columbia
    University Press, 2006.
Schuyler, Eugene. *Turkistan: Notes of a Journey in Russian Turkistan, Kokand,
    Bukhara and Kuldja,* edited by Geoffrey Wheeler. London: Routledge and Kegan
    Paul, 1966.
Scott, Joan. "Gender: A Useful Category of Historical Analysis." *The American His-
    torical Review* 91, no. 5 (1986): 1053–75.
Seltzer, Robert. "Jewish History after the End of Ideology." In *At the Cutting Edge of
    Jewish Studies,* edited by Gershon Hundert: McGill University, 1999, http://www
    .arts.mcgill.ca/programs/jewish/30yrs/index.html.
Shaffir, William. *Life in a Religious Community: The Lubavitcher Chassidim in Mon-
    treal.* Toronto: Holt, Rinehart & Winston of Canada, 1974.
Signer, Michael, ed. *The Itinerary of Benjamin of Tudela: Travels in the Middle Ages.*
    New York: Nightingale Resources, 2005.
Tagger, Nissim. *Toldot Yehudei Bukhara: be-Bukhara u-ve-Yisrael* [The History of the
    Jews of Bukhara in Bukhara and in Israel from the year 600 CE until 1970]. Tel
    Aviv: Nissim Tagger, 1970.
Tilayov, Shulamit. *Shirat Shulamit* [The Poetry of Shulamit]. Tel Aviv: Brit Yotsei
    Bukhara, 1981.

Tolts, Mark. "The Demographic Profile of the Bukharan Jews in the Late Soviet Period." In *Bukharan Jews in the 20th Century: History, Experience and Narration,* edited by Ingeborg Baldauf, Moshe Gammer, and Thomas Loy, 77–89. Wiesbaden: Reichert-Verlag, 2008.

Twersky, Isadore. "The Shulhan 'Aruk: Enduring Code of Jewish Law." *Judaism* 16 (1967): 141–58.

———, ed. *A Maimonides Reader.* New York: Behrman House, 1972.

Wahrman, Dror. *Ha-Bukharim u-Shkhunatam bi-Yerushalayim* [The Bukharans and their Neighborhood]. Jerusalem: Yad Yitzhak Ben Zvi, 1991.

Wolff, Joseph. *Researches and Missionary Labours among the Jews, Mohammedans and Other Sects.* 2d ed. London: James Nisbet and Company, 1835.

Ya'akov Shaul Elyashar archive, *ARC. 4° 1271, Department of Archives, the National Library of Israel.*

Ya'ari, Avraham. *Bibliyografya shel Haggadot Pesah me-Reshit ha-Dfus ve-ad Hayom* [Bibliography of Passover Haggadot: From the Beginning of Print until Today]. Jerusalem: Bamberger and Wahrman, 1960.

———. *Ha-Dfus ha-Ivri be-Artsot ha-Mizrah* [Hebrew Printing in Eastern Countries]. Jerusalem: Ha-Havera le-Hotsa'at Sfarim al-yad ha-Universita ha-Ivrit, 1950.

———. *Ha-Dfus ha-Ivri be-Kushta* [Hebrew Printing in Constantinople: Its History and Bibliography]. Jerusalem: Hotsa'at Sfarim al shem Y"L Magnes (Hebrew University), 1967.

———. *Igrot Erets Yisrael: She-Katvu ha-Yehudim ha-Yoshvim ba-Arets La-Aheihem She-ba-Golah mi-Yeme Galut Bavel ve-ad Shivat Tsiyon she-be-Yameinu* [Letters of the Land of Israel: Written by Jews Residing in the Land, to Their Brethren in the Diaspora, from the Days of the Babylonian Exile until the Ingathering of the Exiles in Our Own Days]. Ramat Gan: Masadah, 1971.

———. *Mah Nishtana: A Selection of One Hundred and Eleven Passover Haggadot,* edited by Harry Hirschhorn. Highland Park: Kol Ami Musuem, 1964.

———. *Shluhei Erets Yisrael: Toldot ha-Shlihut me-ha-Arets la-Gola me-Hurban Bayit Sheni ad ha-Me'a ha-Tesha-Esreh* [Emissaries of the Land of Israel: The History of Emissary Work from the Land of Israel to the Diaspora, from the Destruction of the Second Temple until the Nineteenth Century]. Jerusalem: Mosad ha-Rav Kuk, 1977.

———. *Sifrei Yehudei Bukhara* [The Books of the Jews of Bukhara]. Jerusalem: Kiryat Sefer, 1942.

———. *Toldot Hag Simhat Torah: Hishtalshelut Minhagav bi-Tfutsot Yisrael le-Doroteihen* [The History of the Holiday of Simchat Torah: The Development of Customs amongst the Jewish Diaspora over the Generations]. Jerusalem: Mosad ha-Rav Kuk, 1964.

———. *Zikhronot Erets Yisrael: Me'ah ve-Esrim Pirkei Zikhronot me-Hayei ha-Yishuv ba-Arets me-ha-Me'ah ha-Shva-Esreh ve-ad Yameinu* [Land of Israel Memoirs: One-Hundred-Twenty Memoir Chapters, about Life in the Land from the Seventeenth Century until Today]. Jerusalem: ha-Mahlaka le-Inyenei ha-No'ar shel ha-Histadrut ha-Tsiyonit, 1946/1947.

Yakubov, Yefim. "The 'Declaration of Native Jews'—the Final Legislative Act Induced by the 'Bukharan Jewish Question'." In *Bukharan Jews in the 20th Century:*

History, Experience and Narration, edited by Ingeborg Baldauf, Moshe Gammer, and Thomas Loy, 11–21. Wiesbaden: Reichert-Verlag, 2008.

Yaroshevski, Dov B. "Al Ma'amadam ha-Mishpati shel Yehudei Asya ha-Tikhona" [On the Legal Status of the Jews of Central Asia]. *Pe'amim: Studies in the Cultural Heritage of Oriental Jewry* 35 (1988): 84–97.

Yerushalmi, Yosef Hayim. *Zakhor: Jewish History and Jewish Memory.* Seattle: University of Washington Press, 1996.

Yureva, R. "Vremya Dobrikh Nachinani" [A Time of Good Beginnings]. *Shofar,* February 1992, 3.

Yuval, Tirza. "The Last Celebration." *Eretz Magazine* (November–December 1993): 18–34.

Zand, Michael. "Bukhara." In *Encyclopedia Judaica Yearbook,* 183–92. Jerusalem: Encyclopaedia Judaica, 1975.

———. "Bukharan Jewish Culture under Soviet Rule." *Soviet Jewish Affairs* 9, no. 2 (1979): 15–21.

———. "Bukharan Jews." In *Encyclopedia Iranica,* edited by Ehsan Yar-Shater. Vol. IV, 530–45. London: Routledge & Kegan Paul, 1990.

———. "Yahadut Bukhara ve-Khibush Asya ha-Tikhona bi-Yedei ha-Rusim" [Bukharan Jewry and the Russian Conquest of Central Asia]. *Pe'amim: Studies in the Cultural Heritage of Oriental Jewry* 35 (1988): 47–83.

Zborowski, Mark, and Elizabeth Herzog. *Life Is with People: The Culture of the Shtetl.* New York: Schocken Books, 1952.

Zimmels, H. J. *Ashkenazim and Sephardim: Their Relations, Differences, and Problems as Reflected in the Rabbinical Responsa.* Hoboken, N.J.: Ktav Publishing House, 1996.

Zubin, M. "Yehudei Mehoz Samarkand bi-Shnat 1979—Skira Statistit" [The Jews of Samarkand in the Year 1979—A Statistical Survey]. *Pe'amim: Studies in the Cultural Heritage of Oriental Jewry* 35 (1988): 170–77.

INDEX

Alanna E. Cooper *is an anthropologist and cultural historian who has held research and teaching positions at Harvard University, University of Massachusetts, University of Michigan, and Boston University. Her publications have appeared in, among others,* Jewish Social Studies, AJS Review, Anthropology of East Europe Review, *the* Jerusalem Post, *and* Jewish Review of Books.

Printed in the USA
CPSIA information can be obtained
at www.ICGtesting.com
JSHW011947201024
71961JS00036B/588